Gabby Hartnett

Gabby Hartnett

The Life and Times of the Cubs' Greatest Catcher

WILLIAM F. MCNEIL

McFarland & Company, Inc., Publishers
Jefferson, North Carolina, and London

LIBRARY OF CONGRESS CATALOGUING-IN-PUBLICATION DATA

McNeil, William F.
Gabby Hartnett : the life and times of the Cubs' greatest catcher / William F. McNeil.
p.   cm.
Includes bibliographical references and index.
ISBN 0-7864-1850-8 (softcover : 50# alkaline paper) ∞
1. Hartnett, Gabby, 1900–1972.   2. Baseball players — United States — Biography.
3. Chicago Cubs (Baseball team) — History — 20th century.   I. Title.
GV865.H35M36   2004   796.357'092 — dc22   2004012122
British Library cataloguing data are available

On the cover: foreground Gabby Hartnett (Library of Congress);
background image ©2004 Comstock

*McFarland & Company, Inc., Publishers
Box 611, Jefferson, North Carolina 28640
www.mcfarlandpub.com*

To the memory of Charles Leo Hartnett.
The baseball world knew him as "Gabby,"
but to his family, relatives, and friends, he was always Leo,
which he himself preferred. The genial catcher
of the Chicago Cubs set numerous catching records
during his 20-year major league career and established
himself as the greatest all-around catcher in baseball history.
More importantly, off the field, he was friendly and pleasant,
with a permanent smile affixed to his handsome Irish face.
He made thousands of friends over his 70 years on this planet,
and he left it without leaving a single enemy.
He loved everyone, particularly the children,
to whom he was an outstanding role model.

Great job, Leo.

May you rest in peace.

Acknowledgments

Laure Berthelette, president of the Town of Millville James G. Fitzgerald Historical Society, Inc., was a tremendous help to me in the preparation of this book. She chauffeured me around between Woonsocket and Millville locating photographs and making copies of them. She also spent many valuable hours of her time researching the voluminous files in the Fitzgerald Historical Society, ferreting out other important photos of Gabby Hartnett for use in this book.

Margaret Carroll, Millville town historian, escorted me around the Millville area during my first visits to the town, introducing me to many Millville residents who had Gabby Hartnett stories to tell, filling me in on the early history of the town and showing me the points of interest that related to Gabby's career, such as the "Meadow" ball field, the Hartnett home, the Longfellow Grammar School, and the location of the Millville Rubber Company. She also made her fine book, *The Town of Millville—The First 50 Years*, available to me for research purposes.

Jane McNamara Gilmore, the daughter of Gabby's childhood teammate, Tim McNamara, provided me with several unique photographs of her father and Gabby Hartnett.

Michael Holtzman, reporter for the *Woonsocket Call*, searched the archives at the newspaper to locate some of the important photographs of Gabby's career, particularly the photos of the Baseball Hall of Fame induction celebration. He also publicized my work in an article he wrote for the *Call*.

Jay Sanford came through for me again, as he has done in the past, by loaning me a number of photographs of Gabby Hartnett and his Chicago Cubs teammates from his extensive personal collection.

John W. Outland also provided me with photographs, as he did for one of my previous books. The photos, taken by his father George E. Outland during the 1920s, consisted of candid shots of many of the Chicago Cubs players, including Gabby Hartnett, during the Cubs' visits to Los Angeles for spring training exhibition games.

Sheila Hartnett Hornof, Gabby's daughter, was a joy to talk to, a conduit for many stories of the Hartnett family, and a source of rare family photos, which she graciously loaned me.

Bud Hartnett, Gabby's son, spent many hours talking to me about his father, and about their life in Chicago, both during and after his father's major league career.

Many other people provided me with photographs and/or articles about Gabby, including Roy Hartnett, Lee Gooley, and Linda Butt, distant cousins of Gabby's; Jo Moller, Director of Alumni Programs, Dean College; Kristin Wood, director of the Millville Free Public Library; Barbara J. Bussart, Chief Information and Adult Services Librarian, Woonsocket Harris Public Library; Bryan Strnske, Woonsocket Harris Public Library; and Jocelyn Wilk, Assistant Director, Columbia University Archives.

Pete Palmer, a member of SABR and one of the inventors of the Sabermetrics statistical analysis formulas, provided me with reams of offensive and defensive statistics about many world-class catchers, including Gabby Hartnett, Mickey Cochrane, and Bill Dickey.

Other people who passed on their recollections of Gabby to me, or who related stories they had heard about the great Chicago Cubs catcher, included Gabby's nephew Fred W. Hartnett; John McNamara, a nephew of Tim McNamara; John Dean; baseball researcher Walt Wilson; and former major league players Rene Lachemann, Rick Monday, Harry Danning, Ray Berres, and Doc Edwards.

Many other sources were utilized during the research for this book, including the *Chicago Daily News*; the *Chicago Tribune*; the *New York Times*; the *Berkshire Eagle*; the *Providence Sunday Journal*; the *Boston Globe*; the *Dean Megaphone*; the *Sporting News*; James M. Murphy's unpublished manuscript, *Never Another Like Gabby*; and numerous books relating to Gabby Hartnett's baseball career, as well as the era in which he played.

Table of Contents

Introduction

Major league baseball has been played in the United States since 1876, and during most of that time, fans, writers, and other interested parties have periodically selected their all-time major league All-Star team. At the turn of the twentieth century, the catcher on the All-Star team was usually William "Buck" Ewing, backed up by Michael "King" Kelly.

During the first two decades of the twentieth century, the teams took on a different look, as the backstopping responsibilities were handled by Ray Schalk, Roger Bresnahan, and Wally Schang. When the lively ball came into play in 1920, the composition of the All-Star teams changed again. Now the catchers were expected to provide substantial offensive support, whereas previously they had been chosen primarily for their defensive expertise.

During the first three decades of the lively ball era, the catchers on the major league All-Star teams were either Mickey Cochrane or Bill Dickey, with Gabby Hartnett occasionally added to the mix. In the 1950s and 60s the greatest catcher of all time, as voted on by fans, players, and journalists, was either Yogi Berra or Roy Campanella. And by the 1980s and 1990s, Berra and Campanella were replaced by Johnny Bench.

A review of the major league baseball All-Star teams that were selected by fans, players, and journalists over the years brought several things to light. Fans usually selected players who played during their lifetime, thereby limiting many players who were eligible. Very few of today's fans ever saw Campanella or Berra play, let alone Hartnett, Dickey, or Cochrane. Players, on the other hand, generally chose men they played against, men who played for the same club, or men who played in the same league. Journalists were the most knowledgeable, but they also tended to choose modern athletes over athletes from the early part of the century. And, even more important, they

1

allowed their personal biases to enter into their selections. For example, journalists who did not have a good personal relationship with a particular player might conveniently leave that player off of their ballots.

To determine impartially and scientifically who was the greatest major league catcher of all time, a scientific study was undertaken by the author. This study utilized many of the state-of-the-art Sabermetrics formulas, but went beyond those primarily offensive statistics to include the defensive skills of the contenders, such as fielding average, passed balls, and the individual catcher's success rate gunning down prospective base stealers.

This was both the first study of major league catchers that evaluated each player on both his defensive and offensive skills and the most accurate evaluation of catchers yet conducted. The race quickly turned into a two-man competition, with Gabby Hartnett and Roy Campanella leaving the other challengers far behind. When the smoke cleared from all the individual comparisons, Charles Leo "Gabby" Hartnett, the man from Millville, Massachusetts, emerged as the greatest catcher of all time.

Joe McCarthy, the legendary manager of the Chicago Cubs and the New York Yankees, confirmed that result. He had seen Mickey Cochrane play many times over a 13-year period, and had managed both Bill Dickey and Gabby Hartnett, and he said, "Gabby was the best of the three. He was the perfect catcher."

This is Gabby Hartnett's story.

1

In the Beginning, 1900–1919

The sun rose bright and warm over Otsego Lake in the sleepy little village of Cooperstown, New York, on Monday, July 25, 1955. By mid-morning, throngs of wide-eyed visitors milled around the Main Street area, searching for celebrities and heading toward the portico outside the National Baseball Hall of Fame. At about 11 AM, the main event got underway. It was induction day, and six baseball legends, who had been voted into the Hall earlier in the year, were about to have their plaques placed inside the baseball temple, alongside Babe Ruth, Ty Cobb, Cy Young, and the other 26 mythical figures who preceded them.

A large crowd gathered in front of the portico, while the candidates and the dignitaries filled the small stage. Shirley Povich, President of the Baseball Writers Association of America, welcomed the people to the celebration, and each of the candidates gave short speeches of appreciation for the honor bestowed upon them. The fifth and last inductee to speak was a ruddy-faced Irishman named Charles Leo Hartnett, better known to the baseball world as "Gabby." The big catcher, whom Commissioner of Baseball Ford Frick called "Ole Tomato Face" and "Mr. Personality himself," was overcome with emotion as he strode to the podium. His speech was short but memorable. "I'll never forget this day as long as I live. It's a great feeling to become a baseball immortal and enter baseball's Hall of Fame. I have often said that catching was one of the toughest jobs in the business, and it's nice that the baseball writers have honored me and my profession. I wish every catcher could receive this recognition. They certainly deserve it."[1]

Gabby Hartnett's induction into Cooperstown's gallery of baseball legends was the culmination of a lifetime of major league baseball achievements. At the time of his retirement, he held many records: most games

3

caught (1,826), most years catching 100 or more games (12), most consecutive chances without an error (452), and most career home runs (236). July 25, 1955, was Gabby Hartnett's proudest day; for on this day, he was honored by his peers and the entire baseball world.

His beginnings, however, were much more humble. And they began, not in 1900 when he was born, but 18 years prior, when his father, Frederick Hartnett, first saw the light of day. Gabby Hartnett's pursuit of greatness was a family affair.

Fred Hartnett was born in May 1882 in the Hecla section of Uxbridge, Massachusetts. He quit school after the eighth grade to join the labor force and to help support his family, as was the custom in rural Worcester County at the time. He worked as a laborer for awhile, then went to work in Banigan's Millville Rubber Shop after his family moved to Millville.

Millville, Massachusetts, was a typical New England mill town of 1,700 people at the turn of the twentieth century. The village was divided into two sections — Purcell's Hill on the east, and The Heights on the west. The two residential areas were fiery competitors on the athletic fields, and their baseball games often ended in wild melees. The competition wasn't caused by ethnic or religious differences, however; it was strictly territorial. The Blackstone River and Main Street, with its shiny new trolley car tracks down the center, separated the two contentious factions. The village also had two railroad lines running through it, one at the bottom of Purcell's Hill, which carried passengers between Providence, RI, and Worcester, MA, and the other across the river, which joined Boston, MA, and Hartford, CT. Its two major employers, the Millville Rubber Shop and the Lawrence Felt Company kept the country supplied with rubber boots for decades.

Fred Hartnett was tall, ruggedly handsome, cheerful, and sociable. While he didn't swear or drink, he could always be found in one of Millville's many bars, smoking a big cigar and talking baseball with anyone who would listen. In his younger days, he was known as a man-about-town, a fancy dresser, and a ladies' man. Somewhere along the way, he picked up the nickname "Dowdy," which means sloppy or carelessly dressed. It was obviously meant to be a joke, since he dressed impeccably.

Fred developed a love for the game of baseball as a youth and was soon recognized as the best catcher in the Blackstone Valley. His throwing arm became legendary over the years, and the "Hartnett Arm" was a physical characteristic he passed on to his children. For several years, he caught for Hecla in the Mill League, a semipro league that included teams from Uxbridge, Millville, Whitinsville, and the surrounding communities. Later he played for the Millville Town Team as well as any other valley team that needed a good catcher with a rifle for an arm. Fred's talents were always in great demand. He was rough, aggressive, and cocky — a showboat, according to Jim Murphy.

Ellen "Nell" Tucker was born in Manchaug, Massachusetts, in 1883. The 15-year-old beauty met 16-year-old man-about-town, Fred Hartnett, in 1899, and a romance quickly blossomed. They were married early in 1900 and moved in with Nell's parents on Cottage Street in Woonsocket, Rhode Island. The Hartnetts welcomed their first child into the family on December 20, 1900, less than 11 months after the nuptials. Within two weeks, the proud father, his child-bride, and their new baby boy, moved into a three-story tenement house at 82 Purcell's Hill, just off Main Street, in the Purcell's Hill section of Millville. The tenements like the one the Hartnetts lived in, consisted of a kitchen, dining room, parlor, and two bedrooms. And usually the parlor was closed off and only used for company. Shortly after moving in, Fred and Nell took the baby to St. Augustine's Church to be baptized. They were shocked when the priest, after being told the baby's name was Wilfred Amercy, scowled and said, "That's no name for a boy. We'll call him Charles Leo." And so, the future catcher of the Chicago Cubs became Charles Leo. His legal name, however, was still Wilfred Amercy, and when he applied for social security in 1964, he was turned down. He had to petition the Rhode Island State Registrar to have his name legally changed to Charles Leo before he could begin receiving benefits.[2]

Fred was a hard worker, who supplemented his meager income by gambling. Townsfolk claimed that Fred would bet on anything, even if the sun would come up the next day, if the odds were right. One of his favorite games of chance was poker, and he had a reputation as a smart poker player. Fred and his cronies regularly congregated in the back room of Kilkenny's Store on Main Street for a friendly game. John McNamara, a Hartnett neighbor, remembered, "When I was just a little kid, we'd go into the back room to watch. But most of the time, somebody'd yell, 'Get the hell out of here' to the kids, so we'd scramble out of there. You didn't give anybody any guff in those days. And it'd be filled with smoke — but Fred loved to play cards. Kilkenny's Store was a hangout for the whole town. I still miss it — a place to go, you know — sold cigarettes and ice cream and chewing tobacco, snuff, and all that stuff. Candy or a frappe. And a card game in the back room, and of course they had to put something in the pot for the owner. You know how it went. They were raided a couple of times by the state police, but they never found anything because they got tipped off that they were coming. And they had a slot machine in there once in awhile, and that disappeared quickly, you know. It wasn't so much that. It was just a nice hangout for everybody."[3]

Fred Hartnett played semipro baseball up and down the valley in the late 1890s and early 1900s. He may have had dreams about becoming a major

league catcher when he was young, but if he did, his family responsibilities quickly ended that dream. When he got too old to play the game, he managed the Millville Town Team, which by that time included his son, Charles Leo, and Timothy McNamara, an outstanding local pitcher. Fred taught all his children how to play baseball, boys and girls alike, but he concentrated on Charles Leo. He thought his oldest child had the potential to be a major league player, and he passed his love for the game on to his son, as well as his intensity and desire to be the best player he could be.

When he wasn't involved with baseball, or wasn't playing cards, Fred was buzzing around town on his motorcycle, a 12-horsepower Indian Scout, capable of speeds of up to 60 miles per hour. In the early 1900s, a motorcycle was the only means of personal motorized transportation, and the Scout was the bike of choice for the vast majority of motorcycle enthusiasts around the country. The newly invented automobile was still a plaything for the rich. On weekends, Fred and Nell hit the road, cruising up and down the valley to visit relatives in Manchaug, Uxbridge, Whitinsville, or Woonsocket, with Fred in the pilot's seat and Nell clinging to the sidecar.

Fred also took the motorcycle hunting, which was another passion of his. He loved to hunt rabbits, squirrels, pheasant, maybe deer, but mostly fox. As John McNamara noted, "A lot of fellers had foxhounds, and they would go out by themselves, or they'd get together and let the dogs run. And they'd enjoy being out, and they may not even shoot at the fox, just to give the dogs a good run." Fred often went hunting in the evenings after work with some of his friends. They'd take a dog and the bike and go into the woods around East Blackstone or Uxbridge.[4]

When the electric trolleys became popular shortly after 1900, Fred left his job as a cutter at the Millville Rubber Shop and became a motorman on the Woonsocket-to-Worcester run. While he was busy earning a paycheck, Nell ran the household, cooking and cleaning, caring for the younger children, and supervising the older ones. She delivered 14 children in 16 years, first seven boys, then seven girls, with five boys and five girls surviving to adulthood. The Hartnetts lived on the first floor of the Purcell's Hill tenement when they first moved in, but as the family grew, they took over the third-floor attic also, converting it into additional bedrooms. Nell was the nurturer in the family. She taught the children the important values in life, such as hard work, cleanliness, and love of God and family. And she made sure the Hartnett family attended Mass together at St. Augustine's Church every Sunday. Several of her boys, including Charles Leo, served as altar boys

Opposite page: **The Hartnetts lived in this three-tenement house on Purcell's Hill (later Preston Street).**

at the church. Thanks to Nell's example, her children always maintained close family ties. James Edward Boyle, a family friend, noted, "(Nell) was full of life. She loved her family and lived for them."

All the Hartnett children attended the Longfellow Grammar School, which was located on Central Street, just off Main Street, about a half mile from the Hartnett home. Teacher Mary Harrington noted that the Hartnett girls were "well-scrubbed every day. Their mother never let them out for school unless they were clean and neat."[5] Maintaining that cleanliness was never as easy as it looked, however. Nell said it took her all day Saturday to give the kids a bath, and by the time she got through, the first one was dirty again.

During the 1918–19 flu epidemic, Nell pitched right in to help out any sick neighbors. Margaret (Miles) Gauvin witnessed firsthand Nell Hartnett's concern for people saying, "Nell was a most capable person in so many ways. During that flu epidemic, my mother became very sick. Actually it turned out to be not from the flu. But Nell wasn't afraid — she marched right over to our house and helped us. She had her own large family to think about, but she always wanted to help other people."[6]

She was also one of the neighborhood's most experienced midwives, delivering dozens of babies over the years. Most babies were born at home in those days, because people couldn't afford to go to a hospital. So, when a woman's time was near, one of the children would be sent on a mission of mercy, racing to Nell's house with the message, "Come quick. My mother needs you." Nell's granddaughter, Sheila, said, "I don't know if she was a practical nurse, but she did take care of a lot of people." She had a reputation as a "healer" in Millville.

Everybody in town had a nickname during the early years, and the Hartnett children were no exception. Charles Leo Hartnett's buddies called him "Dowdy," after his father. He was later called "Gabby" by major league players, writers, and fans. But he himself, preferred to be called Leo, and he was always Leo to his wife, his family, and his close friends. Earl Hartnett's nickname was Gisser. Frank, who was born Francis and possessed the "Hartnett Arm," was Sweetie. Herman, who also had a great throwing arm, was Chickie. Harold was Buster. Dorothy was Dottie. Alertina was Tina. Mildred, another of the baseball-playing Hartnetts, was Cooken or Millie. Anna, who was the most talented baseball player among the girls, and who could even challenge her big brothers, was Charlie. She may have been named after Charles Leo, because she was also a catcher who was blessed with the Hartnett Arm. The last girl, yet another ballplayer, was Mary.

It was not unusual that most of the Hartnett children, boys and girls alike, became baseball addicts, because, as Mildred noted in a newspaper interview, "[We girls] heard little more than baseball around the huge kitchen table, and soon [we] too became part of the baseball scene."[7] How strong an influence baseball played in the Hartnett children's lives could still be seen years later. In the 1929 federal census, three of the boys, Harold, Herman, and Leo, ages 22 to 29, all listed their occupation as "ballplayer."

During the period from 1910 to 1925, the Hartnett house was a popular hangout for neighborhood children. Someone was always barging in, looking for a baseball game, a game of marbles, or someone else with whom to go swimming or play hide-and-seek. During the summer months, the children picked blueberries and sold them to the neighbors up and down Main Street for 10 cents a quart. Dowdy brought many of his berries home to his mother, Nell, who loved to bake. She cooked dozens of blueberry pies in season, giving the family a delicacy they couldn't afford to

Nell Hartnett was the nurturer in the family. (Sheila Hartnett Hornof)

purchase. Dowdy's determination to be the best at whatever he did even surfaced when he picked blueberries. "I wanted to be known as the champion berry-picker of New England," Hartnett once recalled. "And I had the reputation as a clean berry-picker; no greenies or crushed berries."[8]

Dowdy and his buddies, Tim McNamara, "Hog 'Em" Boyle, Joe McManus, and Booster McCormick, were typical ten-year-olds, passing the warm summer days fishing for pickeral, bass, and brook trout in the Blackstone River, or swimming in the river or in the Ironstone Reservoir a few miles away. They often ended their day at the railroad tracks, lying in wait for the 5:15 freight that passed through town. They used the boxcars for target practice. One of the boys would yell out a letter from the signs painted on the sides of the cars, and they would all start chucking stones at the car, trying to hit the letter. The closest thrower to the letter was the winner — and Dowdy was hard to beat. His throws were strong and accurate.

The oldest Hartnett boy also had a reputation for being the town's pre-

mier marbles player, like Pee Wee Reese a couple of decades later. Over a
period of time, he reportedly accumulated more than 50,000 marbles, which
he kept in three 25-pound sugar sacks, carefully stored away in the attic.
Years later, on a visit to Millville with his son, he set out to reclaim the marbles but, by that time, they had mysteriously disappeared.

In the winter, the neighborhood activities took the form of sliding on
Purcell's Hill or skating on Cranberry Pond. Dowdy enjoyed sliding, but he
wasn't much of a skater, spending most of the time on his ankles. His favorite
sport was basketball, which was played in the warm, dry confines of a hall.
In his early years, he played for the Knights of Columbus team on the second floor of Temperance Hall. Dowdy was just an average player, but his
brother, Sweetie, who was tall and tough, was a standout. Their main opposition was The Heights team, who played in nearby Foresters Hall, and the
two teams locked horns on numerous occasions. As in baseball, the basketball games between the two adversaries were hotly contested.

When he was home, Dowdy always found time to help his sisters with
their schoolwork. Dottie said, "He used to tell us girls, 'Learn to spell. It's
important.' He was a good brother. He did everything for us. He'd come
home from work or school and he'd stay in and play at anything we wanted."[9]

Baseball was Dowdy's first love, and he always had a ball and a glove
with him, even at Longfellow Grammar School. The boys would have pick-
up games at recess and at lunch, and Tim McNamara and Dowdy began a
pitcher–catcher relationship there, that would dominate the Blackstone Valley scene for almost 10 years. After school, the boys sought out any unoc-
cupied cow pasture or other field that would accommodate a baseball game.
Many times, they played on Lincoln Street, an unpaved street at the top of
Purcell's Hill. The games were played in front of Tom Feeney's house. "The
road right out there (Lincoln Street) was our field. Leo was our leader. He
always wanted to have a scrub game. We'd have strip (taped) balls. Got them
from the rubber shop. They'd soon be lopsided, but that never bothered us.
We used to make chalked circles for the bases and the pitchers box.... Yes,
we broke a few windows, and after awhile we moved up to Smith's Field,
near Billy McCabes, just up Lincoln Street a ways. I remember one day —
Dowdy hit one over the stone wall and I guess we kids thought that was the
longest hit ever made ... Leo could throw! Even then, he'd throw as strong
as people much older. He had a tremendous reach and his arms were powerful. The same with his brother Buster. Buster was a strong, strong kid. I
used to catch Buster, but I quit; he just threw too hard for me.... Sweetie
was a darned good athlete, too. Sweetie and I were classmates. He could have
been a good boxer."[10]

When Dowdy was about seven years old, he had an accident that almost

The Longfellow Grammar School class photograph included Charles Leo Hartnett, who is third from the right in the second row, with his hair parted in the middle. (Town of Millville J.G. Fitzgerald Historical Society, Inc.)

ended his baseball career before it began. His mother recounted the events. "Leo was seven. ...During a baseball game ... a ball went astray ... and Leo legged after it. But an older boy ... threw Leo down. That broke all the bones in his right shoulder and upper arm. The bones were set by a doctor, but the arm was left very stiff. He couldn't lower it (below shoulder height). I was afraid he would be a cripple for life. So I had him carry a flat iron or a pail of stones all the time. He did that for five years."[11] John McNamara recounted a similar strategy used by Fred Hartnett. "He made Dowdy hold pails of sand straight out as long as he could, to strengthen his wrists. He really pushed him."[12]

During Dowdy's early years, Fred made his baseball training a top priority, driving the youngster mercilessly in his efforts to instill good work habits in him. Fred was a perfectionist. Every night after work, he and Dowdy would play catch in the backyard, with Fred pitching and Dowdy catching.

The owner of the original "Hartnett Arm" could still hum the ball. Sometimes, after 15 minutes of catching his father's smoke, Dowdy would be ready to retire, but his father would keep him out there catching for another 15 minutes. One time, the youngster tried to backhand an outside pitch instead of shifting his body in front of the ball, and his father went ballistic. He kicked Dowdy in the seat of the pants, yelling, "Is that the way I taught you to catch a ball. Now, do it again, and do it right this time." "Sometimes Fred would walk up to Smith's Field and watch us," Feeney remembered. "He'd help all of us if he saw us do something wrong."[13]

Baseball filled Dowdy's life. School was actually a distraction for him, keeping him from his goal of becoming the best catcher that ever lived. He spent many days and evenings following the exploits of the Millville Town Team, hounding the manager, John Gibbons, so much, that Gibbons finally made him the team mascot. He sat on the bench during the games, picking up bats and running errands. He also helped carry the equipment to and from the park, which was tough on a little guy, since transportation was nonexistent in those days. The teams had to walk to the game, and an away game in Uxbridge or Slatersville was a five- to seven-mile trek, which could consume the better part of a day.

Fred Hartnett taught his son Dowdy the technique of catching, as well as how to play aggressively and intelligently. (Town of Millville J.G. Fitzgerald Historical Society, Inc.)

When Dowdy was about eight years old, he noticed catching equipment — a catcher's mitt and a mask — in the Gibbons barn, a reminder of when the Millville Town Team manager played the game. Gibbons gladly gave the gear to the young catcher as a gift. "Even at that age, Leo was all baseball…. [At the games,] Leo was always around the team. Such enthusiasm! Such dedication! And he'd watch every move like a hawk. He was only eight or nine, but he was absorbing the finer points of the game even then. I can't remember anyone else his age with the same desire, enthusiasm, and will to make his effort count…. As a young fellow, he was never in trouble. Baseball was first in his thoughts. He'd have been a success in any sport."[14]

Several years later, Dowdy joined the Bluejays, an organized team for boys between the ages of 11 and 14. The Jays played against any junior team that would meet them. One of their opponents was the Cato Street Tigers from Woonsocket. George Egan was a member of the Tigers. "We called him 'Hick' Hartnett because he came from that Purcell Hill part of Millville. Of course, we were from the big city. Hick used to be late for our Sunday games; I think he'd have to serve Mass before he could leave. He could hit, and we always tried to score as many runs early as we could, because we knew once he arrived, he'd knock in some. He could catch, pitch, play the outfield — anything.

Hick was getting his height at this time; he was tall and lean and very quick. He could throw twice as fast and twice as hard as the rest of us. He was a good base runner, and he would steal as soon as he'd reach base. And he could hit the ball a long ways.... I still recall him as a very friendly, likable fellow."[15]

At age 14, Dowdy completed his eighth-grade education at Longfellow Grammar School and joined the labor force. He also played baseball for the Millville Town Team, along with his batterymate, Tim McNamara. McNamara was an overpowering right-handed pitcher, who went on to pitch for Blackstone High School and Fordham University before entering professional baseball with the Boston Braves. But in 1914, he was a member of the Townies. "I was spoiled when Dowdy was catching," McNamara said. "I knew I wouldn't have to worry about runners taking leads. I knew he'd throw them out anyway. I was careless that way, but I could afford to be. Dowdy always had a great arm."[16]

Dowdy's father Fred "never missed a weekend game when [Dowdy] was playing, arranging his [trolley] run so this could be taken care of. He always sat in a tree to watch the games at Millville. From his perch, he would holler instructions to his son on almost every move that [Dowdy] made. When [Dowdy] was up in a pinch, the father invariably would shout, 'It's no beans for you tonight if you don't sock one. This was a pretty dire threat, for in New England, folks don't have much Saturday and Sunday evenings except beans."[17]

Elsewhere, the decade of the teens witnessed many momentous events, both around the world and in the field of athletics. The local newspaper, the *Woonsocket Call*, was the only link between Millville and the outside world, since radio and television were still waiting to be invented. In April 1912, the supposedly "unsinkable" luxury liner *Titanic*, on a voyage from England to New York, went to the bottom of the North Atlantic Ocean, off Newfoundland, after colliding with an iceberg. More than 1,500 of the 2,400 passengers on board were lost.

Two years later, in 1914, the "Miracle Boston Braves," under manager

George Stallings, practically stole the 1914 pennant from John McGraw's mighty New York Giants. In mid-July, the Bostonians were mired in the cellar, 10 games under 500. Then, unbelievably, they began a surge that carried them to the top of the National League by late August. They went on to capture the Senior Circuit flag by a whopping 10½ games over the New Yorkers, then swept Connie Mack's powerful Philadelphia Athletics four straight in the World Series.

Dowdy Hartnett was oblivious to the goings-on in the outside world. He was only concerned with winning baseball games. He was an accomplished catcher, but he still hadn't filled out completely. His 155-pound mass was spread out over a six-foot frame, his thin face framed by two prominent ears, but as McNamara noted, "in that 14–16 age period, he began to develop. Even as a kid, he had an incredible arm. He could always throw."[18]

Forty miles away in Boston, the Red Sox met the Brooklyn Dodgers in the 1916 Fall Classic. The Sox were led by a brash 21-year-old southpaw pitcher named Babe Ruth, who had compiled a glittering 23–12 record in the American League during the season, with a league-leading 1.75 earned run average. In the series, won by Boston four games to one, Ruth went 1–0 with 13 consecutive scoreless innings. Two years later, he would pitch another 16⅔ consecutive scoreless innings to establish a World Series mark of 29⅔ scoreless innings, a record that would stand for 42 years, until it was broken by Whitey Ford of the New York Yankees in 1961.

Dowdy was gainfully employed from 1914 to 1918. He worked on the production line at the Millville Rubber Shop, and he was able to keep a small allowance from his earnings after paying his mother for his room and board. He was beginning to feel like an adult. He was independent, he was working steady, and he had no responsibilities. It was the best of times for the fun-loving teenager. In his free time, he played baseball and hung out with his buddies. "Dowdy was a happy-go-lucky guy. He did well, but never had a swelled head.... Everyone was Dowdy's friend. Even in his younger days, he had a great personality." His mother once said, "Leo wakes up each day with a smile on his face."[19]

Millville, at that time, was a hard-working, blue-collar community. It was a time of frugal living, strict morals, and simple pleasures. It was also a time of close family ties, low crime rates, serious religious affiliations, a drug-free environment, and carefree childhoods. Everyone was equal. No one was rich, and no one was poor. Many families were large, and several members of the family usually worked at the local mills, so there was enough money to pay the rent, buy food, and enjoy an occasional night out dancing or socializing at one of the town's 17 bars. Anyone 14 years or older could always get a job at the Millville Rubber Shop or the Lawrence Felt Company. The pay was small (about $3.60 a week) and the hours were long (55 hours for 5½ days), but the work was steady. It was important to have two or more members of the family working, because the Saturday food shopping trips could fill many grocery bags and cost $3–5.00. It was a hard life, but it was a slower and more relaxed time. It was America at its best.

As Dowdy reached age 18, his interests changed. He started to take an interest in girls. He didn't have a regular girlfriend, but he dated Mary Fitzgerald on occasion, and he regularly palled around with Margaret Miles and Mary Whalen. He often borrowed his father's motorcycle and chauffeured the girls around town to do errands or visit friends. On Friday and Saturday nights, groups of boys and girls would travel to the carnival at Nipmuc Park in Mendon, or to the dances at Rhodes-on-the-Pawtuxet in nearby Cranston, or to Lake Pearl in Wrentham, Massachusetts. And, when the guys wanted to enjoy a "big-city" atmosphere on a Saturday night, they would take the trolley to Woonsocket, a booming metropolis of 28,000, to hang out at the local ice cream parlor, take in a silent movie, or go to a dance.

In the outside world, a savage war had been raging in Europe since 1914, after Archduke Franz Ferdinand of Austria-Hungary was assassinated by a Serbian revolutionary. In 1917, the United States was finally dragged into the conflict after Germany had committed repeated acts of war against American interests. On April 6, the American Congress approved a declaration of war against Germany, and the U.S. armed forces joined the fray almost immediately. The war dragged on for another 18 months before Germany finally accepted defeat, officially surrendering to the allies on November 11, 1918.

Dowdy's buddy, Tim McNamara, graduated from Blackstone High School in 1918 and was awarded a baseball scholarship to Fordham University. That may have made his batterymate sit up and take notice of the opportunities he was missing by dropping out of school, because when he was offered a small scholarship by Dan Sullivan, coach of the Dean Academy baseball team, the Millville youngster jumped at the chance.

In September 1918, Charles Leo Hartnett began his studies at Dean Academy, a prep school in nearby Franklin, Massachusetts. It was rumored that Hartnett was hoping to go to either Holy Cross University or Tufts University after graduating from Dean, but that was never confirmed. During the school year, Dowdy lived at home, getting up at the crack of dawn in order to catch the 7:15 train out of Blackstone. Then he caught another train home in the evening as soon as classes ended. He seldom went out at night during the week, preferring to stay home and study.

Dowdy enjoyed the school life at Dean, but baseball was a grind. Coach Dan Sullivan was a known taskmaster, whose goal was to win at all costs. "Stories are still told that, after his team lost an out-of-town game, he refused

the players a ride and told them to hitchhike back to Franklin.... Once at a football game, a small group from the hometown of one of the second-line players sat behind the Dean bench and chanted throughout the contest: 'We want McIntyre, we want McIntyre.' ...Finally Sullivan got fed up. He yelled from one end of the bench, 'McIntyre, come here!' McIntyre raced toward Sullivan, and the hometown admirers stood and clapped and cheered. 'Mac,' Sullivan said, 'Go up in the stands with those people, will you? They want you to sit with them.'"[20]

When the baseball season got underway, Dowdy was the team's utility man, playing every position except pitcher and second base. The first team catcher was a boy named Inky Sullivan, no relation to the coach, who was four or five inches taller than Dowdy and about 30 pounds heavier. Actually Dowdy was the starting catcher in the opening game and batted cleanup against Worcester Classical High School on April 12. Classical held a 2–0 lead after 3½ innings, but an 11-run uprising in the bottom of the fourth sparked Dean to an 18–4 romp. Sullivan pinch-hit during the big rally and caught the rest of the game. Hartnett, who went 0-for-4, finished up in right field. Dowdy, who was more versatile than the 200-pound Sullivan, caught only two complete games and parts of three others during the rest of the season. Most of the time, he played wherever he was needed.

One day, while hanging out at pitcher Al McCoy's dormitory room after classes, Dowdy announced to his teammates, "I'm going to be a big-league baseball player." That brought hoots and hollers from his buddies, who noted, "How do you expect to hold down a big-league job when you can't even make first-string catcher on our team?" The kid from Millville just grinned and promised, "I'll be a big-leaguer all right, and don't you forget it." According to McCoy, "He was a slugger at the bat and an excellent performer behind it, but the coach was wise enough to see that he could use him almost anywhere on the team, whereas the 200-odd pounds of Inky would only fit into the position of catcher."[21]

In the second game of the season, he was stationed in left field and hit in the seventh slot. He went 1-for-3 in the game, as Dean romped over the Boston YMCA 14–5. And the famous "Hartnett Arm" was one of the features of the game. He gunned down two runners at the plate while the game was still in doubt.[22] One of his biggest days at the plate came against Taft School of Watertown, Connecticut, on April 23. Hitting out of the second slot in the batting order, the rangy catcher led his team to a 21–1 slaughter

Opposite page: **Dowdy Hartnett attended Dean Academy in 1919. As can be seen here, he enjoyed a "prep school" life. (Town of Millville J.G. Fitzgerald Historical Society, Inc.)**

by banging out two singles and a double in five at-bats. He also threw out two runners attempting to steal.[23]

Two games later, he ripped two singles in four at-bats, as Dean once again won comfortably, this time by a 20–5 margin over Boston High School.[24] After four games, Dowdy Hartnett's batting average stood at .313, with five hits in 16 at-bats. But from there to the end of the season, he managed just three more hits in 26 trips to the plate, giving him a season average of .190. It was a disappointing finish to his first year at Dean, but he did excel defensively, making just one error, at first base, in 13 games. And the "Hartnett Arm" was as advertised. The Millville youngster had four assists in four games in the outfield and three assists in two games behind the plate, with no passed balls. He always kept the base runners honest.

Dean won eight games against six losses in 1919, a disappointing record after beginning the year with six straight victories. When asked why Hartnett was playing right field and not catching, the abrasive coach growled, "That guy's got a million-dollar arm and a five-cent head. He has no judgment, no instinct. He'll never make a catcher."[25]

During the summer of 1919, Dowdy Hartnett played baseball for the Millville Town Team. His buddy, Tim McNamara, home from Fordham University, pitched for the team. Dowdy also played for other teams in the area, such as the Rubber Shop and Berkeley, in fact for anyone who needed a catcher. Fred, at this time, was beginning to promote his son all over the county, according to his nephew. "He realized he had some ballplayer there. So what he would do is, in his travels up and down the valley as a motorman on the trolley, he would try to find games where Dowdy could catch. I had people tell me many, many years ago, that he would be in a phone booth at night, dropping dimes in, calling all over the place. And that's how he got seen."[26]

Dowdy Hartnett developed his catching skills during the dead-ball era, when catchers were noted for their defense, not their offense, and the young man from Millville was already a talented defensive receiver in 1919. He called an intelligent game, he kept the pitcher and the infielders on their toes with his constant chatter, and he had the strongest throwing arm ever seen in the Blackstone Valley. At bat, he could hit the dead ball a long way when he connected, but he was a wild swinger who didn't hit for a high average.

One of the biggest events of the summer was a three-game grudge series between Millville and their hated Blackstone neighbors. The first game was played on July 3 at the Clinton Oval in Blackstone, and the home team won, although the score was not published. On the Fourth of July, playing for Berkeley, Dowdy batted sixth and went hitless in five trips to the plate, as his team defeated the Woonsocket Crescents 8–2.

Dowdy Hartnett played on the Dean Academy baseball team in 1919. He is third from left in the back row. (Dean College)

That same night, 800 miles away in Toledo, Ohio, a 182-pound wild man defeated the 245-pound world boxing champion in convincing fashion. Jack Dempsey, known as the Manassa Mauler, pounded Jess Willard into oblivion in three rounds. The relentless challenger dropped the heavyweight king to the canvas seven times in the opening round and continued to hit him at will over the next two rounds. Willard's handlers finally threw in the towel at the end of round three, signaling their man was unable to meet the bell for round four.[27]

The second game of the Blackstone-Millville series took place on the Rubber Shop Oval, or the Meadow as it was called, in Millville, on August 10. A large crowd of 2,000 people crowded the little park next to the mills to witness the event. Blackstone jumped out to an early 2–0 lead over Tim McNamara and his teammates, but the Townies rallied late to tie the game in the bottom of the ninth, then win it in the tenth. The rubber game, one week later, was also played at the Meadow, and an even larger and rowdier crowd jammed the field to support their team. An estimated 3,500 fans were on hand as manager Fred Hartnett handed the ball to Fordham's Tim McNamara to start the game. A disputed call by the umpire in the third inning sent manager Hartnett into orbit and delayed the game for more than 30 minutes, but order was eventually restored and play resumed. Almost immediately, Bunky Kiernan of Millville doubled in the first run of the game. Two innings later, Dowdy Hartnett singled and came around to score another run, giving McNamara a 2–0 lead. The big right-hander held off a late charge by Blackstone to win 2–1.

Emotions ran high in the days following the series, with Fred Hartnett constantly badgering his Blackstone neighbors about their poor showing, and the Blackstone contingent chiding Hartnett to make the series a best three-of-five affair. An agreement was reached between the two parties, and game four took place on Sunday, September 14. Both teams were allowed to hire outside players for this game if they desired, and Blackstone took advantage of the opportunity to pad their lineup with "hired guns," while Fred Hartnett kept his lineup intact. The result was what might have been expected under those circumstances, a 15–5 Blackstone rout.

The final game of the series, which was now deadlocked at two games apiece, took place at the Clinton Oval on October 5. A large crowd filled both the grandstands and the bleachers and overflowed onto the field along the third base line. Both teams used outside players, except that Dowdy Hartnett was still the Millville catcher. Someone named McMullen pitched for Fred Hartnett's crew because Tim McNamara had returned to Fordham for the fall semester. (Unless McNamara returned home over the weekend to play in this grudge match under an assumed name so his coach wouldn't find out.) Whatever the true story was, McMullen was good enough. Millville pushed over three runs in the fifth inning and made them stand up for a 3–2 victory. Dowdy drew the collar in three plate appearances, but had two assists in three stolen base attempts. Millville stole seven bases against the Blackstone catcher, three of them contributing to their fifth inning uprising.

During the summer, Hartnett also played two games for the Millville Rubber Company against the National India Rubber Company (N.I.R.). The first game, played at Bristol on August 24, saw Tim McNamara drop a close 8–7 decision to N.I.R. The Fordham University pitcher held a 7–1 lead after seven innings, but tired in the last two innings, being touched up for four runs in the eighth and three more in the ninth. Dowdy Hartnett, hitting out of the third slot, banged out two hits in five trips to the plate and had two assists. The second game, played on the Asylum Grounds in Bristol on September 13 gave the same results. The game was scoreless for three innings, but N.I.R. pushed over two runs in the fourth and two more

The Millville Town Team was managed by Fred Hartnett in 1919. He is on the left in the back row. Tim McNamara and Dowdy Hartnett are second and third from the left in the front row. (Jane McNamara Gilmore)

in the sixth to win 4–0. McNamara struck out four, but Purvere, a former Eastern League hurler, fanned 11 for N.I.R. Hartnett, hitting cleanup, went 1-for-4.[28]

Millville wasn't the only center of the baseball world in 1919. It was just as exciting in Boston, where the brash, young Red Sox pitcher of a few years ago was now a feared slugger. Outfielder Babe Ruth banged out 29 home runs, breaking Buck Freeman's major league mark of 25, set with the Washington Senators in 1899. And the Babe still took his turn on the mound often enough to rack up nine victories against just five losses.

The World Series of 1919 pitted the powerful Chicago White Sox against the Cincinnati Reds, but betting on the series was light because of rumors that the Fall Classic was fixed. And the rumors turned out to be true as Cincinnati took Chicago to task, five games to three, thanks to the inept pitching of Ed Cicotte and Lefty Williams, as well as the ragged play of first baseman Chick Gandil, shortstop Swede Risberg, and center fielder Happy Felsch. Fred McMullin, Buck Weaver, and "Shoeless Joe" Jackson would also be implicated in the crime.

After the season ended, many of the major league players participated in local exhibition games to supplement their income, which was barely above a blue-collar wage. One of the more interesting series of the fall was a five-game "Little World Series," that was played between Attleboro and North Attleboro, Massachusetts, from September 27 to October 16. Many baseball people have called it the only honest World Series of the year. The Attleboro squad was composed of players from the National League and included such legends as Rogers Hornsby, George Sisler, and Grover Cleveland Alexander. North Attleboro's American League team included the magnificent Babe Ruth, Walter Johnson, and Eddie Collins.

In the opener, North Attleboro took the measure of the visiting Attleboro squad by the score of 5–2 at Columbia Field. "The Big Train" toed the rubber for North Attleboro and was ably supported by the big bats of Joe Dugan, Jiggs Donahue, and Bill McCarthy. The North squad made it two in a row with a 6–3 victory at Brady Field in Attleboro on October 4, the same day the "Black Sox" were dumping one to Cincinnati, 2–0, on two errors by Eddie Cicotte. Babe Ruth, in left field for North Attleboro, went 1-for-4. The third game was a duplicate of the first two games, with North again coming out on top, this time by a 4–3 mark. Braggo Roth had three hits, and Stuffy McInnis and Mike Menoskey had two hits each. Attleboro took the final two games by scores of 6–2 and 8–2, thanks to the overpowering pitching of Alexander, who tossed two complete game efforts. It is conceivable that Dowdy Hartnett and his buddies took in one or more of the games, since North Attleboro was a short 15 miles southeast of Millville and could be reached easily by train.[29]

At the same time the Little World Series was being played, an event of monumental proportions took place in Washington DC. On October 28, "the United States Congress passed the 18th amendment, making the manufacture and sale of alcoholic beverages illegal in the country. It was the culmination of a 200-year effort on the part of various organizations and governments, to control the excessive use of alcohol. Prohibition would have a profound effect on American society during the decade of the 20s, but not in the way it adherents expected."[30]

In September 1919, Dowdy Hartnett returned to Dean Academy for his second year and began the daily train rides back and forth between Blackstone and Franklin. The first term ended in December, and shortly after the Christmas holidays, Hartnett received a letter from the Dean's office, notifying him that he would have to take two final examinations over again before he could begin the second term. He quit school and returned to his production job at the Millville Rubber Shop.

2

On the Road to the Major Leagues, 1920–1921

On January 3, 1920, the city of Boston was stunned by the announcement that Babe Ruth, the worlds' greatest home run hitter, had been sold to the New York Yankees for $120,000 by Red Sox owner Harry Frazee, who reportedly needed the money to finance a Broadway play, "No No Nanette." That move signaled a decline in Boston's baseball fortunes, that has extended into the 21st century. The Red Sox, who captured five of the first 16 World Series played, have never won another one.

As the second decade of the twentieth century got underway, a feeling of despair and hopelessness swept the country, fueled by a depression and escalating prices. After suffering through two years of world war, with thousands of America's young men being killed or crippled, the people began to take a fatalistic approach to life. Hedonism permeated city life. Debauchery, self-indulgence, and self-gratification became the law of the land. The motto of the times was "Eat, drink, and be merry, for tomorrow we die."

January 16 was an important day in U.S. history. Prohibition went into effect — and a small-time Chicago criminal named Al Capone turned 21. Saloons were closed by law, but they were replaced almost immediately by illegal clubs known as speakeasies. The city of Chicago boasted of having over 100 of these dens of iniquity, where drinks that had previously cost 15 cents now sold for 75 cents.

Prohibition, which was intended to reduce the alcohol consumption in the United States, proved to be a complete failure, as bootleg liquor flowed like water. Illegal booze poured into the cities from Canada and Mexico, as well as from thousands of moonshine stills around the country, and gangsters took control of the industry, beginning an age of lawlessness that car-

Dowdy Hartnett worked in the Millville Rubber Shop in the late teens and in 1920. (Town of Millville J.G. Fitzgerald Historical Society, Inc.)

ried well into the thirties. The age eventually became known as the "Roaring Twenties," or the "Jazz Age," where anything went. Wanton young women called flappers compromised the morals of the country. Nothing was too outrageous or degrading.

But the twenties also witnessed a technological explosion across the United States. Industrial automation and new assembly lines made the automobile affordable to most Americans. And the invention of the radio, the telephone, and talking motion pictures provided people with hours of entertainment and enjoyment.

Back in Millville, the Roaring Twenties were just a fantasy that people read about in the *Woonsocket Call*. In the real world, "Dowdy" Hartnett had resumed life as a factory worker and part-time basketball player. He played for the Knights of Columbus (K of C) team with his younger brother Sweetie, who was one of the high scorers on the team and one of its most dominant players, controlling the boards at both ends of the court.

When spring arrived, Dowdy Hartnett was catching for the Millville Rubber Shop team in the semipro Footwear League, composed of teams from plants in Woonsocket, Cambridge, Melrose, Bristol, and Malden. The league schedule called for 10 games, two games against each team, to be played on Saturday afternoons between May 20 and July 22. Games were home and home affairs, and players traveled to them by train. Players were paid their normal hourly rate by their companies. "In the season opener, the Millville Rubber Shop nine humiliated the Alice Mill Team from Woonsocket, 13–4, with Booster McCormick striking out 11 in authoring a four-hitter. Catcher Hartnett went 1-for-4 — a double — and stole a base.

"In another game, around Boston, the umpire had a call to make at second base. This day, on a steal, he went toward second, and was right in line with Dowdy's throw.... The ball hit the ump on the head, and he fell face down on the ground. He was out cold. They had to call an ambulance and take the poor guy to the hospital. Dowdy's throws were like shots."[1]

The final game of the season was memorable, but easily forgettable, as far as Millville was concerned. It was played on Bristol Common between the Bristol National India Rubber team and the Millville Rubber Shop squad on Saturday, July 22. Bristol led the league by one game, but a victory by Millville would force a playoff between the two teams to determine the league champion. Dowdy Hartnett started for the Rubber Shop, and clung to a 10–6 lead after seven innings, but he ran out of gas in the eighth, and Bristol scored eight times to put the game on ice. The final score was 14–10. Hart-

Dowdy Hartnett is seventh from the left in the photograph of the 1920 Millville Rubber Shop team. (Town of Millville J.G. Fitzgerald Historical Society, Inc.)

nett did better with the bat than he did on the mound. Millville's cleanup hitter stroked three singles in five at-bats, scored two runs, and stole one base. His replacement behind the plate didn't fare as well. The Bristol boys swiped nine sacks against him.

The oldest Hartnett boy had a busy summer. In addition to playing in the Footwear League, he played baseball with teams all over Blackstone Valley, as well as for the Pere Marquette K of C in South Boston. He was hitting the ball with authority wherever he played, and his catching and throwing were as sensational as ever. According to the *Call*, major league scouts were becoming aware of the 19 year old backstop and attending some of his games. One story reported that New York Giants manager John McGraw directed one of his scouts, Jesse Burkett, to visit Millville and assess the potential of Dowdy Hartnett. Burkett, who had a sensational major league career between 1890 and 1905, racking up 2,872 base hits, good for a .340 career batting average, reported back to McGraw that Hartnett would never make the grade as a catcher because his hands were too small.

The Pere Marquette Council K of C team visited the Clinton Oval on

Dowdy played for the Millville Town Team in 1920. He is in the front row, on the right. (Town of Millville J.G. Fitzgerald Historical Society, Inc.)

August 22 to battle the Woonsocket Caseys, but they were outgunned by the locals 6–1. Hartnett, batting eighth for Pere Marquette, provided the only fireworks in the game for the South Boston team. As reported in the *Call*: "Hartnett of Millville, who big league scouts are giving the 'Double O,' scored the Boston nine's lone tally. He got a toe-hold on one of Sullivan's benders and rapped it over the left field fence for the circuit."[2]

Dowdy wasn't the only outstanding baseball player in the Hartnett family, according to his nephew Fred. "My father [Harold] and my uncle Chickie, or Herman, played too. They were in the minors, and my grandfather used to say that they were better than Dowdy. The difference was, he had it inside. He had the drive. Chickie played a lot of positions. He was a catcher and a second baseman. He had a lot of ability."[3] One Hartnett friend said that Chickie signed to play pro ball, went to Reading, Pennsylvania where the team was located, got homesick, and came home without ever playing a game.

Dowdy's sisters played ball too, "particularly Anna or Charlie. She ended up with a bad back later in life, and part of it was because she was a catcher. She was catching baseball, not softball. She played on boy's teams. Later on, she played softball. Her brothers said she was a really good athlete, maybe as good as they were."[4] Three of the girls were exceptional on the diamond. They played semipro ball all over New England, and their team was reputed to be one of the best. Charlie caught, Mildred played third, and Mary played short. And they were all blessed with the "Hartnett Arm." Whenever the Millville Town Team played, Charlie was asked to put on a throwing exhibition before the game. That's how good she was.

The major league season was winding down on August 16, 1920, when tragedy struck. Ray Chapman, the shortstop for the league-leading Cleveland Indians, was felled by a fastball to the temple, thrown by New York Yankee submarine pitcher Carl Mays. Chapman died 12 hours later without ever regaining consciousness. Mays' pitch just missed the plate, but Chapman, who was notorious for crowding the plate, couldn't get out of the way fast enough. He remains the only major league player to die as the result of being hit by a pitched ball. Mays, a five-time 20-game winner, was on his way to a 26–11 season when the accident occurred.

Cleveland had battled the Chicago White Sox throughout the season, leading most of the way before the Chapman tragedy. They fell back into second place briefly, then regrouped behind manager Tris Speaker and held a slight ½-game lead over the Sox on September 28. On that date, another bombshell struck. Eight White Sox players were indicted in federal court in Chicago for conspiring to throw the 1919 World Series. The players were immediately suspended from the game by Baseball Commissioner Kenesaw

Mountain Landis, throwing the baseball world into chaos. Kid Gleason's Pale Hose dropped their next two games and were quickly eliminated from the pennant race.

Along the Great White Way, the Yankees' new slugger, George Herman "Babe" Ruth, absolutely destroyed the season home run record by pounding out 54 round trippers, with a big assist from the new lively baseball that was introduced at the beginning of the season.

A momentous event unfolded in Pittsburgh, Pennsylvania, on November 2. The Westinghouse Electric & Manufacturing Company, broadcasting on station KDKA, sent the world's first broadcast across the country, announcing the election returns from the presidential race and declaring Warren G. Harding the winner.[5]

Dowdy Hartnett's date with destiny was rapidly approaching as 1920 drew to a close. He was contacted by a representative of the American Steel & Wire Company's North Works, located in Worcester. They had baseball teams in both Worcester and New Haven in an inter-company league. Dowdy joined the employ of the North Works plant in December and went to work in their Worcester plant in the shipping department at a salary of $35.00 a week.

January 1921 saw young Dowdy Hartnett begin his new job in Worcester, 26 miles from Millville, a boring one-hour train ride away. "I had to arise at 5:30 in the morning to get to my job and I never got home for supper until 7:30 in the evening. One morning it was 20 degrees below zero when I set out for the scene of my employment. When I got into the warmth of the plant, I discovered both my ears had been frozen, causing me the greatest pain. I vowed then and there I'd never work another day in my life. And I never did."[6] He stayed on with the American Steel and Wire Company into the spring and worked out with the baseball team for a short time; but on March 12, he made the move that changed his life. He signed a professional baseball contract with the Worcester Boosters of the Eastern League. One story of how Dowdy Hartnett was signed by the Boosters said the Worcester manager signed him as a favor to his father. Dowdy's nephew Fred laughed when he thought about it. "He probably signed Dowdy because Fred drove him crazy with all his phone calls."[7] The Eastern League had a Class A designation in 1921, but there were also Class B, C, and D leagues. In today's structure, it would be a AA league.

Young Dowdy Hartnett's life took another turn at this time: he fell in love. The object of his affections was Mae Carroll, a beautiful young lady who worked in the office at Summerfield's Furniture Store in Whitinsville. The eight-mile trip from Millville to Whitinsville could be accomplished by taking a train, then transferring to a trolley, but Dowdy preferred to take his father's Indian. The only problem was that the noise from the bike brought numerous complaints from Mae's neighbors on Oak Street, who had to rise early in the morning to go to work in the steel mill. Dowdy solved that problem by parking his bike in the town square and walking two blocks to Mae's house. Dowdy and Mae's romance was not a lasting one, but the two remained friends for many years.

The major league baseball season opened on April 13, and the New York Yankees got off the mark quickly, pummeling the Philadelphia Athletics 11–1. Babe Ruth chipped in with two doubles and three singles in five at-bats. The Eastern League season opened two weeks later, with Jack Mack's Worcester Boosters hosting Hartford. Worcester was hoping to improve on their 1920 season, when they finished in second place, six games behind the pennant-winning New Haven team. Gus Redmond caught, and Dowdy Hartnett watched the game from the bench as the Boosters went down 2–0 before the spitballs of former St. Louis Brown pitcher Kewpie Pennington. On the 28th, they lost again by a score of 4–1.

That same day, Chick Gandil, the former first baseman of the Chicago White Sox, was arrested in Los Angeles, California, in connection with the 1919 World Series conspiracy. Soon, all eight conspirators were rounded up, and they went to trial in July. They were acquitted on all charges, but that didn't stop Baseball Commissioner Kenesaw Mountain Landis. He banned all eight players from baseball for life. None of them ever again played in organized baseball, although several of them, including Joe Jackson, Buck Weaver, and Lefty Williams, continued to play in outlaw leagues and in exhibition games for many years.

Worcester got on the winning track on the 29th, beating the Pittsfield Hillies 3–2, as left fielder Marty Callaghan ripped two base hits. On the 1st, they blanked Waterbury 3–0, and Dowdy Hartnett still hadn't seen any action. But his baptism of fire came on May 2 in Waterbury. The pride of Millville entered the game in the fifth inning, with the Boosters on top 7–5. He singled in his first two professional at-bats, as Worcester prevailed 10–6. Conway and Callaghan each had a triple. The next day, Hartnett caught the entire game. Chief Bender, the former Philadelphia A's pitcher and future Hall of Famer, was the manager of the New Haven team and also its ace pitcher. He took the measure of the Boosters, 4–3, and sent Dowdy back to the bench three times without a hit. Bender tossed a five-hitter and led the Hartford attack with a triple and a home run in three at-bats.[8] Hartnett caught again on Tuesday and went 1-for-3, as Worcester beat Springfield by the score of 5–2. Axel Lindstrom, who had pitched one game for Connie Mack's A's in 1916, threw a complete game seven-hitter. Gabby Hartnett never forgot his Worcester initiation. "In one of my first games, I tried to throw a runner out at second base, and my throw hit the center field fence on the first bounce. After the inning ended, manager Jack Mack said, 'In this league kid, the players run. They don't fly.'"

Two weeks after the season started, fate intervened to accelerate Hartnett's career. On May 16, the Boosters were in Albany to do battle with the Capital nine. Gus Redmond was catching and, in the fourth inning, the big backstop broke his leg sliding into second base. Suddenly, Dowdy Hartnett was thrust into the first-string catcher's job. Worcester won the game 4–3 behind Jerry Belanger's 4-for-4 day. Hartnett drew the collar in two trips to the plate.[9] By the end of May, Mack had his team in second place with a 17–11 record, two games behind Bridgeport and Hartford. When the batting averages were released, Dowdy Hartnett was hitting a respectable .255 with 14 hits in 66 at-bats.

June 3 was a memorable day in the Eastern League in more ways than one. First, the Worcestorites vaulted into first place with an 8–7 win over Albany. Hartnett, batting out of the eighth slot, went 1-for-4. The other memorable event took place in Hartford, where the Connecticut team edged Pittsfield 2–1. The first baseman for Hartford was a man named Henry Lewis, who was making his professional debut. The big, left-handed slugger went 0-for-3 in the game, but broke out of the box with a single and a triple the next night against Waterbury. After the season ended, it was discovered that Henry Lewis was actually Henry Louis Gehrig, a student at Columbia University, who would go on to become one of the most feared sluggers in baseball history. It seems that John McGraw, the crafty manager of the New York Giants, signed Gehrig to a professional contract and wanted to get him some professional experience without affecting his collegiate standing. When the ruse came to light, Gehrig's contract with the Giants was voided, and he had to sit out a season at Columbia before he could resume his college baseball career. Gehrig (or Lewis), who batted .261 in 14 games for Hartford in 1921, terrorized the collegiate ranks two years later, pummeling the ball at a .444 clip, with seven monstrous home runs in 63 at-bats. He also pitched for Columbia, going 6–4 in 11 games.[10]

Once Dowdy Hartnett was elevated to the number one catcher position, he began to take more notice of his deficiencies with the bat. John McNamara noted, "Dowdy wasn't too good with the bat when he was young, but he developed into a good hitter with time."[11] One of the things that set Dowdy Hartnett apart from most of the other young men was his determination to do whatever was necessary to make himself a better ballplayer. He was one of the hardest workers on the Worcester Booster team, and he would go on to be one of the hardest workers on the Chicago Cubs team over a 20-year period. In 1921, Dowdy set out to make himself a better hitter. Every night when the team was home, Dowdy would take the trolley back to Millville and get one of his buddies to pitch to him at the Meadow. Tom Feeney, one of the volunteers, remembered, "Night after night, it was ... curve ... curve ... curve. Occasionally I'd give him a fastball or a change of pace, but mostly it was curves. Dowdy lived for baseball, and he wanted to use every minute to make himself a better player."[12]

As June wore on, Dowdy Hartnett's hitting improved, and the Worcester Boosters went on a hot streak. By month's end, they were on top of the league by a full 3½ games. That was their peak, however. They gradually slipped back into the pack and ended July in third place, two games behind the Pittsfield Hillies. They won the last game of the month, knocking off New Haven 6–4, and Dowdy Hartnett led the attack with 2-for-4, including a triple.[13]

During August, they treaded water and still trailed the Hillies by four games as the month came to an end. The big event of the month for Dowdy Hartnett was a day that was held in his honor: Saturday, August 27. It was officially "Leo Hartnett Day" in Worcester. The town of Millville was almost deserted, as hordes of its residents hit the road north and descended on Boulevard Park. Jim Mulvey, a former Hartnett teammate at the Rubber Shop, acted as master of ceremonies. The fans chipped in to give their favorite son a purse of $100, and a band entertained them between innings. And Dowdy Hartnett didn't disappoint his fans, as reported by Jim Murphy: "In the seventh inning, the Boosters were hanging onto a slim lead, when Bridgeport threatened with two hits and a bunt. Marty Callaghan threw to Hartnett to cut off a run at the plate, but Hartnett, noting that Bridgeport shortstop Wes Kingdon was trying to make third, ran well down into the infield to get Callaghan's throw, and rifled the ball to third, cutting down the runner and ending the rally. The run counted, but the inning was over. Worcester won, 4–1."[14] Hartnett finished the day 1-for-4, and Larry Bennett tossed a complete game four-hitter. The Boosters closed out the month with a doubleheader sweep of Springfield, winning 4–0 and 8–3. Axel Lindstrom did the iron-man bit, throwing two complete games. The twin win left Worcester four games behind Pittsfield, but things were about to get interesting. On September 2, Johnny Bish, in relief of Lefty Bach, defeated Hartford by a score of 12–5, closing the gap between the Boosters and the Hillies to 3½ games. Dowdy Hartnett contributed a single and a double to help the cause. Chief Bender was knocked out of the box in less than two innings by the Mack-men.[15]

As the stretch run began, the Worcester team was still snipping at Pittsfield's heels, with just four games separating the two adversaries. In early September, the Boosters visited Albany. Unknown to the Millville catcher, the Chicago Cubs sent scout Jack Doyle to New York to evaluate his playing skills. Doyle was known as "Dirty Jack" for his rough play during a 17-year major league career, including two years with the battling Baltimore Orioles under Ned Hanlon. He loved players with character in their face, and he was enthralled by Dowdy Hartnett. The Worcester backstop impressed him even more in the game, won by the Boosters 5–4. He went 2-for-3 with the bat and blocked the plate against an oncoming runner like a Greek at Thermopylae. Dowdy remembered what happened next: "Well, one day I went to my manager and asked for a loan of two dollars because I was broke and hungry. He surprised me by passing me a five-dollar bill. 'Take this,' he said with a smile, 'and send me some post cards next spring from California.' 'What do you mean, California?' I asked. 'I mean that you'll be out there next spring because this afternoon I sold you to the Chicago Cubs!' That was the realization of a lifelong dream and I sure was happy. I vowed I'd make good and I'd never stop trying."[16]

As the sun was coming up on September 12, the Worcester Boosters were in Pittsfield to do battle with the Hillies in a six-game home and home series, that would decide the Eastern League pennant race. Pittsfield's lead had been cut to just one game as the series got underway with a double-header. The Hillies made the most of their opportunities, knocking off the challengers in both games by scores of 6–1 and 4–3. In the opener, Colonel Snover, a 6'½", 200-pound southpaw, tossed a three-hitter at Jack Mack's boys, and Johnny Bates homered with two on in the first. Snover had previous major league experience, but it was limited to just two games with the New York Giants in 1919, where he went 0-for-1. In the nightcap, Bates was the hero again. This time, Pittsfield's shortstop, who was 4-for-7 on the day, blasted a game-winning homer. Dowdy Hartnett, now called Leo by his teammates, played in game two and went 1-for-4. The next day, Pittsfield won again, 2–1, and Hartnett drew the collar in three at-bats.[17]

The teams moved on to Worcester to resume their series, but the situation looked bleak for the Worcester team. Pittsfield's three-game sweep at home left the Boosters four games back with just 13 games remaining in the season. They needed a sweep of their own to remain in contention. But that didn't happen. On September 14, the two teams met in another double-header. The Hillies went on a rampage in game one, routing Mack's troops by the score of 16–6. Colonel Snover, pitching on just one days rest, threw a complete game for the win. Twenty-six-year-old Axel Lindstrom from Gustafsburg, Sweden, who had pitched both ends of a doubleheader just two weeks before to keep the Boosters in the race, was obviously physically drained as he was pounded by Pittsfield. He pitched courageously, but he had nothing left and struggled for nine innings. The Hillies ripped him for five home runs, including three grand slams. Howie Baker, a strong, 5'11", 175-pound third baseman with 28 games of major league experience, went 5-for-5 in the game, with two singles, a double, and two home runs. His first homer, a towering blast over the left field fence with the bases loaded in the first inning, was called the longest homer ever hit to left field at Boulevard Park. Bates followed that performance with a grand slam of his own, over the same fence in the second inning, and Snover hit the third grand slam over the right field fence in the ninth. Hartnett, pinch-hitting for Lindstrom in the ninth, singled. In game two, Pittsfield prevailed again, this time by a 10–5 score. The pride of Millville had one hit in three at-bats in the losing cause. In the finale of the series, Pittsfield made it six straight by whipping Mack's team once again, 13–2, and essentially clinching the pennant for the Hillies.[18] Leo Dowdy Hartnett had a single and a triple in four at-bats, but it wasn't enough to derail the Berkshire team. They outscored the Boosters 47–18 in the six-game series, justifying their claim to the throne. Hartnett played in five of the games, one as pinch-hitter, and went 5-for-15.

Worcester closed out its season in Albany and took out their frustrations on the Capital City boys, burying them 26–2 under a 28-hit attack. Lefty Sullivan, who had just been sold to the Philadelphia Athletics, took the brunt of the pounding, which included a big 6-for-6 day by Hartnett. The Boosters jumped on the slender right-hander for four runs in the opening frame and drove him to cover under a 16-run barrage in the second. Larry Bennett held Albany to six hits as he coasted to an easy victory.[19] When the season ended, Pittsfield finished with a record of 92–59, giving them a comfortable five-game edge over the Worcester Boosters. Colonel Snover led all Eastern League pitchers in victories with 25.

Dowdy Hartnett finished the season strong, batting .443 in September, bringing his average up from .225 to .264 when the curtain came down. His final numbers showed 21 doubles, seven triples, and three home runs in 345 at-bats, which would equate to 33 doubles, 11 triples, and five home runs over a full season of 550 at-bats. Apparently, with the help of his friend Tom Feeney, and instructions from Jack Mack and his coaches, Dowdy Hartnett became a hitter in Worcester, where previously he had been known as a hard, wild swinger. As he himself confessed, "When I was a youngster, I wanted to take a wagon tongue for a bat, dig a good toe hold, and swing with all my might. But I smartened up fast when I found out I wasn't hitting well. After I settled on a bat with proper weight and length, my batting average improved quickly. If there's one thing I like better than anything else, it's my base hits.[20]

Under the Big Top, Babe Ruth's tremendous influence on all levels of society became evident when he was arrested in New York for speeding. The judge fined the Bambino $100 and sentenced him to one day in jail. But he let Babe out at 4 PM so he could make that day's game at the Polo Grounds[21].

Babe Ruth continued his slugging in 1921, setting a new home run record with 59 circuit blows. The Yankees captured the American League flag by 4½ games over Tris Speaker's Cleveland Indians. In the World Series, however, John McGraw's Giants, who had nosed out the Pittsburgh Pirates by four games in the Senior Circuit, took care of Miller Huggins' Bombers, five games to three. Leading the Giants' attack were Frank Snyder at .364 and Irish Meusel at .345. Jesse Barnes and "Shufflin' Phil" Douglas each won two games. The Bambino, at .313 with one homer, was the only Yankee batter to solve the Giants pitchers.

Dowdy Hartnett's minor league career was over. From this point on, he would be a major leaguer. His teammate, Marty Callaghan, was also sold to the Cubs, and he would play with Dowdy in Chicago, off and on, from 1922 through 1930. Marty was a journeyman player, who would compile a .267 average in 295 major league games.

Dowdy would not be the first Woonsocket-born baseball player to make it to the major leagues. Twenty-six years before, Napoleon "Nap" Lajoie left his job as a horse-and-buggy driver in the Rhode Island city to join the Philadelphia Phillies, beginning a 21-year journey to the National Baseball Hall Of Fame in Cooperstown, New York. He left behind a lifetime .339 batting average, the seventeenth highest career batting average in major league history.

During this same period, the first coast-to-coast telephone conversation opened the door to yet another American technological breakthrough.[22]

Nap Lajoie is regarded by many baseball experts as the greatest second baseman who ever played the game.

3

Breaking In with the Chicago Cubs, 1922–1923

Dowdy Hartnett spent the winter of 1921–22 relaxing and avoiding manual labor. He did play in one exhibition baseball game, for Rockdale against Whitinsville, as a favor to his Worcester teammate, Jerry Belanger, who lived there. Another Booster teammate, Johnny Bish, pitched for Rockdale. Whitinsville hired two Waterbury players, pitcher Jerry Kahn and catcher George Army. Whitinsville won 2–1.[1]

The rest of the off-season was spent playing a little basketball at the Knights of Columbus, hanging out with his buddies, Tim McNamara, Joe McManus, Booster McCormick, and Chink Duffy; palling around with "the girls," and visiting with his family. He happily made the rounds of the relatives up and down the Blackstone Valley on his father's motorcycle, with his mother as copilot, and he also did a little hunting in the woods around Millville.

In early February, as the northeast was suffering through a typical snowy, frigid winter, twenty-one-year-old Charles Leo "Dowdy" Hartnett set off on the first big adventure of his life. He had spent the first 20 years of his life in relative isolation, never traveling more than 30 or 40 miles from Millville, except for the short trips to Albany during the Eastern League season, and he had never been away from home overnight other than with the Boosters. Now he was setting off on a journey that would take him to an island 25 miles off the coast of California and more than 3,000 miles from home with no friends to accompany him.

One chilly morning, Dowdy Hartnett walked the two blocks to the Millville railroad station accompanied by several family members, including his mother and father, his old baseball buddies, and other close friends like

Chink Duffy and Margaret Miles. As he was leaving, the determined young-ster confided to his sister, "I'm gonna make it, Tina." The overnight trip to Chicago was exciting, but it was also a little nerve-wracking for the big coun-try boy who was alone for the first time in his life. He checked into the Hotel LaSalle on the corner of Madison Avenue, where other Chicago Cubs hope-fuls would be staying, but he arrived well in advance of the other players because he didn't want to be late.

"For three long days I walked around that big city," he recalled years later. "I knew not a soul. I had no friends. I took in all the sights, spent many hours in my hotel, saw a few shows and did anything to amuse myself and kill time. Throughout the three days, I did not speak to a single per-son. At the end of the third day, I found an alley where I knew I was out of hearing distance and let out a great big 'hello.' I wanted to be sure I still had my voice."[2]

While biding his time in the hotel, he wrote a letter to Margaret Miles, using the new fountain pen she had given him as a going-away present. Mar-garet and Dowdy had been Preston Street (formerly Purcell's Hill) pals from early childhood. When he was a teenager, Margaret, who was a talented pianist, tried to teach him the fundamentals of the instrument, but the effort proved fruitless. She had to tell him that he would never be a piano player because his right hand didn't know what his left hand was doing, and vice versa. He wrote: "Friend Margaret: Just a line before I leave for the South [actually he went west] to let you know that I am still in existence. I always adored a fountain pen, and believe me it took me a long time to get one, because I haven't got the brains to think to bring one, not only that I haven't the necessary funds. Well Margaret words can't express how delighted I was to receive it and believe me I'll always do my best to keep in touch with you, providing the ink holds out. Whatever you do, don't get married until I get back because I want to be there. Good-bye old friend until I see you on Pre-ston St. Give my regards to the family, and also Gene. Do not write until I tell you to. Leo."

Within a day or two, other players checked into the hotel, so the affable Dowdy finally had someone to talk to other than the bellhops, the doorman, and the desk clerk. Still, when the train pulled out of Chicago and headed west to Kansas City and Los Angeles on a three-day junket, Dowdy kept pretty much to himself, taking his mother's advice: "Keep your mouth shut, your eyes open, and behave yourself. Don't say anything until you find out what's going on." One of the baseball entourage, which consisted of Cubs executives, manager Bill Killefer, six players, and a few newspapermen, was Dean Sulli-van of the *Chicago Herald Examiner*. After listening to Hartnett's monosyl-labic responses to his questions, Sullivan remarked, "You're certainly a gabby guy."[3] The Chicago writer kept referring to the Cubs catcher as "Gabby" in his columns, and slowly but surely the name caught on in the baseball world. During his first two years in Chicago, he was called Charlie, Dowdy, Leo, George, and Gabby, but eventually it became just Gabby to major league opponents, reporters, and fans. But he was always Leo to his teammates.

From L.A., the Chicago Cubs group, now numbering several dozen people, boarded a passenger ferry for the 25-mile trip to Santa Catalina Island. The entire island, which is 21 miles long, was the property of chewing gum magnate and Cubs owner William Wrigley Jr. who bought it in 1919 and built a spring training site at Avalon on the southern tip of the island. The baseball facilities were primitive in 1922, as was the rest of the volcanic island, but the scenery was spectacular, with ragged peaks stretching 2,000 feet into the sky. Avalon itself was an anachronism. It "had no paved streets. It had no sewage system. It had a poor electric light plant. Its only drinking water came from two wells, which were so inadequate most of the water had to be brought over from the mainland."[4]

There were three catchers in the first group to take the field: Bob O'Farrell, a 25-year-old veteran who was beginning his eighth year with the Cubs and was on the verge of becoming one of the best catchers in the National League; Tom Daly, an eight-year journeyman who, at age 30, was hoping to stay around for one more year; and Gabby Hartnett, an aggressive 21-year-old rookie who felt confident he could make the team. Other players included outfielder Arnold Statz, another 21-year-old rookie who was coming off a fine .310 season with Los Angeles in the strong Pacific Coast League, and Marty Callaghan, Gabby's old Worcester Booster teammate. Within weeks, Bob O'Farrell pinned the monicker "Jigger" on Statz because "he never sat, but was always 'jiggling around.'"[5]

Grover Cleveland Alexander, already a legend at 35 years of age, and coming off a somewhat disappointing 15–13 season after going 27–14 the previous year, was also in the group. The relationship between "Old Alex" and manager Bill Killefer went back a decade. Both men had joined the Philadelphia Phillies in 1911, and Killefer became Alexander's regular catcher, guiding him through three consecutive 30-victory seasons from 1915 to 1917. They were traded to the Chicago Cubs together in 1918, and Killefer kept catching Alexander, even after Bob O'Farrell joined the team. For some reason, Alex didn't like O'Farrell. After Killefer was promoted to Cubs manager, he kept a tight rein on "the alcoholic Alexander. One time, Alex wobbled into the Cub clubhouse just before the game and ducked into the washroom. Killefer followed him in and yelled 'You're still pitching.' Alexander went out and threw a one-hitter. He got the game over so fast, he was still loaded when it was over."[6]

Grover Cleveland Alexander was already a legend by the time he joined the Chicago Cubs in 1918.

The 1922 season was Bill Killefer's first full season as manager, after replacing Cubs legend Johnny Evers at the helm in mid-season the previous year, as Chicago limped home in seventh place in an eight-club league. Nineteen twenty-two was a rebuilding year, with a number of young players on the spring training roster. Rookies Marty Krug at third; Jigger Statz, Barney Friberg, and Hack Miller in the outfield; Vic Aldridge, Tony Kaufmann, and George Stueland on the mound, and Gabby Hartnett behind the plate battled aging veterans for spots on the team.

The first couple of weeks were especially rough, as manager Bill Killefer ran the entire camp ragged, trying to work off the excess blubber that many veteran players added over the winter and introducing the rookies to the sacrifices required to be a major league player. The mountains presented the perfect running track, so it was up and down, up and down, day after day. One day, Gabby told a reporter, "I hope they've got the baselines banked in the National League because one of my legs is shorter than the other from trying to run on these hills." The players also dug long ditches into which sewer lines were layed and worked on other construction projects for Mr. Wrigley. For recreation, they engaged in tug-of-war contests, played golf on Wrigley's new nine-hole golf course, went horseback riding, or went dancing.

Gabby, who didn't have an ounce of fat on him, was a bundle of nervous energy during practice from day one. He was still quiet off the field, as his mother had instructed, and he was initially intimidated on the field, playing alongside veterans like Bob O'Farrell and the legendary Grover Cleveland Alexander. But that feeling soon disappeared, and he became his old self, keeping up a constant flow of chatter, encouraging his teammates, and putting out 110 percent on every play. Killefer was particulary impressed with Hartnett's take-charge attitude and boundless energy. After the Chicago manager had seen him in action a few times, with his enthusiasm, clenched fist, and loud yell after a big play or a strikeout, he said, "Now there's a catcher."

Years later, Bob O'Farrell remembered the young rookie as being "tall and rangy—quite skinny. He filled out well later. I had never heard of Leo Hartnett. I hadn't known about him being bought from Worcester. I first noticed him at camp when he threw. He had a great arm—accurate and strong."[7] O'Farrell knew Gabby was on board for the long haul, but he didn't feel personally threatened by the Millville phenom in 1922, because he figured the kid needed a little more seasoning before he could present a real challenge. Hartnett obviously didn't agree, because when manager Bill Killefer announced the starting lineup for the season, he named O'Farrell as the catcher, to which Gabby replied, "He will if he beats me." That was an unusual remark coming from the happy-go-lucky backstop, who was noted for his geniality. According to one teammate, "He grinned all the time, on the field, off the field, at the dinner table, in the hotel lobby, everywhere. You couldn't help like him, because he so obviously liked you. He liked everybody. But he never talked much."[8]

The Cubs were isolated on Catalina Island, so they had to travel to the mainland to play exhibition games against Pacific Coast League teams like Portland, Vernon, and Los Angeles, as well as the Pittsburgh Pirates who trained in nearby Paso Robles. Originally, manager Killefer planned to farm Hartnett out for more seasoning, but scout Jack Doyle protested, "But he hasn't caught a game yet. Why not give him that chance first?"[9] Veteran pitcher Grover Cleveland Alexander had also taken a liking to the fiery backstop, and he voiced his support for Hartnett. Killefer eventually relented, and Hartnett proceeded to play his way onto the team. The *Chicago Times* reported on Hartnett's progress in glowing terms: "One of the biggest surprises of spring training was the playing of young Hartnett. He displayed excellent judgment in calling for balls, and was fighting all the time. He is the talk of Catalina Island. He is hitting like a fiend. But it is his work behind the bat and throwing to bases that the Millville, Mass. kid is electrifying the camp. He shoots the ball to second just as if driven from the mouth of a cannon. In a game with the Vernon Club of the Pacific Coast League Monday, Leo was credited with five putouts, one assist and no errors. Also a single in the fourth inning driving in two runs. Leo went the full nine innings, receiving Alex in four."[10]

The baseball writer for the *Chicago Tribune* was also high on the new recruit: "Not only is Hartnett an excellent mechanical workman in spite of his youth, but he has the fire and dash of Ray Schalk. He is fighting every minute of the time, fighting with his pitchers, the umpires, and both teams. The harder he fights, the bigger grows his smile. Hartnett first discovers what kind of balls the pitcher throws, and then calls for them all, mixing them up to the consternation of the batters. If he finds the pitcher hasn't control of his fastball, he switches to something else."[11] One of the other reporters was not as optimistic about Gabby's future, writing, "This guy Gabby. His hands are too small. He'll never last two years in the majors."

The Chicago Cubs had two other ballplayers who were poised on the brink of long, memorable major league careers in addition to Hartnett, but their dreams would be shattered by health problems. Charlie Hollocher, a talented, young shortstop would emerge as one of the top shortstops in the National League in 1922, after leading the league in fielding for the second consecutive year. The five-year veteran also became an offensive force in '22, hitting a robust .340, with 90 runs scored in 152 games. He would hit .342

the following year, but would play in only 66 games because of a mysterious stomach ailment that baffled doctors. After dropping to .245 in 76 games the following year, he retired at the age of 28. He owned a bar in St. Louis for several years, but his ailments got the best of him, and he committed suicide in 1940.

Ray Grimes was a hard-hitting first baseman, who had produced a .321 average in 1921 as a 26-year-old rookie and would follow that up with a sensational year in '22, when he tattoed the ball at a .354 clip. He was hitting .329 in June 1923, when he suffered a slipped disc, sidelining him for the season. After two more pain-filled years, the native of Bergholz, Ohio, went home for good at the age of 32, leaving behind a career batting average of .329.

Opening day was Wednesday, April 12, and it found Bill Killefer's Cubs in Cincinnati to do battle with Pat Moran's Reds, who finished in sixth place in 1921, six games ahead of the Bruins and 24 games behind the pennant-winning New York Giants. The Reds had an outstanding pitching staff headed by future Hall of Famer Eppa Rixey and the Cuban sensation Dolf Luque. Their offense was led by Jake Daubert, a lifetime .303 hitter; outfielder

Gabby Hartnett was the backup catcher to Bob O'Farrell in 1923. (Linda Butt)

George Harper, another .303 hitter; and outfielder Pat Duncan, a career .307 hitter. Chicago appeared to be much improved over their pitiful 1921 squad, thanks to the addition of pitcher Vic Aldridge, who went 20–10 with a league-leading 2.16 earned-run-average (ERA) with Los Angeles in the Pacific Coast League; the acquisition of Hack Miller and Jigger Statz from the Boston Red Sox; the continued development of Bob O'Farrell; and the arrival of strong-armed Gabby Hartnett from Worcester of the Eastern League, who was retained as the backup catcher. Tom Daly was released and subsequently retired.

Grover Cleveland Alexander was Bill Killefer's choice to open the season, with rookie catcher Gabby Hartnett behind the plate. Old Alex was opposed by Eppa Rixey, the elongated hurler of the Reds staff. A crowd of 25,000 people packed Crosley Field to view the proceedings. It was Gabby Hartnett's first look at a major league stadium, and he was dazzled by the size of the park, the finely groomed infield, and the acres of green grass. Alex and the Cubs got the season off to a fine start as they captured the game

7–3. The Chicago ace tossed a seven-hitter, with four strikeouts and just one base on balls. John Kelleher, Ray Grimes, and Marty Krug garnered two hits each to lead the attack, and Charlie Hollocher chipped in with several brilliant defensive plays to stall Cincinnati rallies. In the eighth inning, the Reds pushed across two runs to cut the Cubs' lead to four runs, but Hollocher made two sensational stops and throws to gun down prospective base runners. Gabby caught the entire game and went hitless in two at-bats, but his hard ground ball to Ike Caveny at shortstop in the second inning knocked in the run that gave his team the lead. He also laid down two successful sacrifice bunts, which are two more than Mike Piazza has had in his entire career.[12]

Colonel Jacob Rupert and his New York Yankees were not very happy as the new season got underway. Two of their star performers, Babe Ruth (.378 batting average, 59 home runs, 171 runs-batted-in [RBIs] in 1921) and Bob Meusel (.318, 24, 135), had been suspended for playing a post-season barnstorming tour in '21. They had been ordered not to play any exhibition games by Baseball Commissioner Kenesaw Mountain Landis, but they ignored his warning, much to their regret. The two penitent ballplayers were ineligible to play until May 20, but the overall strength of the New York team kept the ship afloat, and when Ruth and Meusel returned, they found their team resting comfortably in their usual position at the top of the league.

In the second game of the Cincinnati series, the Cubs prevailed again, this time by a 5–1 score, behind Vic Aldridge. Bill Killefer's gang battered the Reds' starter, Dolph Luque, mercilessly, ripping him for 12 base hits, including two doubles and a triple in 7⅓ innings. Gabby Hartnett lined a single to left field to start the third inning, his first big-league hit. He eventually came around to score the first run of the game on a single by Charlie Hollocher. The Cubs added another run in the sixth and a trio of runs in the eighth. The Reds' lone run crossed the plate in the bottom of the ninth, depriving Aldridge of a shutout. The scrappy Chicago backstop made his presence felt in another way in the first inning. George Burns led off the game for Cincinnati with a hard single. The next batter, Greasy Neale, hit into a force play, but the throw to first was wild, getting past the first baseman. Neale rounded first and headed for second before he realized that Hartnett had beat him down the baseline and was backing up the first baseman. Neale stopped short and dove back to the bag just as Hartnett's throw to Grimes arrived. Umpire Bill Klem gave the safe sign as the Cubs' dugout exploded. The language was hot and heavy as the Chicago contingent let the umpire know what they thought of his call. Eventually, when the furor carried over into the second inning, an exasperated Klem cleared the entire Chicago bench except for those players who were actually in the game.[13]

The final game of the series was rained out, and the same day, the big umpire in the sky called another Cub, Adrian "Cap" Anson, out at home. Anson, who was 70 years old, was major league baseball's first superstar, holding down first base for the Chicago National League entry, then called the White Stockings, from 1876 to 1897. Chicago won the first National League pennant in history, edging St. Louis by six games. All told, Anson was on five pennant winners, four of them as player-manager. He was the first man to accumulate 3,000 base hits in a career, finishing with 3,081, to go along with a lofty .339 batting average.

Two days later, Gabby entered the game as a pinch-hitter in the sixth inning against the St. Louis Cardinals in Sportsman's Park. He ripped a ball to right center field and was so excited when he saw the ball hit the gap that he tripped over first base, sprawling face-first in the dirt. He still managed to regain his feet and reach second with a double, as the eventual winning run crossed the plate in a 7–5 Cubs victory. And he scored an insurance run a few minutes later. After taking two out of three from the Cardinals, Bill Killefer's troops returned to Chicago for their home opener against the Cincinnati Reds on Friday, April 21. The Windy City lived up to its name for game one, with many people protecting themselves from the wind and the cold with heavy coats and blankets. Grover Cleveland Alexander was on the hill in the opener, opposed by 21-year-old right-hander Pete Donohue. The Cincinnati hurler was on his way to an 18-win season, but on this day, he was second best, as "Old Pete" shut the Reds down 3–1. The Cubs scored all their runs in the third inning on a walk to Krug, a double by Hartnett, an error, and a two-base hit by Hollocher. Gabby also had two assists in his first game in front of the home fans. It was a sign of things to come.

Ray Grimes had two sensational days at the plate in April. On the 27th, "his homer onto Sheffield Avenue in the sixth inning knotted the score 4–4. His two-run single in the seventh paved the way for a 6–4 triumph over the Cardinals. It was the second consecutive day that Grimes drove in both the tying and winning runs. During midseason, he had a stretch in which he drove in at least one run for 17 consecutive games, a major league record. For that period, he knocked home a total of 27 runs."[14]

Vic Aldridge also got into the act as a serious batsman. He had a day that all pitchers dream about on May 6. On his way to an 11–7 victory over the Pittsburgh Pirates, he rapped five singles in five times at bat, drove in one run, and scored one.[15]

The most historic game of the season was played in Detroit on April 30 between the Tigers and the Cubs' crosstown neighbors, the White Sox, as reported by Rich Coberly. Charlie Robertson, a 25-year-old rookie for the Sox, threw a perfect game against the Tigers, winning 2–0. It was the last perfect game in the major leagues until Don Larsen retired 27 consecutive Brooklyn Dodgers in the 1956 World Series. The 6', 175-pound right-hander fanned six and allowed only six balls to be hit to the outfield in his masterpiece. The winning runs crossed the plate in the second inning on a walk, a bunt single by Johnny Mostil, a sacrifice, and a single to left field by Earl Sheely.

The 1922 Cubs were in contention until May 7 and were nestled in second place, just 2½ games from the top, with a 12–6 record. Then they dropped seven of their next eight games and fell to fourth place on May 17. They never rose above fourth again. Hartnett was seeing very little playing time, as manager Bill Killefer went back to Bob O'Farrell on a regular basis. About the only action Hartnett saw the rest of the season was when "Pete" Alexander pitched. He was, however, learning how to be a major leaguer by just being with the club and working out with them. And he was receiving valuable instructions on proper catching techniques and strategy from both manager Bill Killefer and Bob O'Farrell.

During his first couple of years in Chicago, Gabby Hartnett shared an apartment with Barney Friberg and his old Worcester Booster teammate Marty Callaghan. And he had many friends off the field as well as on. One player said he was "the life of the party," a good storyteller and a good listener, with a great sense of humor. He liked to get away to one of the nearest speakeasies after the game with his teammates to unwind with a cold beer. That was quite a change for the kid from Millville, who never had liquor of any kind before he joined the Cubs. His father was a teetotaler who passed his disdain for alcohol on to his son. But that scenario changed when Gabby became a major leaguer. He didn't drink much whiskey, except for a shot now and then, but he did enjoy a good beer.

On May 26, the Cubs and Reds battled to a 2–2 tie in a game that was called after eight innings due to rain. The second game of the doubleheader was also called off. Gabby Hartnett, was once again behind the plate for Old Alex and went 1-for-3, with a stolen base and two assists. Four days later, on Memorial Day, the Cubs hosted the St. Louis Cardinals in a bizarre morning-afternoon twin bill. In the AM game, Chicago won 4–1, and Max Flack, the Cubs' right fielder, who lived only three blocks from Cubs Field, went home for lunch between games. When he returned to the park and began putting his uniform on, "Cub skipper Bill Killefer told him, 'Maxie, boy, you're in the wrong clubhouse.'" Flack had been traded to the Cardinals for Cliff Heathcote while he lunched. In the visitors' clubhouse, Heathcote wept openly when he learned of the trade.[16] The switch didn't help the Cards immediately, however. They lost the PM game by a score of 4–2. Heathcote had a pair of hits for his new team, while Flack got one hit for St. Louis.

At the end of May, Chicago was in fifth place, 5½ games behind John McGraw's New York Giants. Their record was 20–20. Individually, Bob O'Farrell was hitting the ball at a .286 clip, while his backup, Gabby Hartnett, was bogged down at .212 on just 33 at-bats in 13 games. Grimes was hitting .342, with Hollocher at .318. On the mound, Vic Aldridge was leading the pitching brigade with a record of 6–3. Old Alex was 4–5, and and Cheeves was 5–3.

On June 5, Chicago defeated Cincinnati 6–5. Alexander went the route for the victory and scored the winning run after reaching base on an error in the ninth. Hartnett pounded out two hits and had two assists, as enemy base runners were learning firsthand about the "Hartnett Arm." He had a rifle hanging from his right shoulder, and he was not afraid to use it. He was also building a reputation as a catcher who would throw the ball to any base if a runner strayed too far from the bag.

In New York on the same day, Babe Ruth captured the headlines by hitting a monstrous home run over the right field roof at the Polo Grounds. The blast, with two men on base, sparked Miller Huggins' league-leading Yankees to an easy 8–3 victory over the cellar-dwelling Philadelphia Athletics.

The following week, Killefer's Cubs took the Boston Braves into camp with a hard-fought 12–11 victory on the bat of Hack Miller. The Chicago strong-boy, at 5'9" tall and 208 pounds, was reported to be the strongest player in baseball history and had a career day, hammering two home runs and a single, good for seven RBIs. He hit a grand slam in the fifth to tie the game at 7–7 and put another one over the wall with a man on in the sixth to give the Bruins a 9–7 lead. Hack Miller grew up in a tough neighborhood on Chicago's North Side. As a teenager, he worked as a steamfitter and developed his magnificent physique by hefting 250-pound radiators on his shoulders and lugging them around the city streets and up and down stairs. After joining the Cubs, he "would hold fans and teammates breathless with feats of strength. He uprooted trees at Catalina Island, bent iron bars with his hands, and lifted automobiles up by their bumpers."[17]

The Chicago Cubs visited the Brooklyn Dodgers in mid-June, and came away with a split in the four-game series after Alexander won the finale 8–3. Ray Grimes led the Chicago attack with two singles and a two-run home run over Ebbets Field's friendly right field screen. The victory was costly for the Cubs, however, as they lost Gabby Hartnett with a split thumb in the third inning. At the time, Chicago's 24–27 record had them bogged down in sixth place, 8½ games out of first. In one of the few positive notes of the hot summer, the Chicagoans piled up 42 victories against just 25 defeats, from June 13 to August 25, for a .627 winning percentage, moving them into the rarefied atmosphere of third place, five games behind the Giants. Hartnett returned to the wars in early August, but he couldn't break into the lineup. Bob O'Farrell was having a breakout season, one that would gain him recognition as one of the top receivers in the major leagues. He was on his way to a career-best .324 batting average, with 60 RBIs. And, more importantly, he would lead the league with 446 putouts, and 143 assists.[18]

On August 13, the Chicago Cubs buried the St. Louis Cardinals under a barrage of base hits to win going away 16–5. The leading batsman was shortstop Charlie Hollocher, who tied a major league record by smashing three triples. In mid-month, the Boston Braves visited Wrigley Field, bringing together two old Millville Town Team teammates. Pitcher Tim McNamara, now one of manager Fred Mitchell's starters, took the mound for the Beaneaters. Unfortunately, Dowdy Hartnett watched the proceedings from a seat on the bench and saw his buddy get roughed up by an 8–3 count. On August 24, the sixth-place Dodgers came to town to challenge the third-place Cubs. The Chicagoans prevailed behind Alexander 4–1. Hartnett was his catcher as usual and went 0-for-3 with the bat. Second baseman Zeb Terry's triple in the opening frame knocked in the winning runs. Terry, a seven-year big-leaguer, hit .286 in 1922, then retired to his home in Texas at the age of 31.

The next day, the Cubs and Phillies played a game for the ages. Twenty-one-year-old rookie Tony Kaufmann started on the hill for Bill Killefer, and six-year veteran Jimmy Ring hurled for Kaiser Wilhelm's lowly Phils. The game was a donnybrook from start to finish. Ring lasted 3⅓ innings, being raked for 12 hits and issuing five bases on balls. Kaufmann was credited with the victory, although he pitched only four innings, giving up six runs in that span.

Gabby Hartnett and Tim McNamara met in Chicago during their rookie season. (Jane McNamara Gilmore)

By that time, he had a huge 24–6 lead. Even so, his bullpen almost blew it, as the Phils pushed over eight runs in the eighth, and six more in the ninth, before Tiny Osborne could retire the side, saving a heart-pounding 26–23 victory for the exhausted Bruins. The two teams set major league records for the most runs (49) and most hits (51) in one game. The Cubs tied the record for the most runs scored in one inning when they pushed across 14 runs in the top of the fourth. They had previously crossed the plate 10 times in the second inning. Cub outfielder Marty Callaghan tied a record with three at-bats in one inning, two of which resulted in base hits. Cliff Heathcote led the Chicago attack with a 5-for-5 day, two of them doubles. Miller and Krug had four hits apiece, with Miller rapping two three-run homers, and Krug smashing two doubles. Bob O'Farrell had a single and a homer. For Philadelphia, Russ Wrightstone and Curt Walker had four hits each. Once again, Hartnett was a spectator to the proceedings.[19]

From this point to the end of the season, the Cubs dropped 22 of their last 35 games, falling into fifth place and finishing 13 games behind the pennant-winning Giants. They were passed by both the Pirates and Reds down the stretch. On September 23, the Cubs visited Boston, giving Gabby his first chance to play in Braves Field, since he was injured on Chicago's first trip to America's "Hub." The two teams played a doubleheader, with Boston taking the opener 8–4 behind Houlihan and the Cubs winning the nightcap 3–1. Hartnett caught the second game, drawing the collar in two trips to the plate, but the Cubs pushed over all their runs in the top of the ninth on hits by Statz, Grantham, and Heathcote, wiping out a 1–0 Boston lead.

It was a disappointing finish to the season for Bill Killefer and his troops, but it was still a successful season overall, as the team moved up two places in the standings, beating their 1921 record by a full 15½ games. Several members of the team had banner years. Bob O'Farrell, as noted, batted .324. Ray Grimes pounded the ball at a .354 clip, which included a team-leading 45 doubles, 12 triples, and 14 home runs. Hack Miller, at .352, finished right behind Grimes, and Charlie Hollocher not only hit .340, he also led all National League shortstops in fielding for the second consecutive year with an average of .965, cementing his position as one of the top shortstops in the game. Gabby Hartnett caught 27 games, batting a paltry .194 in 72 at-bats, but it was a good learning experience. On the mound, Vic Aldridge racked up a 16–15 slate, Grover Cleveland Alexander had 16–13, and Virgil Cheeves won 12 games against 11 losses.

While Gabby was getting his baptism of fire in the Windy City, his buddy Tim McNamara was receiving his indoctrination into major league baseball, 40 miles from Millville, in Boston. Tim finished the season with a modest 3–4 record, but he had a fine 2.42 ERA, as well as some memorable experiences in the closing days. On September 22, he tossed a six-hitter at the Cincinnati Reds in Braves Field, winning 7–2. Five days later, he shut out the Dodgers 7–0, and on October 1, he blanked the National League champion and defending world champion New York Giants 3–0. It looked like Tim McNamara was on the brink of a long and brilliant major league career, but the fates ruled otherwise. He pitched just five years in the big show, making 98 appearances and compiling a 14–29 log, but, as he said later, he enjoyed every minute of it, and was thankful for the opportunity to compete at that level.

The New York Giants won the National League pennant by seven games over the Cincinnati Reds and met Miller Huggins' New York Yankees in the World Series. The Yanks had edged out the St. Louis Browns by a single game in the Junior Circuit. They took a slim lead over the Browns in early August and held it tenaciously down the stretch. In the Fall Classic, John McGraw's boys swept the Yankees in four games. Brilliant pitching by Art Nehf, Jesse Barnes, Jack Scott, Hugh McQuillan, and Rosy Ryan, plus the slugging of Heinie Groh (.474), Frankie Frisch (.471), and Ross Youngs (.375), carried the Giants to victory.[20] The World Series was enjoyed by baseball fans from New York to California on 220 radio stations that carried Grantland Rice's play-by-play descriptions to three million receivers, making it the first World Series covered by the new medium. The receivers cost their owners almost as much as a new car, setting them back between $50 and $150 each.[21]

The individual batting champions for the season were George Sisler of the Browns at .420 and Rogers Hornsby of the Cards, who rattled the fences to the tune of .401. Hornsby also led the National League with 46 doubles, 42 home runs, 141 runs scored, 152 RBIs, and a .722 slugging average. Ken Williams hit 39 home runs and drove in 155 runs to lead the American League in those categories. The top pitchers were Eppa Rixey of Cincinnati, with a record of 25–13, and Eddie Rommel of the Philadelphia Athletics, with a record of 27–13.

Gabby stayed in Chicago when the season ended to play in the City Series, a seven-game competition between the Cubs and their crosstown rivals, the Chicago White Sox, for the Windy City bragging rights. The City Series had been played since 1903, and the White Sox had won eight of the first 10, including the last seven. In '22, the Cubs broke through, taking the series four games to three. Tiny Osborne was the pitching star for Killefer's team, winning two games. Grover Cleveland Alexander took the deciding game, blanking Kid Gleason's Pale Hose 2–0 in game seven to bring the championship back to the North Side.[22]

When Gabby finally did go back to Millville, "he was thinking what kind of a reception he'd get. Is the high school band going to be out there, all my brothers and sisters? You know, he thought he'd get a little welcome home. And he stepped off the train and looked up and down the tracks, and no one was there. He picked up his bag and started walking, and the crossing guard said, "'Charlie Hartnett. Where have you been all summer?'"[23]

Once he got over the shock of arriving home unnoticed, Gabby was ready for more baseball. While he was away, the Millville Town Team had played Sacred Heart on the Mt. St. Charles field, with a large crowd on hand to witness the battle. Tim McNamara was on the hill for Mil-

Ray Grimes batted .354 in 1922. (George E. Outland)

lville; but without his favorite batterymate, McNamara bit the dust 5–1. In the second game of the Millville-Sacred Heart series, Gabby Hartnett was back in the pads, and he brought with him Freddie Maguire, another Massachusetts boy, to play second base. McNamara added third baseman Frankie Frisch to the roster. "In 1922," Tim recalled, "the Giants had swept the Yankees in the World Series, and Frankie (an old Fordham friend of McNamara's) had had a great Series. Our Millville team was playing a series with our bitter rivals, Sacred Heart of Woonsocket. I asked Frank if he'd play for us, and he agreed. He led off, and hit the first ball over the scoreboard for a homer. Gabby caught for us. We won, 3–0." Tim McNamara pitched and fanned 11.[24]

During his bachelor years with the Cubs, Millville was always Gabby's refuge and safe-house over the winter. It gave him time to celebrate Christmas with his family and visit his old friends and former baseball teammates. He spent many a pleasant evening hanging out with his buddies at Oates Tavern or Corbett's Café, reliving the "good old days." Occasionally the gang would find a cozy table at the Great Western Hotel in Nasonville, Rhode Island, to nurse a beer or two and talk. Gabby often picked up the tab for the evening since he was making the most money. One night, Fred walked in, and, seeing his son drinking, angrily confided to a neighbor, "That will be the ruination of him," a prediction that would prove to be false.

In mid-February 1923, the team assembled at Avalon on Santa Catalina Island again to work themselves back into shape after a winter of eating, drinking, and making merry and to compete for a spot on the roster. After practice each day, the players retreated to the comforts of the St. Catherine Hotel, which was located on the beach just a quarter of a mile from the field. The luxurious old hotel was surrounded on three sides by majestic mountain peaks, with the fourth side gazing out at the ocean. It was a spectacular setting that was an exclusive hideaway for the rich until William Wrigley began to develop it.

During daylight hours or on off-days, the players and their wives could relax on the beach, tour the San Pedro Channel in a glass-bottomed boat, or go horseback riding on the trails that circled the town. Some of the players journeyed into the hills to hunt the mountain goats that were overrunning the island, while others took advantage of Wrigley's new nine-hole golf course that wound its way through and around the nearby canyons. It was a picturesque and challenging layout, and Gabby Hartnett, who had been bitten by the golf bug, played whenever he had the time. Over the years, he became an outstanding golfer, shooting par and better. In the evening, the players could entertain themselves by playing rummy or hearts or some other game of chance in the expansive sitting room or in the privacy of their own rooms.

Gabby was a fixture with the team by this time, but manager Bill Killefer still wasn't sure where he would best fit in, since the Cubs had one of the best catchers in the league in Bob O'Farrell. Killefer considered playing Hartnett in the outfield or at first base, but the outfield was finally ruled out because of Hartnett's lack of speed. Initially, he was tabbed as O'Farrell's understudy and a backup at first base. Eventually, fate would step in and make the final decision.

After six weeks of strenuous exercise, Killefer's well-conditioned troops took the Twentieth Century Limited back to Chicago and prepared for a new season, hoping to improve on their fifth-place finish of 1922. The National League had several strong clubs, including John McGraw's world champion Giants, the pitching-strong Cincinnati Reds, McKechnie's Pirates, and Rickey's Cardinals, making it difficult for the Bruins to climb into the first division. On opening day, Chicago hosted the Pittsburgh Pirates in their newly renovated park, to which owner William Wrigley had added an additional 15,000 seats, increasing the capacity to 33,000. Unfortunately, the extra fan support didn't help the Cubs on this day, as 17-game-winner Johnny Morrison handcuffed the Chicagoans 3–2. O'Farrell had two hits in a losing cause, and Gabby watched the game from the shade of the dugout.

The next day, 1,000 miles to the east, the New York Yankees, in a gala celebration, opened their new park, Yankee Stadium, or as it would become to be known, "The House That Ruth Built." A monstrous crowd of 74,200 screaming fans, jammed into the Bronx ballpark to cheer for the favorite players, while another 25,000 people were turned away, as New York turned out en force, to dedicate baseball's newest and biggest stadium. Miller Huggins' team responded in suitable fashion by beating the Boston Red Sox 4–1, and Babe Ruth put the icing on the cake by smashing a game-winning, three-run homer in the third inning off Howard Ehmke. The Yankees were, once again, the cream of the crop in the American League and were on their way to creating a dynasty. Over the next 40 years, they would win 28 American League pennants and 20 world championships. Their main competition in 1923 was Ty Cobb's Detroit Tigers and Tris Speaker's Cleveland Indians.

Another game of interest was played in New York on the 19th. Williams College defeated Columbia University by the score of 5–1. The losing pitcher for Columbia was 19-year-old southpaw Lou Gehrig, who fanned 17 men during the game. Eight hits, including a double and a triple, and four bases on balls did him in.[25]

Chicago evened their series with Pittsburgh, pounding George Boehler 7–2 behind Alexander's 267th victory. The 36-year-old legend stopped the McKechnie-men on five hits and didn't walk a man. His batterymate, Gabby Hartnett, had a single in four trips to the plate. Shortstop Johnny Kelleher, filling in for the incapacitated Charlie Hollocher, hit the first home run in the new park, a 380-foot shot into the newly constructed left field bleachers.

Gabby Hartnett, now in his second full season with the Chicago Cubs, was just beginning to realize the advantages, as well as the disadvantages, of being a celebrity. The outgoing backstop enjoyed meeting people from all walks of life, and he was happy to talk baseball with them, have his picture taken with them, or just sign autographs. He also loved being around kids and often spent hours talking with them at his hotel or at the park, before and after the game. Sometimes, he sneaked them baseballs. On the negative side, he was beginning to lose his privacy; but for someone like Gabby, that was a small price to pay for all the benefits.

The Millville backstop came into prominence at the start of the "Roaring Twenties," but he was not a participant in the wild, self-indulgent, nightclub scene. Instead, he and his buddies usually sought out a movie, or a quiet speakeasy, so they could just relax from the pressures of the day. Or they would have a nice dinner and hang out at the hotel, talking baseball mostly.

The decade of the twenties was also known as "The Golden Age" of sports, when athletes were mythical figures on the stage of life. Babe Ruth stood astride the baseball scene like the Colossus of Rhodes. Jack Dempsey, at 182 pounds, was king of the ring, knocking out men twice his size, such as 245-pound heavyweight champion Jess Willard. Bill Tilden dominated men's tennis, while Helen Wills did likewise on the women's side. Bobby Jones was the greatest golfer the world had ever seen. Gertrude Ederle became a legend by being the first woman to swim the English Channel. Red Grange and the Four Horsemen of Notre Dame kept the football world mesmerized. Even the animal kingdom had its hero. Man-O-War easily outdistanced all competitors in the Belmont Stakes, winning by 20 lengths and setting a new world record in the process. In his career, the 1,100-pound chestnut thoroughbred entered 21 races, winning 20 of them. His only loss was an accident. It took place before starting gates were used. Man-O-War had his back to the starting line when the starting gun went off, and he still almost pulled off a win.

Following the 7–2 win over Pittsburgh, the Cubs entertained the Pirates in the final game of the series on April 20, and it turned out to be a bonafide war. Whitey Glazner, an 11–12 pitcher in 1922, took the hill for Bill McKechnie, facing southpaw Nick Dumovich of Chicago. Both pitchers should have stayed home. Actually, Glazner pitched fairly well for a few innings, blanking Killefer's boys for the first four innings, then being touched up for single runs in the fifth and sixth. Dumovich was "nickled and dimed to death" by Pirate batters the entire game. Pittsburgh scored in every inning except the third and led by a score of 7–2 after six innings. Dumovich was gone after five innings, and he was followed to the mound by Stueland, Kaufmann, and Osborne. In the bottom of the eighth, the Bruins exploded for seven big runs, turning a 9–4 deficit into an 11–9 lead. After the Pirates tied the game in the top of the ninth, Gabby Hartnett took matters into his own hands in the bottom half, smashing a one-out, game-winning homer over the right field wall, one of the longest homers ever seen in Cubs Park. In all, there were eight homers hit in the game. The Chicago catcher, who was called "George Hartnett" in the *New York Times* story, hit two of them; Barney Friberg hit two; and Heathcote, Statz, Grimm, and Traynor poled one each. Gabby Hartnett led the Chicago attack with three hits, and he had four assists, while surrendering just one stolen base. He also pulled off an unassisted double play.[26] The next day, Hartnett blasted a three-run homer to help his team overcome a 5–0 Pittsburgh lead, with the Cubs winning 10–8. Bottomley, Miller, and Kelleher also hit round trippers in the game, giving the two teams 18 home runs in four games, 12 of them by Chicago.

In Ithaca, southpaw Lou Gehrig pitched Columbia to an 8–3 win over Cornell, fanning 10 men along the way. He also contributed a triple and a home run to the Blue and White cause.

An overflow crowd of 37,000 turned out on April 22 to watch their beloved bombers match bats with the St. Louis Cardinals. Killefer's crew captured their fifth straight game 8–7, but the only homer was hit by Ray Blades of the Redbirds. Tom Osborne struggled all day, finally turning the reins over to Kaufmann in the ninth, when St. Louis tied the game at 7–7. Kaufmann came away the winner after singling and carrying home the deciding run on a single by Ray Grimes. Hartnett contributed a single, a crucial sacrifice, and two assists to the cause. The Cubbies finally got some pitching in their next game, as Alexander whipped the Cards 7–3. Hartnett had a quiet day, going 0-for-4, with no assists. Fortunately, Jigger Statz, with three hits, including a home run, and Ray Grimes, with two hits, carried Chicago to victory. Vic Aldridge followed with a two-hit, 3–0 shutout over Branch Rickey's crew, as reported by the *New York Times*: "Hartnett's home run, his fourth of the season, gave the locals the first run, while hits by Statz and Heathcote, an infield out, and Heathcote's steal of home, accounted for the other two runs. Only one visitor, Mueller who doubled, reached second base. Today's victory was the seventh consecutive victory for Chicago."[27]

After their rapid start, Bill Killefer's wrecking machine was just a ½ game behind the Giants, who had an 8–1 record. From there, however, Chicago hit the skids, losing three straight in the Steel City. On a day when Pittsburgh edged the Cubbies 2–1, Tim McNamara was, once again taking the measure of John McGraw's team at the Polo Grounds. Stuffy McInnis had three singles for the Braves, while Billy Southworth and "Big Bill" Bagwell had two each. Before the game, students from Fordham presented McNamara with "a platinum watch chain, and he showed his appreciation by trimming the world champion Giants, 10–3. McNamara is probably the only athlete in baseball history who received a present before a game, and then didn't prove to be a complete failure in the subsequent proceedings. McNamara wasn't bothered by baseball superstitions. He pitched as coolly and gamely as if it were a college game."[28]

When April came to an end, the Cubs were three games over the .500 mark. Gabby Hartnett was their leading clubber, with four home runs and a .429 batting average in seven games. O'Farrell was hitting .357, and Grimes was tattoing the ball at a .325 clip. Grover Cleveland Alexander had a 2–0 mark for April, as did Aldridge. One month later, the Bruins slipped back into third place, six games off the top rung. O'Farrell had upped his average to .361, Hollocher was at .349, with Hartnett at .314. Gabby's five home runs were still third best in the National League. The Cubs suffered a serious loss in mid-May when first baseman Ray Grimes went out of action with a slipped disc in his back. The injury would limit the Chicago slugger to just 64 games during the season and would eventually cause his premature retirement from the game in 1926. His six-year statistics would show an outstanding .329 batting average and a .480 slugging average.

With the loss of Grimes, the Cubs brought up Allen "Ace" Elliott to play first base. The left-handed hitter platooned at first with Gabby Hartnett the rest of the season. Elliott played in 52 games, batting .250. In 1924, he would play in just 10 games, hitting .194, then disappear from the major league scene forever. Hartnett played 31 games at first base and 39 games behind the plate. Killefer was hoping that Hartnett would solve their first base problem since they already had an outstanding catcher in O'Farrell, and the move would allow the Cubs to keep both big bats in the lineup. But the Chicago manager ended the experiment when he realized that the game's greatest throwing arm would be wasted at first base. Gabby became a full-time catcher, and O'Farrell was eventually traded. First base remained a problem spot for Chicago for two years until they obtained Charlie Grimm from Pittsburgh in a trade. The Philadelphia A's would have a similar problem in 1926 and '27, but they found the ideal solution. In 1925, Connie Mack's team had just found a world-class catcher, in Mickey Cochrane, when a new arrival, also a catcher, roared into camp, seeking a permanent position. The 19-year-old phenom was a solidly built slugger by the name of Jimmie Foxx. The kid was shifted to first base, and he took to it like a duck to water, developing into one of the greatest first baseman in baseball history.

The New York Giants went on a roll in June, reeling off 11 straight victories before running afoul of the Boston Braves on June 30. The New Yorkers captured the first game of a doubleheader 3–2 before dropping the nightcap 1–0 to former Giant pitcher Jesse Barnes. The 30-year-old Barnes, who had won 25 games for John McGraw in 1919, had been traded to Boston just 23 days before. In Chicago, the Cubs beat St. Louis 3–2. A double steal by O'Farrell and Miller, with O'Farrell scoring, was the difference in the game. Gabby Hartnett's batting average nosedived in June to .272, but he wasn't seeing much action because Bob O'Farrell had a hot bat. The first-string catcher was rattling the fences at a .360 pace, trailing league leader Zack Wheat of the Dodgers by just 20 points. The Giants still held a five-game lead over Pittsburgh at month's end, an eight-game lead over third-place Cincinnati, and a healthy 10½ game bulge over Chicago. In the American League, the New York Yankees were eight games better than the Philadelphia Athletics, with Cleveland 9½ out and Detroit 11 games back.

A Fourth of July twin bill against Cincinnati ended in a split, with the Reds taking the morning game 6–3, and the Cubs bouncing back to capture the afternoon game by the same score. Dolf Luque, the crafty Cuban right-hander, on his way to a league best 27–8 record, outlasted Vic Keen in the opener, as both teams pushed across three runs in the ninth. Tiny Osborne, Bill Killefer's 6'4½", 245-pound southpaw, pitched game two and coasted to the victory as his teammates jumped on Donohue for six runs in the first four innings. Statz, Hollocher, Heathcote, and Osborne all collected two singles. The Giants, meanwhile, were sweeping the Phils by scores of 7–3 and 5–3 behind Jack Bentley and Art Nehf.

The Yankees widened their lead in the Junior Circuit by routing the Washington Senators 12–6 and 12–2. The entire Yankee team participated in the slaughter, piling up a total of 29 base hits, including two home runs by Everett Scott and singletons by Whitey Witt, Fred Hofmann, and Aaron Ward. Ruth chipped in with two doubles and a single. Scott's outburst came as a complete surprise, since the 148-pound banjo-hitter put only 20 balls out of the park during a 1,654-game big-league career.

On July 15, Barney Friberg had one of the biggest hits of his career. The Cubs were playing McGraw's Giants in what was always a grudge match, even if the pennant wasn't on the line. On this day, Alexander and Claude Jonnard were knotted up in a 5–5 game in the tenth inning. Then Hollocher singled, Grantham walked, and O'Farrell beat out a bunt to load the bases. Friberg stepped to the plate, picked out a pitch he liked, a 2–2 cripple, and promptly drove it into the left field seats, giving Old Alex a hard-earned 9–5 victory.[29] Three days later, the Cubs bounced the Braves twice 9–1 and 5–3. Alexander pitched a tight nine-hitter in the opener, supported by Hollocher's four hits (two doubles and two singles) and two hits each by Statz, Friberg, and himself. In the nightcap, Tony Kaufmann beat 16-year veteran Rube Marquard. Jigger Statz added three more hits to his day's total, while Bob O'Farrell and Hack Miller rapped two hits each. On August 1, Old Alex whipped the Boston Braves 8–2, both with his arm and with his bat. He ripped a three-run homer plus a single in three at-bats, while holding the Bostonians to just two runs. Hartnett entered the game as a late-inning replacement, but didn't have any at-bats.

The baseball season was interrupted temporarily two days later due to the sudden death of President Warren G. Harding. The President had been in a depressed state for months, after a scandal involving several members of his cabinet rocked his administration. He had been on a tour of Alaska and the Northwest when he was stricken. He took ill in Grants Pass, Oregon, apparently from ptomaine poisoning from tainted crabs he ate in Alaska, compounded by a touch of bronchial pneumonia. He was taken to San Francisco for treatment and seemed to be recovering satisfactorily. Then on the evening of August 2, in his room at the Palace Hotel, he took a turn for the worse. He died at 7:30 pacific time, and Vice President Calvin Coolidge was sworn in as President within five hours.[30]

The Chicago Cubs continued to play a little over .500 ball through August and entered the stretch run with a 69–56 record, good enough for fourth place in the National League behind the Giants, Cincinnati, and Pittsburgh, in that order. New York's record of 80–47 gave them a four-game lead over the Reds, a six-game lead over the Pirates, and a big 10-game bulge over the Cubs. Gabby Hartnett's average was holding at .276, and he had punched out seven home runs in 199 trips to the plate. Bob O'Farrell was hitting .314 with 10 home runs, Barney Friberg had 11 homers to go along with a .323 average, and John Kelleher was hitting .327. Alexander was the leading pitcher with a flashy 19–8 record, followed by Kaufmann at 13–8 and Aldridge at 12–6.

Baseball had to take a backseat to boxing on Friday, September 14, as the eyes of the sports world were riveted on the much-publicized heavyweight boxing championship fight at New York's Polo Grounds between the champion, Jack Dempsey, and the Argentine champion Luis Angel Firpo, better known as "The Wild Bull of the Pampas." A crowd of 85,500 people paid $1,250,000 to see the fight and, although it only lasted two rounds, every person there got his money's worth. The first round was the most ferocious round in boxing history. Dempsey came out fast, but was stopped in his tracks by a Firpo right and sank to his knees. Getting up without a count, he again attacked the Argentine champion and sent him sprawling. Surprisingly, Firpo was back on his feet almost immediately, with fire in his eyes. The champ dropped him six more times, but couldn't keep him down. Suddenly Firpo lashed out with a left and caught Dempsey on the chin. A following right drove the champ completely out of the ring, head first. Ringside spectators hurriedly pushed Dempsey back into the ring, where he managed to weather the storm until the bell. In round two, the champion came out in a fury. A barrage of left hooks put the South American champion down three more times, the third one ending the fight. The whole bloody mess lasted a grand total of three minutes and fifty-seven seconds.[31]

As September wound down, the two New York teams held leads in their respective leagues, setting up another possible World Series confrontation between the two. The New York Yankee lead over the Cleveland Indians had widened to a whopping 18½ games; while in the Senior Circuit, John

McGraw's boys held a still tenuous four-game lead over Cincinnati, with 13 games to play. On September 16, the Giants were in Chicago to tangle with Killefer's Cubs. The game took on the look of another heavyweight fight, as the two clubs hit each other with everything but the kitchen sink, and the fans joined in with a wild bottle-throwing frenzy aimed at umpire Charles Moran. Moran had earned the fans' wrath in the fourth inning by calling Cliff Heathcote out at second base on an attempted steal. After the Chicago outfielder had grabbed Moran by the coat collar and spun him around, he was ejected from the game, bringing hoots and hollers from the big crowd. In the bottom of the eighth, Moran was at it again, this time calling Sparky Adams out at second, ending the inning. That was all the fans could take. They rose in anger and bombarded the field with pop bottles, seat cushions, and anything else that wasn't bolted down. Fortunately, there were no serious injuries, but it took 10 minutes for the police to restore order. The game itself, was a free-hitting affair, with New York scoring in each of the first seven innings, and the Cubs pushing over three runs in the bottom of the sixth to tie the game at 6-all. New York responded immediately, scoring four runs in the top of the seventh to win the game 10–6. Alexander was the losing pitcher in relief, being touched up for the four deciding runs. Irish Meusel was the big gun for McGraw's boys, hitting a single and a home run, while Hack Miller had a 4-for-4 day for Chicago, which included a double and a triple. Gabby Hartnett's action was limited to a nonproductive pinch-hitting appearance in the sixth inning.[32] The next day, the Giants routed Vic Aldridge and the Cubs 13–6 behind a 16-hit attack. "Long George" Kelly, McGraw's 6'4" first baseman, was a one-man demolition crew, banging out five hits in five at-bats, including a double and three home runs. Irish Meusel added a homer, and Bob O'Farrell netted one for the Windy City boys. Jack Bentley was the happy beneficiary of the mauling.

The Giants won six of their next seven games and clinched the pennant on September 28 with a 3–0 win over the Brooklyn Dodgers, or Robins as they were sometimes called. Art Nehf outpitched Burleigh Grimes for the win. All three Giants runs were scored in the opening frame, two of them on a single by Meusel. It was John McGraw's record ninth National League pennant. The same day in Boston, the Yankees set a record of their own, pounding the Red Sox into oblivion 24–4. In the process, they set a new record for hits in one game, with 30, including five-hit games by both Babe Ruth (two singles, two doubles, and a home run) and Wally Schang (four singles and a double). Rookie Lou Gehrig, at the ripe old age of 20, banged out four hits, three of which were doubles, while Jones, Smith, and Dugan had three hits each. Boston pitcher Howard Ehmke absorbed most of the brutal beating, yielding 17 of the runs and 21 of the hits in six innings.

The regular baseball season ended on October 8. The Chicago Cubs won three of their final five games to finish the season in fourth place with a record of 83–71, 12½ games behind the New York Giants and three games better than their 1922 record. On September 29, Alexander downed the Pittsburgh Pirates 5–4, when his team rallied for three runs in the bottom of the tenth to wipe out a 4–2 Buc lead. Gabby Hartnett and Bob O'Farrell were both in the middle of the winning rally. The next day, Bill Killefer's troops took the measure of Pittsburgh again by the same score. Rip Wheeler was the winning pitcher. Barney Friberg had three hits for Chicago, including a double, Hack Miller had a single and a home run, and Jigger Statz had two singles to lead the hit parade. Hartnett made one of his infrequent starts and contributed a key double to the victory.

The world of golf had its own hero on September 30. Gene Sarazen won his second successive P.G.A. championship, beating Walter Hagen on the second extra hole, after the two men completed the 36-hole championship in a dead heat. Sarazen held a three-stroke lead with eight holes to play, but the tenacious Hagen whittled it away with birdies at the eleventh, sixteenth, and seventeenth holes. A Sarazen birdie on the thirty-eighth hole ended the tense struggle.[33]

In the American League, although the pennant race was long over, there were still records to be broken. Tris Speaker, the player-manager of the Cleveland Indians, set a new record for doubles, his 57 two-baggers breaking the record of 56 set by Ed Delahanty in 1899. Babe Ruth didn't set any new home run records, but he did finish with a flourish, hitting three homers over the last week to finish with 41.

Chicago closed out their season in St. Louis, dropping two out of three games. They lost the opener 5–2, with Vic Aldridge taking the loss. Gabby Hartnett went 1-for-4. In the Sunday doubleheader, the Cubs took the opener 10–3 behind rookie Phil Collins, who was making his only appearance of the year. Miller and Elliott homered for Chicago, and Hartnett had a double in three tries. The nightcap was won by Branch Rickey's team 6–3, with Johnny Stuart tossing a six-hitter. Gabby Hartnett sat out the finale, with Kettle Wirtz doing the honors behind the plate.

Rogers Hornsby led the National League in batting with an average of .384, Irish Meusel led in RBIs with 125, and Cy Williams led in home runs with 41. In the American League, Harry "The Horse" Heilmann took the batting crown with an average of .403, and Babe Ruth was the RBI leader with 130 and the home run leader with 41. Heilmann, the Detroit Tigers slugger, had a banner season, with 44 doubles, 11 triples, 18 home runs, 121 runs scored, and 115 RBIs. He was a one-man show and a major contributor to the Tigers' second-place finish.

Individual honors on the Chicago Cubs belonged to Charlie Hollocher and Ray Grimes, who hit .342 and .329, respectively; Hack Miller, who slammed 20 round trippers; and the great Grover Cleveland Alexander, who compiled a record of 22–12. Gabby Hartnett, in his second season, played in 85 games, hitting a respectable .268 with eight home runs in 231 at-bats. He was used sparingly in September and October, primarily as a replacement at first base or catcher, or as a pinch hitter. But his apprenticeship was coming to an end. In 1924, the Millville backstop would stake his claim on the Chicago Cubs catching position.

John McGraw and Miller Huggins met for the third consecutive time in the World Series, and this time, the result was different. The

Jigger Statz pounded out 209 base hits for the Cubs in 1923, batting .319 with 110 runs scored.

New York Yankees won the series four games to two behind great pitching and outstanding hitting. "Bullet Joe" Bush, "Sad Sam" Jones, and Herb Pennock kept the Giants' big bats relatively quiet, while the Babe ran roughshod over McGraw's hurlers, banging out three home runs and driving in eight runs. Aaron Ward hit .417, and Schang and Scott each hit .318 for the world champions.[34]

Hartnett returned to Millville during the off-season, and even played a little baseball for the home team. In one Woonsocket exhibition game, he entertained the crowd with a demonstration of his powerful throwing arm. His tosses to second base either went through the shortstop or second baseman, or turned the players completely around in their tracks — much to the amusement of the crowd.[35]

4

A Major League Star at Last, 1924–1925

The Chicago Cubs had improved their record and their standing each of the three years under manager Bill Killefer. He brought the seventh-place club he inherited from Johnny Evers on August 21, 1921, to fourth place in 1923, with a record of 83–71, 12½ games behind John McGraw's talented New York Giants. Killefer seemed to have the nucleus of a pennant-contending team in 1924: a strong pitching staff headed by Alexander, Aldridge, Kaufmann, and Keen and talented position players in O'Farrell, Grimes, Hollocher, Statz, Friberg, Grantham, Miller, and Adams. And standing in the wings was the 22-year-old catching phenom, "Gabby" Hartnett.

The Giants were still the team to beat in the National League, with the league's most potent offense, led by George Kelly (.307, 16 home runs, 103 runs-batted-in [RBIs]), Frankie Frisch (.348, 12, 111), and Irish Meusel (.297, 19, 125); the league's #1 defense, and its #2 pitching staff. Cincinnati, with the league's top pitching staff, headed by Dolf Luque (27–8), Eppa Rixey (20–15), and Pete Donohue (21–15), was favored to challenge the Giants, as were Pittsburgh and Chicago.[1]

In spite of all the optimism emanating from the Cubs' spring training camp, the year would turn out to be a disappointing mixed bag. Injuries and illnesses would sideline the great Alexander and All-Star receiver Bob O'Farrell for long periods of time, and would lead to the premature retirements of Charlie Hollocher and Ray Grimes. Chicago opened the National League season in St. Louis on Tuesday, April 15, with Vic Aldridge facing Cardinal rookie Johnny Stuart. Baseball Commissioner Kenesaw Mountain Landis threw out the first ball to St. Louis Mayor Henry Kid. Shortstop Charlie Hollocher was on the shelf with a stomach disorder, but the rest of the lineup was intact, with O'Farrell doing the honors behind the plate. Aldridge took his lumps in the first two innings, as Branch Rickey's troops jumped out to a 3–0 lead. The Cubs bounced back with two runs in the third inning and another brace of runs in the fourth, when they knocked Stuart out of the box. Another run in the eighth gave Chicago a 5–3 lead. Bob O'Farrell was in the middle of the Cubs' rallies with two base hits and two runs scored. "Jigger" Statz chipped in with three hits and a run scored, and Adams and Aldridge had two hits each. A near 5–3 victory turned into a tragic 6–5 loss when the Cardinals pounded Aldridge for three runs in the bottom of the ninth before two outs could be recorded. Max Flack and Jack Smith with three hits each, and Rogers Hornsby with two, led the St. Louis attack.

Elsewhere on opening day, the Brooklyn Dodgers nipped the National League champion New York Giants 3–2 behind veteran southpaw Dutch Ruether, who outpitched Giants ace Rosy Ryan. Jimmy Johnston and

Bob O'Farrell was one of the top catchers in the National League until he was injured in 1924. (George E. Outland)

Zack Wheat each had a single and a double for Wilbert Robinson's crew. In the American League, the world champion New York Yankees got off the mark quickly by edging the Boston Red Sox 2–1 in Boston. Bob Shawkey and Waite Hoyt combined on a two-hitter to beat Howard Ehmke, who limited the Yanks to just five safeties. More than 25,000 Fenway Park faithful sat stunned as base hits by Babe Ruth and Aaron Ward combined with two errors by Bill Wamsganns to plate both Yankee runs in the ninth inning, spoiling a superb pitching effort by the Sox big right-hander.

The Cubs rebounded the next day as Grover Cleveland Alexander shackled St. Louis 13–4 behind a 17-hit Chicago barrage. Gabby Hartnett, Alexander's personal catcher, ripped two singles and a two-run home run, and scored two runs in the victory. Grimes and Miller also had three hits as Killefer's Killers ko'd 20-game winner Jesse Haines after just one-third of an inning. Chicago ran its winning streak to three by sweeping the last two games of the series by scores of 7–4 and 6–3. Grantham had a 4-for-5 day, with a double, triple, and home run in game three, and Tony Kaufmann picked up the win with eight strong innings. Vic Keen did the honors in the finale, scattering nine hits. Home runs by Ray Grimes and Hack Miller in the second inning put the Cubs on the road to victory. Gabby Hartnett caught the entire game and contributed a double and a run scored in four at-bats. The Cubs made it four in a row two days later with a 2–1 win at Cincinnati. Grantham and Grimes each ripped a triple, and rookie right-hander Elmer Jacobs tossed a complete game four-hitter. Alexander made his home debut against the Pittsburgh Pirates on April 28 and pitched a gem, winning 2–1 in 11 innings. "Old Alex," a career .209 hitter, lashed a two-out double in the 11th to drive in Barney Friberg with the winning run. Hartnett was 1-for-4, with an assist. Killefer's charges dropped a tough 2–1, 14-inning decision to Pittsburgh on April 30, but finished the month with a 9–6 record, two games behind the Giants. George Grantham at .367 and Ray Grimes at .345 were the top clubbers for Chicago. Grover Cleveland Alexander sported a 2–0 record with a fine 2.37 earned-run-average (ERA).

The Windy City Express struggled in early May, falling 3½ games behind New York; but they recovered nicely to run off a three-game winning streak before welcoming the hated Giants to the friendly confines of Cubs Park. In the opener of the big series, broadcast by Hal Totten on station WMAQ, the cocky New Yorkers took the measure of the young challengers; but in game two, Old Alex struck again. The crafty pitching legend came away with a gutty 6–4 victory, thanks to a five-hit barrage that drove Rosy Ryan to cover after just two innings. Jigger Statz's first-inning single drove in the first run, and his second-inning double brought home runs three and four. Gabby Hartnett laid down a perfect sacrifice bunt in the three-run second-inning uprising. John McGraw's boys didn't roll over and play dead after that defeat. They roared back to take the rubber game, a wild 16–12 war that saw the two teams combine for 34 base hits off 10 harried pitchers. The game was marred by a bottle-throwing incident in the eighth inning when irate Cubs fans, angered at umpire Sweeney's ball-and-strike calls, bombarded the plate umpire with all kinds of glassware. Home runs were hit by Bill Terry (2), Ross Youngs, and George Grantham. Youngs had four of the Giants 21 hits, adding a double to his extra base hit total. Billy Southworth and Heinie Groh had three hits, and three players punched out two. For the Cubs, Sparky Adams had four singles and two runs scored, and George Grantham added a single to his round tripper. Gabby Hartnett viewed the fireworks from the comfort of the dugout.[2]

Chicago lost one of its regular players in May when catcher Bob O'Farrell went down, as he told Lawrence S. Ritter: "A foul tip came back, crashed through my mask, and fractured my skull. It was my own fault. It was an old mask and I knew I shouldn't have worn it." He made several abortive attempts to come back over the next two weeks, but headaches and dizziness sent him back to the sidelines each time. He was limited primarily to pinch-hitting duties for the next four weeks, before returning to the wars on June 18. O'Farrell had played in 15 games with 45 at-bats when he went down. The rest of season, he would play in just 56 games, with 138 at-bats. The catching duties fell on the broad shoulders of the 23-year-old firebrand from Massachusetts, and Gabby Hartnett was more than up to the task. He would go on to hit a solid .299 in 111 games after being over .300 most of the season. He would also slam 16 home runs and drive in 67 runners in 354 plate appearances, numbers that would equate to 26 home runs and 107 RBIs over a full 550 at-bat season. The year 1924 was Gabby Hartnett's breakthrough season. From here on, his reputation would grow year after year.

On May 22, Alexander pitched the Cubs into first place by struggling to an 8–6 decision over the cellar-dwelling Philadelphia Phillies. The 37-year-old hurler was roughed up for 11 hits, but issued just a single base on balls in his complete game effort. Bill Killefer's troops jumped on 18-game-winner Jimmy Ring for five big runs in the opening stanza, and added another deuce in the fourth to open up a 7–1 lead. A four-run Philly uprising in the bottom of the fifth, highlighted by a three-run homer off the bat of left fielder Johnny Mokan, fell short. Gabby Hartnett sparked the Cubs' offense with two singles and a double in three at-bats. He also scored two runs and tossed out one runner attempting to steal. Chicago stumbled through the last nine days of the month, winning five of nine and slipping back into second place, 2½ games behind New York. One game of note was played in Chicago on the 24th. The Boston Braves hammered Vic Keen and the Cubs by an 11–3 score; and in the process, they ran the bases with abandon, challenging the young catcher nine times during the game. They succeeded in stealing five bases off him, but he gunned down four of them along the way.

National League base runners were discovering that Chicago's kid catcher had one of the strongest throwing arms ever seen on a major league diamond. The number of runners who would challenge his arm would decrease rapidly over the next two seasons. Only 136 successful steals would be made against him in 1924–25, compared to a league average of 178. His 54 percent caught-stealing record, which was 9 percent better than the league average, discouraged most would-be thieves.

The statistics for the first two months of the season showed Ray Grimes with a .329 batting average, followed by outfielder Denver Grigsby at .325, George Grantham at .322, and Gabby Hartnett at .313. The young backstop also fashioned six home runs in 83 at-bats. He was second in the league in home runs to Jack Fournier of Brooklyn, who had nine in 132 at-bats. Grantham was a curious case, a lifetime .302 hitter over a 13-year major league career, but a butcher with the glove. His defense made Dick "Strangeglove" Stuart look like a Gold Glove fielder. His 55 errors at second base in 1923 is still the major league record. Grover Alexander was the league's leading pitcher with a glittering 6–1 record. Vic Keen was at 4–2, and Vic Aldridge was bogged down at 3–4.

Gabby Hartnett took advantage of Bob O'Farrell's injury to claim the first-string catching job. (Roy Hartnett)

June was a moderately successful month for Killefer's men, as they went 13–8, but fell 5½ games behind McGraw's sluggers, who ran up a 19–8 slate. The Cubs got off fast by whipping Pittsburgh 2–1 on the first of the month. Vic Aldridge threw a six-hitter at the Bucs, and Chicago touched up Johnny Morrison for a brace of runs in the first inning. Hartnett was 0-for-3, but added another notch to his caught-stealing gun. The following day, the warriors from the Windy City invaded New York to take on the front-running Giants. Three days later, they left town with a two-game sweep under their belts. In the series opener, Keen got the best of Virgil Barnes 6–4. As reported by the *New York Times*, "Barnes threw his famous home run ball twice in the fifth inning and thus ruined what had begun to look like a neat and promising pitchers battle. With the score 0–0 after four innings, Virgil indiscreetly served up his famous delivery to Leo Hartnett, the Babe Ruth of the Windy City, and Leo knocked the pill into the right field stand, with a runner on first base. Barnes fanned Keen and then let Jigger Statz smash another homer into the left field seats." The second game of the series was rained out; but in the get-away game, Alexander was in control all the way, beating Wayland Dean by the count of 3–1. Barney Friberg's two-run single in the first inning gave Alex all the runs he needed, but they added another one for good measure in the fourth on singles by Heathcote, Hartnett, and Alex himself. A sensational shoestring catch by Statz cut off one Giants rally in the fourth, and a fast double play started by Grantham ended a threat in the sixth.

In the American League, the Yankees and the Red Sox were jockeying for position at the top of the league. On June 6, New York beat the Chicago White Sox 5–3 behind Babe Ruth's fourteenth home run of the season to give Sam Jones his second victory. The win, coupled with Boston's 11–4 defeat at the hands of the St. Louis Browns, gave the Bronx Bombers a percentage-point lead in the pennant race.[3]

Nineteen twenty-four was probably the most important year in the life of young Leo Hartnett. He broke into the Chicago Cubs lineup as the regular catcher after the injury to Bob O'Farrell, and he met his future wife. One day, prior to a game in Cubs Park, the Chicago catcher was introduced to Mr. and Mrs. Ed McCullough, Chicago residents and longtime Cubs fans. The McCulloughs invited Gabby to dinner, beginning a friendship that would last throughout their lives. Within a few months, Gabby gave up the apartment he had been sharing with Barney Friberg and Marty Callaghan and moved in with the McCulloughs. Martha Henrietta Marshall, who was living with friends of the McCulloughs, met Gabby at dinner one evening. They hit it off immediately and began a relationship that would culminate in their marriage five years later.[4]

The Chicago Cubs moved on to Brooklyn after the New York series to meet Wilbert Robinson's fired-up Dodgers, who were also in the thick of the pennant race. The first game, played in a driving rainstorm, ended in a Chicago victory when the game was called after seven innings. Vic Aldridge went all the way for the win. The next day, the Dodgers' veteran fireballer, Dazzy Vance, en route to a league-leading 28–6 record, took the measure of Bill Killefer's boys 4–3. Brooklyn held a 2–0 lead after seven innings, but the Cubs pushed over three runs in the eighth on wild throws by Milt Stock and Hank DeBerry, and seemed to have the game well in hand. But Chicago pitcher Rip Wheeler walked Bernie Neis to open the ninth inning, and the game went downhill from there. A sacrifice, an infield hit, and an intentional walk, loaded the bases. Another walk to Jack Fournier forced in the tying run, and Stock's single ended it. Gabby Hartnett drew the collar in four attempts against Vance, which was not unusual, according to John McNamara, who quoted Gabby as saying, "Dazzy Vance was the greatest pitcher I ever saw. He had blinding stuff. I went up to the plate knowing I was gonna come back to the bench pretty soon. If I got a hit, I figured I was pretty lucky."[5]

The Dodgers captured game three behind veteran Dutch Ruether. Vic Keen took the loss. Hartnett went 2-for-4 and had one assist. In the finale, Grover Cleveland Alexander pitched the Cubs to a 7–2 win to gain a split in the series. Killefer's troops left town as they entered, still one game behind the Giants, who split with Pittsburgh, and 2½ games ahead of the pesky Dodgers. Old Alex stopped Robby's team on seven hits and, as usual, didn't walk a man. The account of the game in the *New York Times* pretty much told the story of the type of player Gabby Hartnett was: "The Hartnett-Alexander combination has much to recommend it. Youth and experience are combined. Hartnett has all the enthusiasm of a schoolboy, and Alexander the wisdom that comes only with the years. Gabby worked harder yesterday telling Aleck how well he was pitching than the older man did in actually performing the task. Everything that Alexander threw was a strike with Hartnett, and once umpire Quigley had to walk around in front of the plate and warn him that he would call the balls and strikes and all Hartnett would have to do would be to catch them. That failed to dim Gabby's enthusiasm in the least. He kept right on diving for foul tips and low throws, getting hit and hurt a half-dozen times for his trouble. When it was over, he was bruised and battered, but happy, and the Cubs were so proud of him that they actually tried to carry him off the field like a college boy. Hartnett's most tangible contribution to the game was a home run into the left field bleachers which scored Heathcote ahead of him." Gabby added two singles to his homer, giving him 3-for-4 for the day. Alexander upped his record to 9–1.[6]

The Cubs next visited Beantown, where they pummeled the hapless Braves twice to move into first place, a ½ game ahead of New York. On the 12th, Vic Keen bested Genewich 9–5 behind an 11-hit attack. Hollocher, Friberg, Grigsby, and Heathcote all had two hits, while Hartnett chipped in with a triple and two bases on balls in four trips to the plate. He also threw out two runners on the bases. Game two was won by Chicago 5–1, as Tony Kaufmann stymied the Bostonians most of the day. The game presented the first direct major league confrontation between Gabby Hartnett and his Millville Town Team teammate, Tim McNamara, as Tim recalled, "I was pitching and Leo came to bat. My curve didn't break and the ball hit Leo in the ribs. He made some joking remarks to me as he trotted to first base. We got together after the game, and I remember him telling me that while taking

Tim McNamara (center) played his last full season in the major leagues in 1924. Frankie Frisch is on the left; the player on the right is unidentified. (Jane McNamara Gilmore)

his shower, he saw John Heydler's signature on his side. Heydler, of course, was the National League President, and his name was on every ball."[7]

Jim Murphy recalled how talented Gabby's sister "Charlie" was behind the plate: "Charlie was Anna Hartnett, who also had the 'Hartnett Arm,' and a few years later, toured New England as a member of a top-notch girls team whose lineup included her sisters, Mary and Mildred.... Charlie Hartnett could handle the catching duties so efficiently that Tim (McNamara) brought her to one of the games at Braves Field. She was in uniform and Tim took her onto the field one day. She warmed up Jesse Barnes. She handled him very well. She held her own. Manager Fred Mitchell saw the girl catcher on the sidelines deftly handling Barnes' shots. 'Who's that?' he asked Tim. 'Gabby Hartnett's sister,' Tim replied. 'That explains it,' Mitchell said with a smile. Charlie got a nice hand from the crowd as she finished her warmup of Barnes and headed off the field."[8]

George Kelly's three home runs propelled the New York Giants to an 8–6 victory over the Cincinnati Reds, giving them a first place tie with Chicago. After 51 games, both teams sported 31–20 records, with Brooklyn three games behind at 27–22. Gabby Hartnett was cruising along with a .336 batting average and eight home runs, while Alex topped the league's pitchers with a record of 9–1. Vic Aldridge was close behind at 6–4. The American League pennant race was also wide open, with New York, Boston, and Detroit all in the hunt. The Yankees held a one-game lead over the Red Sox, with the Tigers two games out.

June 14 was the high point of the season, from the Chicago Cubs standpoint. The Giants captured the outright lead the next day with a 4–1 win over Cincinnati and were never headed again. The Cubs' season began to unravel when Grover Cleveland Alexander went down with arm miseries. The 37-year-old right-hander was driven from the mound in the second inning on June 16, absorbing an 8–3 defeat. After having to leave his next start after seven innings and taking another shellacking less than a week later, Old Alex went to the sidelines for more than two months. The Cubs' fortunes disappeared with him. Bill Killefer's men went 6–6 over the last two weeks of June, while McGraw's Giants ran off a 10-game winning streak to create 2½ games of daylight between themselves and their adversaries from the Windy City. Catcher Bob O'Farrell returned to action on June 18, guiding Vic Aldridge to a 9–2 win over the Philadelphia Phillies. The big guns in the Chicago lineup were Statz, Grantham, Grigsby, and Harvey Cotter, with three hits each.

The Giants' winning streak came at the expense of Cincinnati (2), St. Louis (3), Boston, (4), and Brooklyn (1). The losing pitcher for the Dodgers was Dazzy Vance, the National League's leading pitcher with 10 victories. It was the Dodgers' eleventh loss in 13 games to the Giants on the year, and their eighth in a row. Uncle Robby's boys ended the frustration the next day, snapping New York's streak with a 3–2 victory in a game that was decided by the fates as much as by Brooklyn bats. Entering the eighth inning, the Dodgers were holding a slim 3–2 lead, as darkness descended over Ebbets Field. Even though Burleigh Grimes' fastball was nothing but a blur at that time, the Giants managed to push over the tying run on a double by Ross Youngs and a single by Frankie Frisch. Then, with Frisch on second and only one out, the skies opened and a torrential downpour inundated the field. Umpire-in-Chief Bill Klem immediately called time, but when the rain continued unabated, the game was finally called, with the score reverting to the end of the seventh inning, resulting in a 3–2 Brooklyn victory.[9]

While major league teams were battling for the baseball championships, 3,000 miles away in Hoylake, England, America's greatest golfer, Walter Hagen, was competing against 85 other professionals for the British Open Golf Championship. When the sun went down on Friday, June 27, Hagen emerged as the champion for the second time in three years. He defeated E.R. Whitcombe by one stroke after shooting a 36 over the last nine holes.[10]

The Chicago Cubs went into Pittsburgh still in contention for the National League flag, but the fired-up Bucs made them walk the plank four times, 8–7 in fourteen innings, 2–1, 9–0, and 3–0. In the first game of the series, the Cubs Denver Grigsby had five hits in six trips to the plate, including a double and a home run. Chicago catchers had a busy series behind the plate, as Bill McKechnie's rabbits, on their way to a league-leading 181 stolen bases, challenged O'Farrell and Hartnett at every opportunity. In game two, the Pirates swiped three bases in three attempts against Bob O'Farrell; but the next two days, with Gabby Hartnett behind the plate, their fortunes changed. The kid from Millville shot down five base runners in eight attempts in game three, and two out of three in game four, after yielding one stolen base in the series opener, giving him a total of seven runners caught in 12 attempts for a sensational 58 percent caught-stealing percentage against the likes of Max Carey and Kiki Cuyler, who had a 77 percent success rate against National League catchers.

Pittsburgh's sweep extended their winning streak to six games, putting them in fourth place, nine games behind New York. Chicago was still second, their 36–25 record leaving them five games off the pace. Third-place Brooklyn was 2½ games behind Chicago. In the American League, the Washington Senators had surged from fifth place to first place after winning 19 of 27 games. New York dropped 14 of 25 games to fall into third place. The Cubs' leading batsmen through June were Gabby Hartnett (.333, 8 homers), Denver Grigsby (.331), Ray Grimes (.326), and George Grantham (.324). The pitching staff was led by Grover Cleveland Alexander (10–3), Vic Keen (8–4), Vic Aldridge (8–5), and Elmer Jacobs (4–3).

The team managed to keep its head above water in July, going 18–14 to hold onto second place, six games behind the Giants. They missed an opportunity to challenge John McGraw's team for the league lead when New York visited Cubs Park in mid-month. Sparked by George Kelly's five home runs, the Giants steamroller swept the disoriented Cubs in four games to open a big 9½-game lead. Gabby Hartnett's double and home run went for naught in the finale, as Tony Kaufmann was pummeled in a 9–4 rout.

The National League pennant race heated up in August, but the Cubs were on the sidelines as spectators. Their 13–17 record left them floundering in fourth place, 7½ games off the pace. Third-place Brooklyn was just four games out of first. A sign of things to come reared its ugly head in Ebbets Field on August 1 when the Cubs faced Dazzy Vance. The big Iowan farm boy had Killefer's men eating out of his hand, as he blanked them 4–0 on three hits, fanning 14 men along the way, including a major league record of seven in a row. He struck out Hartnett to end the first inning, then fanned the side in both the second and third innings, before Charlie Hollocher drew a leadoff walk to open the fourth. The game was embarrassing in more ways than one for Gabby Hartnett. The Chicago backstop muffed an easy foul pop-up in the seventh inning, leading to the first run of the game. Then in the eighth inning, the Dodgers scored two insurance runs when Hartnett let Heathcote's throw to the plate get by him.[11] Legend had it that Gabby only dropped three pop-ups during his 20-year career. The one in Brooklyn was obviously one of the three.

The cocky New York Giants welcomed the Chicago Cubs to the Polo Grounds on Monday, August 3, and proceeded to dismantle the Midwesterners five times in six games, leaving Killefer's team a distant 11 games behind and, for all intents and purposes, out of the race. Sheriff Blake was the lone victor for the Cubs, beating Claude Jonnard 5–2 with the help of Jigger Statz's home run. Gabby Hartnett, batting out of the cleanup spot, hit safely in all six games, going 7-for-25 with two doubles. Guy Bush pitched the best game of the series for Chicago, dropping a tough 2–1 decision to Wayland Dean in 10 innings.

Guy Bush was a story in his own right. He was a 22-year-old country boy from Mississippi, when the Cubs signed him in 1923. His story was told by Eddie Gold and Art Ahrens. After his signing, "Bush packed his weather-beaten satchel, left town, and pitched under an assumed name in the Kitty League. 'I was scared of Chicago,' said Bush. 'I had heard about all the gangsters and sharp men. I had never ridden an elevator that went up 'n down, and I didn't know about streetcars.' Bush was located three months later, and persuaded to go to Chicago. 'I missed my first train because the porter said it was a Pullman, and I didn't know what a Pullman was, and wasn't going to take a chance finding out.' Bush sat all night in the depot and waited for a day coach. Spring training in 1924 was quite an adventure for Bush, who was shaking from fright when he reported to manager Bill Killefer. While Bush appeared emaciated, he did have broad shoulders and a live fastball. He learned how to throw the curve and screwball from a Cub master, Grover Cleveland Alexander." After his outstanding effort against the Giants, Cubs President William Veeck Sr. "told him to go over to Broadway and buy the best suit he could find. But Bush strolled to Fifth Avenue instead," and bought the best suit in the store, a $135 beauty.[12]

On August 9, while the Cubs were visiting Boston, the fans of Millville gave Gabby Hartnett and Tim McNamara a "Joint Day" at Braves Field. The two men received diamond rings and other gifts from the appreciative citizens prior to the game. The game itself was a tense affair, with Hack Miller's single deadlocking it at 6–6 in the ninth. Jigger Statz brought the Cubs a victory in the tenth with an inside-the-park grand slam homer. Gabby enjoyed his time in Boston because it gave him a chance to visit his family in the evening. He would take the train to Millville, an hour away, spend time with his mother and father, then hit the taverns with his brothers and sisters. It took a lot of the drudgery out of the road trips. In other cities, Gabby's favorite pastimes were bowling, going to the movies, or playing cards in the hotel or clubhouse. On off-days, he and Bob O'Farrell would head for the golf course for a relaxing 18 holes.

The Giants, Pirates, and Dodgers were involved in a knock-down, drag-out war as August came to an end. While New York could do no better than 14–15 during the month, Pittsburgh went 21–10, and Brooklyn was red-hot with a 21–8 log. And the Dodgers weren't through yet. Their five-game winning streak ending the month turned into a 15-game winning streak before coming to an end, by which time the surprising Flatbushers had moved into first place, a ½ game ahead of the Giants. From there to the end of the season, it was a tight, three-team race.

Pittsburgh's 4–5 record early in September dropped them three games behind the Giants. Then they went on an 8–2 tear that brought them back within two games of the top, but that was as close as they could get. They finished in third place, three games off the lead. Brooklyn, on the other hand, wouldn't give in. Not more than 2½ games separated the Giants and Dodgers down the stretch. From August 1 to September 25, Wilbert Robinson's gutty crew racked up 40 victories against just 13 losses, picking up 10½ games on John McGraw's embattled warriors. Unfortunately, the Dodgers ran out of gas at the end, splitting their final four games, while the Giants were taking four of five to win the pennant by a game-and-a-half. One of the Dodgers losses was to the Cubs on the 23rd. Dazzy Vance, who started the game on two day's rest, lost a tough 5–4 decision on a tenth inning home run by Gabby Hartnett. Two days later, Boston scuttled Brooklyn's pennant hopes with a 3–2 win.

In the American League, the Washington Senators came on strong down the stretch to beat the New York Yankees by two games. In the Fall Classic, Washington upset the Giants four games to three in a popular victory. Walter Johnson, the Senators 36-year-old ace, with 376 career victories under his belt, after dropping games one and five, marched in from the bullpen in the ninth inning of game seven and proceeded to blank McGraw's cohorts over the next four innings, eventually earning the victory on Earl McNeely's run-scoring single in the twelfth inning.[13]

Rogers Hornsby won the National League batting championship with an average of .424, the highest batting average in modern major league history. Jack Fournier captured the home run crown with 27, two more than Hornsby and three more than Cy Williams. Dazzy Vance was the leading pitcher, with 28 wins against six losses. In the American League, the batting title and the home run title both went to Babe Ruth, who hit .378 with 46 home runs. Joe Hauser, the Philadelphia A's slugging first baseman, had 27. No one else had more than 19. The old warhorse, Walter Johnson, was the top pitcher, with a record of 23–7. The Chicago Cubs top performers were George Grantham (.316, 12 home runs, 60 RBIs), Cliff Heathcote (.309, 0, 30), Denver Grigsby (.299, 3, 48), and Gabby Hartnett (.299, 16, 67). The pitching corps was led by Tony Kaufmann (16–11), Vic Aldridge (15–12), Vic Keen (15–14), and Grover Cleveland Alexander (12–5).

It was a disappointing season for the Cubs. They went into it with high hopes after their fourth-place finish in 1923, and their fast start heightened those hopes. On July 31, they were just six games out of first place, with a record of 55–40, but from there to the end of the season, they won just 26 games against 32 losses. Part of the decline was attributable to the loss of Grover Cleveland Alexander, who missed more than two months with an injury before going 3–2 in September. Other members of the team slumped badly down the stretch, particularly Gabby Hartnett, who hit a feeble .246 with one home run over his last 40 games, and Denver Grigsby, who hit .247 with no home runs in his last 46 games. Hartnett's problems may have been the result of the severe beating his body took behind the plate during the summer, the result of his all-or-nothing aggressive style.

The brightest moment in the Cubs' season took place at New York's Polo Grounds on September 20. Grover Cleveland Alexander shut down the National League champion Giants by the score of 7–3 in 12 innings. It was the 300th victory of Alexander's illustrious career. He joined Cy Young, Walter Johnson, Christy Mathewson, and Eddie Plank as the only 300-game winners in modern major league history. Five other nineteenth century pitchers also compiled 300 victories. By his retirement in 1930, his 373 victories tied him with Mathewson for third place. Only Young (511) and Johnson (416) recorded more victories since baseball went major league in 1876.

The Cubs miseries continued into the post-season, as they lost another City Series to the White Sox, four games to two. It was their second loss in a row after breaking the White Sox jinx in 1922. Alexander won games one and five for Bill Killefer by scores of 10–7 and 8–3, but Johnny Evers' club won every other game.[14]

While the Cubs were quietly settling in for a winter of quiet solitude, and the New York Giants were contemplating what went wrong in the World Series, football fans in the Midwest were witnessing one of the greatest one-man shows in college football history. On Saturday, October 19, Red Grange, the famed "Galloping Ghost" of Illinois, was shredding the Michigan Wolverines defense with five electrifying touchdown runs in a stunning 39–14 Illinois victory. The pride of Urbana took the opening kickoff and raced 90 yards to pay dirt. He followed that with runs of 65, 55, and 45 yards before the fans were settled in their seats. Playing sporadically the rest of the game, he scored his fifth touchdown on a 10-yard run in the fourth quarter, then passed 23 yards for the Illini's final score. Overall, Grange carried the ball 21 times for 402 yards, and passed twice for 46 yards.[15]

Gabby Hartnett returned home to Millville with his first full season as a regular under his belt, but his body had failed him down the stretch. He was still learning how to pace himself for a strenuous six-month season, and his style of play resulted in many painful injuries. The oppressive heat that rose from the hard clay infields in places like Pittsburgh, Cincinnati, and St. Louis, in July and August, also took its toll.

When Gabby arrived home, he was driving a new pea green Buick Brougham, which cost him $1,500, almost as much as the average Millville resident earned in a full year. His salary for 1924 was $5,000, an impressive figure in the days when a new home cost $7,400, a new car could be bought for as little as $295, a loaf of bread cost $.09, a gallon of gas $.11, and a quart of milk $.13. The Dow Jones Average had reached 100.

One of the first things Gabby did was to gather some of his friends together, pile them into the Brougham, and drive 100 miles over the primitive dirt roads to East Otis, high up in the Berkshire Hills, for two weeks of deer hunting at his expense. It was a ritual he would follow for the next five years. It was a time for hunting, partying, and practical jokes. The entourage, which often consisted of Gabby and cronies like Chink Duffy, Welcome Morey, Jack Powers, Mike Conway, and Jack Whalen, always stayed at a lodge called the Knox Trail Inn. After a long day of trekking through the woods stalking deer, and then eating a hearty meal, the boys loved to gather around the player piano in the bar with a beer and belt out Irish lullabies, while Gabby pumped away with both feet. The raucous joviality often continued well into the night.

One night, according to John McNamara, "Gabby, who was one of the group's biggest practical jokers, needed a watch and Jack Whalen gave him his pocket watch. I think it was an Ingersoll. It wasn't the greatest. And so at the end of the week Gabby and Chink Duffy decided they would have some fun, so they hung the watch up and Gabby went back and blew it to pieces. All that was left was odds and ends, so Gabby put it in his pocket and they went back to the Inn. That night Jack said to Gabby, 'Hey, don't forget to give me my watch back.' And Gabby said, 'Geez, I forgot all about it,' and he gave Jack what was left of the watch, and Jack went bananas. So Gabby took off his watch and handed it to him."[16]

On the more serious side, Gabby was also one of the group's more successful hunters. He grew up around guns and often went hunting with his father in the woods around Millville. He brought down more than his share of deer in the Berkshire Hills, including at least one enormous eight-pointer.

While the hunting party was going on in Massachusetts, hunting of a different kind was underway in Chicago. Gang warfare had broken out in all its bloody violence. The murder of the North Side gang chief, Dion O'Banion, in November, by the South Side kingpin, Johnny Torrio, was the act that precipitated the bloodbath. The war would rage for five years, resulting in the murder of more than 50 gangsters, before local and federal authorities could begin to get the situation under control.

At the same time Al Capone and his thugs were running amok in the city, the Chicago Cubs management was making several changes in an effort to bring the team back to respectability. Gone were Aldrich, Grantham, Hollocher, and Grimes. Hollocher had retired at the end of the 1924 season, and Grimes was released. Aldridge and Grantham were traded to the Pittsburgh Pirates in return for Rabbit Maranville, Charlie Grimm, and Wilbur Cooper. Grimm would solve the Cubs' first base problem for the next decade, and his clubhouse presence was invaluable, as he had a "reputation as a happy-go-lucky, back-slapping guy who loved singing, banjo playing, beer, and German food."[17] Wilbur Cooper would go 12–14 for Bill Killefer in '25, then be exiled to the American League. Bob O'Farrell, Jigger Statz, and Hack Miller would be gone by mid-season, and Vic Keen would be limited to 86 innings pitched because of injuries. It was not the best of times for the Cubs organization. Talent was thin and getting thinner.

Gabby Hartnett's grandmother, Mary (Sullivan) Hartnett, passed away in Millville of natural causes on January 8, at the age of 68, sending the entire family into mourning.[18] The matriarch of the Hartnett clan had lived her entire life in the Massachusetts-Rhode Island area and had attended hundreds of school, amateur, and professional baseball games in which her children and grandchildren played. Not long after she died, Fred and Nell separated, with Nell moving back to Woonsocket, Rhode Island, to live with her daughter Dorothy, while Fred remained in Millville. The separation apparently alienated Fred from many of his children, including Gabby and Sweetie. Several years later, when Fred wanted to attend the 1929 World Series between the Cubs and the Philadelphia Athletics, he tried to contact Gabby for tickets, but his letters went unanswered and his telephone calls were not returned.

The pre-season favorites included the "usual suspects": New York, Pittsburgh, and Cincinnati in the National League, and Washington, New York, and Detroit in the American League. The Chicago Cubs, who were picked to repeat their fifth-

Hack Miller and Charlie Grimm posed for this photograph in Los Angeles in 1925. Hack seems be enjoying the photograph opportunity, but Charlie looks less than enthusiastic. (George E. Outland)

place finish of 1924, were hoping to improve their league standing. The New York Yankees, smarting from their loss to the Washington Senators, were also seeking improvement. But both teams would be greatly disappointed. Miller Huggins' Bombers, on their way north following a successful spring training, had stopped in Asheville, North Carolina, for an exhibition game when their world came crashing down. "The Franchise," Babe Ruth, was taken off the train on a stretcher, with an illness that was alternately identified as the flu or the result of overeating, depending on which story you heard. He was eventually transferred to New York City, where his illness was officially diagnosed as an intestinal infection. He would remain bedridden for three weeks following surgery, and would miss two months of the season, while his team settled back into seventh place, 13 games behind the Philadelphia Athletics.

The Cubs opened their season at home against the Pittsburgh Pirates on April 14. "Old Pete" Alexander drew the opening day assignment and proved too much to cope with for Bill McKechnie's Bucs. As an overflow crowd of 38,000 circling the outfield roared their approval, the big right-hander scattered nine hits en route to a convincing 8–2 decision. He also led the attack on two Pirates pitchers with a single and the season's first home run. His batterymate, Gabby Hartnett, the Cubs' cleanup hitter, handled his responsibilities in equal fashion. The big catcher smashed a double early in the game, then drove a three-run homer over the left field wall in the seventh inning, breaking open a 2–2 game. He also shot down two base runners, further solidifying his reputation as the "top gun" in the major leagues. The victory, #301 for the legendary Alexander, was the first Chicago Cubs baseball game ever broadcast on radio.

The kid from Millville was rapidly becoming a favorite of the fans. He "played ball with the spirit that fired the imagination of the crowd. The fans loved Gabby. They enjoyed his cocky stride to the plate, his sweeping hand wave to the stands, his bellows to the umpires on close plays, his big clenched fist which shot into the air after an opponent's strikeout. He played with everything he had. He handled his pitchers shrewdly."[19]

The same day, in Shibe Park, a 22-year-old rookie named Mickey Cochrane made his major league debut. He entered the game against the Boston Red Sox as a pinch hitter in the eighth inning and grounded out during a four-run Athletic rally. He stayed in the game, replacing Perkins behind the plate, and came to bat again in the tenth inning. This time, he hit a sharp single to left field to move the eventual winning run to third base, from where it scored minutes later on an infield single.[20]

The Cubs had a few bright spots early in the season, but it was all an illusion. Their skills were unable to sustain a winning record. On April 16, Bill Killefer's troops beat Pittsburgh, 8–3, for their second win in three games behind a two-homer game from Gabby Hartnett. Once again, the strong-armed catcher threw out the only two base runners who dared challenge his powerful throwing arm. The next day, the Millville masked-man launched another home run, his fourth round tripper in three games, and the Cubs won going away 9–6. Hack Miller had a big 4-for-4 day for Bill Killefer, and Jigger Statz contributed a single and a homer. Tony Kaufmann was hit hard, but survived to record a complete game victory. Hartnett punched out three base hits in four at-bats, adding two singles to his home run. And he had three more assists, upping his defensive record in the series to seven assists with NO stolen bases allowed. Some of his assists came from picking runners off base when they took too big a lead. His performance was all the more remarkable, coming as it did against the most aggressive team in the major leagues, a team that would go on to steal 159 bases during the season.

Elsewhere in the baseball world, Babe Ruth was improving, but was still hospitalized. And Charlie Ebbets, the President of the Brooklyn Dodgers, who was stricken when the team returned home from spring training, remained in critical condition in his Waldorf-Astoria Hotel suite. He died the next day, April 18.

Gabby Hartnett sent his fifth home run into orbit in his next game, but it didn't help the Cubbies, who were routed by Rickey's St. Louis Cardinals 20–5. Miller also had a homer for Chicago, but the Redbirds smashed five, including two by third baseman Les Bell and one each by Bottomley, Blades, and Douthit. The Cubs hit the road the following week, visiting Pittsburgh and St. Louis. Hartnett stayed hot during the Cubs' visit to the Steel City. His three-run homer in the first inning on the 25th, paced his team to a 4–3 victory. He also claimed two more Pirates base runners and was on the tail end of a double play, preventing a run from scoring. Charlie Grimm's round tripper in the second gave Killefer's team its final run. Sheriff Blake was touched up for three runs in the sixth, but shut the Bucs down over the final three innings. The Chicago clubhouse was livelier than usual after the game, with Charlie Grimm and his musical group celebrating his four-base blast. The Cubs first baseman strummed away on his $450 banjo, while Hack Miller picked the guitar, Barney Friberg did the same on his mandolin, and Cliff Heathcote played the ukulele, much to the delight of the Cubs players, coaches, and manager. In later years, after Friberg and Miller had departed, Kiki Cuyler would join the happy German in a duet, keeping the mood in the clubhouse light and relaxed.

The next week, Gabby's eighth-inning homer helped the Cubs overcome a 4–3 St. Louis lead, propelling them to a 6–4 victory. Killefer's hired gun also took care of two more potential base stealers, although two others got away. Through the first 15 games of the season, Chicago's 9–6 record left them in third place, one game behind the omnipresent New York Giants. Zack Wheat's .462 batting average paced National League hitters, while Gabby Hartnett's eight round trippers topped the home run charts. The Washington Senators were sitting atop the American League, a ½ game better than Cleveland, while the New York Yankees occupied sixth place, 5½ games off the pace. Their missing slugger, Babe Ruth, was still resting comfortably in St. Vincent's Hospital, trying to regain his strength. But he was still weeks away from breaking into the New York lineup.

Left to right: Gabby Hartnett with Helen Collins, Anna "Charlie" Hartnett, and Tim McNamara in 1925. (Jane McNamara Gilmore)

May 5 was a gold-letter day in the career of baseball's greatest hitter, Ty Cobb. The 38-year-old "Georgia Peach," refusing to surrender to Father Time, pounded out six hits in six trips to the plate, including a double and three home runs, to pace the Detroit Tigers to a 14–8 victory over the St. Louis Browns. His 16 total bases were a modern major league record.

The National League celebrated the fiftieth anniversary of its founding on May 8, and the Boston Braves, one of the original members of the league, although they were known as the Red Caps then, celebrated in their own way — by throttling the Chicago Cubs 5–2. Right-hander Joe Genewich limited Killefer's club to eight safeties, all singles, while his team raked Alexander and Keen for 14 base hits, including a double and a triple by Dave Bancroft. Fifty old-time ballplayers attended the game, including George Wright, the shortstop of baseball's first professional team, the 1869 Cincinnati Red Stockings. Wright also played short for Boston in their first National League game on April 22, 1876.[21]

Day by day, it was becoming more apparent that Gabby Hartnett was the best catcher on the Chicago Cubs team and was rapidly gaining recognition as the best all-around catcher in the major leagues. The good-natured backstop had all the tools: a consistent bat capable of driving the ball out of the park on a regular basis, a general's command of the game and the pitching staff, and baseball's deadliest throwing arm — one that was already intimidating the swiftest base runners in the National League. Other than his arrival as a world-class catcher, the Chicago Cubs were a sorry lot. Only Gabby, who was hitting .338, and Charlie Grimm, who was hitting .359, could be found among the league's leading hitters. Kaufmann and Blake, both at 3–1, were the only Chicago hurlers over .500.

On May 21, the A's hotshot rookie catcher equaled the modern major league home run record by putting three balls out of Sportsman's Park in St. Louis. Mickey Cochrane, a 5'10", 180-pound southpaw swinger, connected in the third, fourth, and seventh innings to spark Philadelphia to a 20–4 laugher over George Sisler's Browns. The A's collected 19 hits in all, three each by Cochrane, Poole, Lamar, and Simmons. The same day, Dazzy Vance shut down the Chicago Cubs 5–4. Gabby Hartnett drove a Vance fastball over the 38-foot-high right field screen in Ebbets Field and added a single in a losing cause. The Dodgers bunched four hits for four runs in the third inning. They added another marker in the sixth. Hartnett's homer in the eighth cut the margin to 5–1. Then in the ninth, two singles, a double, and a triple turned the game into a nail-biter, but Vance, still in command, just sucked it up and fanned the dangerous Hartnett to end the game.[22]

Two days later, Charles Leo Hartnett was officially awarded the Chicago Cubs first-string catching position. Bob O'Farrell, his main competition, was traded to the St. Louis Cardinals for catcher Mike Gonzalez and infielder Howard Freigau. The move was beneficial to both principals. O'Farrell caught 147 games in 1926, batted .293, and walked off with the National Leagues Most Valuable Player trophy. In the Fall Classic that year against the New York Yankees, he gunned down three out of four potential base stealers and batted .304. And he threw out Babe Ruth trying to steal second base, with two men out in the bottom of the ninth inning of the seventh game, ending the series.

The same day the trade was made, the Cubs suffered a disastrous defeat at the hands of the Brooklyn Dodgers, aka Robins, blowing a 5–1 lead in the ninth inning. Four base hits, two walks, and a wild throw by Hartnett did the damage. Vic Keen took the loss in relief of Sheriff Blake. The defeat kept the Cubbies bedded down in seventh place, 11 games behind New York. After losing two of three to Brooklyn, Chicago was swept by Pittsburgh before splitting four with Cincinnati, then returning home to beat the Pirates to close out the month of May. In the Pittsburgh game, an 11–2 victory, Gabby Hartnett ripped three hits in three at-bats, including a double and his fourteenth homer in support of a neat six-hitter by Sheriff Blake. In June, Bill Killefer's cohorts played .500 ball, 13 up and 13 down, to cement their hold on seventh place. John McGraw's Giants won only 13 of 27 games played during the month to fall into second place, percentage points behind the red-hot Pittsburgh Pirates, who went 17–8. In the American League, Bucky Harris' Washington Senators held a slight ½-game lead over the Philadelphia Athletics, while the Ruth-less New Yorkers remained in the doldrums, in sixth place, 15½ games from sunlight. The Bambino finally made it back to the team in June after missing more than 50 games.

The fortunes of the Chicago Cubs and the New York Yankees continued in the pits throughout the summer months. The first victim of the disaster was Chicago manager Bill Killefer, who was summarily fired by owner William Wrigley on July 6, leaving the team with a season record of 33–42. His overall Chicago record was 299–292. Surprisingly, Rabbit Maranville, a notorious hell-raiser, was promoted to manager, a move that led to more chaos. After directing his team to a 10–5 triumph over Brooklyn in his debut, the fun-loving Maranville went out on the town to celebrate with several friends; and before the night was over, they were all arrested for disturbing the peace. Maranville's reign lasted only 59 days before he was replaced by George Gibson.

The Yankees' problems with Babe Ruth did not end with his return to duty from his gastro-intestinal illness. His enormous ego surfaced during a road trip to St. Louis in late August, when he confronted his manager, Miller Huggins, challenging the little manager's authority. Huggins, though small in stature, managed like a much bigger man. He would not back down before Ruth's bullying, and finally fined the Babe and suspended him on August 28. Ruth, anticipating the support of Colonel Jacob Rupert, was sadly disappointed when the Yankee owner backed his manager in the dispute. A repentant Bambino finally apologized to his manager a week later and was reinstated on September 7. Showing no ill effects from his losing showdown with Huggins, Babe Ruth came roaring down the stretch, slugging the ball at a .343 clip in September, with 10 home runs in 29 games.

Gabby Hartnett once again sputtered at the end of the season. Over the last two months, he hit just .246 in 37 games, with no home runs, and was benched in favor of Mike Gonzalez for 31 games.

Golf captured the headlines twice during the month of September. On the fifth of the month, Bobby Jones won the National Amateur Championship at Oakmont Country Club in Pittsburgh by humbling his protégé,

Watts Gunn, 8 and 7 in 29 holes. Three weeks later, Walter Hagen, another golfing legend, successfully defended his P.G.A. title by beating challenger William Mehlhorn, 6 and 6 at Olympia Field in Chicago. Jones and Hagen are generally considered to be two of the top golfers in history, along with Sam Snead, Arnold Palmer, and Jack Nicklaus.[23]

As the baseball season came to an end on October 4, both the Yankees and Cubs breathed a sigh of relief. New York edged the Philadelphia Athletics 9–8 in the finale, when Earl Combs stole home in the ninth inning to win it. Babe Ruth and Bob Meusel both homered for Miller Huggins' team, but the Yankees' 69–85 record relegated them to seventh place, 28_ games behind the pennant-winning Senators. Chicago's 7–5 loss to the St. Louis Cardinals dropped Gibson's team into the National League basement. It was a satisfying victory for Cardinals catcher Bob O'Farrell, who hit a home run to drive the final nail into his former team's coffin. Gabby Hartnett closed his season with a double in four trips to the plate.

The individual league leaders were Rogers Hornsby, with a .403 average and 39 home runs, in the National League, and Harry Heilmann, with a .398 average, and Bob Meusel, with 33 home runs, in the American League. Dazzy Vance at 22–9 and Stan Coveleskie at 20–5 led their respective leagues in pitching. The Chicago Cubs' team leaders were Charlie Grimm (.307), Gabby Hartnett (24 homers), and Grover Cleveland Alexander (15–11). Sparky Adams, who batted a healthy .290, led all National League second basemen in fielding average, putouts, and assists.

The Philadelphia Athletics rookie catcher, Mickey Cochrane, caught 134 games, batted .331, led the league with a fielding average of .984, and was selected as the American League's Most Valuable Player. His 40 percent caught-stealing rate, which was not measured at the time, was 5% worse than the league average.

In the World Series, Bill McKechnie's Pittsburgh Pirates defeated Bucky Harris' Washington Senators, four games to three. Walter Johnson was hammered by the Bucs in game seven, absorbing a 9–7 defeat.

The baseball world was saddened by the death of former New York Giants pitcher, Christy Mathewson, on October 7. The man known as "Big Six," succumbed to tuberculosis at his home in Saranac Lake, New York. During his illustrious 17-year major league career, the 6'1½", 180-pound right-handed pitcher won 373 games against 188 losses. His victory total ranks #3 on the all-time list, trailing only Cy Young (511) and Walter Johnson (416). He is among the career leaders in winning percentage (#6), ERA (#5), innings pitched (#6), and shutouts (#3). He is generally considered to be among the five greatest pitchers in major league history, and is frequently rated #1 or #2, along with Walter Johnson.

Gabby Hartnett's overall season was a success, and he continued to develop offensively and defensively. He played in 117 games, the most games he played in one season in the professional ranks. He batted a hard .289, and his 24 home runs represented the first time a major league catcher had ever hit 20 or more home runs in a year. Hartnett's youthful exuberance was still noticeable, however, both on offense and defense. His 24 home runs came at a price. The wild-swinging slugger led the National League in strike-outs with 77. On defense, the twenty-four-year old backstop was absolutely fearless behind the plate. He was quick to throw the ball around the infield in an attempt to pick a runner off base, but occasionally his enthusiasm got the best of him, and he made throws that he probably shouldn't have made. As a result, Gabby led the National League in errors in both 1924 and '25, but he also led the league in putouts and assists in 1925. His 56 percent caught-stealing rate in '25, 13 percent better than the league average, was one of the highest caught-stealing percentages in major league history.

Gabby matured significantly in 1925, learning to play under control rather than with abandon. From 1924 through 1927, he would lead the league in assists twice, and putouts twice, but also in errors three times. But from 1928 through the rest of his career, he would lead the league in fielding average seven times, putouts twice, assists four times, and errors not at all. He would make 73 errors his first six years in the league, but only 70 errors in the next 14. And he was the perennial leader in throwing out base runners. In fact, in major league history, only Roy Campanella could challenge Gabby's success rate in gunning down prospective base stealers. To put his defensive statistics in perspective, Yogi Berra led his league in fielding average twice, assists three times, errors three times, and putouts eight times. Johnny Bench led the league in putouts, assists, and fielding average once each. Both Berra and Bench were better than average at nailing prospective base stealers, but they were not in Hartnett's class.

After the final pitch was thrown in the 1925 baseball season, Gabby Hartnett cleaned out his locker and headed east to his sister's home in Woonsocket, Rhode Island. He spent the next four months socializing and letting his wounds heal. And even though the Cubs forbade him from participating in basketball during the off-season, he ignored the directive and played for the Millville Town Team, managed by his friend, Jack Powers. The team played an average of one game a week around the Blackstone Valley, using Gabby as a drawing card. He also played a little basketball for the semipro Pawtucket Tigers. When not on the basketball court, Gabby usually hung out with his friends. He had inherited his father's love of poker, and could be found many evenings in the back room of Kilkenny's store, playing a little five-card draw.

There was also the annual deer-hunting expedition to Otis, as well as the Christmas celebration with his family, which included Mass at St. Augustine's Church. But Gabby's attention was being drawn back to the Chicago area more frequently, where his girlfriend Martha Marshall resided, and where he had more and more business interests. As time passed, Gabby and Martha grew closer together, and a casual dating relationship slowly became a serious romance. Some nights, they would borrow a car and go to a movie, a nightclub, or the Edgewater Beach Hotel, where they would drink lemonade and dance. Their daughter Sheila said that when they first started dating, "[Martha] didn't have a clue who he was. And they were dancing and she noticed that his hands were calloused. She thought he was a laborer. She had no idea he was a baseball player because she wasn't a big sports fan."

Gabby Hartnett, against the Chicago Cubs' wishes, played basketball for the Millville Town Team in the mid-20s. (Town of Millville J.G. Fitzgerald Historical Society, Inc.)

Beginning in 1925, Gabby Hartnett was torn between two worlds: his childhood home in the Blackstone Valley and Chicago, where his future wife lived. In the years to come, he would spend less and less time in Woonsocket and Millville, and more time in Chicago. And his hunting expeditions would begin to move west also, with turkey-hunting vacations in Michigan's Upper Peninsula and trips to South Dakota in search of elk.

On the streets of the Windy City, the gang war continued unabated. Johnny Torrio, the South Side gang chief, who had been ambushed in January, suffering five bullet wounds, survived the assassination attempt, then spent nine months in jail on a felony count. When he was released, he immediately abdicated his throne and sailed for Italy. His empire was turned over to 26-year-old Al Capone, who had served his boss well over the previous five years. In the first year under Capone, the South Side interests brought in $105 million — $65 million from bootlegging, $25 million from gambling, and the remainder from other interests like loan-sharking and prostitution. Blood would continue to flow in the streets of Chicago for the next four years, as the North Side and South Side criminal empires battled for control of the city.[24]

The most important event in Chicago baseball for the year 1925 was the announcement on October 13 that minor league manager Joseph McCarthy had been signed to manage the Cubs. It was a move that was destined to change the fortunes of William Wrigley, Jr.'s team.

5

Refining His Skills, 1926–1927

When the Chicago Cubs players arrived at spring training camp in February 1926, they were greeted by their new manager, Joseph Vincent McCarthy, also known as "Marse Joe." The 39-year-old native of Philadelphia had been a minor league ballplayer for a dozen years before joining the managerial ranks. He managed Wilkes-Barre in 1913 before moving up to the Buffalo Bisons two years later. In 1919 he assumed the reigns of the Louisville Colonels of the American Association, earning a reputation as an astute baseball man and a superior strategist.

The first moves McCarthy made as manager of the Chicago Cubs were to obtain minor league hitting sensations Hack Wilson and Riggs Stephenson. Wilson was a squat 5'6", 195-pound package of dynamite who, at 26 years of age, had terrorized minor league pitching, hammering the ball at a .370 pace over three years, while winning two home run titles. In two short trials with the New York Giants, he gave signs of future success by hitting .276 with 16 home runs in 573 at-bats. However, when the Giants inadvertently left him unprotected in Toledo, the Cubs drafted him for a modest $7,500. Stephenson, at 28 years old, had spent five years with Cleveland in the American League as a weak-armed infielder who hit a healthy .337 before being optioned to Kansas City. After converting to the outfield and slugging the ball at a .385 clip, the man known as "Old Hoss" was purchased by the Cubs for $20,000 and two players.

Joe McCarthy also called up Charlie Root, who had compiled a 25–13 record with the Cubs farm team in Los Angeles of the Pacific Coast League, and quickly made the right-handed hurler the ace of his pitching staff. He then dipped into the major league reservoir and obtained shortstop Jimmy Cooney from the St. Louis Cardinals to replace the recently departed Rabbit Maranville. Cooney remembered the 1926 Chicago Cubs training camp as the best one he ever attended. There was plenty of hard work, but there was also time for practical jokes, such as the time he and Sparky Adams went around the St. Catherine Hotel collecting all the chairs they could find and piling them all in Gabby Hartnett's room. According to Cooney, "Gabby was busy for quite a time emptying the room of chairs, but he got a kick out of it. He just laughed it off. Gabby was a wonderful fellow, one of the best natured men I ever met. And he had a wonderful arm. Not many stole on him. And hard as he threw, that ball of his was one of the lightest I ever caught."[1]

In a short period of time, manager McCarthy assembled a formidable team, headed by a pitching staff of Root, Blake, Kaufmann, Cooper, and Bush. The infield was adequate, with Grimm, Adams, Cooney, and Freigau, and the outfield was now a potent offensive weapon with Heathcote, Wilson, and Stephenson. But the catching position was the team's most impressive position. Gabby Hartnett was a hardened veteran as the 1926 season got underway. He had evolved as the Cubs' first-string catcher the previous year, had set a new major league home run record for his position, and had cut down opposing base runners at a sensational rate of 56 percent, to certify his reputation as the best all-around catcher in the major leagues. His counterpart in the American League, Mickey Cochrane, hit for a higher average, but lacked Hartnett's power, and had an average throwing arm. Both men were unsurpassed at blocking the plate, handing their pitching staffs and directing their infielders. And both were very aggressive field leaders.

Gabby Hartnett had set two goals for himself in 1926: to cut down on his strikeouts and reduce his errors. He wanted to be more conservative at the plate and concentrate on making contact with the ball instead of trying to drive every pitch out of the park. On defense, he worked hard to play under control and be more selective in his pick-off throws.

As the teams prepared for the new season, the experts were predicting the New York Yankees would once again be the scourge of the American League, with Philadelphia and Washington their primary challengers. In the National League, Pittsburgh and New York were the favorites, with Cincinnati and St. Louis given a slight chance of upsetting the applecart. The Cubs were picked for fifth place, which brought the following angry retort from manager Joe McCarthy. "They tell me we don't look very good on paper. Well, we don't play on paper." But fifth place was still higher than Grover Cleveland Alexander would have picked them. He once told his manager, "McCarthy, you don't have to worry about a runner on second with this club. They just don't get that far."[2]

Marse Joe's new-look Chicago Cubs opened their season in Cincinnati with Wilbur Cooper opposing the Reds' 21-game winner, Pete Donohue. Jack Hendrick's Redlegs prevailed 7–6 in a 10-inning game marked by free hitting and sloppy defense, particularly on the part of the Cubs. Donohue held a relatively safe 6–1 lead before the Cubs exploded for five runs in the eighth. Five Chicago errors, by Heathcote, Cooper, Hartnett, and Cooney (2), led to their downfall. Hartnett contributed a single and a double to the Cub attack and gunned down three reckless base runners. Rookie Charlie Root evened the series the next day with a convincing 9–2 victory, but Red Lucas outpitched Grover Cleveland Alexander 2–1 in the finale. Joe McCarthy's charges moved on to St. Louis where they managed a split with the Cardinals, thanks to a 7–0 shutout by Cooper in the get-away game. Hack Wil-

Sheriff Blake won 10 or more games a year for the cubs between 1925 and 1930.

son, who had ripped two triples and a double in the first six games, hit his first Chicago home run. Grimm, Gonzales, Cooper, and Pete Scott all had two hits.

On April 21, the Chicago Cubs opened their home season in the newly renamed Wrigley Field, with "Old Alex" facing Pete Donohue. This time, the Cubs took Donohue to the cleaners, winning 4–2 before a packed house estimated at 33,000. Cliff Heathcote's two doubles led the Cubs hit parade, and his and Joe Munson's defensive plays short-circuited Cincinnati rallies. Hartnett had a single and two assists in support of his roommate. The next day, McCarthy's warriors pummeled 11-year veteran Carl Mays 18–1 behind a 20-hit barrage. Charlie Grimm poked four singles, Sparky Adams had a single and two doubles, and Howard Freigau had three singles. Heathcote, Wilson, Cooney, and Root chipped in with two base hits each. Two days later, the Cubs captured a 4–3 nail-biter from the Pittsburgh Pirates. Hack Wilson led off the eighth inning with a double to left field, moved over to third on a sacrifice by Freigau, and scored the winning run on a perfectly executed squeeze bunt by Charlie Grimm.[3]

Chicago's 8–7 record for the month of April left them 1½ games behind the Brooklyn Dodgers, still called the Robins by the *New York Times*. On April 29, Joe McCarthy's cohorts welcomed Rogers Hornsby's St. Louis Cardinals to the Friendly Confines and promptly clipped their wings four straight times. In game two, Cubs pitcher Percy Jones doubled in the eleventh inning and carried the winning run across the plate on Hack Wilson's walk-off single. Gabby Hartnett had a single, a double, and two assists in the 10–9 victory. The next day, before a large weekend crowd, Joe Munson's two home runs, including a tie-breaking, three-run job in the eighth inning, propelled the Cubs to an 11–8 win. Former Cub Bob O'Farrell had a single, double, and home run in a losing cause. The Sunday game was another Chicago victory, and another tense struggle, before a festive Windy City gathering. Winning pitcher, Grover Cleveland Alexander's bunt, which was thrown away for an error by Cardinal first baseman "Sunny Jim" Bottomley in the bottom of the ninth, scored pinch runner Pete Scott with the winning run. Gabby Hartnett had led off the inning with his second double of the game, before being replaced by Scott. Hack Wilson had a double and a home run for the Cubs. The final score was 6–5.[4]

The next visitor to Chicago's baseball palace didn't fare much better than the Cardinals. John McGraw's New York Giants took the pipe three times in four games. They captured the opener 2–1, with Virgil Barnes earning the decision over Charlie Root. According to the *New York Times*, "The warm spring day thawed out the Chicago fans, and 20,000 of them were out. The enthusiasm ran wild and was reminiscent of the old days of 1908 when the Giants and Cubs used to battle for supremacy." The Cubs bounced back to take the next three games by scores of 6–0, 6–4, and 8–7. Tony Kaufmann's four-hit shutout stilled the big Giants bats in game two, while Adams, Heathcote, and Kaufmann all had two hits for the McCarthy-men. Old Alex outpitched Hugh McQuillan 6–4 on Saturday before a screaming overflow crowd of 37,000. The Cubs' veteran right-hander had one bad inning, the sixth, when New York bunched four of their seven hits for four runs, but by that time, Alexander held a 5–0 lead, and he slammed the door on McGraw's team over the final three innings. Hack Wilson had a perfect day, with two doubles and a single in three at-bats. Cliff Heathcote chipped in with a single and an inside-the-park homer. In the Sunday finale, 40,000 noisy Chicagoans jammed the park. The *Times* reported, "The fans hung from the rafters, sat on the walls surrounding the park, crowded out onto the playing field in right, center, and left fields, and crowded the aisles and passageways." The game was a donnybrook, with the Cubs jumping out on top early, 5–1, then the Giants roaring back to take a 7–6 lead into the bottom of the ninth. After Hartnett was retired on a fly ball to Ross Youngs, Hack

Wilson, who was sidelined with a leg injury, limped to the plate and promptly drilled a double into the crowd in left field. After Jack Scott walked Sparky Adams, he was yanked in favor of Virgil Barnes, but the Cubs were not to be denied. Heathcote walked to load the bases, after which Joe Munson popped to George Kelly for out #2. The stillness that had settled over Wrigley Field after Munson's at-bat exploded into a deafening roar when Mandy Brooks' ground ball was fumbled by shortstop Travis Jackson, allowing pinch runner Pete Scott to score the tying run. Minutes later, Howard Freigau lined a single to left field to end the game, as the crowd went wild.[5] The victory moved Chicago past Cincinnati into second place, 1½ games behind Wilbert Robinson's Dodgers. In the American League, the Washington Senators slipped past the New York Yankees into first place on the basis of a 6–5 victory over the Chicago White Sox.

Newspaper headlines of May 10 announced the historic flight over the North Pole by American explorer Lieutenant Commander Richard E. Byrd and his copilot Floyd Bennett. They navigated their blue tri-motor Fokker, the "Josephine Ford," to the Pole from Kings Bay, Spitzbergen, circled the Pole several times, then returned home, completing a harrowing 15-hour, 51-minute adventure. The flight also verified observations made by Admiral Peary, the first person to reach the North Pole by an overland route.[6]

The league-leading Brooklyn Dodgers strutted into the Windy City in mid-month to tackle the second-place Cubs. Chicago drew first blood when southpaw Wilbur Cooper blanked manager Wilbert Robinson's boys 9–0 before 8,000 chilled fans. The next day, Brooklyn retaliated behind spitball artist Burleigh Grimes, who came away a 6–2 winner in frigid, windy conditions, which were better suited to Alaska. The Brooks also captured game three when Buzz McWeeny outpitched Charlie Root 2–0. The winning runs scored in the ninth inning when 37-year-old Zack Wheat ripped a double to left and Dodger zany-man Babe Herman sent an outside fastball screaming into left center field for three bases. Herman scored moments later while Gus Felix was grounding out. Chicago tagged McWeeny for eight base hits, including two doubles by Gabby Hartnett and a single and a double by Cliff Heathcote. Herman and Mickey O'Neil had two hits each for Brooklyn.

Both pennant races were up for grabs as May reached the halfway point. Cincinnati took over the top rung from Brooklyn when Uncle Robby's boys dropped a 2–0 encounter with Pittsburgh, while the Reds were defeating the New York Giants. The Chicago Cubs were third, 2½ games off the top. In the American League, five teams were within four games of first place. The Yankees held the top spot, followed by Washington, Philadelphia, Chicago, and Cleveland. Hack Wilson of the Cubs was setting the pace in the National League batting race with an average of .386, while Cliff Heathcote was batting .354 and Gabby Hartnett was locked in at .315. As he had hoped, the big catcher's new conservative batting approach had reduced his strikeouts, but it also reduced his home runs. He had yet to go deep in 18 games. The top Cubs hurlers were Cooper, Bush, and Jones, all with 2–0 records. Root stood at 3–2.

One of the highlights of the Chicago Cubs home games was the pre-game infield drills that featured the sensational throwing arm of Gabby Hartnett. He had already achieved legendary status in baseball circles by 1926 as the possessor of the mightiest arm in baseball history. After terrorizing enemy base runners for four years, Gabby eagerly put his skills on display before every game, relishing the attention of the hundreds of fans who flocked to the park early to see him rifle the ball around the bases, with Hack Wilson and other Chicago players fielding the lightning-fast throws. Wilson delighted the fans by pretending to be spun around by the ferocity of Gabby's throws. Another favorite pre-game drill was called "Burn Out," where Gabby and Charlie Grimm would position themselves at home plate and first base, respectively, and start walking towards each other while throwing the ball as hard as they could, until one of them called it a day. The fans loved it.

Hack Wilson led the National League in home runs in 1926 with 21. (George E. Outland)

Home stands were also important to Hartnett for other reasons. Even though he still hit the speakeasies with his teammates when the club was on the road, he was becoming a strict homebody in Chicago. He spent quiet evenings with the McCulloughs and enjoyed the companionship of Martha Marshall, who was domesticating him and teaching him how to budget his money.

Chicago played .500 ball the rest of May. They beat the Phillies 10–9 on the 16th, took their measures again the next day with a two-run rally in the ninth, and dropped a 5–2 decision to Bunny Hearn of Boston on the 19th. They finished the month with a doubleheader against St. Louis. In the first game, the Cardinals prevailed 5–3 behind Hy Bell, and the Cubs captured the nightcap

8–7, with a five-run rally in the bottom of the eighth. Shortstop Red Shannon led the Chicago attack in game two with three base hits. Adams, Heathcote, Grimm, and Joe Kelly added two hits each. Hartnett was 1-for-2, with a double and an assist in game one, and he pinch-hit in the Cubs' game-winning rally in game two, drawing a walk and scoring a run.[7] Mike Gonzalez, who caught the second game of the doubleheader, was seeing significant action behind the plate, as manager Joe McCarthy tried to give Hartnett plenty of rest during the oppressive summer, so he would be fresh for a possible stretch run. Gonzalez, an outstanding defensive backstop, was hitting .213 after his first 18 games, while Gabby Hartnett was stinging the ball at a .308 pace.

June was a sorry month for the men of McCarthy. Their 9–18 record left them floundering in fifth place, 7½ games behind first-place Cincinnati. The month also spelled the end of Grover Cleveland Alexander's Chicago career. Old Alex, the late-night wanderer, clashed with manager Joe McCarthy from day one. The new Cubs skipper was a disciplinarian who demanded respect from his players, but the alcoholic Alexander frequently ignored his manager's rules and went on his merry bar-hopping way in the evening. Finally, on June 16, after Alexander had failed to appear for series in both Boston and Philadelphia, the tough Irish skipper suspended his star pitcher and sent him back to Chicago in the middle of the road trip. A week later, Alexander was waived to the St. Louis Cardinals after having compiled a 3–3 record with the Cubs in just seven appearances. Alexander's two managers, the old and the new, had differing opinions about the legendary star. McCarthy said, "I liked Alec. Nice fellow. But Alec was Alec. Did he live by the rules? Sure. But they were always Alec's rules. If we finish last again, I'd rather do it without him." St. Louis Cardinals manager, Rogers Hornsby, was thrilled to obtain a pitcher of Alexander's talents, and made his feelings known immediately. "Hell, I'd rather have him pitch a crucial game for me drunk than anyone I've ever known sober. He was that good."[8]

There were very few bright spots during the month. On June 14, the Cubs took the measure of the seventh-place Phillies by the score of 9–7, thanks to a four-homer barrage. Riggs Stephenson blasted two of the round trippers, while Hack hit #9 and Gabby Hartnett put his third into orbit. Bob Osborn was the beneficiary of the outburst. The next day, McCarthy's troops defeated the Phils again, this time by a 4–1 count. Sheriff Blake tossed a four-hitter, while Chicago unleashed a 17-hit attack led by Wilson and Stephenson, with three hits each, and Adams, Kelly, Blake, and Hartnett, with two safeties. The McCarthy-men ended the month with two doubleheader splits. On Sunday, June 28, before a record crowd of 37,000 fans in St. Louis, the Cubbies dropped the opener 3–2, but captured the nightcap

5–0, as Blake tossed a one-hitter. Grover Cleveland Alexander, the former Cub, handcuffed his old teammates in game one, holding them to four hits and one walk, while striking out five. Hartnett went hitless against his old roommate, but he threw out all three base runners who tried to steal. In game two, Blake fanned 10 and walked four in his masterpiece. He was supported by Jimmy Cooney who had three base hits, including a double. The split dropped the second-place Cardinals 2½ games behind Cincinnati, while fifth-place Chicago fell 7½ back. Two days later, the Cubs and Reds divided a pair, with Jack Hendrick's troops winning the opener 3–2, and Joe McCarthy's cohorts taking the nightcap 9–4. Hartnett was hitless in game one, but had a walk, a run scored, and an assist. "Wild Bill" Piercy, Chicago's lanky right-hander, came away the winner in game two, thanks to a powerful Cubs attack. Howard Freigau and Jimmy Cooney pounded three hits each, while Piercy and Heathcote chipped in with two. One of Heathcote's hits left the park.[9]

Riggs Stephenson was leading the Chicago hit parade at month end, with an average of .343, while Hack Wilson was batting .328 with nine home runs. Cliff Heathcote had a .291 average and six home runs in 47 games, and Gabby Hartnett checked in with a .288 average and three homers. Percy Jones was the top pitcher, with a record of 3–1, followed by Kaufmann (5–2), Osborn (2–1), and Root (7–6). Rookie Charlie Root was rapidly becoming the ace of the Chicago staff, a position he would hold, or share with Guy Bush, for the next eight years.

As the oppressive heat of summer settled over the baseball diamonds in Middle America, the Cubs bats got hot, and they began a push that would eventually carry them close to the top of the National League. Joe McCarthy's charges racked up a record of 18–13 in July to move into fourth place in the National League, still seven games behind Pittsburgh, who took over first place from Cincinnati after a five-week run of 22–13. Riggs Stephenson's bat was on fire in July, as he tattooed opposing pitchers to the tune of .402, raising his season average 33 points. Hack Wilson was hitting .313 and had 14 round trippers to his credit. The other leading Chicago hitters were Sparky Adams (.303), Charlie Grimm (.295), Cliff Heathcote (.294), and Gabby Hartnett (.275). Percy Jones had a 7–2 record on the mound, followed by Kaufmann (5–3), Root (13–9), and Piercy (5–4).

August was another big month for the Chicago Cubs, as they rolled to a 19–12 record, but they still trailed the league-leading Cardinals by 7½ games as Labor Day approached. The National League pennant race was a five-team competition, with the Cards, Reds, and Pirates all claiming first place at one time or another during July and August, and Chicago and New York staying within range. The final game of the month saw Percy Jones out-duel Jakie May of Cincinnati 1–0. With the game still scoreless in the bottom of the ninth, Mike Gonzalez sent the Wrigley Field fans home happy when he singled in the winning run. Jimmy Cooney led off the ninth with a ringing double to left and came around to score when the Chicago catcher jumped on a May curveball and sent it screaming into center field.

There were two big stories dominating the headlines around the country in August. One was Gertrude Ederle's conquest of the English Channel. The 19-year-old New York girl, who had failed in her attempt to cross the water bridge between England and France the previous year, battled the wind, rain, tide, and cold for 14 hours, 31 minutes, before emerging from the water at Kingsdown, England, to become the first woman to conquer the channel. In the process, she broke the men's record by more than two hours. She was given a ticker tape parade down New York's Fifth Avenue on her return home.[10] On August 23, movie fans were stunned by the sudden death of Hollywood's silent screen idol Rudolph Valentino. The Latin lover, famous for his torrid love scenes in such movies as *The Sheik*, succumbed to complications from an appendectomy. An estimated 30,000 mourners filed past his casket in Campbell's Funeral Home in New York over a two-day period.

Manager Joe McCarthy's warriors got off the mark slowly in September, as the St. Louis Cardinals proved to be inconsiderate guests, sweeping a doubleheader from the Windy City boys by scores of 2–0 and 9–1. The victories gave Rogers Hornsby's team a two-game lead over Cincinnati in the red-hot National League pennant race. An overflow crowd of 31,000, standing ten deep in left field, watched the tragedy unfold. The day was dark, with intermittent sprinkles; but as far as the Cardinals were concerned, it was bright and sunny. In the opener, Grover Cleveland Alexander gained a measure of revenge against the manager who banished him by throwing a masterful 2–0 shutout against Marse Joe's ace right-hander Charlie Root. The Redbirds got both runs in the third inning when Old Alex doubled into the overflow crowd in left field and scored the first run of the game on Taylor Douthit's triple. The St. Louis center fielder carried an insurance run across the plate minutes later on Billy Southworth's two-base hit. St. Louis made it a clean sweep in the nightcap when Flint Rhem coasted to a 9–2 win, backed by Bob O'Farrell's two singles and a double. Hornsby added two singles, and Chick Hafey punched out a single and a double off Bob Osborn. The lone Chicago run came across on Hartnett's double and two infield outs.[11]

When Chicago whipped the last-place Philadelphia Phillies 3–1 on September 13, they were just 4½ games off the pace. Sheriff Blake outpitched Wayland Dean for the win, with the Philadelphia pitcher's home run their only score. Gabby Hartnett went 1-for-2, with a sacrifice, for McCarthy's team. That was the Cubs' high water mark, as they went on to drop their next four games, beginning with a heartbreaking 5–4 loss to Art Fletcher's Fighting Phils. Hal Carlson, on his way to a fine 17–12 season, held off late Chicago rallies for the victory. Philadelphia chipped away at Percy Jones for single runs in the first and second innings, then drove him to cover with two more in the third. Sparky Adams had three hits, and Cliff Heathcote had two in a losing cause. The Cubs had a scare in the sixth inning when Hack Wilson was knocked unconscious by a Carlson pitch that struck him behind the left ear. He was carried from the field on a stretcher, effectively ending his season. Without Wilson's big bat in the middle of the lineup, McCarthy's demoralized Bruins lost the next four games to Dave Bancroft's lowly Boston Braves. On Wednesday, September 16, they were humbled by the Braves 1–0 and 3–1. The same day, Pittsburgh was all but eliminated from the race after a 2–1 loss to Jesse Barnes and the Brooklyn Dodgers. The Pirates trailed Cincinnati and St. Louis, who were tied for the top spot by 4½ games with just ten games left in the season.

The next day, Boston defeated Chicago again, this time by a score of 4–1. They also took the first game of a doubleheader 3–2 on September 17, before dropping the nightcap 6–0. Percy Jones took the loss in game one on a two-out run-scoring single to right field by Andy High in the bottom of the ninth. Sheriff Blake finally stopped the bleeding by taking game two by a 6–0 count. He held the Beaneaters to three hits while pounding out three hits of his own. Heathcote, Scott, and Stephenson all had two hits, while Hartnett had a double and a run scored.

The exciting pennant races were interrupted briefly on the 19, while a major heavyweight championship fight was being held in Sesquicentennial Stadium in Philadelphia. Jack Dempsey, the champion, who hadn't fought in three years, took on Gene Tunney, a tough former marine, and a man groomed in the manly art of self-defense. While rain poured down on the two fighters, a mammoth crowd of 135,000 people cheered for the challenger. Tunney did not disappoint. According to the *New York Times*, "Through every round of the ten, Tunney battered and pounded Dempsey. He rained rights on the tottering champion's jaw, and he bewildered Dempsey with his speed and accuracy. When the decision was announced in favor of Tunney, the crowd let loose a roar of acclaim for 'the man of destiny.'"[12]

The Cubs ran out the string, winning four of their last seven games, finishing in fourth place with a record of 82–72. Cincinnati's pennant hopes faded as they dropped consecutive series to the Giants and Braves, leaving them two games behind the new National League champions, the St. Louis Cardinals. Two Chicago castoffs sparked the Redbirds to the title, with "Old

Pete" Alexander winning nine big games and Bob O'Farrell having an outstanding season, which earned him the league's Most Valuable Player trophy for 1926.

In the American League pennant race, Miller Huggins' Bronx Bombers held off a late surge by the Cleveland Indians to win the pennant by three games. Babe Ruth paced the Yankees at the plate, batting .372, with a league-leading 47 home runs and 145 runs-batted-in (RBIs). Bob Meusel hit .315, and 23-year-old Lou Gehrig finished at .313. Herb Pennock led the New York Yankees' mound corps with a record of 23–11.

The World Series matched the powerful New Yorkers against the upstart Cardinals, [who won their first pennant since 1888]. The Cards were led at bat by manager Rogers Hornsby, who hit .317; Sunny Jim Bottomley, who stroked the ball at a .299 clip with 120 RBI's; Les Bell, who hit .325 with 100 RBIs; Billy Southworth at .317; and Taylor Douthit, who batted .308. Flint Rhem won 20 games against seven losses for Hornsby's team, while Bill Sherdel chipped in with 14 wins against 12 losses. Radio was coming into its own in 1926, and the Series was carried live by more than two dozen stations coast to coast.

The Series turned out to be an exciting seven-game affair that went down to the last pitch. The Yankees got off the mark quickly in game one, winning 2–1 behind Pennock. St. Louis came back to capture games two and three with Grover Cleveland Alexander taking game two by the score of 6–2. Old Alex was his usual self, tossing a four-hitter at "Murderers Row" and striking out 10, while issuing only one free pass. The Yanks took games four and five and seemed on the brink of clinching the world championship, but the 39-year-old Alexander stymied them again in game six, winning 10–2. Game seven was a true pitchers battle between the Redbirds' Jesse Haines and the Yankees' Waite Hoyt. St. Louis led 3–2 after 6½ innings, thanks to a three-run fourth inning, the result of errors by Mark Koenig and Bob Meusel. In the bottom of the seventh, the Yankees rallied. Mark Koenig led off with a single, and Ruth and Gehrig both walked to load the bases with two out. Manager Hornsby went to his bullpen and waved in the grizzled veteran Alexander, who had already thrown two complete game victories over the previous seven days. Old Pete faced Tony Lazzeri, the Yanks' 23-year-old rookie second baseman, who had hit .275 with 18 home runs and 114 runs-batted-in during the season just completed. Old Pete didn't waste any time. He needed just four pitches to fan the youngster, ending the threat as 38,093 New Yorkers groaned in anguish. The Cardinals veteran proceeded to shut down the Yankees' bats again in the eighth inning, and retired the first two men in the bottom of the ninth before walking Babe Ruth. The Bambino inexplicably took off for second base on the first pitch to Meusel, and Bob O'Farrell calmly gunned him down to end the Series. It was, according to O'Farrell, the most exciting moment in his major league career.[13]

The 1926 league leaders included Heinie Manush (.378), Babe Ruth (47 home runs), and George Uhle (27–11) in the American League, and Bubbles Hargrave (.353), Hack Wilson (21), and Remy Kremer (20–6) in the National League. The Chicago Cubs were led at the plate by Riggs Stephenson (.338), Hack Wilson (.321), and Sparky Adams (.309) and on the mound by Charlie Root (18–17), Guy Bush (13–9), and Percy Jones (12–7). Gabby Hartnett batted .275 with eight home runs.

The easygoing Irishman was generally regarded as the best all-around catcher in the National League in 1926, although he was limited to 93 games behind the plate by manager Joe McCarthy. He had spent his five years in the majors experimenting with his batting stroke in an effort to achieve the best balance between power and average, while minimizing strikeouts. His efforts were successful, as he reduced his strikeouts from one strikeout for every 4.6 at-bats in 1925 to one strikeout for every 7.7 at-bats in '26, but his batting average and home runs both suffered. By 1928, he would put it all together.

A comparison of the caught-stealing statistics of the Philadelphia A's Cochrane-Perkins duo and the Hartnett-Gonzalez combo revealed that the Cochrane team allowed 78 stolen bases against a league average of 81, while the Hartnett team allowed only 42 stolen bases against a league average of 76. The Cubs duo was much more effective than the A's duo in cutting down potential base stealers.

Off the field, Hartnett was still having problems controlling his finances. He was too good-natured, always spent freely, picked up most of the checks, and was an easy touch. And so once again, he had to borrow money to get home after the season ended, even though his salary was almost $10,000 a year.

Chicago, Illinois, was a vibrant metropolis during the career of Gabby Hartnett, but it was also one of America's most corrupt and crime-ridden cities. Mayor William Hale Thompson led a Republican machine that controlled everything from election results to political appointments. Nothing of importance went on in Chicago without Thompson's knowledge and approval, tacit or otherwise. On the other side of the ledger, gang leaders like "Big Jim" Colosimo, Johnny Torrio, Dion O'Banion, and Al Capone controlled gambling, prostitution, and bootlegging in the city, and they protected their interests by making huge payoffs to the highest officials in the city administration, including those in the police department. They also took care of the patrolman on the street. It was government at the expense of the many for the benefit of the few.

Still, Chicago had much to offer in the way of legal entertainment. There were stage shows, operas, movies, museums, large libraries, regattas on Lake Michigan, art shows, a professional football team, and two exciting major league baseball teams. And Gabby Hartnett, who was keeping close company with Martha Marshall, took advantage of many of these centers of entertainment and was slowly becoming, more and more, a year-round Chicago resident.

During the 1926–27 off-season, a second deck was added to Wrigley Field, increasing the seating capacity from 20,000 to 38,396. The new arrangement made it possible to accommodate the large crowds that had been flooding into the North Side park without having them ring the outfield,

Gabby Hartnett was rapidly developing into the best catcher in the major leagues by 1926. (George E. Outland)

necessitating special ground rules for balls hit into the crowd.

Manager Joe McCarthy was still trying to put a championship team together as spring training got underway. He felt comfortable with his catcher (Hartnett), first baseman (Grimm), two of his outfielders (Wilson and Stephenson), and his top two pitchers (Root and Bush), but he was on the lookout for more pitching help, as well as three infielders. He solved one of his problems when he picked up 20-year-old infielder Woody English from Toledo for $50,000. Woody immediately took over the Cubs shortstop job when the incumbent, Jimmy Cooney, came down with a sore arm. McCarthy also added pitcher Hal Carlson, a 17–12 pitcher for the Philadelphia Phillies, in a trade shortly after the season got underway.

One of McCarthy's top priority projects was to gain control over his fun-loving outfielder, Hack Wilson, whose nighttime excursions took him through most of the speakeasies in Chicago, as well as the other seven cities in the National League. At first, "Marse Joe" tried to get Hack to see the error of his ways. The attempt failed, as reported by Gold and Ahrens: "McCarthy took a worm and dropped it into a glass of water. Wilson watched it wiggle around. Then McCarthy placed the worm in a glass of whiskey. It sank to the bottom, stone-cold dead. McCarthy beamed and turned to Wilson. 'Well, did you see that? asked Marse Joe,' 'Yeah,' replied Wilson. 'If you drink whiskey, you won't get worms.'"

Wilson's drinking problem was different than the one Grover Cleveland Alexander presented to his manager. Old Alex resented authority and refused to take orders, frequently missing team meetings, games, and occasionally entire series. Hack Wilson, on the other hand, was a friendly fellow who got along well with McCarthy and always made it to the game on time, albeit with an occasional headache. He once said, "I've never played a game drunk. Hung over, yes. But drunk, no." Regarding his hangover problems, Hack also said, "I see three balls coming at me and always swing at the one in the middle. It's usually the real one."[14] And so, an unusual relationship was formed. The Cubs manager frequently bailed his star outfielder out of jail after an all-night binge and, in return, Hack Wilson always delivered with the bat.

McCarthy also appreciated and respected his All-Star catcher. In later years, after watching Mickey Cochrane in action over a 12-year period, and after managing Bill Dickey for 13 seasons, McCarthy called Gabby Hartnett "the perfect catcher. He was the greatest catcher I ever saw."

Both leagues anticipated tight pennant races, with the American League champion New York Yankees being challenged by Cleveland, Philadelphia, and Washington, and the world champion St. Louis Cardinals under pressure from Cincinnati, Pittsburgh, and Chicago. Miller Huggins was basing his pennant hopes on big seasons from his 23-year-old first baseman Lou Gehrig, who hit .313 with 16 home runs and 107 RBIs, and second baseman Tony Lazzeri, who hit 18 homers with 114 RBIs. The Cardinals were looking forward to having "Old Pete" Alexander for a full season, under new player-manager Bob O'Farrell. Joe McCarthy's Cubs were pinning their pennant hopes on continued strong efforts by the league's top pitching staff, breakthrough seasons by rookies Clyde Beck at second base and Earl Webb in the outfield, and an All-Star performance from catcher Gabby Hartnett.

The 1927 baseball season got underway on Tuesday, April 12, with the Cubs hosting O'Farrell's Cardinals. The *New York Times* recorded the event: "Playing before a crowd of 45,000, the largest that ever was packed into

Wrigley Field, the Chicago Cubs, aided by three home runs, overwhelmed the Worlds Champion St. Louis Cardinals, 10–1 in the seasons opener. Earl Webb, obtained last winter from the Louisville American Association club, led the Cubs slugging attack with two home runs, while first baseman Charlie Grimm, a former Pirate, slammed out the other. Charlie Root held the champions to seven hits, and never seemed in any danger. Grover Cleveland Alexander, the hero of last fall's World Series, started auspiciously, but ran into trouble in the third inning when the Cubs gathered four runs." Mike Gonzalez drew the opening day catching assignment and contributed two base hits to the attack. Gabby Hartnett was behind the plate the next day, going 0-for-3 with two assists as the Redbirds' Jesse Haines outpitched Sheriff Blake 2–0. Another tight pitching duel unfolded on the 15th, with Bill Sherdel tossing a two-hitter at McCarthy's Cubs, but dropping a heartbreaking 1–0 decision on Hack Wilson's home run into the center field bleachers in the second inning. Percy Jones blanked the Cards on six hits, assisted by three double plays.

The Chicago Cubs played .500 ball over the first three weeks of the season, settling into fifth place, three games out of the lead. They picked up the pace as May flowers began to bloom and ran up a 15–10 record for the month, leaving them in third place, 4½ games behind Pittsburgh. On May 3 and 4, they knocked off the Cincinnati Reds by scores of 4–3 and 13–9, an eight-run uprising in the third inning doing most of the damage in the second game. Earl Webb showed the way with a double and a three-run homer. The Cubs hit the road after the Cincinnati series, opening a four-game set in New York under threatening weather conditions. Two of the games were rained out. After sitting through a deluge on May 6, Chicago took the Giants to task the next day by the score of 6–4. Following another rainout, John McGraw's troops came back with a 5–4 win in the finale, before 50,000 wild New Yorkers. Bill Terry won the game with a ninth-inning double, which scored Ed Roush from second base. Hartnett drew the collar again, in three at-bats.[15] Moving on to Philadelphia, the Bruins and Phillies split a four-game series. McCarthy's charges took the opener 6–3 behind a three-homer barrage by Riggs Stephenson, Hack Wilson, and Gabby Hartnett. Stuffy McInnis' Phils won game two by a 5–2 count, and the teams split 4–1 decisions in the last two games. Chicago opened a three-game series in Boston on May 14, finally pounding out a 7–2 decision after 18 torturous innings. Guy Bush hurled the distance for the victory. Charlie Robertson, who pitched a perfect game for the Chicago White Sox against the Detroit Tigers on April 30, 1922, went 17⅓ innings for the Braves. After an off-day on Sunday and a rainout on Monday, the two teams were back in action on Tuesday, playing what would turn out to be a classic. It was a

22-inning drama, which saw Boston pitcher Bob Smith throw a complete game, and Chicago hurler Bob Osborn pitch the last 14 frames. Chicago rapped 20 base hits during the afternoon to 15 hits for Dave Bancroft's team, but the score stood at 3–3 after 21 innings. The Cubs finally broke through with the winning run when Charlie Grimm's base hit scored Hack Wilson, ending the longest game in Chicago Cubs history.

May 20 and 21 were happy days for the Chicago Cubs, and for the entire country as well. In Brooklyn, the Cubs overcame two home runs by Dodgers slugger Babe Herman to win the opener of the series by a score of 7–5. Sheriff Blake recalled how difficult it was to pitch to Herman: "You didn't know what to do with him. You might bounce one up there and he'd swing and miss. Then he might let a good one go by. Then he might knock another bad pitch out of the park. He was dangerous. In one game with us, Babe got four hits and Hartnett picked him off first twice. His manager, Wilbert Robinson, told him, 'The next time you get on base, stay there; stop figuring your batting average.' When a guy got picked off, they would always kid him, saying he was figuring his batting average."[16] The Cubs also won both ends of a morning-afternoon doubleheader the next day, 6–4 and 11–6. A nine-run rally in the ninth inning of the afternoon game carried McCarthy's troops to victory. The outburst was sparked by a bases-loaded triple by the dangerous Hack Wilson and a single and double by pinch hitter Floyd Scott. Gabby Hartnett beat out an infield hit that scored Wilson.

While all this excitement was unfolding in the City of Churches, drama of a different sort was being played out on Long Island. Charles A. Lindbergh Jr. a slender 25-year-old air-mail pilot, took off from Roosevelt Field in a small plane dubbed "The Spirit of St. Louis," and headed north, then east, across the Atlantic Ocean. Thirty-three hours and 29 minutes later, the courageous aviator set his plane down at Le Bourget in France, becoming the first person to fly nonstop from New York to Paris. Lindbergh was overwhelmed by his wild reception in France, as 100,000 people cheered his arrival. A subsequent ticker tape parade on Broadway and Fifth Avenue in New York dumped 1,800 tons of paper on America's newest hero, as tens of thousands of people gave him a typical New York welcome.[17]

The Cubs continued to struggle through May, winning more than they lost and sitting out six rainouts along the way. On the 24th, Alexander beat his old team 8–5. Two days later, Charlie Root coasted to an 11–2 victory over the Cincinnati Reds, then came on in relief the next day and won his own game 3–2, when his single scored Gabby Hartnett. Chicago closed out the month, dropping a 10–9 decision to the first-place Pirates, blowing a 6–2 lead along the way. Pittsburgh outfielder Joe Harris led the barrage with four hits and scored the winning run in the ninth inning after smashing a long triple to center field. Ray Spencer's single ended the game. Gabby Hartnett had a single and a double for the Cubs, and he cut down the only base runner who dared challenge his arm. Pete Scott had five hits in five trips to the plate in a losing cause. Hack Wilson was the leading Chicago hitter, with an average of .313 and nine home runs. Gabby Hartnett was at .276, with five home runs in 127 at-bats. Charlie Root, pitching in 15 of the Cubs' 44 games, had an 8–3 record. Guy Bush stood at 3–0.

Chicago began to click on all cylinders in June, beginning a three-month surge that would carry them to the top of the National League. Manager Joe McCarthy had his team primed to make a run for the roses, even though he was still juggling his infield around, trying to find the right combination. Charlie Grimm was set at first, but the rest of the infield was up for grabs. On June 5th, Clyde Beck was holding down second, Jimmy Cooney and Woody English were sharing shortstop duties, and Howard Freigau was on third. That combination combined for seven base hits, with Beck going 4-for-4, including two doubles and a triple; but the visiting Braves took the slugfest 10–8. Cubs starter Charlie Root was hammered for six runs on 10 hits in six-plus innings.[18] The McCarthy-men played better ball the rest of the month, going 17–10, and closing the gap between themselves and the first-place Pittsburgh to 1½ games. The St. Louis Cardinals held down second place, one game out. Riggs Stephenson paced the Chicago offense in June, batting a torrid .375. He was assisted by Charlie Grimm at .366 and Gabby Hartnett at .333. Charlie Root was their top pitcher with a 5–3 month.

In the American League, the New York Yankees were turning the pennant race into a shambles, running up a record of 49–20 for a glittering winning percentage of .710. Their closest pursuer, the Washington Senators, were 10½ games in arrears. On the last day of the month, Yankees slugger Lou Gehrig walloped his twenty-fifth home run of the season in the first inning against the Boston Red Sox, and Babe Ruth followed suit with his twenty-fifth three innings later, to propel the New Yorkers to a 13–6 victory.[19] The two Yankees sluggers were particularly explosive compared to the rest of the American League. Their combined total of 50 home runs represented 26 percent of all the home runs hit in the entire league. The New York Yankees as a team had 74 homers. The other seven teams combined had a total of 118 home runs.

On July 1, the Cubs scored early and often to whip the St. Louis Cardinals by a 6–2 count. Hal Carlson, a recent arrival from the Philadelphia Phillies, stopped the Redbirds on six hits, while his teammates drove St. Louis ace, Flint Rhem, to cover under a nine-hit barrage in the third inning. Chicago's garrulous catcher, Gabby Hartnett, hit three singles in five at-bats to lead the attack, and added an assist to his day's contribution. The next day, they beat the world champions again, this time by a 7–4 margin. Sheriff Blake tossed a complete game for the McCarthy-men, backed up by a 12-hit bombardment. Sparky Adams had three singles for the North Siders, while Earl Webb and Old Hoss Stephenson each contributed a single and a double to the cause. Hartnett had one walk and one run scored to show for his day's work at the plate, but he excelled in the field. He picked off two base runners, and he cut another run down at the plate on a throw from right fielder Webb.

On the 3rd, they beat the Cards again, this time by a 7–4 score. Hartnett led the offense with a single, double, and triple in three at-bats, with two runs scored and a sacrifice to his credit. Earl Webb went 4-for-5, with a double and a run scored. Charlie Root was the beneficiary of the outburst, upping his record to 14–6. The new Chicago ace was nicknamed "Strongheart" by his teammates because of his dedicated work ethic. He was also a fast worker on the mound, according to Gold and Ahrens: "He didn't waste time peering at the hitter or squinting for signals. He got the ball back, wound up, and threw it again."[20]

Joe McCarthy's troops stayed hot through the Fourth of July doubleheader against Jack Hendrick's Cincinnati Reds in the friendly confines of Wrigley Field, capturing both ends of the morning-afternoon twin bill 2–1 and 6–3. In the morning game, before a small audience of 12,000 fans, Jim Brillheart stopped the Redlegs on three hits for nine innings, and Guy Bush, the eventual winning pitcher, tossed a 1–2–3 tenth. The Cubs won the game in the tenth on a single by Pete Scott and a double by old reliable Hack Wilson. In game two, Guy Bush came on in relief again, this time following Bob Osborn to the mound in the second inning, and won his second decision of the day when the Cubs rallied for three runs in the fourth and singletons in the fifth, seventh, and eighth. Sparky Adams ripped three base hits for the Cubs, while Wilson and Grimm had two each. Gabby Hartnett, who was 1-for3 in the opener, drew the collar in two at-bats, but had two key sacrifice hits, was in the middle of an Osborn-Hartnett-Pick-Grimm double play, and threw out one man attempting to steal. He also kept up a constant chatter behind the plate to keep his infielders on their toes, keep his pitcher focused on the job at hand, and help the umpire call balls and strikes. Charlie Grimm once said, "When Gabby was catching, there were two umpires back of the plate."

The Windy City boys made it seven in a row the next day, with an 8–5 win over these same Reds. Percy Jones, in relief of Osborn, put a "WP" next to his name, with 4⅔ innings of one-run relief. Webb and Wilson had three hits each, including a double, while Hartnett had two walks and a run scored.

Bob Osborn was staked to a five-run lead in the fourth, but was driven to the showers under a four-run barrage an inning later.

Chicago hit the road after the Cincinnati series, invading Pittsburgh for a series against the league leaders. In the opener, Hal Carlson pitched the Cubs into first place, with a tense 2–1 victory over Joe Dawson before a stunned full house in the Steel City. The game was called in the ninth inning after the Cubs had scored two runs in the top of the inning, and the Pirates had scored one run in their half, and had the potential third run on third base with only one out. The score reverted to what it was at the end of the eighth inning, giving the Cubs their margin of victory. Pittsburgh's run was scored in the first inning on a single by Lloyd Waner, a sacrifice, and another single by Lloyd's brother Paul. The Cubs tied the game on a run-scoring double by Hack Wilson in

Guy Bush went 10–10 in 1926, then never won fewer than 15 games a year for the next seven years. (George E. Outland)

the fourth inning, and pushed over the winning tally an inning later on a walk, a single, and a wild throw by Paul Waner. The Chicago winning streak reached nine in a row on the 8th, when Cubs ace Charlie Root blanked the Bucs 1–0 on a brilliant one-hitter. Pittsburgh catcher Johnny Gooch broke up Root's chance for immortality with a two-out single in the eighth inning. Specs Meadows, who scattered eight Cubs safeties, deserved a better fate. The only run of the game came across in the second inning on a wild throw by shortstop Pie Traynor. Gabby Hartnett had a single in four trips and tossed out one base runner. His clenched fist pumping the air accompanied by a piercing yell told the world that all was well with the Cubs. The victory extended Chicago's lead over Pittsburgh to 1½ games.[21]

All good things eventually end, and Donnie Bush's Pirates finally untracked the Chicago express in the get-away game of the series. The score was 4–0, and the villain was an old friend and former teammate, Vic Aldridge, who fashioned a two-hitter in outdueling Chicago's Jim Brillheart. An estimated 20,000 fans witnessed the game and brought the house down with a deafening roar when their Pirates scored three runs in the fourth inning to break a scoreless deadlock. Three base hits, a sacrifice, and an error by Earl Webb in right field did the damage. Hartnett, who was 0-for-3 at the plate, allowed the fourth run to score on a throwing error. The end of the Chicago winning streak coincided with the loss of their big gun, Hack Wilson, who was on the bench nursing a strained side.

The league leaders at the halfway point in the season were Joe Harris of Pittsburgh, who was batting .389; Rogers Hornsby and Hack Wilson, who had 15 homers each; and Guy Bush, who had a record of 6–1. In the Junior Circuit, Lou Gehrig was setting a sizzling pace at the plate with a .399 average and 28 home runs, and Dutch Ruether was the top pitcher with a record of 8–1. Bush, Root (14–6), and Carlson (10–6) paced the Chicago pitching staff, while Stephenson (.333), Wilson (.315), Webb (.315), Grimm (.309), and Hartnett (.302) were the leading Chicago stickers.

The rest of July was an up-and-down battle for Joe McCarthy's troops, as they tried to regain their lost momentum — and their lost offensive sparkplug, Hack Wilson. Fortunately for the Cubs, they had the luxury of a five-game series against the hapless Boston Braves during Wilson's absence, and they made the most of it, winning four of the five. In the opener, Sheriff Blake limited the Beaneaters to three hits, while his mates were pounding out 13, good enough for a 6–2 victory. Charlie Grimm had a double and two singles, Clyde Beck had a double and a single, and Sparky Adams had two singles for Joe McCarthy's crew. Gabby Hartnett had a single and a sacrifice. The Cubs and Braves split a doubleheader on the 13th, with Boston capturing the opener 6–3, and Chicago taking the nightcap 4–1. The split, coupled with Pittsburgh's loss to Brooklyn, gave the Cubs an 11-percentage-point lead in the tight National League pennant race. Hal Carlson was routed under a 12-hit barrage in four-plus innings in game one. Adams and Heathcote had two hits each in a losing cause, and Hartnett had a single, a run scored, two assists, and a double play to his credit. The double play cut down a potential Boston run at the plate. In game two, Charlie Root racked up his 16th victory of the season with a seven-hitter. Eddie Pick and Earl

Webb contributed two hits each to the cause. Chicago catcher Mike Gonzalez nabbed two out of three runners on attempted steals. The Cubs took game four behind Bob Osborn, backed by two hits each from Pick, Heathcote, and Grimm. Gabby Hartnett had a double, a sacrifice, a walk, and a run scored. In the finale, the Bruins unleashed a 16-hit attack against Boston starter Foster Edwards and four relievers for a 9–6 triumph. Jim Brillheart, with help from Guy Bush, took the win. The Chicago fireworks included four hits by Sparky Adams, three hits by Cliff Heathcote (with two doubles), three hits by Gabby Hartnett (with a double), and two hits each by Riggs Stephenson and Charlie Grimm.

On July 19, the Chicago lead stood at one game over Pittsburgh, but over the last week and a half of the month, they dropped seven of 10 contests to fall into second place, a ½ game off the top. Their last big spurt of the month, came against the New York Giants when they took two out of three from McGraw's cohorts at the Polo Grounds. On the 18th, the two teams divided a twin-bill, with the Cubs taking a 10-inning thriller in game one, and the Giants bouncing back to capture game two 3–2. The first game pitted Hal Carlson against Freddie Fitzsimmons, and homers by Mel Ott and Travis Jackson gave the Giants right-hander a 2–0 lead after four. The Cubs came back with a run in the fifth, and added three in the sixth on a walk to Earl Webb, Hack Wilson's single, Charlie Grimm's three-bagger, and Gabby Hartnett's single. After the New Yorkers tied the game at 4-all in their half of the sixth, both pitchers shut the door on further scoring until the tenth. The Giants almost pulled the game out in the bottom of the ninth when they loaded the bases against Carlson with no outs, but the lanky curveball artist bore down and retired the next three batters without any damage being done. That was all Joe McCarthy's boys needed. In the top of the tenth, with Grimm sitting on first base, the man from Millville stepped to the plate and took relief pitcher Don Songer downtown to give his team the victory. In the nightcap, Jesse Barnes outpointed Charlie Root when the Chicago ace grooved a fastball to right fielder George Harper, and the little left-handed slugger deposited it into the upper deck in left field, driving in the tying and winning runs.

The next day was John McGraw Day at the Polo Grounds, celebrating the tough little Irishman's silver jubilee as the New York Giants' manager. The old park rocked as 25,000 fans, including such celebrities as Mayor Jimmy Walker, Commander Richard E. Byrd, Baseball Commissioner Kenesaw Mountain Landis, National League President John E. Heydler, and dozens of luminaries from the fields of theatre, politics, and sports, paid tribute to the grand old man of baseball. Mayor Walker presented the 54-year-old McGraw with a huge silver cup surmounted by a statuette of the

Giants' manager as he was when he played for the old Baltimore Orioles. The other highlight of the festivities was a short baseball game between two teams of Broadway actors, such as Eddie Cantor, "Gentleman Jim" Corbett, and Leon Errol. Somewhere along the line, a jokester substituted a ripe grapefruit for the baseball while Eddie Cantor was at bat, and when the comedian made contact with the pitch, it exploded, drenching him with grapefruit juice from head to toe. The regular game was almost an anticlimax to the festivities, but the Windy City crew ruined the last part of John McGraw's day by whipping his Giants 8–5. The Cubs, who led 4–2 after seven innings, broke the game open in the eighth, as reported by the *New York Times*: "Fay Thomas attempted to pitch the eighth. Gabby Hartnett, who would rather talk than eat, slapped a homer into the upper left field stands with two on, and a second later, young English, a .200 hitter, rammed another four-baser into the right field sector." Hartnett was also involved in two earlier scores. In the fifth, with the Cubs down 2–0, the smiling Irishman hit a groundball to short with Riggs Stephenson on third base. Riggs was cut down at the plate on the play, but the Chicago catcher was able to go all the way to second before the out was made, and he scored minutes later on a hit by English. Two innings later, with the score tied at 2-all, the Cubs jumped in the lead on a walk to Grimm, a ringing double to left field by Hartnett, and singles by English and Osborn. For the day, Gabby was 2-for-5, with a double and a homer, three runs scored, two RBIs, and one assist.[22]

The rest of the month was a struggle. On the 28th, they dropped a 6–5 decision to the Giants when Rogers Hornsby lashed a single, a triple, and a two-run homer. Gabby Hartnett had another good day for Joe McCarthy, banging out three hits in four at-bats and gunning down both base runners who had the temerity to test the cannon that hung from his right shoulder. Hartnett pounded out three more hits on the 30th of July, but once again, it was not enough to stave off defeat. The Phils beat his team 5–3, although Gabby gave them some food for thought on the bases. They attempted a double steal against the Cubs catcher, but the runner on third was cut down at the plate, Hartnett to Beck to Hartnett. Joe McCarthy's troops did end the month with a victory by dumping the Phillies 12–5 before 30,000 exuberant Wrigley Field fanatics. Charlie Root cruised to his eighteenth victory behind a 12-hit fusillade, sparked by Hartnett's single and two doubles, Woody English's double and two singles, and Hack Wilson's two singles and nineteenth home run of the season. The month ended with Pittsburgh holding a slim ½ game lead over the Chicago Cubs in the Senior Circuit, and Miller Huggins' Yankees running away with the Junior Circuit race, a full 13 games ahead of the Washington Senators. The sensational Yankee tandem of Gehrig and Ruth continued to wreak havoc on American League pitchers, with Gehrig having 37 homers to his credit and the Bambino showing 34. The entire New York team had a total of 110 homers in 105 games, an amazing total when compared to the rest of the American League teams, that had a total of 201 homers. Gehrig had outhomered every other team in the league, while Ruth had outhomered six of seven. Hack Wilson was pacing the National League sluggers with 19 home runs. The leading Cubs hitters were Stephenson (.332), Wilson (.323), Webb (.317), Grimm (.314), English (.296), and Hartnett (.296). Charlie Root's record stood at 18–9, Hal Carlson was at 11–7, and Guy Bush was at 7–4.

Joe McCarthy's crew kept the pressure on the Bucs in August, rolling up 16 wins against 11 losses, but they couldn't shake Donnie Bush's squad, who went 14–12 over the same stretch. One of the Cubs' biggest days occurred on August 6, when they defeated the Brooklyn Dodgers 6–2, while the Giants were humbling Pittsburgh 9–2, to give Chicago a healthy three-game lead. Gabby Hartnett had another three-hit day, and his second-inning triple over Gus Felix's head in center field drove in Charlie Grimm with the first run of the game, giving the Cubs a lead they never relinquished. Sheriff Blake captured his ninth victory of the season. The victory was Chicago's seventh straight and 11th in 12 games. "Some 20,000 wildly cheering Chicagoans stormed out of the park singing 'three full games ahead of the Buccos. Bring on the Yanks.'"[23] On August 9, before a raucous overflow crowd of 40,000 in the Cubs' North Side ballpark, Chicago lost not only a game but their catcher as well. Joe McCarthy's team captured the opener of the doubleheader 2–0 behind Hal Carlson, who blanked Brooklyn on six hits. Hartnett went 1-for-3 with an assist, while Scott and Stephenson added two hits each. In the second inning of game two, the Flatbush Flock threatened to score, but were thwarted when Gus Felix was thrown out at the plate by Stephenson after a fly ball. The Cubs lost their catcher, Gabby Hartnett, on the play, however, when Felix's spikes ripped open a gash in Hartnett's foot. Chicago held a 3–0 lead after three innings, but Uncle Robby's boys pushed over five runs in the next two innings off Guy Bush, good enough for a 5–4 win. The split completed Chicago's successful home stand, and they headed east with a three-game lead over Pittsburgh.[24]

Chicago third baseman Sparky Adams had his best day of the season at the plate on August 24. He ripped two doubles in the first inning on his way to a 5-for-6 day, as the Cubs pounded the Philadelphia Phillies 13–1.[25] Both the road trip and the month ended with Chicago still clinging to a tenuous one-game lead over Donnie Bush's stubborn Bucs, with St. Louis just two games out and the Giants only 2½ behind. Pittsburgh swept a doubleheader from the Phillies on August 31, while the Cubs were idle.

September got underway on a somber note. McCarthy's cohorts invaded Pittsburgh for a one-game series and were knocked off the top rung by the determined Bucs. Specs Meadows, on his way to a 19–10 season, edged Hal Carlson by a count of 4–3. Pittsburgh scored two runs in the second on three base hits. Joe Harris hit a long home run over the center field fence in the fourth, and Meadows never lost the lead. Gabby Hartnett went 1-for-3, with a run scored. The loss to Pittsburgh started a downhill slide that didn't end until Chicago's proud Cubs settled into fourth place. On the 2nd, they were blanked by Cincinnati 5–0, with Jakie May taking the measure of Percy Jones. The Chicago offense was held to three hits, singles by English, Wilson, and Grimm. The next day, their offense sputtered again, with Red Lucas tossing a five-hitter to nose out Sheriff Blake 2–1. The lone Cubs run crossed the plate in the sixth inning on a single by Hack Wilson. Hartnett had one hit and an assist. Cliff Heathcote had a single and a triple, with a run scored. The drought continued on the 4th, as 38,000 stunned Wrigley Field fans watched their team's suddenly silent bats fall to the St. Louis Cardinals by another 2–1 score. Southpaw Bill Sherdel, a 17–12 pitcher, scattered seven hits, while outdueling Bruin ace Charlie Root. The loss, Chicago's seventh straight, dropped them into third place, three games behind Pittsburgh. Joe McCarthy's troops had trouble beating anybody as the season wound down. They lost six out of eight games to sixth-place Brooklyn and, on the 18th, they were beaten by the seventh-place Boston Braves, who broke a 15-game losing streak with the victory. Wrigley Field fans again watched their heroes succumb to a less-talented team. Charlie Root, who came on in relief of Sheriff Blake in the ninth inning, was rocked for three runs on four hits to clinch an 11–7 Boston victory. Gabby Hartnett had two doubles in the game and tossed out two men attempting to steal. Adams, English, and Stephenson each had two hits.

When the season ended on October 2, the Chicago Cubs found themselves mired in fourth place, 8½ games behind the pennant-winning Pittsburgh Pirates and a full 6½ games behind third-place New York. Joe McCarthy's club rolled over and died down the stretch, winning only 12 of 30 games in September. Pittsburgh, on the other hand, rolled to a 23–10 record during the month to edge St. Louis by 1½ games. Bob O'Farrell's Cardinals, didn't relinquish their National League crown easily. They compiled a 23–11 record over the last four weeks, but came up 1½ games short. And John McGraw's Giants won 22 games against 10 losses, slipping past the fading Bruins.

The Chicago pitching staff seemed to be burned out by Labor Day, particularly ace Charlie Root, who appeared in 48 games during the season, pitching a total of 309 innings. The big right-hander was hit hard down the stretch, compiling a 2–4 record in September. The rest of the staff was just as tired. Guy Bush was 2–3, Percy Jones was 1–3, and Hal Carlson was 3–3. The Cubs' bats held up reasonably well over the last 30 games, but they were inconsistent, falling silent when they were needed the most. Hack Wilson hit .347 in September, Charlie Grimm .382, and Riggs Stephenson .317. Gabby Hartnett, once again worn down by the constant abuse his body took over 127 games, batted only .205 in September with one home run, but had an outstanding year overall.

His accomplishments were recognized by the baseball experts, who selected him as the catcher on the *Sporting News* Major League All-Star Team. In 449 at-bats, the energetic backstop batted .294 with 32 doubles, five triples, and 10 home runs. He and his backup, Mike Gonzalez, allowed only 52 stolen bases during the season compared to a league average of 81. It was a busy season defensively for Hartnett in other areas as well. He led the league in putouts and assists, but also showed the way in errors for the third time in four years.

Gabby Hartnett became a dangerous clutch hitter in 1927, capable of driving the ball out of the park, while maintaining good bat control. He could hit the ball to all fields and was a skillful bunter as well, able to lay down a sacrifice bunt in a crucial situation. He would hit over .300 six times in the next 13 years, while averaging 24 home runs for every 550 at-bats. On defense, he would dominate the position, leading the league in fielding average six times and gunning down prospective base stealers at a record pace. Never again would he lead the league in errors.

Hack Wilson finished the season with an average of .323 and won his second consecutive home run title, with 30 circuit blows, tying Cy Williams. Riggs Stephenson batted .344, Charlie Grimm hit .311, and Earl Webb .304. Charlie Root had an outstanding season, with 26 victories against 15 losses. He was followed by Guy Bush at 10–10. The Chicago Cubs set one impressive record in 1927: They became the first National League team to draw more than one million fans through the turnstiles, topping out at 1,163,347.[26]

The big news in the American League, as might be expected, was made by the "Sultan of Swat," Babe Ruth, who broke his own home run record. On the next to last day of the season, the Yankees slugger stepped to the plate against the Washington Senators southpaw, Tom Zachary, in the eighth inning of a 2–2 game, with Mark Koenig on third base after legging out a triple. Ruth promptly untied the score with a tremendous shot that landed halfway up the right-field stands. It was his sixtieth home run of the season, breaking his own record of 59 set in 1921.[27] Lou Gehrig finished the year with 47 homers, second to Ruth. The next highest home run total was 18, by Ruth's teammate Tony Lazzeri. The magnitude of Ruth's accomplishment is reflected in the fact that he accounted for 13.7 percent of all the league's home runs. Only eight American League hitters had more than 10.

The World Series pitted Miller Huggins' mighty New York Yankees against the plucky Pittsburgh Pirates. The New Yorkers completely dominated the American League pennant race, winning 110 games, and leaving the second-place Philadelphia Athletics, gasping for air, 19 games behind. Pittsburgh won 94 games to capture the Senior Circuit title by 1½ games. The Fall Classic was no contest. The Murderers Row of Ruth, Gehrig, Meusel, Lazzeri, and Combs routed the Bucs in four games, outscoring the bewildered National Leaguers 23 to 10. Babe Ruth hit the only two home runs in the series while batting .400. Mark Koenig hit .500, Earle Combs .313, and Lou Gehrig .308. Lloyd Waner hit .400 for the Bucs, George Grantham .364, and Clyde Barnhart .313. The rest of the Pirates team combined for an average of .157.[28]

In another athletic arena in September, heavyweight boxing champion Gene Tunney successfully defended his title by winning a 10-round decision over former champion Jack Dempsey in a fight that will long be remembered for the "long count" controversy. The match, held in Chicago's Soldier Field, before 104,943 screaming boxing enthusiasts, was a classic confrontation between a boxer and a slugger. In the seventh round, with Tunney comfortably ahead, Dempsey caught the champion with a devastating left hook, followed by a right and another left, sending Tunney crashing to the canvas. Under the new rules, the standing boxer was required to go to the farthest neutral corner, where previously he could stand over the fallen fighter. Dempsey forgot about the new rule and stood over Tunney until referee Dave Barry motioned him to a neutral corner. Six valuable seconds were lost before the referee began his count. Tunney regained his feet at the count of nine and went on from there to victory, winning the last three rounds. But the controversy will last forever. Was Gene Tunney knocked out? Or was he, as he claimed, clear headed and ready to get up at any time?[29]

In the world of entertainment, talking motion pictures were introduced to the American public on October 6 when *The Jazz Singer*, starring Al Jolson, opened at the Warner Theatre in New York City. An estimated 100 million people a week were rushing to the neighborhood theatres compared to 60 million people a week before the new phenomenon was unveiled.[30]

6

The Best of Times, the
Worst of Times, 1928–1929

Spring 1928 brought renewed hope to the citizens of Chicago. The Cubs team had made a gallant run at the pennant in '27, only to come up short at the end. But management was determined to bring the city a championship and worked diligently to strengthen their club. First they picked up veteran pitcher Art Nehf as a free agent in August. Then they obtained hard-hitting outfielder Hazen "Kiki" Cuyler from the Pittsburgh Pirates on November 28 in exchange for third baseman Sparky Adams. They also purchased the contract of pitcher Pat Malone from the Minneapolis Millers of the American Association and picked up minor league second baseman Freddie Maguire. Art Nehf, at 35 years old, was nearing the end of an outstanding major league career. A two-time 20-game winner, the little left-hander had been John McGraw's meal ticket for six years during the early twenties. Nehf would give McCarthy's Bruins two good years, helping them in their pennant quest.

Kiki Cuyler was the key man in the Cubs off-season wheeling-dealing. The 5'11", 180-pound outfielder was an authentic superstar who could hit for average, hit with power, run, field, and throw. He was a slashing hitter and daring base runner who averaged 33 doubles, 18 triples, 11 home runs, 90 runs-batted-in (RBIs), and 35 stolen bases for every 550 at-bats throughout his career. He had hit .349 for the Pirates between 1924 and 1926, but was benched by manager Donnie Bush in 1927 in a personality clash. Two years before, he had led he National League with 26 triples and 144 runs scored. Cuyler would team with "Old Hoss" Stephenson and Hack Wilson to give the Cubs their greatest outfield in history. All three would end their careers with .300+ batting averages and, in 1929, they would become the first National League outfield trio to drive in 100 runs each. Freddie Maguire was a 27-year-old minor league infielder who had had two short stints with the New York Giants, batting just .238 in 46 games.

Pat Malone was another brilliant pickup by manager Joe McCarthy. He was a big 6' tall, 200-pound southpaw with a blazing fastball. He had gone 28–13 with Des Moines of the Western Association, with a league-leading 190 strikeouts in 1926, and followed that up with a solid 20–18 record with the Millers, once again leading the league in strikeouts with 214. Malone's only weakness was a love of the nightlife. And in Chicago, he found a soul mate in Hack Wilson. According to Gold and Ahrens, "Hecklers at Wrigley Field used to refer to [them] as 'Whiskey Head and Beer Belly.' It was the prohibition era, and the fun-loving pair gave Cub manager Joe McCarthy many a headache with their escapades."[1] Gabby Hartnett thoroughly enjoyed Hack Wilson and Pat Malone, calling them, "two of the most lovable hoodlums in baseball…. Never a dull moment in the dugout, clubhouse, or hotel lobby with either of those Indians around. But I ought to sock Malone, at that, for pinning that 'Puffy' nickname on me with that beer goiter he wheels around."[2]

Hartnett was in excellent physical condition as 1928 got underway. He had added 20 pounds of muscle to his lanky frame over the previous five years and, at 28 years old, was approaching his peak as a hitter. He had also refined his defense to eliminate the careless errors that had plagued him since he entered the majors. A writer for a national baseball magazine, in extolling the virtues of his arm, had noted that recklessness: "Hartnett has probably the greatest throwing arm of any catcher in the National League. What is even more important, he uses his throwing arm wherever the slightest opening offers. In fact, he looks for such openings and he never hesitates to assume a risk in trying to nail a base runner. Not infrequently he shoulders much more than his due share of responsibility, particularly in a tight game where a wide throw would spell disaster."[3]

As he grew older and added weight, the big catcher developed a ruddy complexion, resulting in the nickname, "Old Tomato Face." According to one sportswriter, "There were three distinguishing characteristics associated with the likable Irish-American — a red face, a big cigar, and a laugh in which he simply wound up and let go, laughing all over. His frame shook like a dilapidated jalopy."[4] His daughter Sheila noted, "The manager always had new players and rookies, or any difficult person, room with him because he was easy to get along with."

The Chicago Cubs had a successful spring training camp at Avalon, sparked by the hitting of Kiki Cuyler and Hack Wilson. The former Pittsburgh "Bad Boy" hit over .500 in exhibition games. In one game against his former mates, he hit two home runs and drove in four runs in an 11–5 Chicago victory. In another game, he hit a homer and also made a circus catch in the ninth inning to preserve a 6–4 win over Hollywood of the Pacific Coast League. Wilson seemed to be hitting home runs on a daily basis. He put the ball out of the park against Los Angeles, Hollywood, Portland, and Pittsburgh.

When the season opened, the National League pennant race was considered a toss-up between five teams: Pittsburgh, St. Louis, Cincinnati, New York, and Chicago. The consensus was that the team that had the fewest injuries and the best individual seasons would capture the flag. The Cubs broke from the starting gate slowly, partly because rookie Pat Malone dropped six of his first 10 decisions. But Joe McCarthy stuck with him, and he repaid his manager tenfold by winning 14 of his last 21 decisions. One of the bright spots in the early going was Sheriff Blake, who was 3–0 in April, including a 7–2 win over Pittsburgh on the 24th. Blake had a 17-inning scoreless streak snapped when the Bucs tacked up both their runs in the eighth inning. Gabby Hartnett and Riggs Stephenson homered for Chicago.

As May got underway, Joe McCarthy's troops were back in fifth place, with a 9–10 record, 2½ games behind the Dodgers. They lost the last game in April to the Pittsburgh Pirates 8–7 on a run-scoring single by former Cub, Sparky Adams, in the bottom of the eighth inning. Malone took the loss in relief. Gabby Hartnett was on the sidelines nursing an injury that would keep him out of the lineup for 21 of the team's first 45 games. Donnie Bush's troops completed a sweep of the Bruins by winning games two and three by scores of 4–1 and 9–8 in 10 innings. George Grantham, another former Cubbie, was 3-for-3 with a double in the 4–1 victory. Carmen Hill was the winning pitcher in the game, while Guy Bush took the loss. Maguire, Stephenson, Grimm, and Johnny Butler all had two hits in a losing cause. In the finale, Joe Dawson got the win over Art Nehf. Once again, Sparky Adams was a thorn in Joe McCarthy's side, driving in the winning run with a sacrifice fly in the tenth. Beck, Cuyler, English, and Stephenson each had two hits for the Cubs.

Three teams jockeyed for position in May, with the Cubs racking up a strong 17–9 record. Brooklyn and St. Louis dropped out of contention, while Cincinnati (21–10 in May) and New York (16–11) moved into the first two positions. Chicago dropped their first two games of the month, then went on a tear, running off 13 wins in succession. On the 14th, they captured their ninth in a row, and third straight over the Giants, by an 8–2 score. Charlie Root won his third straight game. Three days later, Joe McCarthy's suddenly revitalized Bruins made it 11 in a row with a 2–0 shutout over the Boston Braves. Pat Malone limited Jack Slattery's boys to five hits in tossing the shutout. Hack Wilson hit his fifth homer of the year in the fourth inning. They extended their streak to 13, beating the visiting Bostonians on Saturday 3–1 behind Art Nehf's five-hitter, then winning the first game of a doubleheader on Sunday 3–2. The Braves ended the streak in the nightcap 4–3. Bob Smith, a converted infielder who played 101 games at shortstop for the Braves in 1923, was the winning pitcher, while Guy Bush took the loss. Chicago tasted the fine wine of first place briefly after their series with the Braves, but four successive losses brought them back to earth in a hurry.

The Cubs' all-world catcher was featured in a national baseball magazine in May, according to the *Call*. The writer called Hartnett baseball's most colorful catcher. He's "not a crab nor a grandstand player, but always straining every nerve to win ball games. Hartnett won his nickname from his running fire of conversation to his own players, particularly the pitcher. That's Hartnett's way of keeping them on their toes, keyed up, tense — ready for action. Hartnett is the most colorful catcher on the diamond and perhaps the most misunderstood. He is colorful because he is always trying, by every means in his power, to win the ball game. To that end, he uses voice, gestures, various kinds of antics, but all with a purpose. When things happen that do not suit him, he shows obvious impatience, and so the fans sometimes call him 'Crabby' Hartnett. They think he's difficult to get along with. This isn't true. Hartnett is a likeable fellow with hosts of friends and few enemies. Off the field, he is the easiest person in the world to talk to. On the field, he's intensely earnest."[5]

Charlie Grimm gave the Chicago Cubs outstanding first base play for 12 years. (George E. Outland)

In the American League, the New York Yankees bolted out of the starting gate like Man-O-War and were 34–8 on June 1, with a big 7½ game lead over Connie Mack's mighty Athletics. They blanked the Washington

Senators 4–0 on May 31, sparked by Babe Ruth's nineteenth home run of the season.

Sheriff Blake's first loss of the year, after a 5–0 start, came on June 1, when he was routed by the Pittsburgh Pirates 10–4. He was hammered for seven runs in 3⅔ innings. Lloyd Waner and Pete Scott each had two singles and a double for the Bucs. The Cubs came back the next day to win by a 10–6 count. Journeyman southpaw Lefty Weinert was the winner for Chicago. It was his only decision of the year. Clyde Beck was 3-for-4 with two RBIs, Hack Wilson was 3-for-5 with an RBI, and Gabby Hartnett was 1-for-4 with two runs scored. The big catcher also had two assists, gunning down one man trying to steal second base and picking off another Pirate runner who strayed too far off second.

The Chicago Cubs treaded water during the month of June, breaking even in 26 games, while St. Louis and Brooklyn were on a roll. When the smoke cleared, the Cardinals were seated in the catbird seat, with a record of 45–25, and Brooklyn had sneaked into third place, just behind the New York Giants, with a record of 37–30. Chicago was fourth at 39–32. The New York Yankees were destroying all opposition in the American League, piling up 50 victories against 16 losses, giving them a nice 11½ game cushion over Connie Mack's A's. By July 1, the lead was up to 13½.

The Cubs did win their last game in June, defeating the Cincinnati Reds 7–5, as Pat Malone took the measure of Pete Donohue. Hack Wilson, Chicago's old reliable, led the Cubs onslaught with two home runs, good for three RBIs. Clyde Beck also drove in three runs. Gabby Hartnett ripped two doubles, had one RBI, and cut down one base runner trying to steal.

On the first of July, Joe McCarthy's cohorts dropped a 4–1 decision to Jack Hendrick's Redlegs. The victory moved Cincinnati into third place and dropped the Cubs back to fifth. The Reds scored all their runs in the second inning, as Eppa Rixey outpitched Sheriff Blake for the win. Third baseman Charlie Dressen led the Cincinnati attack with two hits in four at-bats. Gabby Hartnett had a perfect day at the plate, with three hits. The next day, it was the Cubs' turn, as they walloped the Reds 8–2. Chicago pushed across five runs in the second inning, three of them coming on Hack Wilson's bases-clearing double. Wilson and Cuyler each went 3-for-5, while Grimm, Hartnett, and Beck had two hits each. The win moved the Cubs back into third place, but they were still eight games behind St. Louis. Joe McCarthy's Cubbies moved into St. Louis with a chance to gain ground on the league leaders, and they grabbed the advantage in game one, routing the Redbirds 13–5 behind Guy Bush. Cardinal starter Fred Frankhouse was knocked out of the box after just ⅓ inning, when the Cubs scored six runs. Hack Wilson put #17 out of the park, and Gabby Hartnett went 3-for-5, with a double, a home run, four runs scored, and two assists. In the Fourth of July double-header, the two teams split. The Cardinals took the opener 11–6, and the Cubs came back in the nightcap 16–9. Flint Rhem was the winning pitcher in game one, while Charlie Root was shackled with the loss. Jim Bottomley socked two homers for the Cards, and George Harper hit one. Hack Wilson hit one for the Cubs, and Hartnett went 1-for-3, with a homer and two assists. In game two, Joe McCarthy's warriors unleashed a 21-hit attack, pounding 14-year veteran Clarence Mitchell for six runs in the top of the first. The Redbirds drove Percy Jones to cover in the bottom of the inning with a four-run rally. Pat Malone took the victory in relief. Riggs Stephenson led the Chicago barrage with five hits, including a double and a home run. Hack Wilson had a single, a double, and a home run, and Freddie Maguire also had three hits. Three other Cubs players had two hits each. The loss was even more painful for St. Louis. They lost their hard-hitting right fielder, Oscar Roettger, for the season, when he fractured his leg sliding into third base.

The Chicago Cubs ran up an enviable 19–12 record in July, but they couldn't gain any ground on the leaders, as both the St. Louis Cardinals (18–11) and Cincinnati Reds (17–9) were as hot as the weather themselves. Late in the month, the Cubs and Giants split a doubleheader that left a bad taste in the mouths of the Cubs players. They felt they should have won both games. In the opener, before a wild crowd of 30,000 Giants fans, the Cubs took a 7–2 lead into the bottom of the ninth. Sheriff Blake had two outs, with Welsh on first base following a walk, when the wheels came off his wagon. Mel Ott singled. Freddie Lindstrom singled, and Bill Terry followed suit. When Andy Reese and Andy Cohen also singled, the Cubs lead was down to 7–5, and John McGraw's troops had the bases loaded. Guy Bush was rushed to the rescue. But it was too late. New York had the momentum and wasn't about to give it up. Shanty Hogan, a rotund 240-pound catcher, on his way to a .333 season, jumped on a Bush cripple and drilled a two-run, game-winning double up the alley in rightcenter field, as the delirious fans practically tore the building down. In game two, the Bruins supported a complete game effort by Charlie Root with a 10-run assault against south-paw Bill Walker. Heathcote, Stephenson, and Beck all had three hits for the Cubs. Woody English hit a home run.

Gabby Hartnett played in 26 of 31 games in July, raising his batting average to .274 with 9 home runs. He made up for lost time after returning to the lineup in May, playing in 96 of the club's last 109 games.

Joe McCarthy's troops stayed hot in August, going 16–11 and gaining ground on the St. Louis Cardinals who were trailing by just 4½ games as the month came to an end. The Cubs visited Ebbets Field on July 30 and took the first two games of a three-game series. In the finale, on August 1, they unleashed a 22-hit attack against Watty Clark and a host of relievers to win 16–3, as Pat Malone added another scalp to his collection. Chicago put the game out of reach in the very first inning when they tallied five times on singles by English and Maguire, a double by Cuyler, a sacrifice fly by Wilson, a walk to Stephenson, a single by Grimm, a double by Hartnett, and a single by Beck. Gabby added a single later in the game and had a three-RBI day to pace the Windy City bombardiers.

The American League race was tightening up as August reached its midpoint. A 5–2 Yankee victory over the Boston Red Sox gave them a 4½ game bulge over the Philadelphia Athletics, but things would get even tighter over the next four weeks. The Chicago Cubs went on a four-game losing streak, but rebounded to take two games from the St. Louis Cardinals in St. Louis by scores of 5–1 and 4–2, cutting the Redbird lead to six games. In the first game, Sheriff Blake beat Syl Johnson, with Stephenson and Wilson blasting triples. Hack Wilson hit one out with a man on base in the first inning of the finale to get the Cubs off and running. Gabby Hartnett pounded out three hits, including a double, while Kiki Cuyler had two hits with a home run. Pat Malone tossed a complete game seven-hitter. The second-place Giants trailed by 2½.

Two days later, the Cubs opened a home stand against John McGraw's sluggers, hoping to overtake the New Yorkers. They didn't get off to a good start, however, as they were thrashed in the opener 10–2. Charlie Root was touched up for four runs in four innings, and the relief corps fared no better. Giants outfielder Jimmy Welsh put one into the right field seats. Maguire, Hartnett, and Wilson all had two hits in a losing cause. St. Louis increased its lead over Chicago, defeating the Boston Braves 6–1 behind Grover Cleveland Alexander. The next day, McCarthy's warriors pulled one out of the fire, with a ninth-inning rally. The score was tied 3–3 after eight innings, but the Giants pushed over two runs in the top of the ninth to apparently wrap up the game. The Cubs, however, still had some fight in them. Riggs Stephenson opened the bottom of the ninth with a single against Joe Genewich, and Charlie Grimm followed with a base on balls to put the tying runs on base. Gabby Hartnett moved the runners to second and third with a well-placed sacrifice bunt. The move paid off immediately when Norm McMillan punched a single to left, driving in both runs. Sheriff Blake followed with a single, and both runners moved up on an error. Clyde Beck hit into a force play, with McMillan out at the plate. Then Freddie Maguire sent the fans home happy when he lined a base hit to left field, scoring Blake with the winning run. Chicago took the rubber game of the series, beating New York 6–2 behind former Giants hurler Art Nehf, who scattered nine hits in a complete game effort. Beck, Cuyler, and Grimm had two hits each. Hack Wilson laced a triple, and Gabby Hartnett went 1-for-4. The win left the Cubs six games behind St. Louis and 2½ games behind New York.

In the American League, Miller Huggins' team still clung to a 4½-game lead over the A's after they whipped the White Sox 11–1 behind Waite Hoyt. Lou Gehrig ripped three doubles and drove in five runs. The A's, meanwhile, pounded the Detroit Tigers by an 18–6 score behind the powerful bats of Al Simmons and Jimmie Foxx. Simmons had two singles and a home run, driving in three runs, while "Double-X" ripped two doubles and a home run, also driving in three runs.

Wilbert Robinson's Dodgers were the next visitors to the Friendly Confines, and they were treated kindly by their hosts in the opener of the three-game series. Buzz McWeeny tossed a five-hitter and the Dodgers eked out a 1–0 victory. Sheriff Blake matched pitches with McWeeny for eight innings, but weakened in the ninth, when Brooklyn scored the only run of the game on a single by Flowers, a sacrifice by Herman, and a run-scoring single by Rube Bressler. Hartnett had one hit in three at-bats and threw out the only man who attempted to steal on him. Game two was all Chicago's as Pat Malone rang up another victory, this one by an 11–4 score. Fifteen thousand Cubs fans cheered when their boys scored five runs in the second inning. Singles by Hartnett, McMillan, and Beck got the ball rolling, and Hack Wilson's bases-loaded triple put the icing on the cake. Old Tomato Face had three hits in five at-bats, with two runs scored. He also gunned down two would-be base thieves. The Bruins made it a two-out-of-three series by edging the Brooklynites 3–2 behind a complete game effort by Charlie Root. Bill Doak was the hard-luck loser. A ninth-inning rally sent the 35,000 inmates into a wild frenzy. The Dodgers looked like they were going to make short work of Root when their first three batters in the game all tripled. Root took over from there, however, and he stranded the third runner, limiting the Brooks to just two runs. The Cubs came back with one run in the first and another run in the second. Both pitchers got in a groove after the second inning and proceeded to throw goose eggs at each other until the ninth. With the score tied at 2-all in the bottom of the ninth, Riggs Stephenson reached second base on a throwing error by Dave Bancroft. Grimm sacrificed, and Hartnett and McMillan were both walked intentionally to load the bases, with one out. Pinch hitter Earl Webb grounded to third base, and Stephenson was forced at home for out #2. But the strategy backfired when Clyde Beck lined a single to left field, and Hartnett raced home with the winning run. Meanwhile, in St. Louis, John McGraw's troops were taking the measure of Bill McKechnie's Redbirds three straight times, moving into first place. The Chicago Cubs were third, 3½ games behind.

As often happens after a tough series, a team has a letdown and loses to one of the second division teams. Chicago suffered that fate when the last-place Phillies routed Percy Jones with five runs in 4⅔ innings en route to an 11–6 shellacking of the Windy City boys. Maguire and Cuyler both had three hits, Wilson had a home run, and Gabby Hartnett went 1-for-5, with an assist. The Phils made it two in a row the next day, winning 3–1 behind little right-hander Claude Willoughby. Sheriff Blake was the hard-luck loser. The win was Philadelphia's sixth straight at the expense of the embarrassed Cubs, quite an achievement for a team that had the National League cellar all to themselves and would finish the season a whopping 51 games behind the pennant-winning St. Louis Cardinals. Joe McCarthy's boys finally ended the jinx by winning the get-away game, although it was not easy. They took the contest 3–2 in 12 innings. Woody English had three hits for the day, Gabby Hartnett went 2-for-4 with a home run, and Art Nehf pitched all 12 innings for the victory.

On August 25, the St. Louis Browns stunned the proud New York Yankees by sweeping a doubleheader in New York by scores of 5–2 and 3–1. The twin loss cut the Yankees lead over the Philadelphia Athletics from a once insurmountable 13½ games to just three.

The Bruins welcomed the Boston Braves to Wrigley Field and promptly took out their frustration on the Beaneaters, sweeping two, 4–1 and 4–3. In the opener, Pat Malone, who was rapidly becoming Joe McCarthy's most reliable pitcher, tossed a complete game and shut the Braves down with a single run. Norm McMillan went 2-for-4 with an RBI. Gabby Hartnett drew the collar in three attempts, but tossed out two base runners attempting to steal. In game two, Charlie Root took the measure of Bob Smith, the ace of the Braves staff. Woody English and Root both had two hits. Old Tomato Face went 0-for-3, but had one assist. The Cubs made it a clean sweep of Rogers Hornsby's team, winning the last two games of the series by scores of 7–3 and 6–3. Percy Jones won the 7–3 game in relief of Guy Bush, and Hack Wilson gave him all the help he needed by smashing two home runs, good for four runs. Hal Carlson took the finale with a neat five-hitter. English and Cuyler had three hits each. Gabby Hartnett went 2-for-4 with a double and a triple and two runs scored. And Norm McMillan was sensational in the field, robbing several Boston hitters of base hits with spectacular defensive plays. With an off-day staring them in the face, Gabby Hartnett, Hal Carlson, and Charlie Root put on their best knickers and headed for the golf course to unwind and forget about the pennant race for a few hours.

August was a good month for Joe McCarthy's team, as they ran up a 16–11 record, but they cooled off just four days too soon. The St. Louis Cardinals came to town on the 28th and took the Cubs two straight. Sheriff Blake was treated roughly in the opener, as the Redbirds prevailed 11–3. Gabby Hartnett had a big day with three hits in four at-bats, with a double, a run scored, an RBI, and an assist. In the second game, the Cards came out on top again, this time by a 6–0 count. Clarence Mitchell fired a seven-hit shutout at the Windy City congregation, beating Pat Malone. Hartnett went 1-for-4. New York, meanwhile, dropped two games to the seventh-place Boston Braves, 3–2 and 7–5. In the American League, the Philadelphia A's won a doubleheader from the Chicago White Sox and trailed the Yankees by three games. They won again the next day, 6–2, to trim the lead to 2½ games. Both the A's and the Yankees lost on the last day of the month to maintain the status quo.

The Cubs closed out the month with two wins over the Reds in Cincinnati. On the 30th, they won 2–0 in a rain-shortened game. The Cubs scored two runs in the fifth on hits by Beck and Root. Rain halted play in the top

Hal Carlson won 114 games during his 14-year major league career. (Jay Sanford)

of the seventh, sending McCarthy's boys home happy. Charlie Root outdueled Eppa Rixey with a four-hitter. Gabby Hartnett had 2-for-2 with a double. The next day, they won again, this time by a 5–3 score. Art Nehf pitched six innings for the win, and Hal Carlson finished up with three strong innings of relief. Red Lucas took the loss for Jack Hendrick's team. Hartnett was on the loose again, going 2-for-4 with a triple, a run scored, and an RBI. Wilson and Cuyler both had two singles and a double. Chicago ended the month 4½ games behind the St. Louis Cardinals. In the American League, the A's nipped the Boston Red Sox 3–2 to close to within two games of New York. The Yankees were idle.

The ruddy-faced Irishman went on a rampage in August,

hitting a torrid .345 with two home runs, while playing in 21 of the club's 27 games. He also controlled the game on defense from his position behind the plate, intimidating enemy base runners so much that they seldom challenged his powerful throwing arm. The leading hitters for the Cubs were Stephenson (.316), English (.302), Wilson (.299), Grimm (.290), and Hartnett (.284). Art Nehf had a record of 11–5, followed by Guy Bush at 11–6, Percy Jones at 9–6, Sheriff Blake at 12–10, and Pat Malone at 13–13.

The Cubs started the stretch run impressively, completing a three-game sweep of the Cincinnati Reds, with a 1–0 victory behind Sheriff Blake's tight one-hitter. "Long George" Kelly's double in the fifth inning was the only hit off the Chicago right-hander. Gabby Hartnett stayed as hot as the Cincinnati weather, with two hits in three at-bats, one of them a double. He also took care of the only man who dared test his arm. The next day, Donnie Bush's Pittsburgh Pirates moved into the Wrigley Field snake pit for a four-game series and immediately took the hose in game one, falling before Pat Malone's eight-hitter, 3–2. The game was played in a constant drizzle, but the 32,000 Cubs fanatics who braved the elements didn't care. They went home happy. Kiki Cuyler, who went 2-for-2, brought them to their feet with a home run. Gabby Hartnett had 1-for-2 with an RBI and a sacrifice. On the 3rd, the Pirates pounded Chicago in a morning-afternoon twin bill by scores of 16–1 and 6–3. In the morning game, Erv Brame took the measure of Charlie Root, who was hammered for six runs in 1⅓ innings. Hartnett had 1-for-3, with a double and an assist, although another runner beat his throw to second. In the PM game, Hal Carlson took the loss, while Remy Kremer was the winner. Paul Waner had a home run and two singles for the Bucs. Hartnett had 1-for-4.

The American League pennant race stayed tight as the Yankees split with the Boston Red Sox, winning 8–7 behind Lou Gehrig's home run and 3 RBIs, then losing 4–3. The A's meanwhile dropped a two-spot to the Washington Senators by scores of 6–1 and 5–4. The result left Philadelphia 2½ games out of first place.

Chicago came back to dump Pittsburgh 9–8 in the get-away game scoring the winning run in the bottom of the ninth when catcher Charlie Hargreaves threw the ball into center field on a double play attempt. Old Tomato Face had 2-for-4, with a double, a triple, and a run scored. Stephenson and Grimm homered in support of Blake, who won in relief. In Philadelphia, the Giants and Phils divided a doubleheader, with the Giants taking the opener 9–4, and the Phils winning the nightcap 8–7. Rookie Carl Hubbell, on his way to a 10–6 season, won the opener. Bill Terry had two hits with a home run. In the second game, Cy Williams' two-run homer off Jack Scott in the ninth was the Game-winner. The Cubs entertained the Reds next, and thrashed them 11–1, much to the delight of the big Friday crowd who filled the Friendly Confines. Charlie Root tossed a four-hitter for the win. The Bruins drove Red Lucas to cover under a five-run barrage in the fifth inning, with Gabby Hartnett's two-run homer the big blow. The muscular backstop had another 3-for-5 day, with a double, a homer, two runs scored, two RBIs, two assists, and no stolen bases allowed. English and Stephenson also had three hits. St. Louis defeated Pittsburgh 6–3, leaving them with a 4½ game bulge over Chicago and five games over New York. On Saturday, Joe McCarthy's warriors edged Cincinnati 2–1 in 14 innings. Kiki Cuyler's double in the fourteenth drove in Woody English with the winning run. Hartnett was 2-for-4 with an assist. Pat Malone was the winning pitcher, with six scoreless innings, in relief of Sheriff Blake who gave up just one run in eight innings. When Pittsburgh dumped St. Louis 4–2, the Redbird lead over Chicago dwindled to 3½ games.

In the Junior Circuit, the A's romped over Washington 9–2 on Wednesday, cutting the idle Yanks lead to two games. The next day, Miller Huggins' troops split with the Senators, losing the first game 3–1 and winning the second 8–3. Southpaw Fred Heimach was the winning pitcher in the nightcap. The American League pennant race reached a fever pitch on September 7, when Washington stunned the proud New Yorkers in a twin bill by scores of 11–0 and 6–1. When the Philadelphia Athletics took two games from the Boston Red Sox in Fenway Park, 1–0 and 7–3, they moved into a first-place tie with New York. Lefty Grove dominated the Red Sox in game one, throwing a four-hitter and striking out 11 batters. The only run of the game scored in the top of the sixth, on a walk, Mickey Cochrane's single, and an error. Eddie Rommell was the winning pitcher in game two.

Miller Huggins' team had looked like runaway winners in the early going, taking 39 of their first 48 games and opening a 13½-game bulge over the A's by July 1. But there was no quit in Connie Mack's warriors, and they came roaring back, winning 49 of 66 games between July 1 and September 8, to overtake the Yankees and move into first place. The Yankees whipped the Washington Senators 6–3 on the 8th, on a sixth-inning, game-tying home run by Lou Gehrig and a game-winning, three-run blast by the "Sultan of Swat," Babe Ruth, in the seventh. However, in Boston, the A's humbled the Sox twice by scores of 7–6 (in 10 innings) and 7–4, giving Philadelphia the undisputed league lead by a ½ game over New York. The next day, however, the A's hit a brick wall. "Murderers Row" finally got untracked and swept a doubleheader from Connie Mack's charges, winning 5–0 and 7–3 to reclaim the top spot. The Mack-men entered the zoo at Yankee Stadium under a full head of steam that had gone unchecked for more than two months. This was the moment of truth, and 85,265 boisterous

Bronx patrons let the visitors know the season wasn't over. They yelled themselves hoarse, cheering for their beloved Bronx Bombers and deriding the Athletics at every turn. The hostile atmosphere may have affected Philadelphia, because they were held to just three runs all afternoon. In the opener, tall, lanky George Pipgras, on his way to a brilliant 24–13 season, set the A's down without a run. In the nightcap, Bob Meusel's grand slam in the eighth inning broke a 3-all tie, vaulting the Yankees back into first place by 1½ games. New York kept the lead from there to the end of the season, winning the pennant by 2½ games.[6]

Miller Huggins introduced a new catcher to the world on September 16. William Malcolm "Bill" Dickey, after a fine season at Little Rock in the Southern Association, where he hit .300, was promoted to the big club in time to play 10 games before the end of the season. In his debut, the lanky left-handed batter came off the bench in mid-game and went 0-for-2, as the St. Louis Browns edged the Yankees 6–5. Babe Ruth hit his 500th career home run in the game. Dickey went 3-for-15 over the last two weeks, with a double and a triple. Beginning in 1929, Bill Dickey would catch 100 or more games for New York for 13 straight seasons and be rated one of the greatest catchers ever to play the game.

In the Senior Circuit, Chicago downed Cincinnati 2–0 behind a Bush two-hitter, in what was also their swan song. They made a valiant effort to scale the heights, but just didn't have the firepower to get the job done, finishing four games off the pace. They did have one more shot left in their cannon, however. During the last week of the season, they stormed into the Polo Grounds to take on McGraw's Giants, who were only a ½ game out of first place. They took the first game of a doubleheader 3–2, when Gabby Hartnett stopped Andy Reese trying to score the tying run on a controversial play in the sixth inning. During a rundown, Reese and Hartnett got tangled up near the plate and fell to the ground in a heap, allowing Chicago third baseman Clyde Beck to put the tag on Reese. Giants manager John McGraw protested vehemently, charging interference on Hartnett's part, but the protest was rejected the next morning by National League President John Heydler. McGraw was so enraged by the decision, "He obtained a copy of the picture on which Heydler had based his decision, and had it framed and hung in the Giants office as evidence that the Giants had been robbed."[7] New York came back to capture the nightcap 2–0, but Joe McCarthy's boys took the final two games of the series by scores of 7–2 and 6–2. Those three losses by the Giants, coupled with the St. Louis Cardinals' three-game sweep of the Braves in Boston, gave Bill McKechnie's team the National League Championship by two games.

The New York Yankee Express rolled over the Redbirds in the World

Series to avenge their 1926 debacle. This time, they left no doubt as to which team was the best, as they swept the Series in four games, outscoring McKechnie's crew 27–10 and outhomering them 9–1. Babe Ruth and Lou Gehrig were a two-man demolition crew, with Ruth batting a torrid .625 with three home runs, and Lou Gehrig hitting .525 with four home runs. Rabbit Maranville at .308 was the only Redbird player to bat over .300. Waite Hoyt pitched two complete game victories.[8]

The regular season batting leaders were Rogers Hornsby at .387 and Goose Goslin of Washington at .379. The home run kings were Jim Bottomley and Hack Wilson with 31 home runs each and Babe Ruth with 54. The top pitchers were Larry Benton of the Giants at 25–9 and Lefty Grove at 24–8. Riggs Stephenson (.324), Hack Wilson (.313), and Gabby Hartnett (.302) were the only Chicago Cubs hitters over .300. Pat Malone (18–13), Sheriff Blake (17–11), and Guy Bush (15–6) led Joe McCarthy's pitching staff.[9]

In 1928, Gabby Hartnett finally put it all together. The ruddy-faced Irishman hit .302 with 26 doubles, nine triples, and 14 home runs in 388 at-bats, figures that would equate to 37 doubles, 13 triples, and 20 home runs over a 550 at-bat season. On defense, he had no equal. He led the National League with 103 assists and a .989 fielding average. And he allowed only 39 stolen bases, less than half the league average of 87. His counterpart in the American League, Mickey Cochrane, was only slightly above average, yielding 83 stolen bases against a league average of 87. Gabby also solved the problem of his stamina. In previous years, he had tailed off down the stretch due to the effect of physical injuries and exhaustion. But in 1928, he finished with a flourish. His batting average over the last two months of the season was .337 with five home runs. The big backstop would maintain that edge over the next 14 years, averaging .318 with 22 home runs for every 550 at-bats between 1928 and 1941.

Chicago Cubs owner William Wrigley Jr. took the decisive step to bring his club up to a championship level on November 7, when he obtained the major league's all-time greatest right-handed hitter, Rogers Hornsby, from the Boston Braves for five players, including Freddie Maguire and Percy Jones, plus $200,000 in cash. "The Rajah," at 32 years of age, still had a lot of firepower left in his bat, as shown by his .387 batting average in the season just completed. The move would turn out to be the last piece in the Cubs' pennant puzzle. Their 1929 team would prove to be one of the greatest teams in Chicago Cubs history.

The first event of the new year was the popular Rose Bowl football game in Pasadena, California. And it was an unforgettable contest, highlighted by one of football's most bizarre plays. In the second quarter of the game between the Georgia Tech Engineers and the University of California Golden Bears, center Roy Riegels of the Bears picked up a fumble and started up the field — THE WRONG WAY. He raced 60 yards before he was tackled by one of his own teammates on the two yard line. California immediately tried to punt the ball out of danger, but a Georgia Tech player blocked the punt, and the resulting safety gave Tech a 2–0 lead. That was the eventual margin of victory, as both teams scored touchdowns in the second half, making the final score 8–7. The California center has gone down in football history with the embarrassing moniker of "Wrong Way" Riegels.[10]

In January, an even more memorable event took place in the life of 28-year-old Leo Hartnett. He married his longtime sweetheart, Martha Henrietta Marshall, in the rectory of St. Mary's of the Lake Roman Catholic Church in Chicago on January 28. The wedding could not be held in the church proper at that time because Martha was not a Roman Catholic. The Reverend John Dennison officiated at the ceremony, and Mr. and Mrs. Ira Hartnett, no relation to the groom, served as best man and matron of honor. The guests included Ed McCullough, who had introduced the two, and Chicago Cubs teammates Sheriff Blake and Guy Bush. Gabby and Martha politely posed for the photographers during and after the ceremony, with the groom giving the cameramen some friendly advice: "Shoot fast boys. My heart's sort of fluttering."[11] Mr. and Mrs. Hartnett took up residence in a rented apartment in the 6200 block of North Washtenaw Ave. They almost didn't get the apartment because they landlord wasn't sure that a baseball player was a good enough risk.[12]

The Hartnetts departed for Catalina Island on February 14 for a combination spring training and honeymoon. It was a day that would go down in infamy in Chicago. It was St. Valentine's Day and the weather was frigid, with a temperature of 18 degrees, a cold wind howling, and a light

Gabby and Martha posed for photographers after their 1929 wedding. (Sheila Hartnett Hornof)

snow falling. South Side gang boss, Al Capone, and North Side gang boss, Bugs Moran, had been maneuvering for sole control of the Chicago area for years. Capone proposed a business meeting with Moran, to take place in Moran's North Side garage on the morning of February 14. Moran, sensing that all was not right, did not go to the garage, but seven of his henchman did. Four of Al Capone's hired killers, disguised as policemen, drove up to the garage at 2122 N. Clark Street at 10:30 AM. Once inside, they lined the seven Moran-men up against the red brick wall and sent them to hell with a withering fire from two Thompson submachine guns. The bloody massacre, known as the St. Valentine's Day Massacre, eventually led to the downfall of both the Capone and Moran mobs. The outraged citizens of Chicago forced the police to crack down on the criminal elements in the city. The federal government also joined in, and the famous FBI "Untouchables" eventually brought Capone to justice.[13]

The Chicago Cubs were favored to win the 1929 National League pennant after obtaining Hornsby, and the atmosphere was upbeat when spring training got underway in February. Then disaster struck. The Bruins' all-world receiver, Gabby Hartnett, went down with a sore arm, sidelining him for the inter-camp games. The injury was not considered serious by Joe McCarthy or his coaches at the time, because sore arms were common in the first days of camp. They usually worked themselves out in a week or so.

The players had plenty of time to relax during their four-week stay on Catalina Island, and many of them, like Charlie Grimm, Charlie Root, Hal Carlson, and Cliff Heathcote took advantage of it by fine-tuning their golf game. Some players preferred to stay in the hotel, socializing and playing pinochle. Gabby Hartnett and his new bride spent their time on the beach, with an occasional sight-seeing side trip. One of the more interesting diversions was viewing the numerous underwater sights from the glass-bottom boats that operated out of Avalon. The newlyweds also visited the museum and the casino where weekly dances were held. "One day, [Sheriff Blake] and Charlie Root and their wives decided to borrow one of Wrigley's Cadillacs and drive over the low range of hills to see the other side of the island. Along the way, they passed an old goat and two of its 'kids' standing by the side of the road. Blake was out of the car so fast the others hardly knew he was gone. 'What are you doing,' cried out his wife? 'I'm going to catch me a wild goat,' was the excited reply. 'You people go on your way; I'm staying here to catch that goat.' So they drove off while Sheriff stayed behind. 'I ran down into the canyon after one of the kid goats. When the others came back, I was waiting for them with this goat. We brought it to the clubhouse where we got a baby's bottle and fed it. I gave it to Mrs. Vaughan. The next day she had a little string and a yellow ribbon on the goat and was walking it all around the place.'"[14]

The Cubs' Murderers Row of Hornsby, Stephenson, Cuyler, and Wilson got off to a fast start in the exhibition games, but their pitching was less than sterling, as reported in the *Woonsocket Call*: "In six games with Los Angeles the Cubs have scored 73 runs, yet the best they could do was break even. Yesterday, the Angels collected 18 hits off Ed Lautenbacher and Guy Bush and defeated the Cubs, 12–11. Mike Cvengros and Hal Carlson have turned in the only good pitching of the series." Chicago did get their act together, as the team headed east to begin their quest for the National League title. They beat Bucky Harris' Detroit Tigers five straight. Kiki Cuyler ripped a triple and a

Gabby and Martha honeymooned on Catalina Island in 1929. (Sheila Hartnett Hornof)

homer in one game, as the Cubs prevailed 18–8. In another game, Hack Wilson drilled a grand slam homer into the right-field bleachers in Los Angeles to propel the Cubbies to an 8–5 victory. Two weeks later in Kansas City, Gabby Hartnett told reporters that his arm was better and he was ready to play, but that was wishful thinking on his part. He was still on the bench when the season opened. In fact, the *Woonsocket Call* noted, "The enthusiasm of the Chicago baseball fans has been somewhat dampened by the lack of improvement in catcher Gabby Hartnett's throwing arm. His whip has been treated by all sorts of specialists, but no one seems to know where the trouble lies. Gabby has hardly tossed a ball so far this spring, and it may be some time before he will be able to take his place behind the bat for the Cubs."[15]

There was another false rumor that Gabby was ready to play in late April but, as with previous rumors, it had no merit. Finally, in May, Gabby was sent to Johns Hopkins Hospital in Baltimore, Maryland, for a complete physical examination, but they could not locate the source of his problem either. There was a growing concern in the Chicago Cubs' front office that Gabby would never play major league baseball again. And that concern carried over into the Hartnett household, where Gabby tried to envision a future without baseball, a future that he was ill equipped to deal with. He had no skills that he could utilize in the private sector, and he had no savings thanks to his free-spending bachelor days.

The source of his injury is still a mystery today, although there were several explanations given for it. Woody English claimed he got it from the recoil of his gun while shooting clay pigeons in Lincoln Park in Chicago. Another Cubs player said he hurt it throwing sidearm while playing third base in infield drills at Catalina. And his mother had a completely different story. When she spoke with Gabby in April, she asked him if his wife was pregnant. Receiving a positive reply, she supposedly told him that his arm would get better as soon as the baby was born. Her prophecy proved accurate. Gabby's arm got better after his son, Bud, was born in December. His "ailment" may have been psychosomatic.

Whatever the cause, Joe McCarthy's Cubs were without their spark-plug for the entire season. He appeared in just 25 games, 24 of them as a pinch hitter. He caught one game with disappointing results. As the team's #1 pinch hitter, he hit .273 with one home run. His major contribution to the Chicago Cubs' pennant push was as their head cheerleader and bench jockey, encouraging his teammates and heckling the opposition. He also kept everybody loose with a constant stream of jokes. His daughter Sheila said he loved to tell jokes, and he never told the same joke twice. He especially loved the quick one-liners. He once told a newspaper reporter, "Most catchers are so ugly they don't have to wear a mask, but I have to wear one because I'm so good looking."

During his absence, the Cubs catching position was filled competently by Mike Gonzalez and Zack Taylor. Neither man was considered a strong hitter, with Gonzalez finishing the year at .240 and Zack Taylor checking in at .266, with just one home run between them. But they knew how to handle a pitching staff, and they both had strong throwing arms, allowing only 69 stolen bases against a league average of 87. They weren't up to Gabby's standards, but they were well above average.

Chicago opened their home season on Tuesday, April 16, before 50,000 screaming Cubs fanatics, but the Pittsburgh Pirates took the fans out of the game almost immediately. They scored two runs in the top of the first inning, on an error by Woody English, and went on to defeat Charlie Root 4–3. Six days later, they met an old friend, Grover Cleveland Alexander, and gave him a rude welcome. Pat Malone outdueled the legendary Alex, winning 3–0. Rogers Hornsby's home run in the fourth inning broke a scoreless tie and tagged Old Alex with a loss. To end the month of April, the Cubs dropped a tough 5–4 game to the Cincinnati Reds who scored two runs in the bottom of the ninth off Sheriff Blake. The loss gave Chicago a 7–5 record for the month, leaving them in second place, 1½ games behind the Boston Braves. Joe McCarthy's charges went 15–9 in May, but lost their last four games of the month to dampen an otherwise outstanding run. On May 30, John McGraw's Giants beat the Cubs 7–4 before a large crowd of 40,000 in Wrigley Field. Guy Bush took the brunt of the New York outburst.

From June 1 to the end of the season, the Chicago Cubs exploded. They went 17–9 in June to take a ½-game lead over the Pittsburgh Pirates. Donnie Bush kept his team close for two more weeks: but by July 31, they were five games behind the sizzling Cubbies and could do no better than play .500 ball the rest of the year. On June 30, the red-hot Cubs won their eighth straight game, beating the St. Louis Cardinals by a score of 14–8. St. Louis ko'd Cubs starter Charlie Root after just 1⅔ innings, leading 8–1 after three before the roof caved in. The score was still 8–3 after six, but the men of McCarthy scored three runs in the seventh, five in the eighth, and three more in the ninth to win going away. Hornsby went 4-for-5 with a double and a triple, Wilson was 3-for-5, and Grimm had 3-for-5 with a double. Claude Jonnard was the winner with 3⅓ innings of scoreless relief. The Pirates went back into first place on July 6, after Chicago was beaten 3–2 by the Braves in Boston. The same day, in Philadelphia, the Cardinals set a new major league record for the most runs scored in a single game, with a 28–6 demolition of Burt Shotton's shell-shocked Phillies. The 28-hit attack was led by Taylor Douthit, who went 5-for-6, and Jim Bottomley, who went 4-for-5. Winning pitcher Fred Frankhouse had a 4-for-7 day himself, with two RBIs. In the American League, Connie Mack's A's, at 53–18, held a commanding 8½-game lead over the Yankees.

It was a pleasant summer for everyone on the Chicago Cubs team except Gabby Hartnett, who couldn't fully enjoy the run for the pennant. He had a heartrending summer, not knowing if he'd ever play again. His new wife was pregnant, his $15,000-a-year job was in jeopardy, and his future was uncertain.

The Cubs were playing lethargic baseball in early July, when two incidents in Cincinnati seemed to rouse them from their slumber. Trailing Pittsburgh by three games, they were playing the Reds when words were exchanged between between Ray Kolp and Hack Wilson. According to Holtzman and Vass, "Wilson leaped into the Red's dugout and delivered two rights to the jaw." Later, at Cincinnati's Union Station, while waiting for a train, Wilson got into another altercation, this time with Red's pitcher Pete Donohue, and he "split Donohue's lip with a right uppercut." Almost immediately, the fired-up Cubbies ran off a six-game winning streak against the Dodgers and Phillies. They overtook the first-place Pittsburgh Pirates in less than a week and proceeded to turn the National League pennant race into a runaway. They scorched the playing fields of the northeast United States over the last half of the season, finishing with 98 victories against 54 losses, giving them a comfortable lead over the Bucs. Pittsburgh manager Donnie Bush was fired in August, after his team slumped badly. His replacement, Jewel Ens, had a 21–14 record to show for his tenure, but it was too little, too late.

Joe McCarthy's warriors went on a 24–8 tear in July, running up two more long winning streaks along the way. They won eight in a row to end June and had a nine-game streak stopped by the Braves on July 31. They finished the month with a 63–31 record, good enough for a five-game lead over the fading St. Louis Cardinals. Over in the Junior Circuit, the New York Yankees took their seventh in a row, with a 16–2 rout of the Chicago White Sox. Lou Gehrig was 3-for-5 with a home run. The win kept Miller Huggins' boys five games behind the 74–26 Philadelphia Athletics.

On August 4, Hal Carlson beat Buzz McWeeny, as the Cubs walloped the Brooklyn Dodgers 12–2 before a small Sunday gathering of 18,000 in the Friendly Confines. Norm McMillan had a 3-for-5 day with a double, while Hornsby, Wilson, Cuyler, and Taylor all had two hits. Babe Herman, Brooklyn's all-time leading hitter, smashed a tremendous home run over the right field fence. The stretch runs were nonexistent in both leagues, as the Cubs and A's sprinted for the finish line. Joe McCarthy's troops cooled off slightly in September, winning 15 games against 13 losses, but still finished 10½ games ahead of Pittsburgh. Gabby Hartnett's arm was still a subject of conversation in the Chicago clubhouse as well as the front office. A number of people, both players and executives, thought his sore arm was all in his head. So on Sunday, September 9, it was put to the test. The Chicago Cubs were hosting the New York Giants, and a large gathering of 40,000 Cubs fans pushed their way through the turnstiles to watch Gabby in action. His performance was less than noteworthy. His throwing arm was only a shadow of its former self, and even his bat was a noncontributor. No one tested his arm by trying to steal on him, but when he attempted a pickoff at third base, his throw had nothing on it. At the plate, he was 0-for-3 with a walk, as the Giants beat the Cubs and Guy Bush 5–4.

Hornsby, the Cubs' new second baseman, sparked the team all season and won the league's Most Valuable Player Award for his contributions. He ripped the ball at a sensational .380 clip, with 47 doubles, eight triples, 39 home runs, and 149 RBIs. He also led all second basemen in double plays and assists. But he was by no means a one-man army. The Chicago outfield was truly amazing. Kiki Cuyler slugged the ball for a .360 average, with 15 homers and 102 RBIs. Hack Wilson batted .345, with 39 homers and a league-leading 159 RBIs. And Old Hoss Stephenson hit .362, with 17 homers and 110 RBIs. They were the first National League outfield trio in history to have more than 100 RBIs each. Cliff Heathcote hit .313 as a part-timer. Pat Malone was the league's leading pitcher, with a record of 22–10. Charlie Root was 19–6, Guy Bush was 18–7, Hal Carlson was 11–5, and Sheriff Blake was 14–13 for Joe McCarthy's club. As a team, the Cubs led the league in fielding average, double plays, runs scored, doubles, and shutouts, and they were second in earned-run-average (ERA). Most baseball experts have called the 1929 Chicago Cubs team the greatest Cubs team ever assembled.

In the American League, Connie Mack's Philadelphia Athletics ran away from the rest of the pack, winning their first of three successive pennants. The A's jumped out front almost immediately and raced to a 104–46 record, giving them a huge 18-game bulge over the New York Yankees. Miller Huggins' club was hampered by pitching problems all year and had only one man with more than 13 wins. Ruth, Gehrig, Lazzeri, and Combs all had typically fine years, but the mediocre pitching was too much to overcome. The A's had some outstanding bats, with Jimmie Foxx, Bing Miller, Mule Haas, Al Simmons, and Mickey Cochrane all hitting over .300, and Simmons leading the league with 159 RBIs; but it was the phenomenal pitching that made the difference. Their staff allowed almost one run per game less than the Yankees. George Earnshaw was the league's top pitcher with a record of 24–8. Lefty Grove, who might have been the greatest left-handed pitcher in the history of the game, went 20–6, Rube Walberg was 18–11, and three other pitchers won in double figures.

The 1929 World Series looked like a toss-up, with both the Cubs and A's having a balanced combination of hitting, defense, and pitching. Manager Connie Mack shocked the world in the opener when he started a 35-year-old right-hander named Howard Ehmke to oppose Chicago Cubs ace Charlie Root at Wrigley Field. Ehmke, who had pitched in only 11 games during the season with a 7–2 record, was nearing the end of a 15-year career. He would pitch just three games in 1930 before retiring. This was his swan song, and he made his manager look like a genius. According to *The Ballplayers*, "Mack reasoned that the side-arming Ehmke had the perfect mix of control and slow stuff to keep the predominantly right-hand hitting Cubs off balance, and gave Ehmke time off near the end of the season to personally scout the Cubs."[16]

Ehmke was sensational. He throttled the Chicago hitters, scattering eight hits, striking out 13 batters in nine innings, and winning 3–1. Charlie Root pitched a strong game for the Cubs, holding the A's to just one run on three hits in seven innings. His only mistake was serving up a cripple to Jimmie Foxx, and Double-X sent it screaming into the left-center field bleachers in the seventh inning. The A's continued to dominate the series in game two, routing Pat Malone in less than four innings and walking off with a 9–3 decision behind Earnshaw and Grove. Joe McCarthy's warriors bounced back in game three with Guy Bush, outdueling George Earnshaw 3–1. Philadelphia took a 1–0 lead in the bottom of the fifth on singles by Cochrane and Miller, but after being held to four runs in 23 innings, the Cubs exploded for a three-spot in the top of the sixth. A walk, an error, and two singles did the damage.

Game four was the key game of the series, and one of the greatest games in World Series history. Charlie Root started on the mound for the visiting Cubs, opposed by 19-year veteran Jack Quinn, who had compiled an 11–9 record during the season. The Chicago sluggers got to Quinn in the fourth inning and hit him hard and often. They took a 2–0 lead in that inning on a two-run homer by Charlie Grimm and put a big five-spot on the board in the sixth on five successive singles and an error. By the time the bottom of the seventh rolled around, the Cubs were comfortably in front 8–0, nine outs away from tying the series. Then the roof caved in as Charlie Root suddenly lost his stuff. Al Simmons led off with a long home run onto the roof in left field. After Foxx singled to right, Miller hit a fly ball to center field that Hack Wilson lost in the sun, the ball dropping in for a single. And the stampede was on. Three of the next four batters singled, and Root was on his way to an early shower. Art Nehf took the mound,

Mickey Cochrane batted .320 during his 13-year major league career.

but couldn't stem the tide. Mule Haas hit a long drive to center field. Once again, Hack Wilson lost the ball in the sun, and it went over his head and rolled all the way to the wall, as Haas circled the bases with an inside-the-park home run. The Chicago lead was now down to a single run, 8–7. When Nehf walked Cochrane, Joe McCarthy brought in Sheriff Blake. Simmons singled Cochrane to second, and Foxx singled him in with the tying run. "Marse Joe" quickly rushed Malone to the mound to stop the deluge, but the rookie right-hander was not up to the task. He hit Miller with a pitch to load the bases, then grooved one to Jimmy Dykes, and the Philadelphia third baseman ripped it down the left field line for two bases, scoring both Simmons and Foxx. The carnage finally ended when both Boley and Burns went down swinging, but the A's had stunned the Chicago team with a 10-run inning, the biggest comeback in World Series history. The demoralized Cubs were retired in order in both the eighth and ninth innings by Lefty Grove, who struck out four of the six men he faced.

Chicago tried to regroup in game five, and for awhile it seemed as if they might succeed. They led 2–0 after eight innings, but the A's rallied one more time. Pat Malone, the Cubs starter, fanned French to open the inning. Max Bishop followed with a single, and Mule Haas hit a game-tying home run over the right field wall. Cochrane grounded out, but Simmons hit a long smash off the scoreboard in center field, which missed being a home run by inches. Foxx was walked intentionally, but Miller ruined the strategy by ripping another double off the scoreboard, sending Simmons home with the winning run. There were many heroes for the Athletics. Five players had four or more RBIs, and three players — Foxx, Haas, and Simmons — each had two home runs. Jimmy Dykes led the team at bat with an average of .421, followed by Mickey Cochrane at .400. The pitching staff had a meager 2.40 ERA; compared to the 4.33 ERA put up by the Cubs pitchers. Hack Wilson was the big bomber in the series, with an average of .471. Rogers Hornsby could do no better than .238. Gabby Hartnett's participation in the series was limited to pinch-hitting duties, and the dejected catcher struck out in all three appearances. Guy Bush was credited with the Cubs only victory and sported an excellent 0.82 ERA in 11 innings pitched.[17] Manager Joe McCarthy was livid at the performance of his All-Star aggregation, remarking, "Sometimes I think that nine trained monkeys could do better in a Series than the apes we pay salaries."[18]

Things were looking good for the citizens of the United States in October 1929. The Roaring Twenties were still in full bloom, speakeasies were doing a booming business in bootleg booze, and automobiles were becoming affordable necessities for many working Americans. There were 23 million automobiles on the road in 1929. The Ford Motor Company, with its new automated production lines, had increased employees' wages sevenfold since 1910, and the new Model T could be purchased for less than $1,000.

But the good times came to an end with brutal suddenness. Many Americans were active in the stock market, and it was common practice in those days to buy on credit, with just 10 percent down. The strategy worked well during most of the twenties, and people became more prosperous; but in 1929, the dream ended. Between October 21 and November 12, the stock market plummeted, and thousands of people saw their life savings slipping away. On the 13th, "Black Tuesday," the market dropped from 312 to 164. Millionaires across the country were suddenly broke. Small investors were wiped out. Suicides were common occurrences. And mobs of people rushed to Wall Street to try to salvage what little they could. The American economy collapsed. A severe depression descended over the nation, as people no longer had extra money to purchase luxuries; manufacturing production was reduced drastically, and 25 percent of the workforce lost their jobs. It would take most of the next decade, and a World War, to revitalize the country.[19]

Gabby Hartnett was one of the lucky ones who didn't suffer either financially or personally during the depression. He wasn't heavily invested in the stock market, and he had a steady job with a good income, playing baseball. His family also survived with a minimum of discomfort, thanks in part to Gabby. He sent his mother money for rent and other expenses every month, and he was always there to help out his brothers and sisters in emergencies, medical or otherwise.

William Wrigley Jr. decided to stand pat in 1930. He felt that, with Gabby Hartnett back, his team would be even stronger than the club that won the recent National League pennant. He was probably correct, but fate would intervene in an unkind way to sabotage his strategy.

During the off-season, Gabby Hartnett operated his own insurance business to keep busy and earn some extra money, but he never made it a full-time job. It was during this time that Frank "Sweetie" Hartnett moved to Chicago to be near his big brother, who was his hero. He lived with Gabby and Martha for about a year until he found a job as a salesman. Then he moved to his own place in Oak Park. Sweetie and Gabby were not only brothers, they were also best friends, and they spent a lot of time together over the years.

7

The "Year of the Hitter" and Beyond, 1930–31

The year 1930 is known as "The Year of the Hitter" because changes in the manufacturing of the baseball produced a ball with the seams at the same height as the leather cover, instead of being raised. As a result, pitchers could not grip the ball properly to throw a curve, and their fastballs were straight as an arrow. And batters like nothing better than to hit balls that do not break. The entire National League, including pitchers, batted .303 for the year, and the American League hit .288. Seventy-one players hit over .300, with 12 of them exceeding .354. The Philadelphia Phillies, who hit .315 as a team and scored 944 runs, came in dead last, 40 games behind St. Louis. Their pitchers were touched up for 1,199 runs, an all-time major league record.

"Gabby" Hartnett had his own problems to worry about during the off-season — his sore arm. After his son, Bud, was born on December 4, 1929, Gabby was anxious to find out if his mother's prediction, that the soreness in his arm would disappear after the baby arrived, would come true. To this end, he maintained a strict training regimen through November, December, and January. Every morning he would leave his North Washtenaw Avenue apartment and go to the Northwest Lions Club where a trainer would put him through a rigorous program of weight lifting, calisthenics, and heat treatments. He also did some light throwing, but never cut loose with a "Hartnett throw."

By the time spring training began on February 22, his arm felt much better; but he was still protective of it during the first two-hour drill, which was mostly a press session. The 500 people who were milling about the field included only 19 ballplayers, mostly catchers and pitchers. The rest were reporters, photographers, and fans. There was a short training session where the players did some throwing, hitting, bunting, and base running, but most of their time was spent posing for pictures and giving interviews. Although Gabby didn't display his powerful arm, his throws were made with an over-the-top motion, instead of the sidearm motion he used in 1929 when his arm was sore, a good sign that was not missed by his manager.

February 24 was a gold letter day for Gabby Hartnett and the Cubs, as reported by Irving Vaughan in the *Chicago Tribune*: "For the first time in almost exactly a year to the day, Gabby Hartnett's famous throwing arm swung into action this afternoon. With all the power and accuracy that one time gave him a rating of the peer of backstops, he whipped four balls down to second base. The ease with which he did it, convinced camp followers that when the Cubs line up April 15 for their maiden effort in the flag campaign, the effervescent Gabby will be among those in action. Hartnett's exhibition of throwing wasn't his own idea. He was behind the plate catching Carlson when McCarthy said 'I'll find out whether he can throw.' McCarthy grabbed a glove and ran to second base. Then he called to Gabby to throw

Gabby Hartnett was always a stylish dresser during his Chicago career. (Town of Millville J.G. Fitzgerald Historical Society, Inc.)

a couple in that direction. His first throw was perfect but it wasn't caught that way. McCarthy didn't expect the ball to come burning toward him like a meteor. He misjudged its speed and it whacked him on the right wrist. The second was just as deceptive. It smashed him on the left wrist. The second two pitches breezed past McCarthy just as if he wasn't there, but nevertheless he was pleased."[1] Apparently "Old Tomato Face" had cured his throwing arm during the winter, but he had neglected other aspects of his training and was several pounds overweight when he first arrived at Avalon. His punishment was to join Pat Malone, Sheriff Blake, and the other "fatsoes," for an accelerated exercise program to sweat off the winter's suet.

Another of manager Joe McCarthy's projects was to restore

the confidence of his top slugger, Hack Wilson, whom McCarthy thought must have been devastated after his World Series debacle. But he didn't have to worry about Hack. The happy-go-lucky outfielder had taken the embarrassing episode in stride. One morning at breakfast in the St. Catherine Hotel dining room, he even asked the waiter to dim the lights so he wouldn't misjudge his soup.[2]

The Cubs traveled to Los Angeles on March 16 to play an exhibition game against the Angels, and Hartnett was back at his old stand behind the plate. Chicago belted L.A.'s best by a score of 10–5, and Hartnett was on top of his game, handling the chores behind the plate and going 2-for-4 with the bat, including a triple. Riggs Stephenson had a three-hit day with a home run. Back at camp after the west coast visit, a jubilant Joe McCarthy gave Gabby Hartnett's throwing arm a clean bill of health after watching him throw the ball around during three exhibition games. "Marse Joe" also predicted that his Cubbies would win another National League pennant, and he hoped the Philadelphia Athletics would win the American League flag so he could gain revenge for the 1929 World Series loss.

The Chicago Cubs' 1930 National League season opened in St. Louis on April 15, with Sheriff Blake facing Flint Rhem, the Cardinals' former 20-game winner, who had spent the 1929 season in the minors. Blake carried a 5–1 lead into the seventh, but a pulled leg muscle forced him to the sidelines after the first two Redbirds reached base. Guy Bush relieved Blake but was ineffective, and he gave way to Pat Malone in the ninth, with the Cubs hanging on for a 9–8 victory. Gabby Hartnett had a banner day. He went 2-for-3, with a double and two runs scored. He also shot down three men who decided to test his arm, one of them on a "strike 'em out, throw 'em out," double play. The next day, the Cards got even, belting Charlie Root for five runs in 2+ innings, en route to an easy 13–3 win. Gabby went 1-for-4 and picked off two more base runners. Chicago ended the month of April with a 9–8 record after defeating the Pittsburgh Pirates 5–2 at home. Woody English and Hack Wilson homered in support of Pat Malone, who pitched a complete game. "The Pirates then tried to find out how good Hartnett's revived arm really was. They started a double steal. Gabby whipped a bullet-like peg to English and English snapped it over to third to get Paul Waner who, when he saw he couldn't reach the plate, tried to get back to the far corner."[3] The Bruins start left them in third place, 2½ games behind Pittsburgh. In the American League, the big story was the New York Yankees' sluggish start, which had them in the basement with a 3–9 record. The Washington Senators were leading the league with an 11–3 record. Gabby Hartnett was off to a sizzling start for Chicago, batting .340 with four home runs in 47 at-bats.

The Cubs players, in addition to their baseball responsibilities, donated a significant amount of their time to youth programs in the Windy City. One of the programs they participated in was the *Tribune's* Baseball School for Boys, which offered professional instructions in the art of hitting, throwing, and fielding a baseball. The sessions, held at Wrigley Field on Saturday mornings, drew more than 5,000 boys each week. On April 26, Gabby Hartnett was the main attraction, and he gave a demonstration in the art of catching and throwing a baseball from a squat position. The good-natured Irishman loved working with kids, and he felt baseball was a wholesome outlet for a young boy's energy, preparing him for life by teaching discipline, teamwork, and a strong work ethic. Gabby's concern for young people was in evidence one day when he was entering a building to attend a baseball banquet and noticed a group of boys waiting outside to get players' autographs. He immediately went to one of the organizers of the event and asked him if the kids could come inside. He said, "I'd rather disappoint a president of the United States than disappoint a kid." The kids were invited in, and were treated to turkey and ice cream.[4]

On May 3, Rogers Hornsby, the greatest right-handed batter in the history of baseball, conducted the *Tribune's* clinic and gave the kids pointers on hitting. The day after his session, the Cubs blanked the Phillies 1–0 in 10 innings. Charlie Root hurled the complete game shutout, striking out five and walking one. The Phillies had a big chance to win the game in the eighth inning, but were thwarted by Hartnett. They put together three singles in the inning, but after the first one, the runner trying to steal second was gunned down by Gabby. Root took matters into his own hands in the tenth, leading off with a double and coming around to score the winning run when former Cub, Barney Friberg, let a double play grounder go through his legs.[5] Joe McCarthy's charges nipped the Cincinnati Reds 6–5 on May 28, but a tragedy turned the Chicago clubhouse into a somber place. Their 36-year-old pitching ace Hal Carlson died suddenly of a hemorrhage of the stomach at his North Side hotel, following a two-year illness. The big right-hander had a 4–2 won-loss record at the time of his death. He left a wife and a four-year-old daughter.

A less-serious tragedy befell the team on May 30, when Rogers Hornsby broke his ankle in the first half of a morning-afternoon doubleheader against Gabby Street's high-flying Cardinals. The injury happened in the third inning of the morning game, with the Bruins up 2–0. Hornsby's two-base hit drove in the second run. The next batter, Hack Wilson, lifted a fly ball to right field, and Hornsby tried to go to third after the catch. He started to slide, changed his mind, and twisted his leg as he went in standing up. His left ankle snapped as he fell to the turf. Root completed the shutout, with Gabby Hartnett going 2-for-3. In the afternoon half of the twin bill, the Cubs prevailed 9–8 in 10 innings in a real dogfight. First one team, then the other, took the lead, with 27 base hits rattling around Wrigley Field. The winning run scored on a double and two errors by the St. Louis infield. Hartnett had a single in four trips to the plate, scored one run, and threw out the only man who tried to steal on him. Hack Wilson and Hornsby's replacement, Footsie Blair, hammered home runs for the home team. The Cubs finished the sweep the next day, dumping the Cards 6–5.[6] May was an up-and-down month for Joe McCarthy's boys, and their 14–11 record for the month had them in third place, three games from the top. In the American League, the New York Yankees had vacated the basement and moved all the way up to third place, three games behind the Washington Senators and Philadelphia Athletics, who were tied for the top spot.

Joe McCarthy's charges visited Brooklyn in early June while riding a nine-game winning streak. But the Dodgers put an end to that in a most unseemly manner. Southpaw Watty Clark entered the game as a relief pitcher in the fifth inning, with the Dodgers on the short end of a 9–8 score: two innings later, he launched a three-run homer over the 38-foot right field screen to propel his team to a 12–9 victory. Two home runs by Woody English and singletons by Hack Wilson and Clyde Beck were wasted. The next stop on the eastern junket was Philadelphia, and the Cubs came away with a split in the four-game series after gaining a hard-fought 7–5 win in the finale, thanks to Gabby Hartnett. Guy Bush was trying to hold a 4–2 lead in the eighth, when "Old Tomato Face" picked out a cripple from Hal Elliott and deposited it in the left field seats. After Burt Shotton's team had narrowed the score to 5–4 with a two-run outburst in the bottom of the eighth, Gabby stepped to the plate again in the ninth, with Charlie Grimm on first base and two men out, and promptly drilled the first pitch high over Baker Bowl's 60-foot-high barrier in right field. The Cubs' catcher finished the day with two hits, a walk, and three runs scored.

Kiki Cuyler had a big day in Wrigley Field on June 27. A Ladies Day crowd of 51,556, including 30,476 screaming females, came to see their idol, and he didn't disappoint them. He hit a walk-off two-run homer in the bottom of the tenth inning to beat the Brooklyn Dodgers 7–5.[7] The Bruins took three out of four from Uncle Robby's boys, ending a run of 24 victories in 31 games, and vaulted over Brooklyn into first place. They closed the month with a 10–3 rout of the New York Giants in a dazzling display of baseball. Sheriff Blake coasted to the victory after an eight-run Cubs' first quickly turned the game into a laugher. Gabby Hartnett had a 2-for-4 day, with his seventeenth homer, two runs scored, and three runs-batted-in (RBIs).

On July 1, the Chicago Cubs tasted the rarefied air of first place, with a 1½-game lead over Brooklyn and a healthy 7½-game lead over John McGraw's team. The Philadelphia A's had taken over first place in the American League, followed by Washington and New York. July was an up-and-down month for Joe McCarthy's charges, as they were in and out of first place the entire time. Their 15–15 record for the month left them looking up at the Brooklyn Dodgers, who won 25 of 39 games. The Fourth of July doubleheader cost them first place, when they could do no better than split with Jewel Ens' Bucs. Rookie southpaw Bud Teachout, on his way to an 11–4 season, stopped Pittsburgh in game one by the score of 10–1, with Riggs Stephenson's home run the big blow. In the afternoon half of the AM-PM twin bill, Charlie Root was battered for 12 base hits, as Pittsburgh gained the split 5–1. Hartnett had a single in three trips to the plate, after sitting out the opener. The Cubs regained the top spot the next day when they ripped Larry French 12–3 behind a 19-hit attack. English, Cuyler, Wilson, Danny Taylor, and Hartnett all had three hits, with Taylor and Hartnett smashing home runs in the rout.

Chicago beat the Braves on the 12th, with Teachout throwing a complete game in a 7–3 victory. Charlie Grimm, who had been hitless in the previous five games, slammed two singles and a double to pace the offense. Every Cub player had at least one hit, with the exception of Hack Wilson. The most disappointing day of the month was the 13th, when the Cubs dropped a doubleheader to the fifth-place Boston Braves, 2–1 and 3–0. In the opener, diminutive right-hander Socks Seibold kept the Bruin sluggers in check until the ninth, when three singles gave them their only run. Sheriff Blake, the losing pitcher, could have sued for nonsupport as both Braves runs were unearned, coming on errors by English and Beck. But the real tragedy of the day occurred in game two, when Boston's Sunday law prohibiting baseball being played after 6 PM cost Joe McCarthy's charges four runs. In the top of the ninth, singles by Wilson, Stephenson, Grimm, and

Kiki Cuyler was one of the top hitters in major league history, batting .321 over an 18-year career. (George E. Outland)

Doc Farrell chased two runs across the plate. Gabby Hartnett's double drove in two more, giving Chicago a 4–3 lead. In the bottom of the ninth, George Sisler singled, Chatham struck out, and Jimmy Welsh doubled, putting runners on second and third. At this point, the game was stopped, and the score reverted to the end of the eighth inning, with Boston winning 3–0.[8] Chicago ended the month in second place, two games behind Brooklyn. The Giants were third, another three games out. In the American League, Connie Mack's powerful A's had opened up a big eight-game lead over Washington, and 9½ over New York.

Hack Wilson hit seven home runs during the first two weeks of August, putting him within three of Chuck Klein's record. Meanwhile, "Unser Joe" Hauser, the former Philadelphia A's slugging first baseman who had finished second to Babe Ruth in the 1924 home run race before breaking his knee and ending his big league career, pounded his fifty-fourth home run for Baltimore in the International League, on his way to a 63-homer season. Three years later, Hauser would raise the bar to 69 homers while playing for Minneapolis in the American Association.

Joe McCarthy's cohorts welcomed Wilbert Robinson's big bad Dodgers to the Friendly Confines for a critical four-game series on August 12, with the Brooks holding a percentage-point lead in the National League title scuffle, after leading the Cubs by 3½ games just a week ago. Chicago captured the opener of the series, only to see the Dodgers roar back for a 15–5 win on Wednesday. Pat Malone took matters into his own hands in game three and shut the visitors down 5–1 on eight hits. Blair, Wilson, and Hartnett had two hits each, as the Cubbies took a one game lead in the pennant race. The next day, they upped the lead to two, by nipping the Dodgers 4–3 in 10 innings. Danny Taylor was the batting star of the game with three hits, including two doubles. He knocked in a tying run in the sixth with a single, and drove in the game winner in the tenth with a double. Gabby Hartnett chipped in with two singles. Charlie Root went the route for the victory. The four-game series set a new National League attendance record for a series, with 122,000 people viewing the four games.

The Cubs hosted the Philadelphia Phillies for a five-game series beginning on the 16th, and the big news of the series was Hack Wilson tying the National League home run mark of 43 set by Chuck Klein in 1929. Hack hit a two-run homer in the opener of the series, and drove in another run with a single. He knocked in two more runs in game two, and four more in game three, the last one coming on a solo homer. In the fourth game, he hit a solo homer in the seventh inning, his forty-third of the season. He drove in two more runs in the finale, on two sacrifice flies. Hack went homerless in three games against the New York Giants, but stormed the heights against the Pittsburgh Pirates on August 25th. Home run #44 was a solo shot in the seventh inning. The Chicago strongman also had 148 RBIs, just 22 short of Klein's record, and Hack still had 29 games left to play.[9]

The Chicago Cubs' 17–12 record for the month gave them a season record of 77–51, a five-game lead over New York, a six-game lead over Brooklyn, and a 6½ game lead over St. Louis. The Dodgers, who led the Cubs by two games at the end of July, lost 19 of 31 games in August. Hack Wilson had a sensational month. He slugged 13 home runs, giving him 46 for the year, and he had an unbelievable 53 RBIs, a major league record for one month. The A's still held a 6½-game lead over the Senators in the American League.

September would prove to be a bitter month for the men of McCarthy. They would lose seven of their first 11 games during the month, and 12 of their first 20, to fall out of first place. Gabby Street's high-flying Cardinals got as hot as the weather in mid-August and, after trailing by 12 games on August 9, they went on a torrid pace over the next seven weeks, winning 39 of their last 49 games. The Bruins' decline began at Wrigley Field on September 1, when they dropped a doubleheader to the Cincinnati Reds by scores of 5–0 and 2–1. George Kelly, acquired by the Cubs from Minneapolis in August rapped a single and a double in game two and scored the only run of the day for his team. They had only six other hits all day. Charlie Root pitched the Cubs to an 8–2 win in the finale. The Cubs got three runs in the first inning, sparked by Danny Taylor's triple, and added two more in the fifth on Gabby Hartnett's twenty-ninth home run of the season. On September 3, the Cubs took a 9–6 shellacking from the Pirates, with Teachout and Blake blowing a 5–2 lead in the sixth inning, when the Bucs pushed over six runs. They had one run in and two men on base, with just one out, when Blake came in for Teachout. He retired the first man to face him, walked the next two men to force in a run, then gave up a single to Brame to plate two more. The next day was a nail-biter, with the Cubs prevailing 10–7 in ten innings, thanks to Gabby Hartnett. As the Cubs trailed 6–2, the big catcher stepped to the plate with two men on base in the sixth inning and promptly unloaded his thirtieth home run of the year to cut the Buc lead to a single run. The Cubs went ahead with two in the eighth even though Hartnett was robbed of a triple on a circus catch by Lloyd Waner in center field. The Waner brothers tied the game at seven apiece in the bottom of the ninth when Lloyd doubled and came around to score on a triple by Paul. In the top of the tenth, Chicago put two men on base with one out, and Gabby Hartnett cleared the bases with a towering home run over the left field wall. The victory maintained the Bruins' lead of 4½ games over New York and St. Louis.

The Cubs blew another big opportunity on the 5th when they lost a heartbreaking 8–7 decision to Pittsburgh. Pat Malone was given a 7–1 lead after six innings, but wilted down the stretch. His relief, Bob Osborn, came in with a 7–4 lead, but was touched up for three runs in the seventh and one in the tenth. Gabby Hartnett continued his hot hitting, smashing his thirty-second home run to deep left center field, with a man on base in the fourth. With the score tied and one man out in the bottom of the tenth, Paul "Big Poison" Waner hit a line drive to right field. Kiki Cuyler tried for a one-handed catch, but the ball got by him and rolled to the wall, as the Pirate slugger rounded the bases for an inside-the-park game-winning homer. In the get-away game, another 1930 donnybrook, the Cubs came out on top, bloody but unbowed. The final score was 19–14, and the two teams pounded out 32 hits between them, with the Cubs getting 17. Four Chicago players had three hits, and three Pittsburgh players had three. Hack Wilson had two singles and his forty-seventh home run, and he drove in four runs, giving him 140 RBIs for the year. Two Cubs starters, George Kelly and Gabby Hartnett, went hitless.

During the first week of September, Woody English stroked the ball at a .379 clip, while Kiki Cuyler hit .333. Gabby Hartnett hit only .250, but hammered four home runs in seven games. Joe McCarthy took his embattled Bruins into the Ebbets Field snake pit on September 9, and they were humiliated by manager Wilbert Robinson's surprising Dodgers. "Their pitching was overpowering. Ray Phelps, Dolf Luque, and Dazzy Vance combined to hold the Windy City sluggers to just one run in three games. Phelps led off with a scintillating 3–0 shutout, pulling the Brooklyn crew to within 2½ games of the top. Babe Herman got the big blow, a home run in the fifth. Dolf Luque blanked the Cubs again, this time 6–0. A five-run first routed Root. Babe Herman had three more hits including a double. Dazzy Vance finished off Chicago's hopes in game three, fanning a National League high 13 batters, en route to a hard fought 2–1 decision. Glenn Wright's twentieth home run into the left field circus seats with Herman on base in the first inning was all the big redhead needed. A solo four-bagger by Hack Wilson kept Chicago from suffering the ignominy of a triple whitewashing."[10]

The Dodgers followed up the Chicago sweep with a four-game sweep of the Cincinnati Reds at home to move back into first place by one game over the St. Louis Cardinals. And they were hosting the Redbirds in a crucial three-game series, with just 12 games left in the season. The Cincinnati series was expensive for the Dodgers, however, as they lost their star centerfielder Johnny Frederick with a broken ankle. The Cubs, meanwhile, dropped two of four to the lowly Phillies, taking the opener 17–4, losing 7–5 and splitting a doubleheader, losing the opener 12–11, and winning the nightcap

6–4. In the opener of the twin bill, the two clubs combined for 37 base hits, 19 by Chicago. Sheriff Blake was staked to a 10–5 lead after 7½ innings, but couldn't hold it. Burt Shotton's boys ripped him for six runs in the eighth to grab an 11–10 lead. After the Cubs tied the game at 11 apiece in the top of the ninth, Lefty O'Doul, one of baseball's all-time greatest hitters, slugged a home run off Teachout to end the game. English and Heathcote had homered earlier in the game for the Bruins. Gabby Hartnett was 2-for-4 with a sacrifice. In game two, Guy Bush stopped the Cubs' slide temporarily, with a 6–4 victory, and even that wasn't easy. He had a 6–1 lead after 8½ innings, but had to withstand a three-run Philly rally in the bottom of the ninth before he could enjoy the win. Cliff Heathcote smashed another homer for Chicago, and Chuck Klein hit one for Philadelphia. Hack Wilson sent #50 soaring out of Baker Bowl to become the first National League player to hit 50 or more home runs in a single season, and just the second major leaguer to do it, behind the great Bambino.

The Brooklyn Dodgers' world came crashing down around them when the unbeatable St. Louis Cardinals roared into Ebbets Field and proceeded to dismantle the Bums in three games, by scores of 1–0 in 10 innings, 5–3, and 4–2. In the opener, "Wild Bill" Hallahan of the Cards faced off against the great Dazzy Vance and matched the Dodger ace pitch for pitch for nine innings. In the tenth, Andy High sliced a double down the right field line and came around to score the first run of the game on a looping single by Taylor Douthit. Brooklyn came right back, loading the bases with just one out, but Al Lopez bounced into a 6–4–3 double play to end it. When the Cards took game two 5–3, the two teams were deadlocked at the top of the league. In the finale, former Dodger pitcher Burleigh Grimes scuttled his old teammates 4–2, putting the Brooks in a position from which they never recovered. They lost five of the last seven games to finish fourth, six games out.

The Chicago Cubs moved into Boston and were humbled by Bill McKechnie's Braves 3–2. Bob Smith beat Jess Petty in a pitchers duel. The Cubs were held to just six hits by the former infielder. For the week, only Hack Wilson at .400 and George Kelly at .333 hit with any authority. Gabby Hartnett batted .273 with no extra base hits. The loss dropped Chicago three games behind St. Louis, with just six games remaining in the season. To the Cubs' credit, they regrouped and ran off a six-game winning streak, but the Cardinals won five of their last six to take the flag by two games. The Cubs won the second game of the Boston series, 4–2, behind Pat Malone's nineteenth victory of the season. The game was tied at 2–2 after eight innings, but Gabby Hartnett blasted his thirty-fourth home run in the ninth inning, with Cliff Heathcote on base, to win the game. In the get-away game, Guy Bush stopped the Beaneaters 6–2 behind Hack Wilson's fifty-third homer of the season. Hack also added to his major league RBI record, by driving in two men to give him 182 on the season. In the opener of the final series of the year, at home against Cincinnati, Pat Malone won his twentieth victory of the season, 4–3. Hartnett had a single and a home run for the Cubs. The next day, Chicago won again, this time by a 7–5 score, with Sheriff Blake doing the honors. Hack Wilson hit #54 and drove in three more runs. The stocky center fielder put two more balls out of the park the next day before going homer-less in the finale. The St. Louis Cardinals ended the season in a rush, clobbering Philadelphia 15–7 on the 22nd, then coming back to manhandle them again, 19–16. The two teams combined for 75 hits in two games. Gabby Street's marauders moved on to Pittsburgh where they clinched the pennant with 9–0 and 10–5 wins over the Bucs.

It was a disappointing finish to an exciting season for the Cubs and manager Joe McCarthy. The team was a prohibitive favorite to repeat as National League champions, and McCarthy took the blame for the failure from owner William Wrigley Jr. He was replaced as manager by Rogers Hornsby with four games remaining in the season. Hack Wilson ended his season in a blaze of glory, smashing three home runs in the last three games, sending the Wrigley Field faithful into a frenzy. He finished the year with 56 home runs and a major league record 191 RBIs. According to Cincinnati catcher Clyde Sukeforth, "Hack really hit 57 home runs. He hit one up in the Crosley Field seats so hard that it bounced right back. The umpire figured it must have hit the screen. I was in the Reds' bullpen, and we didn't say a word."[11]

One of the oddities of the season, pointed out by researcher Walt Wilson, and reported by Cliff Kachline, was that it took 37 innings to finish one game between the Cubs and the Philadelphia Phillies. The Cubs-Phillies game of May 5 was rained out after one inning. The makeup game on August 16 ended in an 11-inning 3–3 tie. Another attempt to play the game to a conclusion three days later resulted in another tie, this one 6–6 in 16 innings. The next day, in their fourth attempt to reach a decision, the Phillies defeated the Cubs 10–8.[12]

In the American League, the Philadelphia Athletics coasted to the pennant, with an eight-game bulge over the Washington Senators. The New York Yankees finished 16 games back. The World Series matched the powerful Connie Mack A's against the up-and-coming St. Louis Cardinals. McKechnie's team, which would gradually evolve into the hell-for-leather "Gashouse Gang" a year later, still gave Philadelphia all they could handle. Lefty Grove, baseball's legendary southpaw, outpitched Burleigh Grimes in the opener before 32,295 excited fans in the City of Brotherly Love. The final score was 4–2 and was sparked by home runs off the bats of Al Simmons and Mickey Cochrane. The A's took game two behind George Earnshaw, before Wild Bill Hallahan slowed their momentum with a scrambling 5–0 shutout. After the Cardinals evened the series at two games apiece with a 3–1 win in game four, Philadelphia won the next two by scores of 2–0 and 7–1 to claim the world championship. Lefty Grove, who lost game four to Jesse Haines, relieved Earnshaw in the eighth inning of game five with the game still scoreless, and came away the winner when Jimmie Foxx hit a long, two-run homer into the left field seats in the ninth. Earnshaw closed out the series two days later with a complete game five-hitter. Al Simmons led all hitters with a .364 average.[13]

The individual league batting titles were won by Bill Terry, who hit .401, and Al Simmons, who hit .381. Terry is the last National League hitter to hit .400. Ted Williams, who would hit .406 in 1941, is the last American Leaguer to reach that rarefied level. Hack Wilson with 56 homers and Babe Ruth with 49 led the sluggers. The top pitchers were Pat Malone at 20–9 and Lefty Grove at 28–5. The Chicago Cubs had six .300 hitters led by Riggs "Old Hoss" Stephenson (.367), Hack Wilson (.356), and Kiki Cuyler (.355). Woody English had a career season, batting .335 with 36 doubles, 17 triples, and 14 home runs. Gabby Hartnett had his greatest season as a major leaguer, batting .339 with 37 home runs and 122 RBIs. And he showed his newfound stamina by swatting the ball at a .328 clip from August 1 through the end of the season, with 14 home runs in 198 at-bats. "Old Tomato Face" also dominated the defensive statistics for major league catchers. He led all National League catchers in putouts, assists, and fielding percentage, and he allowed only 47 stolen bases against a league average of 60. Mickey Cochrane led the American League in putouts, assists, and fielding average, but he and Bill Dickey were below average in defending against stolen bases, allowing 79 and 82 stolen bases, against a league average of 75. All three members of the Chicago outfield had driven in more than 100 runs in 1929; but in 1930,

Hack Wilson's 191 RBIs in 1930 is still the major league record.

Stephenson drove in only 68 in spite of his lofty batting average. When he was questioned about it, he said, "I batted behind Wilson. He cleaned the sacks and didn't leave any for me."[14]

Money was always a problem — or an incentive — for Gabby and the other major league players. In addition to his salary, Gabby also picked up $2,000 as his share of the Cubs second-place finish money and $1,235 as the winners' share of the Chicago City Series, won by the Cubs over the White Sox, four games to two. And he signed a new contract for $20,000, a veritable fortune in the depression year of 1931. Gabby was not a miser, however. He was very generous with his money, especially where his family was concerned. Sweetie Hartnett went into business for himself with a loan from Gabby. He started the first tire recapping business in Chicago and eventually became affiliated with British Petroleum in the fuel and oil business. He was a very successful businessman in Chicago and, in later years, was Gabby's frequent golfing companion. After Gabby died in 1972, Sweetie moved to Portland, Oregon, where his son lived.

Before one of the City Series games in Comiskey Park, Gabby had his picture taken with Al Capone and his son, "Sonny," and the photographer who recorded the event sent wire-photos of it to newspapers from New York to California. The next day, Gabby got a telegram from Baseball Commissioner Kenesaw Mountain Landis that read, "You are no longer allowed to have your picture taken with Al Capone." The fun-loving backstop wired the commissioner right back with the tongue-in-cheek message, "OK, but if you don't want me to have my picture taken with Al Capone, you tell him."[15]

Martha hated that photograph with a passion. It seemed to her the press always used that photo whenever they ran a story about Gabby.

After the City Series ended, Gabby was recruited by Kiki Cuyler to join him, Cliff Heathcote, and Hack Wilson on a vaudeville tour, a popular off-season venture for professional athletes. The vaudeville gig had been going on for 50 years or more and had attracted such luminaries as Mike "King" Kelly of the old Chicago White Stockings, heavyweight boxing champions John L. Sullivan and Jack Dempsey, and Babe Ruth. The Chicago Cubs foursome toured the country advertised as a singing group, although they only "mouthed" the words, with the actual singers standing backstage. The four teammates had a great time, performing, mingling with their public, and partying.

In another sporting venue, Bobby Jones, the precocious golfing prodigy, won his fourth major golf title of the year on September 28 by soundly thrashing Gene Homan 8 and 7 at the Merion Cricket Club in Ardmore, Pennsylvania, to win the National Amateur championship. At 28 years of

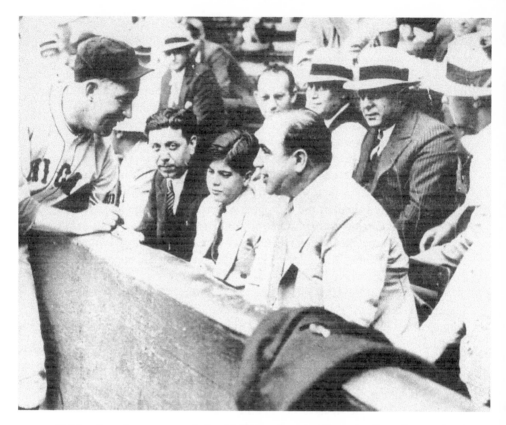

Gabby signed an autograph for Al Capone's son, Albert, in Comiskey Park in 1931. Albert's infamous father is seated at right center.

age, he was the first man to hold all four major titles at the same time. He was also the American Open champion as well as the British Amateur and British Open champion. Three months later, he announced his retirement from competition to enter the motion picture industry.[16]

Other news around the country included the invention of radar, which was announced by the U.S. Navy and described as being able to detect approaching vessels even in fog or darkness. In Washington, DC, President Hoover's National Commission on Law Observance and Enforcement reported that prohibition was a failure. It said "that controlling the production and distribution of liquor has failed and that the law cannot be enforced."[17]

The Hornsby era began in earnest in the spring of 1931. The team was basically the same team that had represented Chicago the previous two years, but Wrigley and Veeck were hoping that, with Hornsby healthy again, they could recapture the title they lost in 1930. If they did, they would have to do it with a less-powerful offense because the baseball had been changed once again. "It wasn't the same ball. It had been deadened with the introduction of the cushion cork center and a thicker cover. Also, to allow the pitchers a stronger grip, crucial in the delivery of breaking pitches, the seams were raised."[18]

Gabby Hartnett was at the peak of his career in 1931, and after his sensational season the previous year, he was in demand by press agents for publicity photos during spring training. His rugged good looks and his Irish smile came across beautifully on film, so he was often photographed in the company of young Hollywood starlets like Arleen Judge and Rochelle Hudson. He also continued to fine-tune his golf game on Wrigley's handsomely groomed 18-hole course.

The big catcher picked up where he left off in September, unleasing a devastating pyrotechnic display in exhibition games. One of his most impressive games was played against the Los Angeles Angels in Wrigley Field on March 15. The Cubbies pounded Jack Lelivelt's club by the score of 25–6. Kiki Cuyler had five hits in seven at-bats, while Gabby smashed two home runs and drove six runners across the plate.

When the season opened in Chicago on April 14, "Rajah" had his team ready. The Pittsburgh Pirates came to town and were welcomed by 43,000 Cubs fanatics. They were also welcomed by Charlie Root and Gabby Hartnett who gave them a lesson in how the game should be played. Root tossed a four-hitter at Jewel Ens' team, setting them down with two runs, while fanning five. Hartnett had a big day, going 2-for-4, with two runs scored and two assists. He put his team on the board first by slamming a two-run homer over the bleachers in left-center field in the bottom of the second. In the top of the third, he caught Rollie Hemsley napping on second base and picked him off with a bullet to Hornsby. Five innings later, after the Bucs had narrowed the lead to 3–2, Hartnett doubled to drive in Wilson who had walked, and later came across the plate himself. The final score was 6–2. Unfortunately a few fans created incidents that dampened the victory celebration. Hack Wilson, who had misjudged two fly balls in the 1929 World Series, was bombarded with lemons his first time at bat. And Hornsby, who was not generally liked, received more than his share of boos.[19]

Rogers Hornsby's reign as manager of the Chicago Cubs was destined to last less than two years. There were already rumors of dissension in the club, even before the first ball was thrown in the '31 season. Hornsby and Hack Wilson clashed constantly, as the teetotaling manager was infuriated by the off-field antics of his most dangerous hitter. He also crossed swords with Kiki Cuyler and Charlie Root. Hornsby was "blunt, crude, sometimes

Gabby posed with Hollywood starlets Rochelle Hudson and Arlene Judge at Avalon in 1931. (Roy Hartnett)

arrogant, and as diplomatic as a sawed-off shotgun. Impatient and sarcastic to the nth degree, he expected perfection and nothing less. He berated players for drinking and smoking. With his razor tongue, he alienated nearly every player on the club."[20]

The Cubbies made it two in a row on the 16th, edging the Pirates 6–5 behind former Boston Braves hurler Bob Smith, who came to Chicago in an off-season trade. Hornsby's cohorts jumped out to a 5–0 lead after three innings, and barely held off a late charge by the Bucs. Hartnett was at it again in this game. He hit a tremendous drive to center field in the third inning that bounced off the scoreboard more than 400 feet from home plate. The big catcher coasted into third base as Wilson and Stephenson scored. Hornsby's homer in the fifth was the last Cubs score of the day. The National League champion St. Louis Cardinals visited the Friendly Confines next, and they suffered the same fate as Pittsburgh. Charlie Root held Gabby Street's team to six hits and beat them easily 4–1. Woody English had two hits for the Cubs. Hartnett went 1-for-3 with a stolen base and a sacrifice. The Cards got even the next day when Burleigh Grimes outpitched Bob Smith 3–2. Johnny Moore had three hits for the Cubs, and Les Bell had two. Hartnett was hitless in three trips to the plate, but had an assist and was on the tag end of a double play from Hack Wilson.

Root racked up win #3 six days later, taking the Cincinnati Reds to task, 3–1. It was another six-hitter for the Chicago ace, who struck out four and walked only one. Rogers Hornsby had three singles to lead his team, and three other players had two hits each. Gabby Hartnett was 1-for-3 with a walk and a stolen base. He also tossed out two base runners, one of which was a "strike 'em out, throw 'em out" double play. According to one of his teammates, Gabby dared base runners to try to steal on him. The Bruins won again on the 29th, beating the Redlegs by another 3–1 count. Big Ed Baecht scattered 11 base hits and three walks while outdueling Red Lucas. Baecht would see action in parts of six major league seasons and retire with a career record of 5–6, including 2–4 in '31. On this day, he was at his best and was supported by Riggs Stephenson, who had a single and a double.

The same day, in Cleveland, Ohio, 25-game winner Wes Ferrell threw a no-hit game at the St. Louis Browns, winning 9–0. The big 6'2", 195-pound fireballer struck out eight and walked three in his gem. He also cracked a double and a home run, driving in four runs. The home run was the first of nine he would hit during the year, a major league record. His career total of 38 home runs is still the major league record for a pitcher.

The Chicago Cubs boasted an 8–3 record for April, putting them in a first-place tie with St. Louis. The biggest news story of the month was the wet weather that greeted the Cubs in every city. They encountered six rainouts in the last 10 scheduled dates. They had two off-days in both Pittsburgh and Cincinnati, one in St. Louis, and one in Chicago. Their April record would be the high-water mark of the year. The rest of the year would be lackluster. Rogers Hornsby's charges could never gain momentum. They always seemed to follow a winning streak with a losing streak. A mid-May eastern road trip was a disaster, as they dropped series to Boston, Philadelphia, and Brooklyn. Single wins over the Braves and Phils were all they could show for their trouble. They lost their only encounter with the Dodgers, when Bob Smith was raked for four runs in the fourth inning, wiping out an early 4–1 Chicago lead. "Pea Ridge" Day, the acclaimed hog-calling champion of Arkansas, picked up the victory. They did finish the month with a five-game winning streak, four of them over Pittsburgh, the last one being a slick 5–0 whitewashing by Bob Smith. A Wrigley Field gathering of 30,000 delighted home fans cheered Smith's every pitch, as the right-hander limited the Bucs to three base runners, two hits, and one walk. Woody English, the Cubs' .300-hitting shortstop, cracked three hits, including a double, and scored two runs. Moore and Grimm each had a double and a single. The victory left Chicago in third place, three games behind the Redbirds. Hornsby made one personnel change in May. He recalled Billy Jurges, the 23-year-old slick-fielding shortstop from Louisville, to fill in for third baseman Les Bell, who was injured.

Brooklyn moved into the Friendly Confines in early June, bent on improving their 19–20 record. Ray Phelps toed the rubber for Wilbert Robinson's team while Pat Malone was Hornsby's choice. The game bounced back and forth, with first the Dodgers, then the Cubs, taking the lead. A 4–4 game after six innings turned into a 6–4 Cubs lead after eight, as the Windy City boys unleashed a four-hit attack, good for two runs. But the Bums weren't done. In the top of the ninth, Wally Gilbert hit a two-run triple and scored minutes later on a sacrifice fly by Babe Herman, sending the Hornsby-men to a crushing defeat. Jurges, Grimm, and Cuyler had two hits for the Cubs. Hartnett was 1-for-3 with a walk and two runs scored. The Bruins, who outhit their opponents, 12 to nine, hit into four double plays. One of the biggest distractions for the Cubs players during the year was the conflict between Hornsby and Hack Wilson. The fun-loving Wilson slumped at the plate under the constant harassing from Hornsby, seeing action in only 117 games, with 360 at-bats. His batting average dropped from .356 in 1930 to .261, his home runs went from 56 to 13, and his RBIs tailed off from 190 to 61. He was suspended for violating the team curfew, and didn't play after September 6.

Bob Smith tossed another gem on June 7, whipping John McGraw's Giants 5–1, thanks to a four-run rally in the bottom of the eighth. Ten thousand hardy souls braved the wintry conditions to watch the New Yorkers drop their seventh game in nine starts and fall from first place to a second-place tie with the Cubs in the tight National League race. Grimm opened the big inning with a ringing double to left center field. Smith bunted and reached on a fielder's choice. Kiki Cuyler brought Grimm home with the tie-breaking run with a single to left. After English bunted into a force play at third and Hornsby was retired on a fly ball to center field, Stephenson doubled to right for one run, Johnny Moore beat out an infield hit for another run, and the fourth run came across when Hughie Critz threw wild trying to get English at the plate.[21]

The Chicago Cubs had a team batting average of .301 in early June, the only National League team over .300, and they led the league with 221 runs scored. But their erratic pitching was keeping them from dominating the standings. They had four players batting over .345, but only Les Sweetland at 5–0 and Guy Bush at 3–1 had pitched consistently good ball. The team's

15–14 record in June left them struggling in third place, 5½ games behind the St. Louis Cardinals. One of their most impressive games was played on June 30, when they battered the lowly Phils 14–3. Pat Malone was the beneficiary of a 19-hit attack led by himself, Hornsby, and Danny Taylor, with three hits each. Hornsby's output included two home runs and seven RBIs. Gabby Hartnett was 1-for-5.

July was another humdrum month for Chicago, who had a mediocre 17–15 record. They did slip past New York into second place, but they trailed the red-hot Redbirds by 8½ games. Gabby Street's Gashouse Gang went 21–13 in July, and they would turn on the afterburners down the stretch, winning 38 of their last 54 games, to win the National League title by 13 games. The Fourth of July doubleheader was a typical Chicago Cubs performance. In the morning half of the AM-PM twin bill, Charlie Root beat Benny Frey in a classic pitchers duel, blanking the Reds on five hits and driving in the only run of the game himself. Gabby Hartnett doubled in the seventh inning and came around to score on a single by Root. In game two, Guy Bush was hammered for six runs and 14 base hits by the last-place Reds, who won easily 6–2. The loss dropped the Bruins into fourth place, 5½ games out. One of the more humorous incidents of the month took place on July 31 in Babe Ruth's Boston hotel room. The Bambino, who was entertaining some friends, smelled smoke, and when he looked out the window, he saw an awning on fire two floors below. Racing to the bathroom, he filled a pitcher with water and poured it out the window, on the fire below. He repeated this action several times until the fire was out. "The blaze attracted many passersby who gave the Babe a lusty cheer. 'I only hope,' said the Babe, 'that none of you guys were throwing cigar butts out my window.' 'You were the only one smoking in this room,' Ruffing pointed out. 'Well,' Babe thoughtfully replied, 'then let's say no more about it.'"[22]

Cubs President Bill Veeck, in an effort to strengthen the club for a possible stretch run, purchased the contract of second baseman Billy Herman from the Louisville Colonels of the American Association, where he was hitting a torrid .350. The Cubs gave Louisville $50,000 and two players. In addition, they had to send Billy Jurges to the Colonels for the last two months of the season. Herman's debut with Chicago was memorable. "Batting against Cincinnati Reds hurler, Si Johnson, Billy dug into the batters box. Johnson threw, and Bill took a tremendous swing. The ball hit the ground in back of the plate and, with a wicked reverse english, bounced straight back, smacking Billy right on the head. So a sterling career started out in the most ignominious way possible. Billy Herman was carried off the field on a stretcher — knocked out cold by his own foul ball!"[23] Herman recovered nicely from his first exposure to major league pitching and finished the season batting .327 in 27 games. He would go on to play 15 years in the big time and retire with a career batting average of .304.

Billy Herman was a 22-year-old impressionable kid at the time, and he was in awe of the Cubs pitching staff. "It was a bad club to be breaking in with, because of that pitching staff. Biggest bunch of head-hunters you ever saw. Charlie Root. Off the field, a very quiet man. Out on that mound, he was mean. So was Pat Malone. And so was Lon Warneke. Guy Bush too. That was a mean staff. Every time they'd throw at a hitter, naturally somebody on our club would get it right back. I think I must've had my tail in the batters box as often as my feet. But I was young and agile then, and it didn't bother me. Not much."[24]

Rogers Hornsby's charges entered September without much hope of catching the St. Louis Cardinals, who now owned a 10-game lead over New York and a 14-game lead over Chicago. The American League race was also a runaway, with Connie Mack's powerful juggernaut opening up a 15½ game lead over the Washington Senators. Their 90–35 record was one of the best records in modern times and put them in position to challenge the record of the 1927 New York Yankees who won 110 games. The major league record belonged to the 1906 Chicago Cubs who won 116 games.

The Cubs' season continued on a downward spiral when they dropped a Labor Day doubleheader to the eighth-place Reds by scores of 7–4 and 8–4. Charlie Root and Guy Bush were both routed by the revitalized Cincinnatians, who pounded out 12 hits in each game, led by shortstop Leo Durocher, who went 6-for-8 with three doubles and four RBIs. Rookie Billy Herman had four hits for the Cubbies, and Vince Barton and Charlie Grimm had three each. Hartnett was just 1-for-6 and had one assist on a strikeout double play. Chicago lost eight games in a row at the beginning of September, dropping them 17½ games behind St. Louis. But instead of just playing out the string, Hornsby's cohorts played their best ball of the year over the last three weeks of the season. It was too little, too late, but it was something to build on for next year. On the 10th of the month, Pat Malone coasted to a 17–4 win over the Philadelphia Phillies in the Friendly Confines. Gabby Hartnett and Kiki Cuyler led the hit parade with four hits each. "Old Tomato Face" rapped two singles, a double, and a home run, good for six RBIs. He also cut down one runner trying to steal. Malone chipped in with a single and a fifth-inning home run to aid his own cause. Two days later, Johnny Welch, recently recalled from the Reading club of the International League, stopped the Phils on seven hits, winning 5–2, to sweep the three-game series. The only runs off Welch came in the ninth inning on a walk, a triple, and a double, with no outs; but the 24-year-old southpaw settled down and retired the last three men to end the game.

The next day, they swept a doubleheader from the Boston Braves. Charlie Root was not at his best in the opener, but his offense presented him with an 11–7 victory, with manager Rogers Hornsby giving him the biggest present of all. After the Braves tied the score at 7-all in the top of the ninth inning, Hornsby, batting for Rollie Hemsley in the bottom of the eleventh, with two men out and the bases loaded, smashed a grand-slam home run into the right field seats, sending the 33,000 fans into a wild celebration. Game two was much quieter, as Guy Bush threw a one-hitter at the Beaneaters, winning easily 8–1. Gabby Hartnett paced the Chicago barrage with a single, a double, and three RBIs. Les Bell's two-run homer in the first gave the Cubs a lead they never relinquished. On the 17th, they ran their winning streak to eight games, with a 4–3 squeaker over the Brooklyn Dodgers. The Cubs had a 3–1 lead after eight innings, but the never-say-die Bums pushed across two runs in the ninth to deadlock the game. Then in the bottom of the ninth, Hornsby's cohorts came back. Woody English was hit by a pitch, went to second on a sacrifice, and moved over to third when "Sloppy" Thurston walked two men. Then, with two out and the bases loaded, Danny Taylor slapped a single to left field to plate the winning run. Hartnett was 1-for-3 and gunned down two would-be base stealers. The next day, the streak was history, as a 6'2" rawboned right-handed flamethrower with the rhythmic name of Van Lingle Mungo, outpitched Charlie Root 3–2. Lefty O'Doul and Babe Herman were all the offense Mungo needed. In the first inning, O'Doul walked and Herman lifted a home run into the right field seats. Then, after the Cubs had tied the game in the fourth, the Dodgers came right back with the game winner. O'Doul lined a one-out double to left center field in the fifth, and Brooklyn's Babe rescued him with a single to left field. Gabby Hartnett had a double in three trips to the plate and racked up two more assists. Chicago got back on the right track two days later, taking the Dodgers to task by the score of 9–1. Guy Bush enjoyed a breather for a change, as his teammates raked Dazzy Vance and a reliever for 12 base hits. The Dodger ace, who was usually poison to the Windy City boys, didn't have it on this day. Woody English had a single, a double, and a walk off Vance, then added a single and a triple off Cy Moore. Billy Herman, the exciting new Cubs second baseman, added three singles to the Chicago attack. Danny Taylor and Brooklyn's Johnny Frederick homered. Hartnett was a spectator to the proceedings, drawing the collar in three trips to the plate.

The Chicago Cubs closed out their season with a doubleheader victory over the Pittsburgh Pirates, 3–1 and 8–4. The two wins gave Hornsby's team 13 wins against only two losses after September 9. Charlie Root got the ball rolling for the Cubbies in game one, tossing five innings before turning the

ball over to Bob Smith. Danny Taylor's home run into the right field bleachers in the third, and Charlie Grimm's circuit clout off the top of the right
field screen in the fifth, gave Root his winning margin. Taylor added another
homer in the second game, putting a ball over the right field screen in the
second inning. The Pirates got to Bush for three runs in the third and, with
the score 3–2 in Pittsburgh's favor after five innings, Bush turned the ball
over to Malone. He was touched up for a run in the top of the seventh, but
the Cubs turned the game around in the bottom of the inning. A single and
two walks loaded the bases for Cuyler, who doubled to right field to drive
in two runs, tying the game at 4-all. A walk to Bell loaded the bases again,
and Vince Barton promptly unloaded them with a grand-slam home run to
right field, his thirteenth of the year. The season ended on a happy note, but
it was far from a happy season. The turmoil in the Chicago clubhouse,
brought on by manager Rogers Hornsby, probably contributed to the poor
showing of a team that was supposed to challenge for the pennant, but who
struggled all year just to keep their heads above water.

The St. Louis Cardinals coasted to the pennant, winning 101 games
against 53 losses, for a 13-game bulge over the New York Giants and a 17-
game spread over the Chicago Cubs. The Philadelphia Athletics won the
American League pennant going away, their 107–45 record leaving the New
York Yankees gasping for breath, 13½ games behind. Both teams were geared
up for the World Series, although Connie Mack's bombers appeared to have
too much firepower for St. Louis. The A's were installed as heavy favorites
by the baseball experts, and they were envisioning a repeat of their 1930 victory, but Gabby Street's battling Redbirds had a surprise in store for them
and for the entire baseball world. They had, after all, won 101 games during
the season, and had a well-balanced attack that led the league in fielding,
and was second in runs scored and earned-run-average (ERA). And their
fleet-footed runners swiped 114 bases during the season compared to 27 for
Philadelphia.

The two teams split the first six World Series games, with Lefty Grove
winning two games, and Wild Bill Hallahan and George Earnshaw each
tossing shutouts, but the pitching hero of the series was the Cardinals' 38-
year-old spitball artist Burleigh Grimes, who won two games, including a
4–2 decision in game seven. Pepper Martin, "The Wild Horse of the Osage,"
was the Redbirds' offensive sparkplug, batting a torrid .500 with 12 base hits
and generally causing chaos on the bases. He personally drove the Athletics'
Mickey Cochrane crazy, swiping five bases off the future Hall of Fame
catcher.[25]

The regular season batting champions were Chick Hafey of St. Louis
at .349 and Al Simmons at .390. Chuck Klein of the Phillies with 31 homers

and Babe Ruth with 46 led the sluggers. And Bill Hallahan (19–9) and Lefty Grove with a sensational 31–4 record and a barely visible 2.06 ERA topped the pitchers. Grove's performance was one of the greatest pitching feats in baseball history, coming in a year when the league ERA was a lofty 4.38. The Chicago Cubs were led at bat by Charlie Grimm and Rogers Hornsby with averages of .331 each, Kiki Cuyler at .330, and Riggs Stephenson and Woody English at .319. English had set a record for the most runs scored by a shortstop, with 152 in 1930. And over the three-year period from 1929 through 1931, he scored 400 runs, another record for shortstops. Hornsby's 16 home runs led the sluggers. And Charlie Root (17–14), Guy Bush (16–8), Pat Malone (16–9), and Bob Smith (15–12) were the top pitchers. Gabby Hartnett batted .282 with 70 RBIs in 117 games and once again played solid defense. He permitted only 49 stolen bases against a league average of 58. His American League counterparts gave up 66 and 71 stolen bases, respectively, against a league average of 78. Both American League catchers had outstanding years with the bat, however. Cochrane hit .349 with 17 homers and 89 RBIs in 122 games, while Dickey came in with a .327 average and 78 RBIs in 130 games.

At the same time the World Series was being played, the Chicago Cubs and Chicago White Sox were battling it out for the supremacy of the Windy City. Donnie Bush's Pale Hose, who finished in last place in the American League, 51½ games behind the A's, beat Hornsby's Cubbies in seven games. Red Faber set the tone for the series when he blanked the Cubs 9–0 in game one. Guy Bush returned the favor in game two, winning 1–0. The Cubs won game three 2–1, lost games four and five by scores of 4–3 and 13–6, took game six 3–2, and were finally beaten in game seven 6–0.[26]

Gabby Hartnett was a full-fledged celebrity by this time, a 10-year big-league veteran recognized as one of baseball's greatest catchers. He supplemented his income by permitting his name to be used on various products, such as baseball bats and gloves. The Wilson Company, manufacturers of sporting goods, sold the Gabby Hartnett model 508 catcher's mitt, complete with a facsimile signature of Gabby, for $16.00. The full-page magazine ads, which included his photo and biography, stated the mitt was "endorsed by the peppery catcher of the Chicago Cubs." It also said the mitt, which fit the left hand only, was made from the "finest select cowhide."

By now Gabby and Martha were living in their own house at 2638 Albion Avenue in the Rogers Park section of Chicago, thanks to the generosity of Hack Wilson, according to their daughter Sheila. "They wanted to buy the house. My mother of course wanted it, and my Dad wanted it right away and they needed a few bucks for a down payment, and they didn't have it, because in those days you had to wait to get a few dollars together.

And they were in the Edgewater Beach Hotel in Chicago, riding down in the elevator with Hack Wilson. And Hack said to my mother, 'What's the matter, Martha? You look kind of glum.' She told him, 'I need x-number of dollars to put down on the house.' So he just pulled a wad of bills out of his pocket, peeled off the money and said, 'Pay me back when you get it.'

"The house was a large two-story house with a large living room, dining room, and kitchen on the first floor, and four bedrooms on the second floor. The basement was unfinished, but Dad had a room down there with pictures and trophies all over the place. That's where he used to play cards with his friends.

"We went to church at St. Timothy's Roman Catholic Church on North Washtenaw Street. Dad went to confession every Saturday and to Mass every Sunday. It was a ritual with him. Mom, who I think was brought up Lutheran, converted to Roman Catholicism after Bud was born."[27]

Gabby with his mother Nell and his 1-year-old son Bud. (Sheila Hartnett Hornof)

Gabby's mother Nell came to Chicago in the fall to see her son and her two-year-old grandson Bud, who had fond memories of her. "We lived in a two-story house, and one day I climbed to the top of a ladder that was leaning against the side of the house. Grandma came right up behind me and dragged me down. She wasn't very big — a tiny lady — but she was as tough as nails."[28]

Al Capone was back in the clutches of the law again in 1931, after being indicted for income tax evasion in the spring of the year. The trial took place in October, and Capone was found guilty and sentenced to 11 years in prison plus $80,000 in fines and court costs. The Chicago gangster would spend two years in the federal penitentiary in Atlanta, then be moved to Alcatraz, where he would spend another five years in cell #85. He would eventually be pardoned in January 1939 and spend his remaining days at his palatial estate in Miami Beach. He would die there from the effects of syphilis on January 25, 1947.[29]

8

The World Series — and
Gabby Plays, 1932–1933

The tumultuous times that defined the Hornsby era continued into the 1932 season. Dissension was a regular visitor to the Chicago locker room. And bad luck stalked the team from day one. Billy Herman, who was beginning his first full year under the hard-boiled skipper, was one of the players critical of him: "He was all business. You couldn't smoke or even drink a soda in the clubhouse or read a paper or anything like that. If you were a rookie, he wouldn't talk to you. Never say hello. The only time you'd hear his voice with your name in it was when you did something wrong, and then you'd hear it loud and clear."[1] Hack Wilson, Chicago's slugging center fielder, who had as much fun off the field as on it, was one of the main targets of Hornsby's wrath in 1931. The manager finally benched his star in September, then traded him to the St. Louis Cardinals for pitcher Burleigh Grimes.

The entire Chicago Cubs organization was thrown into mourning on January 26 with the news that owner William Wrigley had passed away from a stroke in Phoenix, Arizona. The 70-year-old Wrigley left a $50 million estate, including the Cubs. His son, Philip, assumed control of the baseball team, although President William Veeck made most of the baseball decisions. The change in ownership was not good news for Rogers Hornsby, who was favored by William Wrigley, but was not popular with Veeck.[2]

The Chicago Cubs advance guard, consisting of pitchers, catchers, and rookies, arrived at Avalon on February 16 and were met by Hornsby and his coaching staff, who put them through a series of torturous conditioning drills to prepare them for the long season. The first few days of drills had to be held in the gymnasium because a constant rain had made the new practice diamond unplayable. Players in the advance guard included the 1931

159

rookie sensations, Billy Herman and Billy Jurges, plus rookie infielder Stan Hack, who was called "Smiling Stan" because he had a permanent grin affixed to his face. Gabby Hartnett was also in the group. He was accompanied to Catalina by his wife Martha and son Bud.

John McGraw and his New York Giants also trained in California in 1932, using Washington Park, the home of the Pacific Coast League Los Angeles Angels. "The weather was good and the conditions under which the Giants trained was perfect. They beat the Los Angeles club, the Cubs, and the Pirates, whose base was at Paso Robles, north of L.A. The newspapermen boldly predicted the Giants would overthrow the Cardinals, pennant winners for two years and now champions of the world. The schedule kept the Giants busy, but took them to pleasant places. They visited Catalina for Saturday and Sunday games with the Cubs, and after the Saturday game there was a barbecue at William Wrigley's Center Ranch and later a dance at the casino in Avalon."[3]

Hornsby, who was one of the game's celebrated sore losers, drove his team hard in Catalina. He was still testy over their sorry performance in 1931 and was determined not to let it happen again. He was constantly at odds with the press and usually responded sarcastically when interviewed, such as his comment to a reporter who suggested the Cubs had a strong bench: "I don't care what kind of bench I've got. A carpenter can give me a good bench."[4]

While the Chicago Cubs and other major league teams were preparing for the new baseball season, the country was shocked by events taking place in New Jersey. Charles A. Lindbergh's son, two-year-old Charles A. Lindbergh Jr. was taken from his crib at the family home in Hopewell on March 1, and held for ransom. The Lindbergh's complied with the $50,000 ransom demand, but the baby was never returned. His body was found in nearby woods two months later. The trail of evidence led to a Bronx carpenter named Bruno Richard Hauptmann, and he was convicted of the crime on September 18, 1934. He died in the electric chair in Sing Sing Prison in 1936.[5]

Early in March, the Cubs traveled to Los Angeles for the first game of a six-game series against the New York Giants. The schedule called for the Cubs to follow the Giants series with two games against the Portland Beavers, then move up the coast to do battle with the San Francisco Seals, the Oakland Oaks, and the Pittsburgh Pirates. John McGraw's charges won the series from the Cubs, five games to three. The Bruins took game six by a score of 11–5, pounding Carl Hubbell for eight runs in five innings. Gabby Hartnett hit a tremendous home run off the New York screwball ace, sending a drive across the street beyond the left field fence. The Giants closed out the series by winning the last two games. They beat rookie Lon Warneke 8–7, scoring four runs in the bottom of the ninth before two outs could be made. In the finale, they jumped on Charlie Root for three runs in the first inning and won 5–4. Woody English hurt his finger on March 27, but the injury was not considered serious until April 9, when it was discovered that the joint was broken. Billy Jurges was moved to shortstop, and did such a good job there that when English returned on May 6, he took over third base.

The baseball experts picked the Cardinals and Yankees to win the titles in their respective leagues. St. Louis was considered the cream of the crop in the Senior Circuit, with strong pitching, good hitting, and a well-balanced defense. The Giants were picked for second place

Charlie Root won 201 games for Chicago over a 17-year career.

because their pitching was suspect. And the Cubs were picked for third because it was felt they lacked power. Brooklyn was slotted in at #4 and Pittsburgh #5. In the Junior Circuit, the experts accurately picked the first four positions: New York, Philadelphia, Washington, and Cleveland. The choice of the Yankees was based on Philadelphia going into a decline rather than on New York improving.

Opening day found Hornsby and his charges in Cincinnati to tangle with the cellar-dwelling Redlegs. Charlie Root was on the mound for the Cubs, facing Si Johnson, a workhorse who had the misfortune of pitching for the worst teams ever to represent major league franchises. Dan Howley's team shocked the Windy City boys by scoring four runs in the bottom of the ninth, winning the game 5–4. Root was sailing along with a 4–1 lead after eight innings, when things went sour. With two men on base and no outs, Root tried to stop a line drive with his hand, getting nothing but a bruise, and having to depart in favor of Guy Bush. A strikeout followed by two doubles ended the game, as 26,000 stunned Cincinnati fans screamed with delight. In the American League, Joe McCarthy's New York Bombers visited Philadephia and routed their hosts 12–6 behind a five-home run outburst. Babe Ruth and Sammy Byrd had two homers each and Lou Gehrig had one. Lefty Gomez got the decision over George Earnshaw.

Pat Malone changed the scenario the next day by tossing a complete game six-hitter, winning 3–2. Unfortunately, the lowly Reds bit their keepers again in game three, hammering Bob Smith for five runs in the opening stanza, and coasting to a 5–3 victory behind Red Lucas. Rookie Lon Warneke, the "Arkansas Hummingbird," on his way to a brilliant 22–6 season, allowed his team to leave town with a split in the series by scattering eight hits and winning 6–2. "Old Hoss" Stephenson was the big gun for manager Hornsby, ripping three doubles and setting up Charlie Grimm for three runs-batted-in (RBIs). The Chicago Cubs next visited the National League champion St. Louis Cardinals, hoping to recover from their early season malaise. Guy Bush was Hornsby's choice to face Gabby Street's club because Burleigh Grimes was still bedridden with the flu. Three runs in the top of the seventh earned Bush a 4–1 victory over Redbird rookie Tex Carleton. Stephenson led the charge again with two base hits and three RBIs. Charlie Root stepped up the next day and handcuffed the Cardinals on four hits, while his mates got to Flint Rhem for seven hits, good for three runs and a 3–1 victory. Vince Barton homered for the Cubs in the second inning, and doubles by Johnny Moore and Gabby Hartnett plated two more in the sixth. "After Frisch had singled in the fourth for the first hit off Root, he started to steal second, and Hartnett, as he drew back his arm to make the throw, let the ball fall from his grasp. Under a new wrinkle in the scoring rules, Hartnett was charged with a passed ball and Frisch was not credited with a steal."[6] The pesky Cincinnati Reds came to town on April 20 and, showing no respect for their superiors, trounced the Cubbies 7–2. Pat Malone was knocked out of the box in the third inning when Howley's cohorts pushed across five runs. Red Lucas, enjoying the luxury of a big lead, held Chicago to five hits and coasted to the victory. Gabby Hartnett went hitless in three trips to the plate, but threw out two runners trying to steal and doubled one runner off first base after a strikeout. The champion St. Louis Cardinals were hitting on hard times as they set out in quest of another National League pennant. Their 7–6, 10-inning loss to Pittsburgh was their sixth loss in a row. Lloyd Waner's double drove in the winning run.

Chicago rebounded behind Bob Smith to beat the Reds in game two, 3–2. Si Johnson, who pitched good enough to win most games, held the Bruins to four hits, but two runs in the eighth caused his downfall. Hornsby's charges did it again the next day in another one-run nail-biter. Guy Bush, known as the "Mississippi Mudcat," started for Chicago and was presented with a 5–0 lead after three innings, but he needed the help of Charlie Root to gain a 5–4 decision. Riggs Stephenson had three singles and an RBI, Jurges had a triple and two RBIs, and Kiki Cuyler had a double and two RBIs. Billy Herman had two singles and scored two runs. The two teams played another one-run game on April 23, their fifth one-run game in seven meetings, and the Cubs prevailed 2–1 in 12 innings. It was another outstanding pitchers duel between Lon Warneke, Ray Kolp, and Si Johnson. The Reds scored in the second inning, the Cubs tied it in the fifth, and the game was still 1–1 after 11 innings. At that point, Redleg manager Howley pinch-hit for Johnson, who had relieved Kolp in the ninth. And two outs and two relief pitchers later, the game ended on a wild throw by Reds shortstop Leo Durocher.

The injury gremlin visited the Friendly Confines again on April 24, when outfielder Kiki Cuyler broke his foot in the first inning of a game against the Pittsburgh Pirates. The Cubs put a three-spot on the board in the bottom of the first, to take a 3–0 lead over George Gibson's team, but the rally became costly when Cuyler twisted his left ankle rounding third base. He would be shelved for the next month, while the Cubs struggled to survive the loss of two of their best players. Fortunately, the infield "Kiddie Korps" of Jurges and Herman were performing magic with their gloves, giving their pitchers sensational inner defense. Johnny Moore, who replaced Cuyler in the lineup, pounded out two base hits, including a home run, and drove in two runs. Stephenson had another 3-for-4 day, with three doubles and two RBIs, and Grimm and Jurges chipped in with three hits of their own. Hartnett was 1-for-4, with an RBI, a run scored, and an assist. The final score was 12–3 in favor of Chicago. Pat Malone was rattled for four runs in the first inning in his start against Pittsburgh, then settled down and blanked the Bucs the rest of the way. In the meantime, Malone's teammates pecked away at Steve Swetonic for two runs in the second, three in the fifth, two more in the sixth, and a singleton in the eighth, to win 8–4. Herman, Taylor, Hartnett, and Grimm all crunched two base hits for the Cubs, while Jurges and Lance Richbourg knocked in two runs apiece.

The next victim to enter the not-so-friendly Confines was Gabby Street's Redbirds, who had bounced back from their 0–6 start to win five of their next eight games. They couldn't make it six in the opener of the series, however, as Hornsby's troops put together two big innings for a 12–7 victory. A five-run fourth by the Cubs was offset by a five-run outburst by the Cardinals in the sixth. But a six-run Chicago rally in the seventh iced the game for winning pitcher Charlie Root, who relieved Bob Smith in the sixth and held the Cards in check the rest of the way. Hack, Herman, Richbourg, and Taylor, at the top of the order, had nine of the Cubs' 13 hits and scored nine of their runs. Riggs Stephenson had a home run and a walk, two runs scored, and three RBIs. Richbourg had four RBIs. The Bruins ran their winning streak to seven when they took the measure of the Cardinals again, this time by a 5–3 score, with Lon Warneke beating Flint Rhem. Billy Herman had three base hits, Grimm had a home run, and Hartnett had an RBI and gunned down two base runners. Chicago finished the month of April in first place, but the Redbirds knocked them off the perch the next day and ended their seven-game winning streak in the process, routing Guy Bush 7–1. "Wild Bill" Hallahan stymied the Cubs with just three hits, while his mates were ripping an even dozen off the slants of the Chicago starter. George Watkins had a single, double, and home run for St. Louis. The top batsmen for Chicago in the early going were Riggs Stephenson (.353), Kiki Cuyler (.308), and Johnny Moore (.308). Gabby Hartnett was bogged down at .160. On the mound, Charlie Root was 3–0 and Lon Warneke was 2–0.

Rogers Hornsby's charges lost their first two games in May, then came back to beat the Pittsburgh Pirates 8–6, thanks to a five-run rally in the top of the seventh inning. Billy Herman, the sensational young second sacker, rapped four base hits, including a double, while third baseman Stan Hack put one into orbit. Hartnett had a single in four at-bats. Bob Smith struggled to the victory. Rookie Lon Warneke kept his perfect slate intact at 3–0, when he rolled over the Bucs the next day by a score of 4–1. Gabby Hartnett was 1-for-4 with an RBI and an assist. Shortstop Billy Jurges had a triple and two RBIs. One of the Chicago reporters asked the lanky right-hander to pose for a photo before the game, but he declined. When the reporter kidded him about being superstitious, he remarked, "I never pose for any pictures on days when I'm going to pitch. Superstitious, hell! I just think it's unlucky."[7] Brooklyn followed Pittsburgh into the Friendly Confines, and they were treated just as badly. Max Carey, the new Dodgers manager, cheered his team on to victory in the opener, as Watty Clark, his lanky southpaw, set the Cubbies down with nine scattered hits en route to a 2–1 win. Charlie Root, the losing pitcher, was the victim of shoddy fielding on the part of Johnny Moore and Stan Hack, but it was Watty Clark's double in the seventh that drove in the winning run. Hartnett was hitless, but threw out three reckless base runners. That was the only game Brooklyn could win, as the Cubs captured the next three, 3–1, 3–0, and 12–5. Pat Malone tossed a six-hit shutout in game three and was ably supported by Billy Herman, who went 3-for-3 with a double. In the finale, an 11-hit attack led by Grimm with three hits, and Hemsley and Stephenson with two each, gave Burleigh Grimes, the last of the spitball pitchers, the victory.

The Cubs closed out their home stand with a series against the Philadelphia Phillies, who were no longer the doormats of the National League. Manager Burt Shotton had developed a decent ball club in the City of Brotherly Love and was ready to take on all comers. They managed only one win in four games in Chicago, but they battled Hornsby's troops every inch of the way. They took the opener 8–6, handing Lon Warneke his first loss of the season along the way. The Bruins took the last three games, 11–10, 9–4, and 6–4. The Phillies had a 7–3 lead in game two after 5½ innings, but the Cubs scored in each of the last five innings, including two in the ninth, to pull out the victory. Pat Malone was the winning pitcher in relief. Gabby Hartnett had a single and a double in four at-bats and laid down a perfect sacrifice bunt in the Cubs' two-run rally in the eighth. English, Stephenson, and Grimm all had three hits in the slugfest. Chicago took the next game on the strength of a big eight-run seventh inning that wiped out a 4–1 Philly lead. Lance Richbourg had four hits for the winners, and Charlie Grimm once again added three to the pot. Hartnett was 1-for-4, with an RBI and two assists. Bud Tinning, in relief of Root, took the win. The Windy City boys took the get-away game behind Guy Bush.

The wins over Philadelphia kept the Cubs in first place and gave them a 2½-game lead over the Boston Braves. In the American League, meanwhile, the New York Yankees were on a roll. Lefty Gomez's 8–0 whitewashing of Cleveland was the team's fourth consecutive shutout, tying the American League record. The other three shutout pitchers were Red Ruffing, George Pipgras, and Johnny Allen. Two days later, the Yanks nipped the Cleveland Indians 3–2 on Babe Ruth's tenth-inning home run. Bill Dickey also homered in the game, which kept New York 1½ games ahead of the Washington Senators.[8]

Chicago opened a short six-game road trip in Cincinnati on May 20. They took the opener 4–3 in 12 innings, with Burleigh Grimes going the distance for the victory. Herman, Moore, Stephenson, and Jurges all chipped in with three hits. Moore and Stephenson had two RBIs each. The next day was the Reds' turn. They beat the Cubs 3–2 in 11 innings. Lon Warneke, the 23-year-old right-hander, who won his first five games in the big leagues, was beaten for the third straight time. He had two opportunities to win the game, leading 1–0 after 8½ and 2–1 after 10½, but couldn't nail it down. Johnny Moore had two singles for the Cubs. Hartnett was hitless, but he had two more assists, as he continued to cut down opposing base runners at a sensational rate. Dan Howley's Redlegs sent the Bruins out of town with scowls on their faces after administering two more defeats on them, by scores of 6–5 and 4–3. A run in the eighth and two in the ninth snatched victory from defeat in game three. Then Ray Kolp outpitched Charlie Root in the finale. After a day of rest, Chicago tried to right their ship, but came up short. They outhit the St. Louis Cardinals 14 to 10, but three errors did them in, 8–6. Gabby Hartnett had a career day in defeat for the Cubs. The big catcher went 5-for-5, with three doubles, two runs scored, an RBI, and two assists. They finally snapped their three-game losing streak in game two, as Burleigh Grimes threw nothing but goose eggs at Gabby Street's sluggers, winning 3–0. Moore, Herman, and Grimm had two hits each. The Bruins returned home with a slim ½-game lead over Boston and a 4½ game lead over St. Louis. They moved back into the top spot when Philadelphia out-slugged Boston 17–13. Four Philly players had three hits each, and three other players chipped in with two. Home cooking didn't help the Cubs, however, as they could play no better than .500 ball in the Friendly Confines. They split two games each with the Reds, Cardinals, and Pirates, giving them a record of 16–13 for the month.

June 1 found them still in first place, their 27–16 mark 2½ games better than Boston; but George Gibson's Pittsburgh Pirates, who languished in fifth place most of the first two months of the season, had quietly moved up to fourth place and were about to light the afterburners. In June, they would turn a 5½-game deficit into a ½-game lead in the National League race. The Yankees, meanwhile, had opened a 4½-game lead over the Detroit Tigers, who had moved ahead of Washington in the American League. The defending champion Philadelphia Athletics held down fourth place, six games out.

The Brooklyn Dodgers came to town on June 15, and it turned out to be an historic day for Dodger outfielder Johnny Frederick. The Cubs won the game 8–3 behind Lon Warneke, but Frederick banged out a pinch-hit home run for the losers in the eighth inning. It was Frederick's second pinch-hit homer in three days, and he would hit four more over the next three months, giving him a new major league record of six pinch-hit home runs in one season.[9] As far as the Cubs were concerned, June was a month to forget. They slumped to a 9–14 record and fell into second place behind the red-hot Pittsburgh Pirates, whose 14–7 record gave them a ½-game lead. The Cubs leaders were Riggs Stephenson (.333), Charlie Grimm (.311), and Johnny Moore (.301) in batting, and Moore (8) in home runs. Gabby Hartnett had brought his batting average up to .233, but had just four home runs in 190 at-bats.

Pittsburgh poured it on in July, roaring through the month with a 25–13 mark, to open up a 5½-game lead over second-place Chicago. Rogers Hornsby's charges went 17–15 for the month, but couldn't put a long winning streak together. And in their big series against the Pirates, they were swept 3–0. On July 3, Heine Meine beat Pat Malone 4–3 in a game called after six innings because of rain. The win sent George Gibson's Bucs into first place by a ½ game over Chicago. The next day, Pittsburgh lengthened their lead by winning both ends of the holiday doubleheader by scores of 9–6 and 6–5 in 11 innings. In the morning half of the twin bill, Grimes was raked for eight runs in less than three innings, after being handed a 4–0 lead in the top of the first. Hartnett was 2-for-3, with a double, an RBI, and a run scored in a losing cause. In the nightcap, Pittsburgh tied the game off Guy Bush in the bottom of the ninth, then tagged him with the loss in the eleventh. "Old Hoss" Stephenson had two singles and a double, Charlie Grimm had two singles, and Kiki Cuyler had a two-run homer for the Cubs. Hartnett drew the collar in five at-bats. The month of July was even more depressing than the league standings showed. The Cubs lost their fancy fielding shortstop due to a gunshot wound. Violet Popovich Valli, a Chicago showgirl who had been spurned by Billy Jurges, went to his room at the Carlos Hotel on July 6 with a 25-caliber revolver in her hand and murder on her mind. She fired three shots, wounding Jurges in the ribs, back, and hand, before he could subdue her. The Cubs' shortstop was sidelined for three weeks, while his team struggled to stay afloat.[10]

The hot, humid days of summer began to take their toll on teams less well conditioned than Hornsby's Chicago Cubs. The heat and humidity were oppressive, according to Billy Herman: "Here's how you went from Chicago to St. Louis to Cincinnati — and I'm talking about July and August when it's always 90 or more degrees. You got on a train at midnight, and maybe that train has been sitting in the yards all day long, under a broiling sun. It feels like 150 degrees in that steel car. You get into St. Louis at six thirty in the morning, grab your own bag, fight to get a cab, and go to the hotel. By the time you get to the hotel, it's seven thirty and you have an afternoon ball game to play. So you hurry into the dining room — and it's hot in there, no air conditioning — and you eat and run upstairs and try to get a few hours rest. Then you go to the ballpark, where it's about 110 degrees. You finish the game about five or five thirty and go into the clubhouse. It's around 120 degrees in there. You take your shower, but there's no way you can dry off; the sweat just keeps running off of you. You get back to the hotel and go up to your room. You try to sleep but you can't because you're sweating so much. This goes on for four days in St. Louis, and you go on to Cincinnati and it's the same thing. For eight days you haven't had a decent nights sleep."[11]

August was the key month in the Chicago Cubs' pennant drive. The final scenario began to unfold on the second of the month when President William Veeck Sr. fired manager Rogers Hornsby, with the Cubs five games behind the Pirates and 55 games remaining in the season. Charlie Grimm, a popular choice, was appointed manager for the last two months. Not many players were sorry to see the hard-driving Hornsby leave, although some, like former Cub Les Bell, thought highly of Hornsby: "I've heard a lot of ball players say he was a tough man to play for. I never found him that way. All he ever asked was that they gave him all they had out on the field."[12] Hornsby's dismissal also brought to light a horse betting scandal, as noted by Holtzman and Vass: "He [Hornsby] told Veeck he wanted the remaining money due on his contract in a lump sum. An inveterate horseplayer, Hornsby was in debt to six or seven of his players and wanted to repay them. The Chicago papers ran banner front-page headlines. The caption under a photograph of Guy Bush contended the Cub players owed $38,000 to bookmakers. Landis probed but made no charges."[13]

The Grimm era got off to a promising start as they took three of four games in Philadelphia. They beat the Phillies in the opener of a four-game series, dropped the second game, 9–2, when Charlie Root was ko'd in 3⅔ innings, then swept a doubleheader on the 6th by scores of 10–9 and 10–8 in 11 innings. In the opener, Guy Bush blew a 6–1 lead after six innings, as the Phils jumped in front, 7–6. Base hits by Cuyler and Stephenson and a sacrifice fly by Demaree tied the game in the eighth, and another single by Hartnett, followed by a double by Gudat and a single by Root, gave the Cubs the winning margin. Gabby was 2-for-4 with a run scored. The second game was a back-and-forth affair, with first one team, then the other, grabbing the lead. The Phils scored two runs in the bottom of the ninth to deadlock the game at 8–8, but Grimm's shock troops pushed over two in the eleventh for the win. Leroy Herrmann, who would pitch in only seven games all year, was the winning pitcher with 2⅔ innings of scoreless relief. There were many heroes for the Cubs on this day, including Billy Herman who went 7-for-11 with an RBI in the twin bill. Riggs Stephenson was 7-for-11 with three RBIs. And Kiki Cuyler was 5-for-10 with four RBIs. The Cubs were now back in the race, as they had cut the Pittsburgh lead from five games to just 2½ in three days. Hours after the game ended, catcher Rollie Hemsley was arrested in Philadelphia for drunken driving and immediately suspended and sent home by manager Charlie Grimm.[14]

On August 6, the Cubs bought former New York Yankee shortstop Mark Koenig from the Mission club of the Pacific Coast League for added infield insurance. The 28-year-old Koenig was hitting .335 for Mission at the time of his purchase. Ten days later Chicago began the streak that would bring them the National League pennant. They ran off 20 victories in their next 21 games, including 14 in a row at one point. Their overall record for August was 23–5, while the Pirates stumbled badly, winning only 10 of 30 games. The second and third games of the Cubs' streak were torturous extra-inning affairs against the pesky Boston Braves. On the 17th, the two teams battled for 19 innings before the Bruins pushed over a run to win 3–2. Frank Demaree's bases-loaded single in the bottom of the 19th made a winner out of Guy Bush, who pitched the last inning. The next day, Charlie Grimm's warriors pulled out another nail-biter, this one by a 4–3 score in 15 innings. Riggs Stephenson singled to drive in Woody English with the deciding run, giving the Mississippi Mudcat another one-inning victory. It was Bush's third win in a relief role in a week, since he had pitched the final three innings of a 3–2, 10-inning win over Pittsburgh on the 11th.

The Pirates couldn't do anything right in August. They lost their last two games in July and dropped their first eight games in August, knocking them off the top perch. Along the way, they lost four to the third-place Phillies, three to the fourth-place Braves, and three to the fifth-place Dodgers. The miseries continued until late in the month. After beating the Braves 5–2 on the 11th, George Gibson's harried charges lost 12 of the next 16 games to fall into third place, seven games behind the red-hot Cubs, before rebounding to win their last five games.

Kiki Cuyler was practically a one-man team down the stretch, batting a sizzling .365 over the last four weeks of the season. On August 27, he hit a three-run homer, as the Cubs won their eighth game in a row, a 6–1 win over New York in the first game of a twin bill. The Bruins won the second game also, and Cuyler chipped in with two more hits. The next day, he added three hits to his total, including a homer, and drove in the game winner in a 5–4 win over the Giants. He kept up the barrage a day later, banging another homer in a 4–3 win over New York.[15]

On August 31, Charlie Grimm's warriors staged another stirring comeback to beat the hapless seventh-place Giants 10–9. Cuyler singled in the tying run in the bottom of the ninth, but New York appeared to take command in the top of the tenth when they scored four runs off Guy Bush, who walked one batter, hit two others, and was touched for two singles. In the bottom half of the inning, the Cubs turned it up a notch after two men had been retired. Mark Koenig got the ball rolling when he "knocked a homer into the right field stands at the expense of pitcher Sam Gibson. Taylor singled to right center and Herman singled to center. English singled to center scoring Taylor. Then Cuyler socked his fifth hit of the game, a homer into the center field stands, about thirty feet to the right of the scoreboard, driving in Herman and English ahead of him and winning the ball game.

Cuyler was mobbed by a crowd of admirers who had stayed through the rain that fell on the last three innings. As soon as he entered the clubhouse he was boosted on a round table in the center of the dressing room and advised he better give a speech. Cuy did the best he could, but his pals weren't satisfied. They ripped off his uniform, stretched him on the floor, and scrubbed him with the shower brushes until he was pink as a baby. Mark Koenig was accorded a similar heroic treatment. While several mates held him on the floor, others took turns slapping his body with bare hands."[16]

On September 2, Cuyler hit his fifth homer in six games, as the Cubs beat St. Louis 8–5.

Gabby Hartnett contributed two singles, a double, and two RBIs to the Chicago attack. And Billy Herman had a single, a triple, and two RBIs. The next day, a large crowd of 45,000 pennant-crazy Chicagoans overflowed the Friendly Confines and had to stand around the outfield, hoping to see two more victories against the Redbirds. The team accommodated them in the opener, winning their fourteenth straight game with yet another extra-inning win. Gabby Hartnett, who had a 2-for-4 day with an RBI and two assists, led off the eleventh inning with a single, and Stan Hack, who went in to run for Hartnett, eventually came around to score the winning run on a single by English. Dizzy Dean, on his way to becoming the greatest pitcher in the National League, brought the Cubs' winning streak to an abrupt halt with a brilliant 3–0 shutout in game two. The big fireballer from Lucas, Arkansas, scattered eight hits and fanned seven Cubs along the way. The Cubs' home stand ended with a record of 18–2, which gave them a comfortable 5½-game lead over Pittsburgh. Billy Herman was the biggest gun in the Chicago arsenal, slapping the ball at a torrid .395 pace, followed by Mark Koenig at .377 and Kiki Cuyler at .326. Cuyler led the team with five home runs and 26 RBIs, while Herman led in runs scored with 17. Cuyler and Koenig scored 13 runs each.

Kiki Cuyler's heroics didn't end with the St. Louis series. He blasted an eleventh-inning home run to beat the Giants 8–7 on the 15th, giving Lon Warneke his twenty-second victory in relief. Gabby Hartnett had a single and a home run and batted in two runs in the game. Five days later, the Chicago Cubs clinched the pennant when they defeated the Pittsburgh Pirates 5–2 before a packed house of 38,00 delirious home fans. Another 15,000 fans, who were hoping for standing-room tickets, had to be turned away by eight police squads of Chicago's Finest when Cubs President William Veeck refused permission to put up ropes around the outfield. The Cubs' championship was their thirteenth National League pennant and their seventh in the modern era. Kiki Cuyler's bases-loaded triple in the seventh brought home the winning runs. Some Chicagoans didn't sleep for days, as the partying went on endlessly. On the 22nd, Charlie Grimm's amazing Bruins were honored by Mayor Cernak and the city council with an automobile parade from Wrigley Field to city hall via Lake Shore Drive and Michigan Boulevard. The usual speeches followed.[17]

In the American League, the New York Yankees coasted to a 13-game margin over the Philadelphia Athletics. Their 107 victories were exceeded in the American League by the 110 wins of the 1927 Yankees, in the National League by the 116 wins of the 1906 Chicago Cubs, and by the 110 wins of the 1909 Pittsburgh Pirates.

The New York Yankees were installed as heavy favorites to vanquish the Cubs in less than six games, with their explosive offense, which scored 1,002 runs during the regular season, aided by 160 home runs. Charlie Grimm's charges could muster just 720 runs and 69 home runs against National League opponents. Chicago had a slight advantage in fielding and pitching, but not enough to offset the Yankees "Murderers Row." Billy Herman admitted that the Cubs were intimidated by the big New York sluggers: "You know, you hate to say it, but we were overmatched, strictly overmatched, and we were a damn good ball club. We had a lot of fire and spirit on the Cubs, but when we went out that first day and watched the Yankees take batting practice, our hearts just sank. They were knocking those balls out of sight. We were awestruck."[18]

The Series opened in New York on September 28, and the script was followed to a "T." After the Cubs put up a two-spot in the top of the first, it was all New York thereafter. Guy Bush was raked for eight runs in 5⅓ innings on just three hits. In the fourth inning, a walk, a single, and a two-run shot into the right field bleachers by Lou Gehrig gave Joe McCarthy's team a lead for the first time. Two innings later, Bush was chased after walking four men and yielding a two-run single to Bill Dickey. The final score was 12–6. Gabby Hartnett had two doubles for the Bruins. In game two, Lefty Gomez scattered nine hits and fanned eight men en route to a 5–2 victory. Once again, the Yankees took advantage of bases on balls from the cautious Chicago pitchers, to score the decisive runs. They took the lead in the bottom of the first when Lon Warneke walked the first two men to face him, and they both came around to score. Ruth walked and scored in the third as New York built a 4–1 lead. The final run of the game was scored in the fifth inning on singles by Gehrig and Dickey.

The Series moved to Chicago for game three, and it was a game that would go down in baseball legend. George Pipgras, who was 16–9 during the season, toed the rubber for Joe McCarthy's team, facing Charlie Root, who was 15–10 for Chicago. It turned out to be a sluggers day. The Yankees put three on the board in the top of the first on an error, a walk, and a

Opposite page: **Billy Herman scores the first run of the 1932 World Series as Kiki Cuyler and Bill Dickey look on.** *Above:* **Babe Ruth grounding out to first in game one of the 1932 World Series as Gabby Hartnett looks on.** (Jay Sanford).

tremendous home run into the right field bleachers by Babe Ruth. The Cubs countered with one in the bottom half of the inning on Kiki Cuyler's run-scoring double. Lou Gehrig led off the third inning with a long shot into the right field bleachers, but Charlie Grimm's cohorts scored two in their half to narrow the margin to 4–3. Cuyler's home run and Grimm's double did the damage. The Cubs tied the score an inning later on a double by Jurges and a single by English. The Yankee fifth produced the hit that has become a myth over the years. With one out, Babe Ruth hit his second home run of the game, a monstrous blast over the bleacher screen in straightaway center field. The Yanks and Cubs had been hurling insults at each other throughout the Series, with the New York bench jockeys calling the Cubs "cheapskates" for voting Mark Koenig only a half-share of their World Series pot. The verbal abuse accelerated in the fifth inning, with Babe Ruth at bat. Fifty-thousand Chicago fans hurled insults at the Yankee slugger, and he responded in kind. He was exchanging obscenities with the Cubs bench while he batted. According to Cohen & Neft and other historians: "He took a strike, pointed out into the field, took another strike, again pointed, and then belted a Root changeup into the center field seats." The hit has gone down in baseball lore as "The Called Shot," but the facts in the case are still not clear. Babe Ruth was happy to take credit for calling the shot, but never actually said he did call it. Gehrig and a few other New York players claim he pointed to center field. The Cubs' public address announcer and sports writer Grantland Rice also supported the Called Shot story. The Cubs perspective was entirely different. Gabby Hartnett, who was the closest player to Ruth, said "I don't want to take anything from the Babe, because he's the reason we made good money, but he didn't call the shot. He held up the index finger of his left hand, looked at our dugout, not the outfield, and said 'It only takes one to hit.'" Charlie Root of Chicago, who had a reputation as a mean pitcher who would knock his mother down if she crowded the plate, said, "He didn't point. If he had, I'd have knocked him on his fanny. I'd have loosened him up. I took my pitching too seriously to have anybody facing me do that."[19] The film of the incident is inconclusive. The actual intentions of the Babe are in the eye of the beholder. But, whatever the facts of the case are, the homer gave the Yankees a 5–4 lead, and Lou Gehrig extended it to 6–4 moments later when he sent a Root fastball over the right field wall. Both teams scored in the ninth, the Cubs' run coming on a home run to right field by Gabby Hartnett, making the final score 7–5.

In game four, after New York tallied one run in the top of the first, Charlie Grimm's charges sent Johnny Allen to a quick shower with four runs in the bottom half of the inning. Four singles, an error, and Kiki Cuyler's three-run homer did the damage. Unfortunately, Cubs starter Guy Bush couldn't stand the prosperity. Tony Lazzeri's two-run homer in the third cut the Chicago margin to a single run, and a sixth-inning single by Gehrig plated two more, giving New York its first lead at 5–4. After the Cubs tied the game in the bottom of the sixth, Murderers Row unloaded against southpaw Jakie May, with four singles and a double, good for four big runs and a 9–5 lead. Earle Combs homered for New York in the ninth, and Lazzeri hit his second of the game, as Joe McCarthy's powerful lineup clinched the Series sweep with a 12–6 victory. The Yankees batted .313 as a team, outscored the Cubs 37 to 19, and hit eight home runs in four games, with Gehrig getting three, and Lazzeri and Ruth banging out two each. Gehrig led all hitters with an average of .529, while Bill Dickey hit a solid .438. For the Cubs, Riggs Stephenson hit .444, Billy Jurges hit .364, Charlie Grim hit .333, and Gabby Hartnett hit .313. Another controversy arose after the series ended, when the Cubs players, openly hostile to their former manager, Rogers Hornsby, did not vote him a World Series share. He appealed to Baseball Commissioner Kenesaw Mountain Landis, claiming he was a major contributor to the Cubs' National League championship, but his appeal was denied.[20]

The individual league leaders for the season were Lefty O'Doul of Brooklyn who batted .368, Dale Alexander of the Boston Red Sox who hit .367, Chuck Klein and Jimmie Foxx with 38 and 58 homers, respectively, and Lon Warneke (22–6) and George Crowder of Washington (26–13) on the mound. Jimmie Foxx challenged Babe Ruth's single-season home run record all summer before falling two short. "Double-X" was consistent from start to end, hitting seven homers in August and 10 in September. The 37-year-old "Sultan of Swat" was on the decline, but still had enough left to put 41 balls into orbit. His total would drop to 34 in 1933, then to 22 the following year, and finally to six in his farewell season with the Boston Braves.

Riggs Stephenson was the leading Chicago Cubs hitter with an average of .324, followed by Billy Herman at .314, Charlie Grimm at .307, and Johnny Moore at .305. Moore (13), Hartnett (12), and Cuyler (10) were the leading home run hitters, and Warneke (22–6), Bush (19–11), and Root (15–10) topped the pitchers. Stephenson would be one of the main cogs in the Chicago offense for nine years, with a career average of .336. He led the National League in doubles in 1927 with 46 and in 1932 with 49. He drove in 110 runs in 1929, and he hit .316 and .444 in two World Series. Gabby Hartnett finished strong once again, batting at a .333 clip in September with five home runs. He had a sensational season behind the plate, allowing only 29 stolen bases against the league average of 56. His American League counterparts, Mickey Cochrane and Bill Dickey, were victimized 68 and 65 times, respectively, against the league average of 68.

After the Series ended, Lon Warneke headed for his home in Ida, Arkansas. When several people asked him to stay in Chicago, Warneke said, "Heck, I can live a whole winter down home for $50. I can't live a week up here for that."[21] Gabby Hartnett cleaned out his locker and spent some quiet time with Martha, dining and dancing at the Edgewater Beach Hotel, taking in a few movies, and nightclubbing. Later, he went hunting for pheasant in Michigan's Upper Peninsula with Kiki Cuyler. The only player transaction Chicago Cubs President William Veeck made after the 1932 season was to obtain outfielder Babe Herman from Cincinnati for $75,000 and four players, including Johnny Moore, Rollie Hemsley, and Bob Smith.

Baseball was a pleasant diversion for millions of Americans around the country and a lucrative income for several hundred talented ball players. But the country in general was still in the throes of a severe depression. It had been growing since 1929 and was at its worst in 1932, but, according to an article in the publication, *News of the Nation*: "Beneath the tragic realities of massive unemployment and hunger is an under-girding of faith, honesty, integrity, and industriousness. Americans have shown they are willing to do any sort of work to keep their families fed, housed, and together. They will

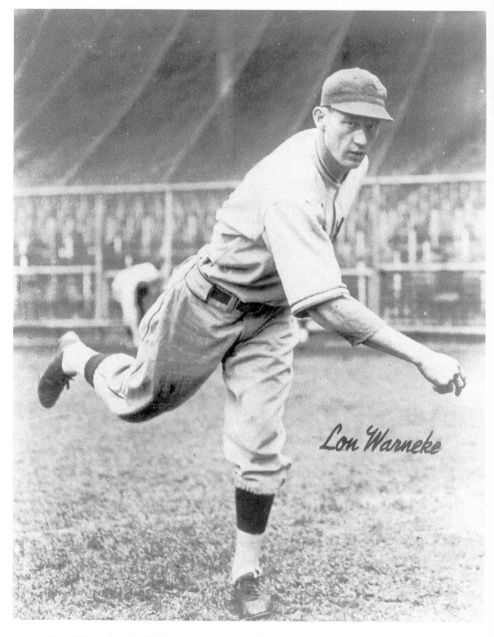

Lon Warneke, the "Arkansas Humming Bird," went 22–6 in 1932 to spark the Cubs to the National League pennant.

sell apples, scrub floors, wash dishes, pick fruit, drive trucks, or keep on trying to scratch a hard living out of dry ground."

Franklin Delano Roosevelt, the newly elected thirty-second President of the United States, promised to take immediate action to alleviate the situation in the country. At his inaugural address, he said, "Our greatest task is to put people to work." As he spoke, there were 12 million people out of work, about one-fourth of the workforce. During his first 100 days in office, Roosevelt pushed an unprecedented number of relief and recovery bills through Congress. The Works Progress Administration (WPA) and other federal agencies put people to work for the government, building roads, parks, dams, and other public facilities. Other legislation introduced by the new President protected bank deposits and provided aid to farmers. In other legislation promised by Roosevelt, the 18th Amendment, which prohibited the manufacture and sale of alcohol, was repealed in February 1933. The repeal went into effect on November 7.[22]

Middle age was beginning to creep up on Gabby Hartnett in 1933, and it was becoming more and more difficult for him to stay in shape over the winter. To prepare himself for the rigorous season ahead, Gabby traveled to Hot Springs, Arkansas, in January to sweat off the suet before going to spring training. When he finally departed for the west coast, he was accompanied by Martha and Bud, who welcomed the break from the frigid and snowy weather conditions in Chicago. But mother and son didn't stay in California the entire six weeks. The team traveled to Los Angeles for a series of exhibition games in Washington Park in early March, and the first night in the Biltmore Hotel was Martha and Bud's last. At approximately 5:55 PM, while Gabby was taking a bath, an earthquake struck the Los Angeles area, causing the hotel to sway like a palm tree in the breeze. According to Tot Holmes, "An aftershock shook the city the following day and one of the Cub Players was so terrified that he ran out of the hotel barbershop half shaved and with the barber's apron still on him. The frightened player slept that night in the park across the street from the hotel."[23] Martha didn't bother to sleep in the park. She gathered up Bud and took the next train back to Chicago.

The baseball experts ignored the Chicago Cubs' dash for the pennant in 1932 and installed the Pittsburgh Pirates as the favorites to win the National League championship. The New York Yankees were considered a shoo-in to win another American League title. One reason the experts dropped Chicago into second place was because their all-world right fielder, Kiki Cuyler, fractured his ankle sliding into second base during an exhibition game in California and would be out of action until July. He would play in just 70 games during the season. His outfield mate, Riggs Stephenson, had health problems of his own. Assorted injuries and an attack of malaria limited his action to 97 games. The Cubs' exhibition schedule included eight games against the Pittsburgh Pirates, who had led the 1932 National League race during the dog days of summer, only to be overtaken by the red-hot Cubs down the stretch. The Cubs won the spring series, five games to three. They took the opener on St Patrick's Day by a 4–3 score, and followed that with a 14–7 rout the next day. George Gibson's charges took game three 10–4, but the Cubbies won game four 6–4, and took the next one 16–10 on March 30. In April, Pittsburgh won 6–5, but the Cubs bounced back behind a four-homer attack to win 12–5. The Pirates took the last game of the series 8–7, on a home run by Gus Suhr. Babe Herman broke out of a prolonged slump by slamming a double and a long home run, helping the Cubs overcome a 7–1 Pirate lead in the eighth inning, before losing in 10. "My stride has been wrong for two weeks," said Mr. Herman. "I was not depressed, for I have never been in poor stride for more than two weeks, but just the same I was happy to see me become myself once more. I will be very tough on pitchers from now on."[24]

Charlie Grimm announced that Lon Warneke, the Arkansas Hummingbird, would pitch the opener for his team: "I figure Warneke, as the leading pitcher of the National League in 1932, deserves the honor of pitching the season opener." It was a good choice on the manager's part. The string bean right-hander blanked the St. Louis Cardinals 3–0 in Wrigley Field while 25,000 Cub fans voiced their approval. Gabby Hartnett accounted for three of the Cubs' 11 base hits, driving in two of the three runs. In game two, the Redbirds' Wild Bill Hallahan outpitched Guy Bush in a pitchers duel, winning 3–1. Ripper Collins, the Cards' miniature slugger, had two singles and a home run, good for three RBIs, supplying all the offense Hallahan needed. Babe Herman had three doubles for the losers and was robbed of a fourth when George Watkins made a sensational backhand catch of his long drive to right center field in the seventh inning. The rubber game of the series was postponed due to rain, leaving a lot of questions unanswered. In other action, the New York Yankees won their first game of the season when Lou Gehrig brought the home crowd to its feet by smashing a three-run homer in the first inning, overcoming an early 1–0 Boston Red Sox lead. Lefty Gomez, Joe McCarthy's crafty southpaw, made the runs stand up for a 4–3 win. Two days later, Babe Ruth duplicated Gehrig's feat by launching a three-run homer in the first inning, leading his team to a 7–3 win over the Philadelphia Athletics.

Pittsburgh was the next visitor to the Windy City, and they had revenge on their minds after losing the close pennant race the previous year. Heinie Meine, who was the victim of the four-homer game in New Mexico, started the opener for the Bucs, but was relieved by Bill Harris in the seventh inning when the Cubs scored three runs to take a 4–3 lead. Burleigh Grimes, who relieved Charlie Root in the eighth, gave up the tying run in that inning, as well as the winning runs in the tenth, as the Bucs prevailed 6–4. Billy Herman's four base hits and Woody English's three were wasted in the end. Gabby Hartnett had a single in three at-bats. After splitting the four-game series with Pittsburgh, the Bruins moved into Sportsman's Park in St. Louis for a series against the Cardinals, and the animosity between Cardinals manager Rogers Hornsby and the Cubs erupted. St. Louis won the game 2–0 behind Tex Carleton, which was a bitter pill to swallow, since both runs were unearned. The scores came in the fourth inning when a great throw to third base from right fielder Babe Herman skipped past the Cubs third baseman, whose view of the play was blocked by the base runner. One run came across on the play, and the second one followed moments later on an infield out.

Before the game, Hornsby had made comments to the press, saying that Cubs' manager Charlie Grimm and Hartnett had been stool pigeons for Chicago President William Veeck during Hornsby's managerial tenure with the Cubs, and that Veeck fired him so he could promote Grimm, who was his pet. After the game, Grimm wanted to go into the St. Louis clubhouse and challenge Hornsby to a fight in front of his team. Hartnett also wanted to confront the Cardinals manager, but gave Grimm first dibs. Veeck defused the situation by advising Grimm against such action, telling him that the results of the 1932 pennant race spoke volumes about the relative managerial skills of the two adversaries.

The feud simmered for a few days, then quieted down as the Cubs moved on to Cincinnati to battle the Reds. A 6–1 loss to the Redlegs didn't help the attitudes of the Cubs, as they returned home to meet the St. Louis Cardinals for the third time in two weeks. Grimm's cohorts battled the Redbirds in a doubleheader on April 30, and the confrontation ended in a dead heat. The Cubbies captured the opener 7–5 behind Charlie Root, and the Cards took the nightcap 5–3, with Tex Carleton chalking up the win. In game one, Chicago pounded Bill Hallahan for five runs in six innings, during which time the game was suspended for one hour and 41 minutes due to rain. Frank Demaree, with a triple and two doubles, and Babe Herman with a home run and two infield singles, sparked the Chicago offense. In game two, the Cardinals were outhit 10 to 5, but nine bases on balls issued by Pat Malone spelled the difference in the game. A walk and a single put one run on the board for St. Louis in the first inning. Another walk, a single, and a two-run homer by Rogers Hornsby in the third inning overcame a Cubs lead fashioned by a two-run homer by Gabby Hartnett in the second. Tex Carleton, with relief help from Dizzy Dean, made the lead stand up. The split gave the Cubs a record of six and eight for the month. St. Louis was even worse at 6 and 9. Pittsburgh was on top of the heap with a 10–3 mark. In the American League, the Yanks' 11–4 record led the White Sox and the Senators, both of whom had 10 wins and six losses.

The Bruins struggled in May, but a 5–1 win over Pittsburgh on the last day of the month gave them a 16–13 record for the month and a fourth-place spot in the standings, 4½ games behind the first-place St. Louis Cardinals, who had run up a 20–9 log during the month, replacing the Pirates as the league leaders. June began on a promising note when Lon Warneke stopped Hornsby's Redbirds 8–6 in a route-going exhibition that required more guts than talent. After his team had presented him with a nice 4–0 lead after four innings, the Arkansas right-hander gave them back, and more, in the top of the fifth. The Cardinals scored five runs after two men had been retired to put themselves in the driver's seat with a 5–4 lead, which took the Ladies Day gathering of 26,000 screaming fans out of the game. The Cubs, however, were made of sterner stuff, and they rebounded in the bottom half of the same inning. Si Johnson entered the game in the fifth and proceeded to walk the first man to face him. Babe Herman made him pay for that mistake by ripping a triple to right field to tie the game. The next batter, Riggs Stephenson, put the Cubbies in front by launching home run #4 into the right field seats. Later in the inning, Gabby Hartnett unloaded on Johnson, sending a dinger over the left field wall, making the score 8–5. Warneke settled down after his fifth-inning sabbatical, holding the Cardinals to one run over the last four innings.

The juggling act for first place in the National League continued in June, as the Chicago Cubs knocked Hornsby's Redbirds off their perch with a 4–3 victory on June 10. Bill Terry's New York Giants sneaked past St. Louis after beating the Phillies 5–2. In St. Louis, a big Saturday crowd was silenced in the top of the first inning when Charlie Grimm's charges hung a big three-spot on the board. Billy Herman's double and singles by Stephenson and Grimm did the damage. In the ninth inning, with the Cubs up 4–3, St. Louis threatened. Frankie Frisch singled, and Ernie Orsatti sacrificed him to second, but when Frisch overran the base, an alert throw from Herman to Koenig cut him down. The weekly averages published by the Chicago statisticians showed that Hartnett was leading his team in hitting (.322), home runs (10), and RBIs (39) in 49 games. Babe Herman had joined Gabby in the .300 circle, with an average of .304.

Another ho-hum month was coming to an end for the Cubs when they visited Ebbets Field to take on the Dodgers and their Flatbush Faithful, who gave their boys loud vocal support from the first pitch to the last. In the opener, Charlie Root topped Walter "Boom Boom" Beck by a score of 7–2.

Babe Herman slammed a double and a three-run homer to pace the Cub attack. He also threw a runner out at the plate. In game two, Chicago was beaten by a 6–3 count. Van Lingle Mungo, Max Carey's big fireballing right-hander, scattered seven hits and held the Cubs to a single run after the first inning. Gabby Hartnett's two-out double to right field drove both runners across the plate, giving Charlie Root a 2–0 lead. But the Cubs' righty didn't have it on this day, and the Dodgers picked him apart systematically over the next 2⅓ innings. They plated one run in the bottom of the first, then drove Root to cover with a two-run outburst in the third. Chicago had one last volley in their cannon, tying the game with a run in the sixth. Babe Herman sent a towering drive to straightaway center field, good for three bases, and he scored on a single by Demaree. The Dodgers tried to execute a double steal in the first inning, but Joe Stripp was cut down at the plate, Hartnett to Jurges to Hartnett. Not many teams were successful in completing double steals against Gabby Hartnett. His quick release and powerful throw usually resulted in an easy out at the plate. The big Irishman threw out another runner trying to steal later in the game. The Cubs' 14–14 record for June left them floundering in fourth place, a full seven games behind the front-running Giants.[24]

On July 1, the Cubbies were back with their hitting shoes on. With big Bud Tinning throwing nothing but strikes and the sluggers hitting the ball to all parts of Ebbets Field, Charlie Grimm had a relaxing day. The final score was 13–3, as 18 base hits sailed off Chicago bats, seven of them by the battery. Tinning went 3-for-3, with a double and an RBI, while his catcher, Gabby Hartnett, pounded out four hits in six trips to the plate, including two doubles, good for four RBIs. He also had an assist on a strikeout pickoff double play to Grimm. The playing manager also chipped in with four hits and two RBIs. The next day, Max Carey's Flock swept a twin bill from the Cubs, beating Pat Malone 7–3 when Grimm's troops wasted 15 base hits, then hanging a 4–3 loss on Charlie Root, when he ignored the slow-footed Al Lopez on third base in the bottom of the ninth and the alert catcher stole home with the winning run.

Major league baseball added something new in 1933, an All-Star Game. Arch Ward, sports editor of the *Chicago Tribune*, suggested to league owners that an All-Star Game be played in Chicago during the city's World's Fair. The owners heartily endorsed the suggestion, scheduled the game for July 6, and selected the managers and players themselves. The game was such a success that it was made an annual event, to be played in early July each year at the halfway point in the season. After 1934, the All-Star teams were selected by the managers. By 1946, the fans were selecting the teams except for the pitchers, who were still chosen by the managers. The All-Star managers were the managers of the previous year's World Series teams.

Sweetie Hartnett drove his brother and Martha to the All-Star Game at Comiskey Park, joining 47,593 other fans who braved the sweltering weather to see the legends of baseball compete against each other. Connie Mack, the grand old man of baseball and a major league manager since 1894, and John McGraw, a big league skipper since 1899, were chosen to lead the two teams. The American League won the game 4–2, as starting pitcher Lefty Gomez, a notoriously weak hitter with a career average of .147, singled off Bill Hallahan in the second inning, driving in Jimmie Dykes with the first run in All-Star history. Babe Ruth upped the margin to 3–0 in the third with a two-run shot into the right-field stands. Frankie Frisch homered for the National League in the sixth inning. One of the curious aspects of the game was that none of the top three catchers in baseball, Hartnett, Dickey, or Cochrane, started the game. In fact, only Hartnett played in the game, and he entered it in the sixth inning. In the fan's poll, which was

unofficial, Dickey and Cochrane ran one-two in the American League, and Hartnett led the National League voting. However, because of the rule that every team had to be represented, Mack chose Rick Ferrell to represent the Boston Red Sox and did not select Cochrane. Dickey was on the team, but did not play, as Ferrell caught the entire game. Jimmie Wilson of the Cardinals started the game for the National League. Hartnett and the two legendary pitchers, Hubbell and Grove, all entered the game in the late innings. Gabby went 0-for 1, while Hubbell tossed two shutout innings and Grove threw three.

Gabby Hartnett was the premier catcher in the major leagues between 1924 and 1938.

When the baseball season resumed after the All-Star Game, the Bruins hosted the Brooklyn Dodgers to open a long home stand. The game was a tight pitchers duel for 7½ innings, as Ownie Carroll, Brooklyn's string bean right-hander, held a slim 1–0 lead over Charlie Root. Then in the bottom of the eighth, Chicago exploded for six big runs and a 6–2 win. Jim Mosolf, a journeyman outfielder, knocked in two runs, and Babe Herman's monstrous triple to right center field plated Mosolf. Hartnett had 1-for-3 plus a key sacrifice in the big inning. Charlie Grimm's charges took the next game also, 5–3, pulling within three games of the New York Giants. Guy Bush was the winning pitcher, beating Ray Benge. Hartnett was the big gun in the Cubbies' offense, with two doubles in four at-bats and three RBIs. The Windy City boys made it three-in-a-row by beating Clyde "Boom Boom" Beck 4–1 behind Lon Warneke's eleventh victory of the season. The win was also Chicago's eighth in a row. Grimm, Jurges, and Hartnett all had two base hits, with one of Gabby's going for two bases. The pride of Millville, leading his team with his excited yells and his clenched fist pumping the air, also scored two runs and threw out one foolhardy base runner. Brooklyn ended the Cubs' winning streak on get-away day, by pinning a 5–3 defeat on Bud Tinning.

Grimm's charges righted the ship immediately and captured seven of their next nine games. On July 20th, one of the big games of the month, Chicago welcomed the Philadelphia Phillies to the Friendly Confines and promptly blasted them into submission by a 10–1 count. The executioner was Babe Herman who had a career day. After hitting a single in the first inning, the big left-hander drove a home run over the left center field wall onto Waveland Avenue with a man on base in the third inning, launched another four-bagger to right center field in the fifth with a man on, and put #3 deep into the right field seats in the eighth. His eight RBIs gave him 55 for the year, just three behind the team leader, Gabby Hartnett.[25] Then, without any warning, the Bruins went into the tank, dropping their last six games of the month, three in St. Louis and three in Pittsburgh, to turn a spectacular 17–5 run into a modest 17–11 month. Their finish knocked them out of second place, and dropped them back to fourth, 6½ games from the top. Still the Chicago fans were optimistic, remembering the previous year's run for the roses, when they overcame the same deficit to win the National League pennant by four games. Things looked better when Pat Malone handcuffed the Cincinnati Reds for a 3–1 win. It was Malone's seventh win of the season against nine defeats, and the Cubs' ninth victory in 15 starts against the Redlegs. The Cubs scored all their runs in the third inning. Malone, a lifetime .188 hitter, drove in the first one with a single, Cuyler drove in #2 with another single, and Babe Herman laced a double to right for the last run. Charlie Grimm's charges made it a clean sweep by taking the next two games also, then laid out the welcome mat for the tough Pittsburgh Pirates, hoping to jump past the Bucs into second place and narrow the gap between themselves and the New York Giants. That didn't happen. This was a new year, and things generally don't repeat themselves. Big 6'3", 195-pound Hal Smith stopped the Cubs on five hits, and his teammates ripped Lon Warneke and Lynn Nelson for 12 safeties. Gabby Hartnett tried to keep his team motivated by lashing out two singles and driving in one run, but it all went for naught when the top of the batting order went 0-for-12. The latest Chicago Cubs batting statistics showed Riggs Stephenson as the leader with an average of .306, followed by Babe Herman at .287 and Gabby Hartnett at .286.

Chicago had a reasonably good month in August, winning 16 games against 12 losses, but it wasn't pennant material. They kept pace with Bill Terry's Giants who went 16–11 during the month and gained on the Pirates who lost 13 of 25. But they still trailed the New Yorkers by seven games. According to Tot Holmes, the reason for the Cubs' lukewarm summer can be traced directly to their home and away records. They played like world champions in the Friendly Confines, winning 42 and losing only14, a sizzling .750 percentage. But on the road, they were a sorry 19 and 37. One hot August day, a "Boston outfielder came over to Babe [Herman] and pointed out a man sitting in the left field box seats. 'Do you know who he is' [the player] asked? 'Nope,' said Babe. 'That's John Dillinger, the famous bank robber.' Dillinger, his girl friend, and a cluster of what appeared to be bodyguards attended the games throughout the entire week. Other members of the Cub team told Herman that the local police knew he was there but wouldn't tell the federal agents. In a related incident, Woody English had the same type of car that Dillinger drove and was stopped four nights in succession by agents with drawn guns."[27]

The first of September was a down day for Charlie Grimm's boys. They lost to the Cincinnati Reds by a count of 7–3, as Pat Malone was treated roughly by Donnie Bush's cellar dwellers. Six base hits and four bases on balls were all the Redlegs needed to corral the Cubbies. Chicago put together a 10-hit attack, but three double plays short-circuited their rallies. Gabby Hartnett had two singles and an RBI, Billy Herman had two doubles, and Hack and Cuyler also had two singles. The sun finally came up on September 3, as Bud Tinning tossed a four-hitter en route to a 4–0 whitewashing of Cincinnati. Once again Hartnett led the attack with three singles in four at-bats, an RBI, and two runs scored. Stan Hack, with a single and a double, was the only other Cub with more than one hit. Paul Derringer, a tall, rugged right-hander, who would go on to win 223 games over a distinguished 15-year career, including four years with 20 or more victories, went down to his twenty-third defeat on this day. He would finish the season with a record of 7–27. The win left the Cubs a distant 8½ games behind New York with 25 games to play.

Gabby Hartnett tailed off down the stretch, but it was primarily in his batting average, which was just .241. He still led the team with four home runs and 17 RBIs in 87 at-bats. Babe Herman finished strong when he played. But he was benched for long periods of time after earning Grimm's wrath for a couple of fielding lapses. On September 8, Babe whacked four base hits, including a double, and drove in three runs in the Cubs' 5–3 victory over the Boston Braves. The next day, however, he dropped a fly ball and misplayed another ball, as the Braves beat Chicago in 13 innings. From that point to the end of the season, Babe played sporadically, which hurt the Cubs' offense significantly, since their collective bats went silent down the stretch. Herman slugged the ball at a .346 clip, with two home runs and 16 RBIs in September. Ten of his RBIs came in his last 11 games of the season, when he went 19-for-38. He finished with a flourish, hitting for the cycle against Dizzy Dean on September 30. The Cubs lost the pennant by six games, but it was primarily the loss of Riggs Stephenson and Kiki Cuyler to injuries that did them in. Their two top outfielders, both with 100+ RBI capabilities, played in only 167 of a possible 308 games, with 86 RBIs between them.

Chicago stayed hot during the first half of September, going 10–3, but only shaved a ½ game off the Giants' lead. The moment of truth for Charlie Grimm's charges came when the two teams faced each other six times in Chicago, from September 13–16, in an OK Corral-style shootout. It was a wild affair, as every Cubs' fan for miles around converged on Wrigley Field to encourage their team and hurl insults at the visiting Giants. Chicago drew first blood when they scored two runs in the first inning and made them stand up for a 2–0 win. Guy Bush scattered nine base hits, and the New Yorkers stranded 10 men along the way. Screwball artist Carl Hubbell started for the Giants, and the Cubbies got to him before he found his groove. Singles by Billy Herman, Cuyler, and Stephenson, and an error, accounted for the two runs. In game two, another pitchers duel, a steady drizzle kept the crowd down to a paltry 5,000, but the Cubs played like it was sunny and 80. They jumped to a 2–0 lead in the third inning off Freddie Fitzsimmons, but the Giants bounced back with one in the fourth and two in the seventh off Charlie Root, to take a 3–2 lead into the ninth. Riggs Stephenson started the Chicago ninth by lining a single to right field. Babe Herman came out of Grimm's doghouse for one pinch-hit at-bat and "whistled a two-bagger right past Terry's feet. Strategy demanded that Camilli be passed, filling the bases with none out. Hartnett did not produce the grounder that the Giants had hoped would lead to a double play. He ran the count to 3–1 and then bounced a single over Fitzsimmons, sending Stephenson and the Babe home with the deciding runs."[28]

The Cubs had the momentum now. They trailed New York by 5½ games and had two successive doubleheaders against the league leaders the next two days. But hope turned to despair almost immediately as the Chicago offense went into early hibernation. On Friday, September 15, "Prince Hal" Schumacher and Roy Parmalee held the Bruins to just one run and 10 hits for the afternoon. Bill Terry's Giants won both games by scores of 5–1 and 4–0, essentially ending Chicago's pennant hopes. In the opener, Schumacher outdueled Tinning and Malone for eight innings, hanging onto a narrow 2–1 lead. Then in the ninth, they pushed over three runs without the benefit of a hit. A walk, two errors, and a wild pitch put the game away for the New Yorkers. Parmalee and Hi Bell combined for the shutout in the nightcap, with Bell, who came in with the bases loaded and two out in the third, picking up the win. The next day was more of the same. Only the names were different. Carl Hubbell, who pitched only two innings in the opener, went the distance this time, giving up 12 hits but keeping the big Cubs bats at bay when the chips were down. The Giants managed only seven hits off Lynn Nelson, but a wild pitch and a bases-loaded walk cost him dearly, as the two runs gave the Giants a 2–1 win. In the finale, journeyman right-hander Bill Shores went the route and gained the decision over Guy Bush by a count of 6–3. The double loss, coupled with the double loss the previous day, dropped Chicago into third place, 9½ games behind the high-flying Giants. The culprits in the disaster were the Cubs bats, which went silent all up and down the lineup. As a team, they were outscored by Bill Terry's troops 20–11 over the six games. Babe Herman played in just two games, one as a pinch hitter, and had two hits in four at-bats with a double. He was sorely missed.

The New York Giants went on to win the National League pennant by five games over the Pittsburgh Pirates and six games over Chicago. The Washington Senators raced to the American League title, finishing seven games ahead of Joe McCarthy's Yankees. The Senators were led by 26-year-old playing manager, Joe Cronin, who not only led the team to victory in the tough American League race, but also played a solid shortstop and batted .309 with 118 RBIs. He was ably supported by Heinie Manush (.336), Joe Kuhel (.322), and Buddy Myer (.302). Goose Goslin was in the thirteenth year of an 18-year career, but he was still dangerous, hitting .297 with 10 homers and 97 RBIs. George Crowder (24–15) and Earl Whitehill (22–8) gave the Senators a formidable pitching duo. Bill Terry's Giants were led by Terry himself (.322) and Lefty O'Doul (.306). Mel Ott, who slugged the ball at a .283 clip with 23 homers and 103 RBIs, supplied most of the power. The New York pitching staff was solid, with a 2.71 earned-run-average (ERA) and 22 shutouts. They were led by Hubbell (23–12), Schumacher (19–12), and Fitzsimmons (16–11).

The World Series looked like a tossup, with the big Washington bats matching blows with the New York pitching staff. But John McGraw's Giants made short shrift of the experts' predictions, as they disposed of Joe Cronin's crew in five games with their superior pitching. Carl Hubbell went 2–0 with a 0.00 ERA, pacing a staff that compiled a 1.53 ERA for the Series. Mel Ott spearheaded the batting attack with a .389 average and two home runs.[29]

The league batting champions for the season were Chuck Klein at .368 and Jimmie Foxx at .356. Klein with 28 homers and Jimmie Foxx with 48 led the home run parade, and Carl Hubbell (23–12) and George Crowder (24–15) were the top pitchers. Charlie Grimm's Cubs were led by Old Hoss Stephenson at .329 and Kiki Cuyler at .317. Babe Herman and Gabby Hartnett hit 16 homers each, and Guy Bush (20–12) and Lon Warneke (18–13) paced the mound corps. Gabby sparkled on defense yet again, as he made just seven errors and fielded .989. And he allowed only 35 stolen bases against a league average of 51. In the American League, Cochrane and Dickey allowed 67 and 35 stolen bases, respectively, against a league average of 56, making Cochrane's performance well below average and Dickey's well above average and slightly better than Gabby's.

The biggest news in the country in the fall of 1933 was the passage of the 21st Amendment by Congress, once again legalizing the manufacture, sale, and distribution of distilled liquor. Prohibition had been a major disaster that never slowed the flow of liquor into the country. It was just carried out in secret, and the government didn't have enough agents to prevent it. In fact, the only winners were the gangsters who controlled the flow and sale of the liquor, the moonshiners who manufactured much of the liquor in the hills of Kentucky and other southeastern states, and the bootleggers who moved the booze to market.

9

The National League's MVP, 1934–1935

When Gabby Hartnett left for California on March 1, 1934, he was not alone. He was accompanied by his brother Chickie, who wanted to see what a real major league spring training camp was like. Gabby outfitted his brother with a Cubs uniform and arranged to have him work out with the team for several weeks. Chickie, who was 27 years old at the time, could play any position and play it well. Many people felt he was the best ballplayer in the Hartnett family, and the Cubs might have offered him a contract if he was younger, but his time had passed. He had his opportunity to play professionally back in the mid twenties, but he blew it. After signing a contract to play for Reading of the International League, he joined the team in Pennsylvania, but got homesick almost immediately and returned to Millville without ever playing a game.

Martha and Bud also accompanied Gabby to Catalina for a pleasant four-week vacation in the sun. Bud remembered that many famous people visited the Chicago training camp, including Edgar Bergen, Charlie McCarthy, and Ronald Reagan. Bud recalled that Reagan, who did re-broadcasts of the Chicago Cubs' games for radio station WHO in Des Moines, Iowa, was called "Dutch" by his parents. Bud also became a celebrity of sorts at Avalon. He was recruited to do a photo shoot with his father and two Hollywood starlets, Ann Sheriden and Toby Wing. The photo showed Bud trying to pull his father away from the two pretty girls who were getting too friendly.

Babe Herman was among the missing when camp opened. He stayed home, complaining about his contract. "I ain't a holdout. I just don't want to sign this contract the Cubs sent me because the dough ain't big enough."[1] It was a typical Herman ploy. He held out frequently because he didn't like

spring training. But after meeting with
President William Walker in Los Angeles, he signed his contract and joined
his teammates in Avalon. One new
arrival was outfielder Chuck Klein,
who was obtained from the Philadelphia Phillies for three players and
$65,000 in cash. The 6', 185-pounder
had dominated the National League
slugging statistics for the past five years,
leading the league in home runs four
times, runs-batted-in (RBIs) twice, and
runs scored three times. His five-year
averages, based on 550 at-bats, showed
41 doubles, eight triples, 32 home runs,
116 runs scored, and 123 RBIs — a devastating performance. The Cubs would
discover that Chuck Klein's statistics
were a mirage, however. His numbers
were greatly influenced by playing in
Baker Bowl, a bandbox ball field with
the right field wall just 281 feet from
the plate. The 28-year-old left-handed
hitter had become an expert at lofting

Chickie Hartnett (right) visited his
brother at Avalon in 1934 and
worked out with the team for six
weeks. (Sheila Hartnett Hornof)

fly balls over the 60-foot-high tin fence in Philadelphia.

The baseball world lost one of its early pioneers when John McGraw
died on February 25 at the age of 60. "Muggsy," as he was known in his
younger days, was a pugnacious ballplayer who was a member of the famed
Baltimore Orioles, a team of feisty players who revolutionized the game in
the 1890s, popularizing such strategic plays as the hit-and-run, the squeeze
bunt, bunting for base hits, and the famous "Baltimore Chop." Muggsy
played third base for 16 years, compiling a batting average of .334. After his
playing days were over, McGraw managed the New York Giants for 33 years,
utilizing the same strategy and winning 10 National League pennants and
three world championships. During his managerial tenure, he won a National
League record 2,840 games.

As the Cubs played their way across the country, Gabby Hartnett had
to leave the team temporarily to be with his son Bud who was seriously ill
in Chicago with a strep throat. In the days before penicillin was discovered,
a strep throat could be fatal, and Gabby spent many anxious hours at his
son's bedside in quiet prayer. During his meditations, he promised God he

would quit drinking whiskey if Bud survived, and when that came to pass, Gabby swore off whiskey forever. He did like a little Harvey's Bristol Cream Sherry in later years, and he did drink beer, however. Once Bud's recovery was assured, Gabby left Chicago to rejoin the team in Cincinnati, leaving his son in the capable hands of his mother, his grandmother, and Signe, the maid. The Hartnetts had three maids between 1929 and 1943. Hazel or "Hay" followed Signe, and Amelia followed Hazel. The maids received a small stipend and room and board.

The Reds and Cubs opened the 59th National League season in Cincinnati on April 17, with Si Johnson facing "The Arkansas Hummingbird." A capacity crowd of 30,247 wild Rhinelanders were out in force to root for their favorite players, and for their new manager, former Cubs catcher Bob O'Farrell, whose predecessor, Donnie Bush, had finished last in 1933. The Reds' fans didn't have much to cheer about on this day, as Lon Warneke pitched a near-perfect game. He shut the Reds down without a hit for 8⅓ innings, while his mates were picking away at Johnson and Larry Benton for six runs on 11 base hits. Gabby Hartnett had two singles and a walk in four at-bats, with a run scored, an RBI, and an assist. Chuck Klein had an auspicious debut, sending a home run screaming over the right field wall with a man on in the sixth inning, as the Cubs scored four times to break open a close 1–0 game. In the ninth inning, with Warneke knocking on the door to immortality, Adam Comorosky stepped to the plate with one out and poked a bloop single to center field, breaking up Warneke's no-hit bid. The Cubs won the game 6–0. The next day, they pounded 43-year-old Dazzy Vance for eight runs on 10 hits in eight innings, winning 8–4. The former Brooklyn fireballer was one year away from retirement, and he was pitching on nothing but memory by this time. Guy Bush was the benefactor of the Chicago barrage, which was led by Chuck Klein who had a single, a home run, and three RBIs. Billy Herman had three hits and two runs scored for the Cubbies. Charlie Grimm's charges made it a clean sweep on the 19th when Pat Malone outgunned Paul Derringer by a 4–1 count. Chicago made the most of their nine hits, scoring single runs in the fourth, fifth, sixth, and ninth, offsetting Cincinnati's first inning score. Gabby Hartnett launched a home run in the ninth inning for the final run. Babe Herman went hitless, but made a leaping catch against the right field screen in the sixth inning, taking an extra base hit away from Jim Bottomley.[2]

The good times kept coming for the Cubs when they visited St. Louis. Charlie Root and Lon Warneke pitched complete games as the Windy City

Opposite page: Gabby hit a solid .344 in 1935, with 13 homers and 91 RBIs, en route to winning the National League MVP award.

boys chalked up wins #4 and #5. In the opener, they scored a run in the top of the ninth inning to snap a 1–1 tie. The winning run came across on a single off the right field wall by Woody English, a sacrifice by Billy Herman, and a run-scoring single by that man Klein. The first Cubs run was the result of a home run by "Chinski," as Root was called in the Cubs clubhouse. Tex Carleton was the hard-luck loser for St. Louis. In the Sunday get-away game, Chicago drove Dizzy Dean from the box in three innings and buried the Redbirds by a 15–2 count, with Warneke pitching his second successive one-hitter. Rip Collins' double in the sixth inning was the lone hit off the Chicago righty. Babe Herman broke out of a 1-for-18 slump by banging out three base hits.

The big bad Bruins won their sixth consecutive game on the 24th, when they opened their home season in frigid Wrigley Field before a meager turnout of 16,000 fans. They beat Dazzy Vance for the second time in a week, but this time they had to work for it, as the "Dazzler" kept the Cubs at bay after the first inning with his "nothing" ball. Grimm's charges pushed across three runs in the bottom of the first and held on to win 3–2. Cincinnati played victim again on the 25th, as Pat Malone beat Derringer for the second time, this time 6–1. Babe Herman had two base hits, Billy Jurges socked a home run, and Malone knocked in two runs to help his own cause. O'Farrell's slumbering Reds finally came to life after five successive losses at the hands of the Cubs and turned back their tormentors, 5–4, with two runs in the ninth. Bud Tinning took the loss. Klein had another homer, but this time in a losing cause.

Chicago finished the month by taking three out of four from St. Louis and one from Pittsburgh. They took the opener from Frankie Frisch's team, but it was a tense struggle all the way before they pushed over the winning run, with one out in the bottom of the eleventh inning, on a game-winning single by Gabby Hartnett. Guy Bush took Dizzy Dean to task for the second time, beating the Cards' ace by a 7–1 score in game two. Dean, who saw his record drop to 1–2, would recover nicely after his two meetings with the Cubs and finish the season with a sensational 30–7 mark, the last major league pitcher to win 30 games until Detroit's Denny McLain went 31–6 in 1968. Chicago's Babe hammered out three hits, including a double, and Klein added to his home run total by sending a tremendous shot 436 feet into the center field stands to the right of the scoreboard. The Cards gained some measure of revenge by pummeling Grimm's cohorts 9–4 in the finale. Pat Malone took the brunt of the attack, yielding seven runs in a little over six innings. Gabby Hartnett was the only Cub to give Bill Walker any trouble, touching him for a single and two home runs, with two runs scored and two RBIs. The Cubs backstop also shot down one attempted base stealer.

Billy Jurges was a sensational defensive shortstop for the Cubs during the 1930s.

The Cubs whipped the Pittsburgh Pirates 8–6 in 12 innings on April 30. Hartnett was once again the big gun for Chicago, rapping a single, double, and home run; driving in three runs; and scoring one. His twelfth inning single drove in the game winner. Jurges and English also had three hits for the winners, and Billy Herman had a single and a home run. Guy Bush pitched the last 4⅓ innings for the win. Charlie Grimm had his team sitting atop the National League standings as the month came to an end, their 10–2 record giving them a 1½-game cushion over the New York Giants. The Cardinals were 5½ games behind in sixth place. In the American League, the Yankees held a slim ½-game lead over the Detroit Tigers, who were building a powerhouse in Navin Field. The Tigers had future Hall of Famers Charlie Gehringer, Hank Greenberg, Mickey Cochrane, and Goose Goslin, plus such outstanding pitchers as "Schoolboy" Rowe, Eldon Auker, and Tommy Bridges. The early season batting leaders for the Cubs were Chuck Klein (.353, 5 home runs, 15 RBIs) and Gabby Hartnett (.268, 5, 10).

May was a 50–50 month for the Cubs as they struggled to a 15–14 record, while Frisch's Redbirds posted a sizzling 21–6 mark to capture the top spot in the league. Chicago began the month by losing two out of three to Pittsburgh in the Steel City, then splitting a four-game series with the Boston Braves in the Friendly Confines. On May 5, the Beaneaters took the measure of the Cubbies 5–4 on the strength of a late-inning five-run rally. Charlie Root kept the Bostonians under wraps for seven innings, but they knocked him out of the box before he could retire the side in the eighth. The defeat was particularly expensive for the Cubs as they lost Gabby Hartnett, who went down with a cracked right index finger. Rookie Babe Phelps was sent behind the plate to fill in while Hartnett was recuperating.

The threat of rain, or maybe the presence of the seventh-place Philadelphia Phillies, held the Wrigley Field attendence to a paltry 1,500 on the 8th, and it was just as well the way the Cubs played. Lynn Nelson was in the shower before he could retire a man in the first inning, as a walk and three base hits gave the Phils a four-run start. They completed the massacre against Malone and Dick Ward, running up 13 runs on 18 hits, with the Cubs chipping in with four errors. The final score was 13–6 with Chuck Klein going 3-for-3, with a double, a home run, an RBI, and three runs scored for the losers. Charlie Grimm's Bruins gave the Wrigley Field fans something to cheer about four days later, when they beat the Brooklyn Dodgers 5–0 on a two-hitter by rookie Bill Lee. It was the high-kicking Lee's second major league start and his second shutout, as he had blanked the Phillies on four hits the previous Sunday. The big right-hander had his blazer working to perfection, as he fanned seven Dodgers en route to the win. Billy Jurges hit one out of the park with a man on for the Cubs, and Dolph Camilli doubled home two more runs, as the Cubs scored all their runs in the sixth inning. Losing pitcher Van Lingle Mungo struck out 11 Chicago batters.

Chicago opened a series in New York with a victory over "Prince Hal" Schumacher. It was a 10-inning thriller with Lon Warneke going the route for the 3–2 win. Dolph Camilli homered for the Cubs and Bill Terry hit one for the Giants. It was an expensive win for Charlie Grimm's troops as they lost Gabby Hartnett again, this time with a bruised elbow, courtesy of an errant Schumacher pitch in the second inning. The Cubs were back in first place with an 18–8 record as the month reached the halfway point, and Gabby Hartnett was back in action behind the plate after being sidelined for five days. Pittsburgh and St. Louis were both within two games of the top. The New York Yankees had widened their lead to 3½ games over Cleveland and 4½ over Detroit.

The Windy City boys went on siesta the last two weeks of May, going 7–8 to fall back into second place, 1½ games behind St. Louis. They did register a victory on May 31, defeating the Pittsburgh Pirates 11–5 behind a four-hit outburst by Babe Herman. The big left-handed hitting slugger ripped two singles and two doubles, good for three RBIs and three runs scored. Gabby Hartnett did his part also, banging out two hits in four at-bats, with a double and three RBIs. For the month, the Chicago backstop hit the ball at a .341 clip with four home runs. And his defense was impeccable. Chuck Klein was the leading Cubs slugger with 14 home runs and 40 RBIs, in 43 games. Babe Herman was batting .316 with four home runs.

On June 1st, "Big Jim" Weaver, all 6'6", 230 pounds of him, shackled last-place Cincinnati 3–1. It was the Reds' twenty-eighth loss in 36 games. Bob O'Farrell's team actually held a 1–0 lead after seven innings, but the Cubs scored two in the eighth when Billy Jurges cracked a double down the left field line and Gabby Hartnett followed with a tremendous home run to left center field. The ball cleared the 50-foot-high scoreboard, 400 feet from home plate, but not many people saw it because the attendance at Crosley Field could have been counted on two hands and two feet — almost. It was 700. The next day, the Cubs were stopped by Ted "Lefty" Kleinhans, 3–1, with Bud Tinning taking the hard-luck loss. Chicago managed only seven hits off the Red southpaw, and left most of them on base. Hartnett was 0-for-3.

In the midst of the exciting pennant race, manager Charlie Grimm was blindsided by Chicago Cubs President William Walker, who traded first baseman Dolph Camilli to Philadelphia for Don Hurst. It was one of the worst trades in Cubs history. Hurst would bat just .199 in 51 games for Chicago and would never play another major league game after 1934. Camilli would go on to have nine outstanding seasons with Philadelphia and Brooklyn, leading the Dodgers to the pennant in 1941 with 34 home runs and 120 RBIs. Walker kept the trade a secret from everyone until it had been completed. "Babe Herman awakened in his Cincinnati hotel room on June 11 and found Don Hurst, former Phillies first baseman, sleeping in the other bed. Looking around for his roommate Dolph Camilli, Herman asked, 'Where did you come from?' 'I don't know, they just traded me for Camilli,' Hurst said. When Hurst reported to the Chicago dressing room that afternoon, the manager thought he was there looking for tickets to the game."[3] After the Cincinnati series ended, Pat Malone and his wife decided to go to Milan, Ohio, to visit friends on his off-day. They hailed a cab outside the park instead of waiting for the night train and convinced the driver to take them on their 200-mile journey. The trip was completed in record time, at a cost of $32, a weeks pay for most people.[4]

Chicago moved on to Philadelphia for a three-game series, with Hurst and Camilli facing each other for the first time. In the opener, Bud Tinning took the measure of Jimmie Wilson's team, 6–5, aided by Chuck Klein's fifteenth home run of the season. Gabby Hartnett went 1-for-4 with an assist. The Phils came back to win the second game 2–1 when Ethan Allen homered off Charlie Root in the eighth inning. Gabby Hartnett had a perfect day with three hits and an RBI. He also chalked up three assists, two taking out would-be base stealers, and one as the middle man on a short-to-home-to-first double play. The Cubs won the next day by a score of 6–4 on home runs by Klein, Hurst, and Babe Herman. Hartnett shot down two out of three base runners. In the get-away game, Camilli pounded a game-tying homer in the ninth, and the Phils won it in the tenth. The Cubs were up and down during June, but finished the month with an eight-game winning streak. Win #8 was a 6–4 win over Pittsburgh in Forbes Field. Bill Lee went the distance for Chicago, and his teammates blasted Pirates starter Ralph Birkofer for all their runs in less than four innings. English had three base hits to lead the Chicago attack. Babe Herman was the top gun for Chicago during the month, with an average of .382. According to Tot Holmes, "He slammed homers in the first and second game of the St. Louis series on June 5, then knocked in Billy Herman with the winning run in a 1–0 victory on the final day, dropping the Cardinals out of first place."

Chicago trailed the Giants by one game on July 1, and the Cardinals were another two games out. In the American League, the Yankees were one game better than the Tigers, with Washington six games out. The second All-Star Game was the top attraction of the summer. It was played at the Polo Grounds in New York, with the 1933 World Series managers, Bill Terry and Joe Cronin, selecting the players, in conjunction with the fans. The top vote-getter in the National League was Bill Terry with 7,144 votes, and in the American League, it was Charlie Gehringer with 7,315. Gabby Hartnett held a big lead over Al Lopez for the catcher's position, 4,792 to 1,148. In the American League, Mickey Cochrane outpointed Bill Dickey, 3,830 to 2,772. The game was played on July 10, and it was one of the more memorable games in All-Star history. A capacity crowd of 48,363 filled the little oval on Coogan's Bluff to overflowing. Hartnett, who would catch the first five All-Star Games, was behind the plate for Carl Hubbell as the game got underway. Gabby recalled, "After the first two batters got on base in the first inning, I called time and went out to Hub and said, 'Why don't you throw the screwball? It always gets me out.'" Hubbell took a tuck on his belt, reared back and struck out Babe Ruth, looking, on the "scroogie." Gehrig followed the Bambino to the plate and went down swinging. Jimmie Foxx was the next batter, and he fared no better. He fanned to end the inning. As Hubbell walked to the dugout, the big crowd exploded with screams, yells, and whistles. After the National League scored a run in the bottom of the inning on a homer by Frankie Frisch, "King Carl" went back to the mound for round two. The first batter was Al Simmons, a lifetime .334 hitter. Simmons took the first pitch for a ball, then waved at three in a row for strikeout #4 for Hubbell. Joe Cronin of Boston, another .300 hitter and a perennial 100+ RBI man, followed Simmons to the plate, and he also fanned, giving Hubbell five strikeouts in a row against some of the most dangerous hitters in base-ball history. Bill Dickey broke the string when he sliced a single to left field. That brought Lefty Gomez to the plate, and a friendly repartee between the Yankee pitcher and the Cubs catcher ensued. Gomez glanced down at Gabby and said, "I'm a .190 hitter. What the hell am I doing up here?" To which Hartnett added, "Are you trying to insult Hubbell, coming up here with a bat?" Gomez promptly fanned. Gabby said it was the greatest exhibition of pitching he ever saw. "What a gent that Hubbell is. He wouldn't even shake me off. He'd just make it a little wide and give me a chance on the next one to call for what he wanted to pitch. He'd rather have let them hit one than make me look bad before that big crowd by standing out there wagging his head to shake me off. There's a guy for my money."[5] Hubbell pitched three scoreless innings for the National League, but his successors didn't fare nearly as well. Warneke was raked for four runs in a little over one inning, and Mungo suffered the same fate. A 14-hit barrage by Gehringer, Foxx, Simmons, Cronin, and Averill gave the American League a 9–7 victory.

When the action resumed after the All-Star Game, the Cubs visited the City of Churches to engage the always-dangerous troops of Casey Stengel. As Tony Cuccinello of the Dodgers remembered, "We were getting the hell knocked out of us, 10–1 in the first game and about 12–2 late in the second game. Casey was up and down the bench screaming like it was 1–1 in the ninth inning. The rest of us were pretty quiet. The big Chicago pitcher, Lon Warneke, the guy with that high kick, had nailed a couple of our guys. Sten-gel thought we were too timid about it. 'Do I have anybody here who will take a crack at them?' All of a sudden, Van Mungo, our best pitcher says, 'I'll take a crack at them skip.' He picked up his glove and went to the bullpen. He threw a few pitches and Casey called him in. He hit Gabby Hart-nett right in the ribs with the first pitch. Mungo was a little smashed when he did that, see, because he had pitched the day before and he was known to take a drink once in awhile after a game. I don't think Mungo could ever do anything wrong in Casey's eyes after that."[6]

Next on the agenda for Charlie Grimm's cohorts were the Boston Braves, and the Windy City brigade was ready. They captured the first three games of the series to move to within one game of New York in the standings. Warneke won the third game 7–4, beating Fred Frankhouse. Hartnett had a single and an RBI, but Babe Herman stole the show with a single, a home run, and three RBIs. English, Grimm, and Stainback all had two hits. The same day in New York, Bill Terry's Giants were humbled by Pittsburgh 3–1 in the opener of a doubleheader, but bounced back to take the nightcap 11–1. The Cubs dropped the finale to Boston 7–6, while the Giants were edging the Pirates by the same score behind two home runs off the bat of Joe Moore and a singleton by Lefty O'Doul. The New York Yankees beat the Detroit Tigers in a historic game by a 4–2 count. Babe Ruth, probably the greatest home run hitter the game will ever see, sent his 700th home run screaming into the Michigan sky. His closest competitors were Lou Gehrig with 314 homers and Rogers Hornsby with 301. Gehrig, in the midst of his history-making iron man string, played his 1,426th consecutive game, but took himself out of the lineup in the second inning with a sore back.

The Chicago Cubs moved into the Polo Grounds on July 14 for the first crucial series of the year, with just two games separating the two adversaries. Big Jim Weaver got the Cubbies off and running with an 11–7 victory. Charlie Grimm had a four-hit day, and Billy Herman had three. Gabby Hartnett was 2-for-4, with two RBIs and an assist. The win, the Cubs' fourth in a row over New York (going back to their June series in Chicago) pulled them to within one game of the top. Grimm's charges couldn't maintain their momentum, however, and the Giants stayed in control over the last two weeks of July, going 10–5 before dropping the last game of the month to the Braves 4–1. The Cubs struggled with a 6–8 slate before breaking out against the Cardinals on July 31, sweeping a twin bill by scores of 7–1 and 7–2 before a packed house in Wrigley Field. The opener was actually the completion of a protested game, beginning in the bottom of the seventh inning with two men out, runners on second and third, and the Cubs up 5–1. They added two more runs in the eighth to give Lon Warneke a hard-earned victory, his first win in 19 days. Gabby Hartnett was 1-for-4 with an assist. Warneke and English each had three hits. In the scheduled game, Warneke came back to record a complete game victory, his fourteenth of the year. Kiki Cuyler had two doubles and a single, and Woody English had three singles for Chicago. Charlie Grimm had a homer and three RBIs. The wins, coupled with the Giants' loss, pulled the Cubs back to within 2½ games of first place. The "Gashouse Gang" from St. Louis was five games out. The New York Yankees and the Detroit Tigers were still jockeying for position in the tight American League race, with New York holding a .002 lead after sweeping the Boston Red Sox by scores of 11–2 and 2–1, while the Tigers were splitting with Cleveland, losing the first game 9–7 and taking game two 4–2. Lefty Gomez was the winning pitcher for New York in the first game, tossing a three-hitter. Lou Gehrig hit two home runs with three RBIs in support of Gomez. Johnny Murphy outpitched Fritz Ostermueller in the nightcap. Hal Trosky and Joe Vosmik powered Cleveland to their victory over Detroit in the first game before a large home crowd, but Tommy Bridges shut them down with seven hits in game two, to earning the Tigers a split.

Kiki Cuyler was the leading Chicago batsman at the end of July, hitting a lusty .342. Babe Herman, after scorching enemy pitchers for four homers and a .382 mark in July, had his season average up to .338. Chuck Klein had 19 home runs and 72 RBIs to go along with a .327 average, while Gabby Hartnett was ripping the ball at a .319 clip with 15 home runs and 69 RBIs.

Sunday, August 12, was the last shot the Cubs would fire in the 1934 pennant race. They marched into Sportsman's Park and humbled the St. Louis Cardinals twice, 7–2 and 6–4. In the opener, Bill Weaver took the decision over Paul Dean, thanks to two home runs and a double by Babe Herman and a homer and a single by Billy Herman. Pat Malone beat Paul's older brother, Dizzy, in game two. Cuyler had two singles, a double, and a triple for the Cubbies. Gabby Hartnett sat out both games, nursing an injury. He had tried playing through the injury for two weeks, but could manage just a .118 batting average during that time. That double loss by the Cardinals was actually the beginning of a sensational run that would culminate in the National League championship. After the game, "When Frisch counted perspiring noses on the train that was taking the team to Detroit for an exhibition game, not a Dean was in sight. It so happened that at that particular time, Dizzy was eating fried chicken under a tree in the countryside, laughing over how mad he figured Frisch was by then. Frisch was mad enough to fine Dizzy $100 and Paul $50. Notified of the fines, the Deans refused to go on the field. Frisch suspended them and Dizzy tore up two uniforms, registering great anger for a photographer. The players rallied around Frisch in the emergency. They vowed to play harder so the Deans wouldn't be missed. They won seven of the next eight games. The boys, especially Dizzy, had to take a public spanking before Commissioner Landis, to whom Dizzy confidently appealed. But they took the spanking like men. After the rebellion there was ability plus team spirit and team determination, plus two invincible Deans."[7] From there to the end of the season, the Cardinals went on a 33–12 rampage, with the Deans contributing a combined 16–7 record to the total. Gabby Hartnett returned to the wars on the last day of the month and homered and singled off Dizzy Dean, but the Cardinals prevailed in the game 3–1, pulling into a second-place tie with the Cubs.

Bill Terry's New York Giants held on to their lead during the last two weeks of August, finishing the month with an 80–46 record, good enough for a 5½-game lead over both Chicago and St. Louis. As September began, Frankie Frisch's Gashouse Gang kicked it up a notch and roared down the stretch, winning 21 of their last 28 games. Both the Giants and Cubs played less than .500 ball over the last four weeks. In the American League, the Detroit Tigers had opened up a 4½-game lead over Joe McCarthy's New York Yankees by Labor Day. The Cardinals began their final run by whipping the fading Cubs 7–1 behind "Old Diz." Rip Collins and Bill Delancey homered, and the Redbirds pounded Bill Lee into submission in a little over two innings, opening up a 6–0 lead. Gabby Hartnett had to leave the game in the third inning when he aggravated an old injury. The Cardinals took a big step toward the pennant when they nipped the New York Giants 2–0 in 12 innings on New York's home grounds. Paul Dean went the distance for Frisch's troops, holding the Giants to six base hits. St. Louis got to Freddie Fitzsimmons for nine safe blows, with three of them coming in the fateful 12th. Ducky Medwick started the rally with a one-out single to left. Rip Collins singled to right, sending Medwick to third, from where he scored on Bill Delancey's sacrifice fly. Collins came across minutes later on a single by Leo Durocher.

Charlie Grimm's Cubs dropped out of the race when they lost 13 of 21 games, including three of four to the seventh-place Philadelphia Phillies in mid-September. On September 21, the Dean brothers humiliated the Brooklyn Dodgers when Dizzy stopped Casey Stengel's charges on three hits in game one, and Paul came back to no-hit them in game two. Dizzy, who had a no-hitter himself with two out in the eighth, modestly told the reporters after the second game, "Shucks, if I'd a known Paul was gonna throw a no-hitter, I'd a throwed one too."

The Cardinals won again on the 24th and 25th to narrow the Giants' lead to one game. Bill Terry's weary warriors dropped two games to the Phillies in the last week of the season, and when Dizzy Dean blanked the Reds 4–0 on Friday the 28th, the two teams were tied for the lead. The Dean brothers beat the Reds again on Saturday and Sunday and claimed the National League pennant when the Dodgers, still smarting from a remark made by Giants manager Bill Terry over the winter, when he asked, "Is Brooklyn still in the league?", marched defiantly into the Polo Grounds and dismantled the Giants by scores of 5–1 and 8–5 in 10 innings, as hundreds of signs around the Polo Grounds, reminding Terry of his ill-conceived remark, read, "Yes, Terry, Brooklyn Is Still in the League."[8]

The American League race went to Mickey Cochrane's powerful Detroit Tigers, who left the New York Yankees inhaling their dust, seven games behind. The 1934 World Series, which opened in Detroit on October 3, was a classic. Both teams had led their respective leagues in batting average and runs scored and were second in earned-run-average (ERA). St. Louis had six .300 hitters and one 30-game winner, while Detroit had seven .300 hitters and two 20-game winners. In the Series opener, Dizzy Dean beat General Crowder 8–3 behind Ducky Medwick's three singles and a home run. Detroit took a hard-fought 3–2 decision in 12 innings in game two, with Goslin's single off Bill Walker driving in Gehringer with the winning run. Paul Dean captured game three 4–1, but Eldon Auker came back to even the Series once again, with a 10–4 win. Dizzy Dean entered the game as a pinch runner in the fourth inning and "failed to slide while running to second and caught shortstop Billy Rogell's throw right on the head. They carried Diz off the field on a stretcher, x-rayed his head, and found nothing," according to teammates. Mickey Cochrane's charges won the key fifth game 3–1 with Tommy Bridges tight seven-hitter gaining the decision over Dizzy Dean. The younger Dean kept the St. Louis Cardinals in the race with a 4–3 win, setting up a final matchup between Auker and Dizzy Dean, who pitched on just one days rest. In the third inning of a scoreless game, the Redbirds jumped on Auker for seven runs on three doubles, three singles, and three walks. Joe Medwick drew the ire of the hostile Detroit crowd when he slid hard into third baseman Marv Owen in the sixth inning, precipitating a brief confrontation. When he took his position in left field in the bottom of the inning, Medwick was pelted with fruit and other objects. After several minutes, Commissioner Landis ordered Medwick from the game for his own protection. The Cardinals won the game and the world championship by an easy 8–3 margin.[9]

The league batting champions for the season were Paul Waner at .362 and Lou Gehrig at .363. Mel Ott with 35 round trippers and Gehrig with 49 were the home run kings. And the top pitchers were Dizzy Dean with a record of 30 and 7 and Lefty Gomez with a record of 26 and 5. The leading hitter for the Cubs was Kiki Cuyler with an average of .338. Gabby Hartnett batted .299 with 22 home runs and 90 RBIs. He was hitting .319 at the end of July, but was in and out of the lineup over the last two months nursing nagging injuries. Playing while hurt, he hit just .269 in August and September, but still managed to send six balls out of the park. He once again dominated the defensive statistics for his position, leading the league in putouts, assists, and fielding average. He allowed only 37 stolen bases against a league average of 45. Mickey Cochrane and Bill Dickey were victimized 43 and 68 times, respectively, against a league average of 68, making Cochrane well above average and Dickey just average in that category. Neither man led the league in any defensive statistic. Cochrane hit .320 with two home runs and 76 RBIs. Dickey hit .322 with 12 homers and 72 RBIs.

The Cubs went into the trade market in a serious way after the 1934 season ended, determined to strengthen their lineup for a run at the National League pennant in 1935. Their first act was to trade 32-year-old Pat Malone to St. Louis for catcher Ken O'Dea. Malone didn't stay in St. Louis long. When he returned his contract with the statement "You made a mistake and sent me the batboy's contract," Branch Rickey went ballistic and quickly shuffled him off to the New York Yankees. He won only three games for New York in 1935 and retired two years later.

The Chicago brass followed that deal by obtaining big right-hander Tex Carleton from St. Louis for Bud Tinning and Dick Ward on November 21. The next day, they dealt Babe Herman, Jim Weaver, and Guy Bush to Pittsburgh for pitcher Larry French and outfielder Freddie Lindstrom. French, a 6'1", 195-pound southpaw, had been a consistent winner for the Pirates for six years, and would do the same for the Cubs over the next six years. Chicago management had been disenchanted with Herman for some time, considering him to be a defensive liability, and they felt Bush was nearing the end of the trail at 33 years of age. Lindstrom was actually a throw-in in the deal, but he would make a significant late-season contribution to the Cubs' pennant chase. Frank Demaree, a Chicago farmhand who had batted .383 with 45 home runs for Los Angeles in the Pacific Coast League in 1934, was called up to the big club and would be another important piece of the pennant puzzle in '35.

The biggest baseball news of the off-season was the release of Babe Ruth by the New York Yankees on February 26. He immediately signed with the Boston Braves, expecting it to lead to a managerial position, but, in fact, the Braves only wanted him as a drawing card. He would play 28 games for the Braves, batting .181 with six home runs before retiring as an active player on May 30.

Spring training went without incident for Charlie Grimm and his coaches and players. Augie Galan, who had batted .260 in 66 games for the Cubs in 1934 was a standout in the exhibition games, adding his name to the list of outfielders vying for jobs: Cuyler, Lindstrom, Klein, and Demaree. And rookie Phil Cavaretta, who had seen action in seven games at the end of the previous season, won the first base job over Grimm, who would play in only two games in '35 and then 39 games in '36 before hanging up his spikes for good. Gabby Hartnett, who had recently celebrated his 34th birthday, was in his fourteenth year as a major league catcher and was beginning to show signs of middle age, particularly around the middle. His weight had ballooned to the 220-pound range over the past couple of years and, more and more, he was being referred to in the newspapers as "plump" and "roly-poly." Although his speed was almost nonexistent, his bat was as deadly as ever, and the famous "Hartnett Arm" was still feared by enemy base runners.

As opening day approached, the baseball experts, who had been covering the spring training activities, made their predictions for the upcoming season. They selected the Yankees to win the American League pennant, followed by Cleveland, Detroit, and Boston. In the Senior Circuit, they predicted a championship for the New York Giants, followed by St. Louis, Chicago, and Pittsburgh, in that order. Pitching seemed to be the reason for the top selections. The experts felt the Giants had the best pitching staff with Hubbell, Schumacher, Parmelee, and Fitzsimmons. They didn't think the Dean brothers could repeat their 1934 performance when they won 49 games between them. And they felt the Cubs' pitching would have to exceed expectations in order for them to challenge the Giants for the top spot. The experts backed the wrong horse in both races.

The season opened at home on Tuesday, April 16, and the Cubbies came out with all guns firing. Lon Warneke gained the decision over Ray Harrell of St. Louis, 4–3. Dizzy Dean started for the Cardinals, but left in the first inning after taking a line drive to the left leg off the bat of Freddie Lindstrom. His injury was not deemed serious. The Chicago hero was Gabby Hartnett, who began his season in fine style, homering in his first at-bat, then driving home the game winner in the bottom of the eighth with a 400-foot drive that just missed being another home run, hitting the top of the screen. In between, he had a single, giving him 3-for-4. He also added an assist to his daily worksheet.[10] Charlie Grimm's charges finished the month as they began it, beating the Pittsburgh Pirates on April 30 by a 3–0 score. In between, they went 6–5. Southpaw Roy Henshaw, on his way to 13–5 season, blanked the Bucs on eight hits. Hartnett once again led the attack with a single, a double, a run scored, and an assist. Lindstrom and Galan also had two hits for the Cubs. Shortstop Billy Jurges did not play in the game. He watched from the stands after being fined $50 and suspended for three games by National League President Ford Frick for an altercation on the field two days before. Chicago's 8–5 record for April had them in third place, a ½ game behind New York. Cleveland led the White Sox by one game in the American League race.

The Cubs beat the Boston Braves on May 12 by a 14–7 score. Larry French coasted to the win, with relief help from Root in the eighth. Freddie Lindstrom led an 18-hit attack with three singles and a triple. Chuck Klein had three hits with a home run and three RBIs. Babe Ruth went 0-for-2 for the Braves, but had two walks and scored two runs. When the team was on the road, the Chicago Cubs often passed the time with a friendly game of cards, like rummy or hearts. Manager Charlie Grimm, trainer Andy Lotshaw, Gabby Hartnett, and even owner P.K. Wrigley, enjoyed the competition. According to Edward Burns at the *Chicago Tribune*, "Among card players of the Cubs traveling parties, it is not considered cheating to look into an adversaries hand. When you play cards with the Cubs the first thing you find out is that you must hold the cards very close to the bosom. Assistant manager Gabby Hartnett is the champion at the lightning peek. He is a marvel at what, we believe, psychology professors call perception. Gabby can take one flash and have a perfect mental photograph of a 13 card hand without missing a card. Gabby is proud of this gift. Just to show he is frank and above board, Gabby frequently makes such remarks as 'You'd have a helluva hand if it wasn't for that singleton ace of spades.'"[11]

Babe Ruth had one big day left in his bag of tricks before he retired. It was May 25 at Forbes Field and the Boston Braves were in town to tangle with the Pittsburgh Pirates. Babe Ruth hit a home run his first time at bat. The next time he came up, former Cub Guy Bush was on the mound for the Bucs. Ruth hit a pitch on the handle of the bat, and it just cleared the fence down the right field line for another home run. Bush, upset about what he considered a cheap home run, vowed it wouldn't happen again. When he faced Ruth a second time, he was determined to put three fastballs right past the old man. Ruth took one strike, then caught the next one on the fat part of his bat and sent it on a high arc over the triple-deck stands and completely out of the park. Years later, Bush would say, "I had never seen him hit a long ball and I wanted to challenge him."[12]

On June 1, the Cubs were still ensconced in third place, their 18–14 record leaving them 6½ games behind Terry's Giants. The second-place Cardinals were 5½ out. In the American League, the Yankees had a game-and-a-half lead over the Chicago White Sox and a 2½ game lead over the Cleveland Indians. June got off to a slow start for Charlie Grimm's team as they dropped a doubleheader to the St. Louis Cardinals in the not-so-Friendly Confines by scores of 4–3 in 12 innings and 4–1. Paul Dean beat Lon Warneke in the opener, and "Fidgety Phil" Collins bested Bill Lee in the nightcap. Gabby Hartnett smashed a homer and a single with two RBIs in the first game, and he went 1-for-4 in the second. Paul Dean won his own game by leading off the twelfth inning with a double and eventually scoring on a sacrifice fly by Frankie Frisch.

On the 11th, with his team mired in fifth place, 8½ games behind the streaking New York Giants, manager Charlie Grimm read the riot act to his charges. He banned poker-playing completely and put severe restrictions on pinochle. Card-playing had become almost obsessive with many players, with pinochle games lasting until midnight and poker games going on until 4 AM. "Joe McCarthy never would stand for poker when he was manager of the Cubs, and Rogers Hornsby insisted upon small stakes. Grimm at first tolerated small stakes only, but recently the lid has been off. Some of the boys have been taken for merry rides and there have been growls from trimmed lambs that at least one of the fellows had a superhuman knack for filling his hand just when pots were the largest. The objection to pinochle is that the Cubs, in their zeal for pinochle, virtually have forgotten about the charm of baseball. Instead of the usual banter about base hits, screwballs, and other such matters. Mr. Grimm has heard naught but talk of melds, 60-queens, 80-kings, etc."[13]

Following the managerial tirade, the Bruins went out and routed the Phillies in game one of a doubleheader, 15–0, before dropping the nightcap 11–8. Freddie Lindstrom piled up five hits in the two games, while Augie Galan chipped in with four. The next day, the Cubs were on the winning side of a doubleheader, beating the Phillies in the City of Brotherly Love, 12–6 and 9–7. Warneke and Clay Bryant were credited with the victories although the hitters should have gotten the credit for both wins. In the opener, Billy Herman pounded out five hits in six at-bats with four runs scored. Augie Galan went 3-for-6 with a double. Chuck Klein had a home run and two RBIs. In game two, the Cubs had only seven base hits, but they were the beneficiaries of 10 free passes issued by Orville Jorgens. Bryant and Galan homered for Charlie Grimm's troops. Because Hartnett was ailing, Ken O'Dea caught both games and did an outstanding job, going 4-for-7 with a double and four RBIs.

That night, in Long Island City, New York, the world's heavyweight boxing champion was dethroned. Max Baer lost a unanimous 15-round decision to James J. Braddock, a former longshoreman and journeyman boxer since 1928. Braddock, whose record was a mediocre 50 wins and 22 losses, dedicated himself to winning the heavyweight championship of the world one year before the fight, and by the sheer force of his will, he climbed Everest on this night. Baer, who held the championship for exactly one year, said he was retiring from the ring. Braddock would fight just one exhibition match before losing his title to Joe Louis two years later.

Gabby Hartnett was back in action the next night and went 1-for-4 with an RBI, but on the 16th, his injury forced him out of the game in the 5th inning. The Cubs whipped the Dodgers 9–4, and O'Dea chipped in with a single, a home run and three RBIs. Two weeks later on June 28, Gabby was present at the birth of his daughter, Sheila Ann Hartnett, in Evanston. He stayed at the hospital until he saw the baby and was sure that both mother and daughter were fine. Then he drove to Wrigley Field for the game against the Pittsburgh Pirates. In his first at-bat, the new father stepped to the plate with Phil Cavaretta on first base and drove the ball into the right field stands, giving Chicago a 2–0 lead and presenting his new daughter with her first birthday present. Roy Henshaw further added to the celebration by throwing a one-hitter at the Pirates, winning 8–0. The next night, the Bruins

The first family photograph of Gabby and Martha with their two children, 5-year-old Bud and his baby sister Sheila. (Sheila Hartnett Hornof)

stopped Pittsburgh twice by scores of 1–0 and 2–1, and Hartnett, who sat out the opener, went 4-for-4 in game two, including a double that drove in the winning run. The Cubs ended the month by dropping a 9–7 decision to the Pirates as Bill Lee and Fabian Kowalik were raked for 17 base hits, including four by Woody Jensen. The New York Giants were still showing the way in the National League race with a record of 44–18. Pittsburgh was in second place, a distant 8½ games in arrears. The Cubs were another ½ game behind. New York was also on top of the American League, with Cleveland 2½ games behind and Detroit 3½ out. Gabby Hartnett was still the Cubs' leading hitter with an average of .330. Stan Hack at .316 and Augie Galan at .301 were the only other .300 hitters in the club. Galan and Phil Cavaretta each had seven home runs. And Bill Lee had a record of 7–3 to pace the Cubbie's pitchers. Tex Carleton was at 6–3, and Larry French was at 7–5.

July started slowly for Grimm's club as they dropped four of their first six games. On July 6, they thought they had an easy win under their belt as they led Pittsburgh 8–2 after 8½ innings, but Pie Traynor's veteran team didn't know the meaning of the word quit, and they just kept hammering away at Larry French in the bottom of the ninth until they had pushed over six runs to tie the game. The struggle went into the thirteenth inning when the Cubs finally put a two-spot on the scoreboard, winning 10–8. Phil Cavaretta knocked in the eventual winning run with his fourth hit of the game. Galan and Herman contributed two hits each, while Gabby Hartnett also chipped in with two, including a double.

The third major league All-Star Game was played in Municipal Stadium in Cleveland on July 8, and the Cubs were happy to see it come, as they had fallen 9½ games behind the New York Giants, and they needed time to regroup. The All-Star Game turned out to be another American League celebration as they walked off with their third straight victory, this time by a score of 4–1. Lefty Gomez, who pitched a record six innings, was the winning pitcher, and Bill Walker of the Giants was saddled with the loss. The National League had only four hits, one of them by their starting catcher, Jimmie Wilson. Gabby Hartnett caught the last two innings, but didn't come to bat. Jimmie "Double-X" Foxx launched a two-run homer in the first inning to get the American League off and running, and he also drove in the fourth run with a single.

When baseball resumed again, the Chicago Cubs were fresh and eager to get going. The rest of the season was much more to Chicago's liking, as they made a determined effort to overtake Bill Terry's team. Charlie Grimm and his cohorts welcomed the cellar-dwelling Braves to Wrigley Field on July 14 and promptly swept them under the rug twice by scores of 10–2 and 3–1, increasing the Cubs' winning streak to six in a row. Gabby Hartnett's defensive skills saved the Cubs from disaster in another game against the Braves. It happened in the ninth inning and the victim was Boston rookie Elbie Fletcher. "Part of my job is to try to get a batter's mind off his work," Gabby said. "Their first baseman was at bat. The score was tied, three men on, two out in the ninth inning, and the count three and two. Tex Carleton was on the mound when I went to work on Elbie. I told him to watch the next one because he was sure going to see something different from anything that had ever been served up to him before. The pitch cut the heart of the plate and Fletcher just stood there looking at it, being struck out without ever taking his bat off his shoulder. We won the game in the last half of the inning." Fletcher later told Arthur Sampson of the *Boston Herald*, " That darned Hartnett was to blame. He told me I'd see something astounding and I got to wondering what it could be, and that pitch whizzed by me before I knew what happened. It was a lesson I won't forget."[14]

The Windy City boys roared through the rest of July, compiling a 26–8 record for the month, and picking up 8½ games on the league-leading New York Giants. They could have gone into first place on July 31 by sweeping a doubleheader against the Pittsburgh Pirates, but they dropped the second game 6–5 in 11 innings, after winning their eleventh straight game in the opener 4–2. The Giants lost to Philadelphia 5–3, and the Cardinals were on the short end of a 4–3 10-inning game against Cincinnati. Roy Henshaw won the first game for Chicago when they scored four runs in the top of the eighth inning to erase a 1–0 Buc lead. Gabby Hartnett, who was 2-for-4, singled with the bases loaded in the eighth to drive in the eventual winning runs. The victory was an expensive one for Chicago, however, as it was discovered after the game that Hartnett had broken a bone in his left ankle in the fifth inning. At the time of his injury, he was leading the team with a .347 batting average and 66 RBIs. According to the *Tribune*, "An x-ray examination revealed the fracture. Dr. J.J. Schill found the ankle bone sheared off and the ligaments separated. 'Even with the best of luck, Hartnett who has been hitting .347, will be unable to resume play for ten days,' Dr. Schill said." Hartnett left immediately for Chicago for further medical care.[15]

As August got underway, Chicago found themselves just a ½ game off the top rung of the ladder and five games ahead of the defending National League champion St. Louis Cardinals. In the American League, the Detroit Tigers were on the verge of blowing away all opposition. They held a three-game lead over the New York Yankees on August 1, but after a 23–7 run in August, their lead would be a more comfortable 8½ games, and they would coast home from there. The Cubs cooled off slightly after their sensational July run, and the Giants also treaded water, picking up just 3½ games on

Charlie Grimm's charges. But the St. Louis Cardinals caught fire, determined to repeat their 1934 championship. They ran off a 22–7 record in the heat of the summer to wrest first place away from the Giants by .008 points. The Cubs went five and seven while Gabby Hartnett was on the mend, dropped the first two after his return, then went 10–6 the rest of the month. On August 10, the Cubs were humbled by the Cardinals 4–2, as Dizzy Dean, on his way to a 28–12 season, picked up his nineteenth victory. Gabby's nephew Fred Hartnett told a humorous story about an encounter Dizzy had with Phil Cavaretta during one Cubs-Cardinals game: "Dean was pitching for St. Louis and Phil Cavaretta was a rookie. The Cardinals were winning by some fantastic score. And Cavaretta had struck out three times and comes up in the ninth inning and Dean says, 'Here kid, see if you can hit this,' and he underhands the ball to the plate and Cavaretta hits it down the right field line and takes off, and Dean takes off right behind him, and Cavaretta goes around first and Dean goes around right behind him, and they both slide into second base, and wouldn't you like to see something like that today? They used to have fun playing ball in the old days."[16]

The Cubs moved into the Polo Grounds on August 22 to challenge the league-leading Giants, with New York four games to the good. Chicago took the first two games of the series to cut the Giants lead in half, but Bill Terry's troops bounced back to take game three 9–4, with an eight-run barrage in the second inning off Tex Carleton. On get-away day, the Bruins eked out a 5–4 victory to knock the New Yorkers off the top rung for the first time since April 27. But it was the Cardinals, not the Cubs, who claimed first place. The red-hot Redbirds, who won for the nineteenth time in 22 games during the month, grabbed a ½-game lead over New York and a 2½-game lead over Charlie Grimm's warriors. Four days later, Frank Demaree enjoyed a career day as the Cubs and Phils divided a doubleheader. In the opener, he pounded out three hits, but the Cubs dropped a 13–12 decision to Jimmie Wilson's team. In game two, he stepped up the pace, ripping five hits, and the Cubs won by a score of 19–5.[17] The Windy City boys ended the month on a down note, losing to Birkhofer of the Pirates by a 5–0 count. When the stretch run got underway, they were just 1½ games behind the Giants and 2½ games behind St. Louis. Chicago beat Pittsburgh 8–2 on the 1st, split with the Reds 3–1 and 2–4 on the 2nd, and rested on the 3rd. When the sun came up on September 4, Chicago still trailed the Cardinals by 2½ games, but they were about to begin one of the most amazing winning streaks in the history of major league baseball. Over the next three weeks, the Cubs would win 21 consecutive games, second only to the New York Giants' 26-game winning streak in 1916. A curious thing about the Giants' streak was that they were in fourth place when the streak began, and

they were still in fourth place when it ended. That would not be the case
with the Chicago Cubs.

September 4 began like any other day, with the Cubs and their fans
hoping that their team could begin to whittle away at the Cardinal lead.
Charlie Grimm and his fellow ballplayers hosted the Philadelphia Phillies in
the first of a four-game series, but Jimmie Wilson's team drew first blood,
scoring one run off Larry French in the top of the first on a three-base error
by Chuck Klein and a sacrifice fly. The score was still 1–0 after 3½ innings.
Then the Cubbies came to life, scoring two runs on a single by Hartnett, a
walk to Hack, a single by Jurges, followed by walks to French and Galan.
Augie added a run in the sixth on a homer and finished a five-run rally in
the eighth by hammering a grand slam home run into the right field seats.
The win was French's thirteenth of the year against nine losses. Hartnett was
1-for-4 and had two assists, one of them on a "strike 'em out, throw 'em out"
double play.[18] The next day, the Cubs edged the Phils 3–2 in 11 innings on
a one-out, bases-loaded single by Frank Demaree, who had a three-hit day.
Chicago had taken a 2–0 lead early in the game, but the Phils tied it up with
single runs in the sixth and eighth. Charlie Root picked up his twelfth win
of the season. The Cardinals also won, pummeling Boston 15–3, but the
Giants were beaten by Cincinnati 4–1. The seventh-place Phillies were giving the Cubs all they could handle, although they weren't getting any victories. In game three, Philadelphia took Chicago into extra innings for the
second consecutive day; but once again, the men of Grimm hung on for the
victory by a score of 3–2. Lon Warneke went the distance for the win. They
finished off the sweep of the Phils the next day when Bill Lee blanked them
by a score of 4–0.

The Cubs next opened a four-game series against the cellar-dwelling
Boston Braves, beginning with a doubleheader on September 9. The Chicago
pitching was superb as Tex Carleton tossed a four-hitter for a 5–1 win in the
opener before a small week-day crowd of 11,500, and Larry French followed
up with a 2–1 victory in game two, scattering nine base hits. Gabby Hartnett had 1-for-2 with two walks and two runs scored, in game one. The
nightcap was a tense struggle from start to end. The Bruins got their two
runs in the first inning and French made them stand up. Boston narrowed
the count to 2–1 with a run in the fifth, but that was all they would get.
Freddie Lindstrom banged out two hits for the Cubs, with a double and a
run scored. It was a big day for Charlie Grimm's charges; the Giants were
idle, and the St. Louis Cardinals were beaten by the Phillies 4–3. Chicago
vaulted over the New York Giants into second place, only one game behind
the Cardinals. With their winning streak at six games, the Cubs' confidence
was increasing, and their goal of overtaking St. Louis now looked more real-

istic. Detroit still had a comfortable 8½-game lead over the New York Yankees in the American League, so this was the only real race left as the 1935
baseball season wound down.

Charlie Root was the next Chicago pitcher to take the mound, and he
proved to be as unhittable as his predecessors, throwing a 4–0 whitewashing at Bill McKechnie's outgunned crew. The Cubs broke a scoreless tie with
a run in the fourth, and then put the game out of reach with a three-spot
in the fifth. Lindstrom was the big gunner with a single, a double, and two
RBIs. Hartnett went 1-for-4 with a double and an assist. A small crowd of
4,500 enjoyed the proceedings. The standings remained unchanged as the
Redbirds won and the Giants took two from Pittsburgh. The Cubs ran their
streak to eight with a 15–3 thumping of the Beaneaters in the series finale.
"Big Bill" Lee was the beneficiary of two big innings, a six-run fifth and an
eight-run eighth, as he coasted to his seventeenth victory of the season against
six losses. Chicago piled up 19 base hits led by Stan Hack who went 4-for-
5 and Gabby Hartnett who went 3-for-5. Both men had a double, two runs
scored, and two RBIs for the day. St. Louis kept its one-game lead by trounc-
ing Philadelphia 10–2, but the New York Giants fell 3½ games out after
absorbing a 10–7 drubbing at the hands of the Pittsburgh Pirates.

Casey Stengel brought his Brooklyn Dodgers into the Friendly Confines
on September 12, but if he knew what lay in store for him and his team, he
would have gone fishing. Manager Charlie Grimm, with the pennant now
on the line, announced that he would go with a four-man rotation the rest
of the way, with Warneke, French, Root, and Lee carrying the load, and Carleton and Henshaw in the bullpen for emergencies. The big, bad Bruins still
had their hitting shoes on as the series got underway, and they made Lon
Warneke's day a pleasant one, erasing a 2–0 Brooklyn lead with four runs
in the bottom of the second inning and going on to a 13–3 victory. Fifteen
base hits shot off the Cubs' bats, with Augie Galan accounting for four of
them, with a double, a home run, and five RBIs. St. Louis continued to protect their slim lead with a 5–2 win over the Giants that put New York closer
to elimination, 4½ games behind with just 21 games to play.

The Cubs were on a roll now, and their all-world catcher was enjoying
every minute of it. In the clubhouse, he kept the players loose with his jokes
and funny stories. During the game, he was intense, pacing the dugout, urg-
ing his team on when they were at bat, and keeping up a constant chatter
behind the plate when the enemy batted. Victory #10 was a 4–1 win over
the Dodgers, with Larry French taking the measure of George Earnshaw and
Dutch Leonard. Brooklyn had a 1–0 lead in the fourth when the Cubs suddenly exploded to take control of the game. With one away, Gabby Hartnett drew a base on balls, and that started the avalanche. Before the second

out was recorded, the Cubbies had a 3–1 lead on successive singles by Demaree, Cavaretta, Hack, and Jurges. The Cardinals meanwhile were dropping a 13–10, 10-inning decision to the New York Giants, cutting their lead over Chicago to just four percentage points. Dizzy Dean took the loss in relief. After the game, French was questioned about what went on in the pitcher-catcher conferences that he and Gabby had during games. "Well, let's say we're out in front by a couple of runs in late innings. I'm a bit tired because it's very hot and my control suddenly gets shaky. So Gabby will walk out to me, and he'll say, 'Listen Larry, it's awful hot and this game is dragging. Now the quicker we end this, the quicker we can have a tall, cold glass of beer.' We'll talk about that cold glass of beer until I can almost taste it. Then Gabby will laugh and he'll say, 'I know a swell place around the corner. Let's get the ball game over and get ourselves a couple.' You may not believe it, but when Gabby walks back behind the plate after that, I feel like I've had a good rest and I find that my control has come back. Gabby kids a pitcher along and nurses him and bellows at him and somehow he gets more out of a pitcher than any catcher I ever saw."[19]

The Cubs moved into first place by one full game over the St. Louis Cardinals with an 18–14 win over the stubborn Dodgers on the 14th, while the Redbirds were losing a tough 5–4 game to the Giants in 11 innings. Charlie Root was the starter and winner for Chicago, but with a 16–4 lead after six innings, he got careless and was roughed up for five runs in the seventh. His relief, Roy Henshaw, gave up another five-spot in the ninth before Fabian Kowalik could stem the tide. Gabby Hartnett, his teeth clenched and his fist pounding the air to spur his team on, ripped three base hits, drove in two runs, scored two himself, and took care of one base runner in a double play with Jurges. This was the only game during the 21-game winning streak where the opposition scored more than three runs. It was also the first game that required relief help after 10 straight complete games. St. Louis, perhaps feeling the pennant pressure for the first time, blew a 3–2 lead in the ninth inning before succumbing two innings later.

Bill Lee pitched the Cubs to a 6–3 win over the Dodgers for victory #12, and watched their lead climb up to two full games as the Giants once again humbled the defending champion Cardinals by a score of 7–3, with Carl Hubbell taking the measure of Dizzy Dean. It was Dean's third loss in four days. With just 11 games remaining on the schedule, all eyes were focused on the five-game series between the Cubs and Cardinals that would close out the season beginning on September 25. The Cubs weren't buying into that scenario, however. They were taking it one game at a time, although they felt, to a man, that the National League pennant was theirs for the taking. Gabby Hartnett, with his infectious grin, and Stan Hack, with his con-

Stan Hack was an outstanding defensive third baseman and a lifetime .301 hitter.

stant smile, kept the Chicago clubhouse loose as they pursued their dream. When a reporter asked Hack about his hometown of Grand Detour, Illinois, the Cubs third baseman lamented, "It's so small, we don't even have a town drunk. Everyone has to take a turn."[20]

The first crucial series of the month got underway on September 16 when Bill Terry brought his never-say-die Giants into the "House That Wrigley Built," determined to claw their way back into the National League pennant picture. They trailed Chicago by 3½ games after taking three out of four from St. Louis, but they were even with the Cubs in games lost, so their fate was still in their hands. New York had gained some momentum over the last three days, but Terry had depleted his pitching staff in the process, and he had to gamble on rookie right-hander Harry "Gunboat" Gumbert in the opening game. He lost the gamble. Gumbert had a 2–1 lead over Lon Warneke, the Cubs' 18-game winner, after 3½ innings, but that disappeared in a big six-run Bruins uprising in the bottom of the fourth, and Warneke took control from there. Herman, Cavaretta, and Warneke all had two RBIs for the winners. Hartnett banged out two hits and carried over the tying run in the fourth after singling. Cavaretta's home run closed out the Cubs' scoring in the fifth. In St. Louis, Paul Dean kept the Cardinals close by beating Van Lingle Mungo in a classic pitching duel, 1–0. The Giants desperately needed to win the last three games of the series to stay in contention. Hal Schumacher faced Larry French in game two, and Charlie Grimm's charges put another nail in the New York coffin with a 5–3 victory. "Prince Hal" left the game with an injury, which was later diagnosed as a strained muscle that would put him out of action the rest of the season. The Cardinals fell another ½ game behind Chicago when they split a doubleheader with the pesky Brooklyn Dodgers. Paul Dean saved the first game for Jesse Haines when he stepped to the mound in the ninth inning with one run in, two men on base, and no outs and proceeded to snuff out the Dodgers' rally to protect a 4–2 victory. Unfortunately, his brother Dizzy didn't fare as well. He relieved Ed Heusser in the seventh and last inning of game two with the Cards up 6–5, but he couldn't hold the lead, being raked for three runs in an 8–7 Brooklyn win.

Wednesday's pitchers were Charlie Root (14–8 for the Cubs) and Clyde Castleman (14–5 for Bill Terry's harried crew). Castleman was not up to the challenge as the Windy City Bombers jumped on him for eight runs in the fourth inning, erasing a 2–1 Giants lead and igniting a 15–3 Chicago rout. The loss dropped the New Yorkers 6½ games off the lead with time running out. Billy Herman scorched the Giants pitchers with four base hits, while Demaree and Lindstrom cracked two of their own in a 20-hit Chicago barrage. Hartnett had 1-for-4, with a run scored and an RBI. St. Louis beat Brooklyn 6–3 to stay two back. The next day, Charlie Grimm's charges beat the Giants again, 6–1, behind Bill Lee. And the Cardinals kept pace as Dizzy Dean, who had absorbed four losses in eight days, finally marked up a victory, beating Brooklyn and Ray Benge 9–1.

September 20 was a day of rest for all the teams, so Hartnett and Root drove to the Sunset Hills Golf Club for a day of relaxation. By this time in his career, Gabby was an excellent golfer, capable of shooting par on occasion. The big catcher was noted for his long, booming drives, but he was not a one-dimensional player. He had a strong short game as well as a deadly putter.

When the wars resumed the next day, the Cubs met the Pittsburgh Pirates in a short two-game series, while the Cardinals faced the Reds in St. Louis. Roy Henshaw, with help from Lon Warneke, brought the Cubs closer to the National League pennant by stopping Pie Traynor's team by a 4–3 count. A wild crowd of 38,624 Wrigley Field patrons cheered their team repeatedly as they sensed a championship in the near future. Demaree and Herman had two hits each, while Galan socked a two-run homer. The win was a big one for Chicago because Cincinnati beat St. Louis 9–7 and the Giants split with Brooklyn, widening the Cubs' lead to 3½ games with just six games left in the season. On September 23, more than 40,000 people streamed into the Friendly Confines to watch Larry French win his seventeenth game of the year, a neat 2–0 shutout of the Bucs. Cy Blanton, Pittsburgh's 18-game winner, was a tough opponent, but a run in the first and another in the eighth sent him down to defeat. The St. Louis Cardinals stubbornly refused to fold, as they swept two from the sixth-place Reds by scores of 14–4 and 3–1. Hallahan and Dizzy Dean were the winning pitchers. The New York Giants, however, packed it in for the season, as they were mathematically eliminated after coming out on the short end of a 5–2 score against Brooklyn. The victory ended the Chicago Cubs' home season and reduced their magic number to two, since all five of their remaining games were against St. Louis. Frankie Frisch's Redbirds would have to win four of five to capture the pennant. Chicago had two days to rest their weary bones and heal their wounds before doing battle. Warneke, Lee, and Root were set to take the mound for Charlie Grimm, while Frisch had the Dean brothers ready to go in the first two games. Charlie Grimm was already looking ahead to the World Series as he got ready to play St. Louis. He vowed to keep the team active over the last few games of the season so they wouldn't lose their edge: "The only regular who is going to get any letup in his routine is Gabby Hartnett. The big boy's fingers are all banged and his lame ankle continues to bother him. So the minute we are over the top, out comes Gabby. All he needs is about the amount of rest he'll get before the World Series starts."[21]

While Chicago was resting, the Redbirds had to play Pittsburgh in a makeup game on the 24th. Bill Hallahan took care of business in that one, keeping the Bucs at bay, while his mates thrashed Pittsburgh pitching to the tune of 11–2. The next day, Paul Dean faced off against Lon Warneke, as Charlie Grimm's warriors went after their nineteenth consecutive victory and a share of the National League pennant. The contest was befitting a championship game, as both pitchers rose to the occasion and threw some of their best ball of the season. But Warneke was just a little better. Dean scattered seven Cubs hits, but the Arkansas Hummingbird held the Cardinals to just two safeties. Neither pitcher issued any bases on balls and, with one Chicago double play, St. Louis had only one man left on base. It was an overpowering performance by Warneke. Paul Dean was good, but not perfect. He started the game like Walter Johnson, fanning the first five men he faced; then he made his only mistake of the day, and it cost him. He grooved a pitch to Phil Cavaretta and the Cubs 19-year-old first baseman drove it to the roof of the right field pavilion. That was the ballgame.

Game two was rained out, so a doubleheader was scheduled for the next day. The Cubs magic number was down to one, and Dizzy Dean was the man chosen to make sure that didn't happen. His mound opponent was Bill Lee, looking for his twentieth victory of the season. Dean, who appeared to tire down the stretch after pitching 324 innings during the season, was no match for the Cubs' towering right-hander. St. Louis got on the board first, catching Lee cold with a two-run outburst in the first inning, but that was the extent of the Redbird offense. Lee shut them down over the last eight innings. Dean, on the other hand, gave up the tying runs in the third inning; the tie-breaking run in the fourth; and singletons in the seventh, eighth, and ninth, as the Cubs prevailed 6–2 to clinch the National League pennant. Freddie Lindstrom, with four hits and three RBIs said, "Dean's fast one didn't have a thing on it. He's one tired ball pitcher." Galan and Hack, with three hits each, also took no mercy on the Redbird ace. The pennant celebration had to wait until the second game of the doubleheader was over, and the Cubs took that one as well, beating rookie Mike Ryba 9–5. Roy Henshaw, in relief of Charlie Root, was the winning pitcher. True to his word, Charlie Grimm replaced Gabby Hartnett in game two and sent him back to Chicago, along with Warneke, Root, and Lee, to scout the Tigers. While he was at Comiskey Park, Gabby spent some time with his adversary and friend, Mickey Cochrane. They congratulated each other on the season's accomplishments and welcomed the opportunity to face each other in the World Series. They also posed for photos together to satisfy the press corps.

The Chicago clubhouse was a wild scene after the doubleheader ended, with men yelling and singing, hugging each other, and dousing each other with beer and other liquids. It was a glorious day in Chicago Cubs history, as the new National League champions roared back from a 10½-game deficit, which found them resting in fourth place on the Fourth of July, to nail down the flag on the enemy's turf. The 21-game winning streak, which didn't end until the pennant was clinched, was a total team effort, as shown by the statistics. The Cubs outscored the opposition by an average of 6.4 runs per game to 2.3 runs per game. The pitchers threw 18 complete games in 21 starts and had the following records: Lee and French won five games each, Warneke and Root won four games each, Henshaw won two games, and Carleton won one game. Six of the eight position players batted over .350, and seven of the players batted in 11 or more runs. Stan Hack batted .400 with 13 RBIs, Billy Herman batted .396 with 11 RBIs, Augie Galan batted .384 with 21 RBIs, Frank Demaree batted .366 with 12 RBIs, Gabby Hartnett batted .356 with 10 RBIs, Freddie Lindstrom batted .354 with 18 RBIs, and Phil

Cavaretta batted .250 with 12 RBIs. Defensively, the Cubbies were sensational, leading the league in double plays. The infield of Cavaretta, Herman, Jurges, and Hack has since been called the greatest infield in Chicago Cubs history.

Years later, Billy Herman looked back at that season and reminisced: "The 1935 team, damn it all, we had everything. It was one of the two best I ever played on — the '41 Dodgers was the other. In September we suddenly got hot. I don't mean just hot — we sizzled. How do you explain a team getting that hot? I don't know. Maybe it's the power of positive thinking. All of a sudden we got the notion that we couldn't lose; there was no way we could lose. Winning can become an infection, just like losing. We rode that streak right into the World Series."[22] Phil Cavaretta put it another way: "You ever go 75 miles an hour on the highway while everybody else is doing 50? That's how we felt."[23]

The World Series matched two evenly balanced teams, with Detroit capturing the American League pennant by three games over the New York Yankees. Both teams boasted of strong hitting, a tight defense, and outstanding pitching. The Cubs led their league in runs scored, ERA, and double plays. The Tigers led their league in runs scored, fielding average, and shutouts. The official betting line in New York City called the Series a tossup, even money, and take your pick. The Chicago Cubs had five .300 hitters, while the Detroit Tigers had four, but the American Leaguers scored a half a run more per game that their rivals. The Cubs appeared to have the stronger pitching, allowing half a run per game less than Detroit. Both defenses were sensational. Manager Mickey Cochrane, being superstitious and remembering that his team won both games in Chicago during the 1929 World Series when he stayed at the Edgewater Beach Hotel, booked his team there.

The World Series got underway at Navin Field in Detroit on October 2, with Lon Warneke (20–13) matching pitches with Schoolboy Rowe (18–13). An overflow crowd of 47,391 fans crowded into the little park along Michigan Avenue, which had a seating capacity of only 29,000. This game was the Cubs' finest hour, as Warneke stopped the powerful Detroit offense dead in its tracks, blanking them on four hits. Rowe held the Cubs to seven hits, but two of them came in the first inning and, coupled with a Detroit error, gave the Grimm-men two runs. Gabby Hartnett knocked in the second run with a single after the first run scored on the misplay. Gabby added another single later in the game, and Frank Demaree crushed a home run in the ninth to bring the final score to 3–0. Mickey Cochrane read his team the facts of life before game two, and they responded with a convincing 8–3 victory. Tommy Bridges was never in serious danger after his team ko'd Charlie Root in the opening stanza before the Chicago right-hander could retire a batter. Two singles, a double, and a two-run homer off the bat of Hank Greenberg sent Root to an early shower.

The Series moved on to the Windy City for game three, and 45,532 of the Cubs faithful filled Wrigley Field. Eldon Auker, an 18-game winner for Detroit, was opposed by Big Bill Lee, who was 20–6. It was a nail-biter with the Cubs jumping out to an early 3–0 lead while their fans went crazy in the stands, only to have the Tigers come back with a run in the sixth and four in the eighth to take a 5–3 lead into the bottom of the ninth. But the Cubs fought back. Singles by Hack, Klein, and O'Dea, and a sacrifice fly by Galan, sent the game into overtime. With Rowe opposing French, the Tigers broke through in the top of the eleventh on a single by Billy Rogell and a single by Jo-Jo White, which brought home the eventual game winner. George Crowder, who was 16–10 during the season, was Mickey Cochrane's choice to still the Cubs bats in game four, while Charlie Grimm countered with 11-game winner, Tex Carleton. It was another classic pitching duel as both men left nothing on the table. Chicago managed only five base hits off Crowder, while Detroit touched Carleton and Root for seven. The teams traded runs in the second and third innings, with the Cubs' marker coming on a home run into the right field stands by Gabby Hartnett. The Tigers pushed across the deciding score in the sixth on two errors by the usually flawless Cubs defense. Billy Herman led off the sixth with a double, but was left stranded. Hartnett was robbed of a base hit in the ninth when his line drive was grabbed by Rogell with a sensational leaping catch. Demaree and Cavaretta followed with singles, but Hack hit into a game-ending double play. Game five went to Chicago and saw another outstanding pitching performance by Lon Warneke, who pitched six shutout innings before being relieved by Bill Lee. Schoolboy Rowe went the distance for Detroit, yielding three runs, two of them earned, but lost a 3–1 decision. Chuck Klein accounted for the two winning runs with a homer into the right field bleachers in the third inning.

The Series returned to Detroit for game six, and Mickey Cochrane's Tigers closed it out with a close-fought 4–3 win, scoring the world championship run in the bottom of the ninth with two men out. The game went back and forth for six innings, with Detroit scoring the tying run in the sixth on a two-out double by Rogell and a single by Marv Owen. Billy Herman was a one-man show for the Cubs, raking Bridges for three hits, including a two-run homer, and driving in all three Chicago runs. In the ninth, with Larry French still on the mound for Chicago, Cochrane singled, went to second on an infield out, and scored the championship run on a single by Goose Goslin. The Cubs had wasted an opportunity in the top of the inning when Stan Hack led off with a triple, but stayed there as Jurges fanned, French bounced to the pitcher, and Galan flied to left. Charlie Grimm has been raked over the coals ever since for allowing French, a .141 hitter, to bat for himself in the ninth, in a game the Cubs had to win.

Pete Fox was the leading hitter in the Series with an average of .385. He was followed by Charlie Gehringer at .375 and Billy Herman at .333. Tommy Bridges of Detroit and Lon Warneke of Chicago both posted 2–0 records. The much-publicized confrontation between baseball's two greatest catchers, Gabby Hartnett and Mickey Cochrane, ended in a draw. Both men batted .292. Hartnett had one home run and two RBIs, while Cochrane had one RBI. On defense, Hartnett threw out one of two attempted steals, picked off one man, and had three other assists. Cochrane threw out two out of three attempted steals and had one other assist. But Cochrane's team won and Hartnett's team lost.[24]

The individual statistical leaders for the regular season were Arky Vaughan (.385) and Buddy Myer of Washington (.349) in batting, Wally Berger (34) and Jimmie Foxx (36) in home runs, and Dizzy Dean (28–12) and Wes Ferrell of the Boston Red Sox (25–12) on the mound. For the Cubs, Gabby Hartnett led all hitters with an average of .344, followed by Billy Herman at .341 and Frank Demaree at .325. Chuck Klein's 21 home runs led in that department, and Bill Lee at 20–6 and Lon Warneke at 20–13 paced the mound corps. Augie Galan, in just his first full season in the major leagues, established a record that will never be broken. He was the first man to play an entire season without hitting into a double play. He played 154 games with 646 at-bats. Dick McAuliffe of Detroit tied the record in 1968, but had 76 fewer at-bats.

Gabby Hartnett had one of his most dominating seasons both offensively and defensively. Despite being crippled with numerous injuries to his fingers and ankle during the season, he still managed to hit a lusty .344 with 13 home runs and 91 RBIs, in 413 at-bats. He once again led the league in assists and fielding average. And he allowed only 45 stolen bases against a league average of 50. Mickey Cochrane batted .319 with five home runs and 47 RBIs in 411 at-bats, and he allowed 44 stolen bases against a league average of 41. Bill Dickey batted .279 with 14 home runs and 81 RBIs in 448 at-bats. He led the league in putouts and fielding average, and he also allowed 44 stolen bases.

Elsewhere in the world, the famous humorist Will Rogers was killed in a plane crash on August 16. The Oklahoma native was on his way to the Far East on vacation when his small plane, piloted by Wiley Post, crashed on takeoff from a small airfield in Point Barrow, Alaska. Will Rogers, America's highest paid entertainer at the time of his death, was a popular movie actor, radio personality, and newspaper columnist. Wiley Post had gained fame in 1933 when he became the first person to fly around the world alone.

In the political arena, Congress passed the Social Security Act on August 14. The most important parts of the Act included unemployment insurance, disability pensions, and old-age pensions. Both employers and employees would make contributions to the federal government to fund the programs. Old-age pension benefits would begin at age 65.[25]

On October 23, the Baseball Writers Association of America voted Gabby Hartnett the Most Valuable Player in the National League for 1935. As noted above, Gabby had a magnificent all-around season, leading his team to the National League pennant with his clutch hitting, sensational defensive play, and overall leadership. He was an intense competitor on the field and a take-charge guy behind the plate; but in the clubhouse, he was a happy-go-lucky warrior who kept his team loose during the pressure-packed days of the stretch drive.

The National League held their annual meeting in Chicago in December, and Gabby Hartnett attended as the Cubs' assistant manager. The daily agenda dealt with rule changes, personnel movements and vacancies, and the effect of the country's economic conditions on the game. After the work sessions ended, Gabby and Charlie Grimm found time to shoot some pool in the game room and pose for publicity photos. One photo showed Gabby leaning over the pool table lining up a shot, while Grimm stood by observing his technique. Another photo showed a grinning Gabby with a large sack, supposedly full of money, slung over his shoulder. Later in the evening, the genial backstop had a chance to socialize with representatives of the other major league teams in the lounge. Gabby was in his element there, swapping small talk with his friends and enjoying his two favorite pastimes, a good cigar and a glass of beer.

It was a busy winter for the pride of Millville, Massachusetts. He was invited to speak at dozens of banquets around the country, and he tried to accommodate as many of them as possible. Major league baseball players were always popular after-dinner speakers, and one as colorful as Gabby Hartnett, especially one who had just won his league's Most Valuable Player award, was in great demand.

10

Reaching for the Top, 1936–1937

The sins of the banquet circuit caught up to Gabby Hartnett in February when he arrived at spring training. The National League's Most Valuable Player looked a little bulky around the middle when he took his suit jacket off, and when he stepped on the scales in the clubhouse, the needle hovered around the 235-pound mark. It took a lot of sweat and tears to cut Gabby down to a relatively svelte 218 pounds, but the old warhorse worked hard to get it done. He also worked hard off the field, hiking around the golf course with Charlie Root and Charlie Grimm in the late afternoon, or climbing the hills around Avalon to hunt mountain goats with Charlie and Stan Hack. Still, he didn't move as fast as he did in his younger days, and he confided to Edward Burns in the *Sporting News*, that he had rabbit ears on the ball field: "I can hear and just about locate any fan that shouts anything at me. The most common razz I get is when I fail to beat out a hit to deep short. This never fails to cause several customers to bark, 'Why don't you get a pair of roller skates, you big bum.'"[1]

One player was missing when the camp opened. Freddie Lindstrom, who had stepped in when Chuck Klein was injured late in 1935 and made a significant contribution to the Cubs' 21-game winning streak and eventual National League pennant, was released in January. The move, orchestrated by the front office, stunned manager Charlie Grimm as well as most of the players. The Chicago Cubs had a busy spring training, and Grimm was in high spirits as he looked forward to another trip to the World Series. The experts made the Windy City boys the favorite to repeat, but their South Side neighbors might have questioned that prediction based on their spring exhibition series. The White Sox, who finished fifth in the American League race in 1935, and who were picked to finish third in '36, swept the last three games of the pre-season series from the Cubs, to take the series three games to two. They won the final game by a lopsided 7–1 count on April 12.

Opening day saw the Cubbies in St. Louis to take on the dangerous Cardinals, who battled Charlie Grimm's team right down to the wire in '35 before succumbing to the blistering pace set by Hartnett and company. A week-day crowd of 17,000 paid their way into Sportsman's Park to see their hero, Dizzy Dean, take on Chicago Cubs ace, Lon Warneke, the man who had dominated the Detroit Tigers in the World Series. Dean, who had been a holdout most of the spring and wasn't able to pitch much before the season started, didn't have it on this day as the Cubs raked him for 14 base hits in six innings, scoring three runs in the top of the first, and adding another six runs to their total over the next five innings. Warneke was not at the top of his game either, but he didn't have to be. He retired after seven innings with a 12–6 lead. Billy Herman blistered Dean and his relievers for five base hits in five at-bats, including three doubles, a home run, and three runs-batted-in (RBIs). Gabby Hartnett had three hits with a home run and two RBIs, and Frank Demaree also had three hits with two homers and three RBI's. The next day, Roy Parmelee put the Cubs back in their place, taking a 3–2 decision from Bill Lee in a tight pitchers duel. Frankie Frisch's two-run homer in the bottom of the fifth inning overcame a 2–1 Cubs lead and carried the Redbirds to victory. Chuck Klein had two hits in a losing cause. The rest of the month continued in the same vein, and Grimm's troops finished the month with an 8–6 record, leaving them in second place ½ game behind Bill Terry's Giants. Tex Carleton was one of the bright spots for the Cubs during the month, tossing a four-hit shutout in one start, then scattering 11 base hits for an 11 inning 2–1 win over Brooklyn on April 30. Gabby Hartnett blasted a long home run to right field in the bottom of the eighth inning off Dodgers southpaw Ed Brandt, to wipe out a 1–0 Brooklyn lead. Then Woody English, pinch-hitting for Carleton in the 11th, hit a sacrifice fly to drive in Frank Demaree with the winning run. Billy Herman sizzled in April, batting a lofty .433 with 11 doubles and 12 RBIs in 14 games.

The month of May was more of the same, as the Bruins struggled to a 12–14 month, slipping into fourth place behind St. Louis, New York, and Pittsburgh. Their 8–7 10 inning win over the Pirates on May 31, after dropping a twin bill the day before, left them 6½ games off the top spot. Larry French carried a 7–3 lead into the ninth, but faltered, and the Bucs pushed over four runs to tie the score before Tex Carleton could stem the tide. Charlie Grimm had three hits and two RBIs for Chicago. There was one personnel move made during the month. Chuck Klein, the slugger who disappointed the fans by showing he was only human and not the mythical figure Baker Bowl made him out to be, was traded back to Philadelphia for

Gabby still had a powerful swing, even as his career was winding down. He batted .307 in 1936 and .354 in 1937.

outfielder Ethan Allen and pitcher Curt Davis. Frank Demaree had vaulted
to the top of the hitters list for Chicago, batting .337 in 40 games. He was
followed by Billy Herman, who had cooled off after his blazing start in April,
and whose average was now a more modest .328. Gabby Hartnett was third
at .322. Hartnett and Herman were tied for the RBI lead with 31 apiece.
Billy was still showing the way in doubles with 20, and Demaree had five
home runs.

The New York Giants came to town on June 3 and rode Hal Schumacher's three-hit masterpiece to a fast one-hour-and-39-minute 3–0 victory. It was the Giants' first victory in Wrigley Field after nine straight losses.
All the runs were scored in the first inning as Curt Davis was slow off the
mark. He settled down after that to blank the New Yorkers over the next
seven innings, but it was too late. Gabby Hartnett had one hit in four at-
bats and threw out one would-be base stealer on the back end of a double
play. Billy Jurges, who had been nursing a sore arm for weeks, and had been
in and out of the lineup, had to take himself out of the game after two
innings. He would miss 36 games during the season because of the nagging
injury. The Cubs bounced back the next day to take an 8–5 win over New
York and Clyde Castleman. Lon Warneke did not have one of his better
days, but managed to stay the full nine innings for the win. He also punched
out two base hits and scored a run. Billy Herman had another big day, ripping four hits in five trips to the plate, including his twenty-first double of
the season. Gabby Hartnett went 2-for-5 with an RBI and a run scored.

The first results of the All-Star ballots were released and showed Gabby
Hartnett with a wide lead over Gus Mancuso for the National League catching spot. Billy Herman also had a big lead at second base over Stu Martin
of the St. Louis Cardinals. Hack, Jurges, Demaree, and Warneke were in
close contests for positions on the team. Mickey Cochrane held a sizable
lead over Bill Dickey in the American League balloting.

Casey Stengel's sassy Dodgers filed into the Friendly Confines on June
5 and were promptly dispatched three times in three days by the struggling
Cubs. In the opener, the Bruins pummeled Dodgers ace Van Lingle Mungo
by a 12–3 count. A big seven-run fifth inning put the game away, and gave
Bill Lee the victory. Ethan Allen had three hits for the Cubbies, while five
other players had two hits each. Gabby Hartnett, after being called out on
strikes in the first inning, was so upset with the call that he let umpire Lee
Ballanfant know about it in no uncertain terms. Ballanfant took the abuse
for a few minutes, then thumbed the irate Hartnett to an early shower. Hartnett was back the next day and the Bruins pounded the Bums 10–4, as Tex
Carleton coasted to the victory. Every Chicago player had at least one hit
with the exception of Woody English. Galan, Demaree, and Carleton had

two hits each, and Phil Cavaretta rapped a double and a home run, good for four RBIs. Hartnett had a double in four trips to the plate and gunned down two base runners who were bold enough to test the "Hartnett Arm." The next day looked like déjà vu, as Charlie Grimm's sluggers took the measure of Tom Baker, a journeyman right-hander en route to a 1–8 season. The final score was 4–3, with the winning run crossing the plate on a bases-loaded walk. Ken O'Dea, who was the recipient of the final walk, was replacing Gabby Hartnett, who missed the next 10 games with assorted injuries. On the same day in New York, the Yankees defeated the Cleveland Indians 4–2 behind home runs by Lou Gehrig and Tony Lazzeri. Rookie phenom Joe DiMaggio saw his consecutive-game hitting streak come to an end after 18 games. The fleet-footed center fielder, who was leading the American League in batting with an average of .379, would set an all-time consecutive-game hitting streak of 56 games five years later, on his way to being recognized by many experts as the greatest all-around player in baseball history.

On June 7, Larry French blanked the Phillies 3–0, scattering eight hits along the way. Ken O'Dea continued to pound the ball, slashing a double and a single and scoring one run. French was not only a valuable asset on the mound, he was also in demand in the clubhouse. According to Gold and Ahrens, "French possessed good business acumen. He was the advisor of many of the Cubs in transactions of all kinds and served as an income tax consultant. Off the field he dabbled in real estate, owning several apartment houses and an auto loan business."[2] When Roy Henshaw took a 6–3 decision from the Phillies the next day, it was the Cubs' sixth consecutive victory. Demaree and Herman once again paced the attack with two hits each. Lon Warneke continued the good times by defeating former Cub Fabian Kowalik by a score of 4–3. Kowalik had a 3–2 lead with two out and no one on base in the bottom of the ninth inning, but couldn't finish off the stubborn Cubbies. Minutes later, with the bases loaded, Ken O'Dea singled to snatch victory from defeat for Charlie Grimm's charges. The 23-year-old backstop had three hits in all, with a triple and three RBIs. The winning streak hit eight when "Big Bill" Lee took the measure of the Phils 6–4, thanks to two-hit games from Hack, Galan, Demaree, and Allen. Stan Hack's home run in the seventh inning broke a two-all tie and propelled the Bruins to victory. The winning streak moved Chicago past the New York Giants into second place, still 3½ games behind the Redbirds. In the American League, the Yankees and Red Sox were involved in a dogfight, with New York clinging to a 1½-game lead. Detroit was 7½ games out of first.

On June 12, the sixth-place Boston Bees (formerly the Braves) sneaked into the Friendly Confines and were quickly routed by Charlie Grimm's charges 17–1. The star of the day, as Irving Vaughan noted in the *Chicago*

Tribune, was "...Ken O'Dea. Continuing in the stride that has kept old Gabby Hartnett in temporary obscurity, Ken contributed two singles, one double, one triple, and one pass to the day's carnival. His triple cleaned up a full house. One of his singles also appeared with the bases loaded. And his double inaugurated the final Cub scoring spree in the seventh. Woody English amused with a pair of two-baggers, both run producers. Ethan Allen, who also tripled with the bases full, figured in another profitable incident by doubling. Phil Cavaretta poled a homer as the first incident in a six-run fifth inning, and singled to assist in a two-run affair in the sixth. And while the battle was funny enough without this one, Tex Carleton, who did all the pitching, hit a homer which accounted for one of the half-dozen runs in the fifth."[3] Victory #10 was a 7–2 whipping of the Bees, who scored both their runs in the top of the first, catching Curt Davis before he was warmed up. The rangy right-hander shut Bill McKechnie's charges down over the last eight innings, while his teammates raked Ben Cantwell and Tiny Chaplin for seven runs on 10 base hits. Herman had two singles, a double, an RBI, and two runs scored. The Cubs beat Boston again the next day, with Frank Demaree knocking in all the runs with two homers in a 3–1 victory. Lon Warneke limited the Bees to seven safeties in a complete game effort.

Mickey Cochrane, Gabby Hartnett's American League counterpart since 1925, was hospitalized in Detroit with a nervous condition after collapsing in Philadelphia. The rest and relaxation worked wonders with the 33-year-old manager, and he was released from the hospital within a few days.

The Chicago Cubs hit the road after the Boston series. The first stop was Philadelphia, and Charlie Grimm's charges treated their hosts shabbily. In their initial meeting, Larry French outpitched Fabian Kowalik for a 4–1 win. The Cubs righty was in and out of trouble all day, but he bore down in the clutch to strand 10 runners. Phil Cavaretta clipped Kowalik for three hits, while Herman, O'Dea, Demaree, and Allen all had two. In game two, the Cubs used three pitchers to contain the Phils, with Lon Warneke picking up the win with 3⅔ innings of relief. Roy Henshaw, who yielded five base hits and three walks before leaving the game with two outs in the fifth, broke a string of 12 consecutive complete games thrown by the Chicago pitching staff. Ken O'Dea once again led the Bruins attack with a single, a double, and two RBIs. Hack, Herman, and English also had two hits.

While the ferocious Cubbies were manhandling Jimmie Wilson's outgunned troops, the New York Yankees were in Cleveland, annihilating the third-place Indians in a doubleheader by scores of 15–4 and 12–2 behind Red Ruffing and Monte Pearson. Ruffing led the Yank attack in the opener with four hits, including two home runs. Frank Crosetti also had four hits. In the nightcap, Monte Pearson punched out four base hits, giving the Yankee hurlers eight hits in 10 trips to the plate for the day, with two home runs and six RBIs. New York blasted the Cleveland pitching staff for 38 base hits, including 13 for extra bases.

Yankee Stadium was a popular place while the Yanks were away, hosting a much-celebrated heavyweight boxing match between the young Detroit sensation, Joe Louis, and the former World Heavyweight champion, Max Schmeling. The "Brown Bomber" went into the match a heavy favorite, but the German slugger upset the odds by smashing Louis into oblivion in the twelfth round of a scheduled 15-round fight. Schmeling took control of the fight early and gave the American boxer a savage beating before finally putting him down for the count.

On June 20, Gabby Hartnett donned the tools of ignorance for the first time in two weeks, but went hitless as the Bruins broke a four-all tie with the Dodgers, scoring two runs in the ninth inning to win 6–4. Ken O'Dea, in a pinch-hitting role, singled with the bases loaded in the ninth inning to drive in the winning runs. The next day, Chicago and the Brooks met in a doubleheader, and the Windy City boys captured their fifteenth consecutive victory in the lid-lifter by a score of 7–2, with Curt Davis tossing a neat five-hitter. Billy Herman paced the Cub attack with a single, a triple, two runs scored, and two RBIs. Gabby Hartnett had a double, an RBI, and a run scored, and English and Davis had two singles each. The Chicago victory string was finally snapped in game two as Brooklyn fireballer Van Lingle Mungo took a 6–4 decision over Bill Lee. Charlie Grimm hit a pinch-hit home run in the eighth inning. The Chicago Cubs' 15-game winning streak began with the Cubs in fourth place in the National League, eight games behind the league-leading St. Louis Cardinals. When it ended, they were in second place, just a ½ game off the top rung, with Pittsburgh a game behind Chicago. Frank Demaree at .345 and Billy Herman at .338 were the top Cubs hitters. The New York Yankees held a 4½-game lead over the Boston Red Sox in the American League.

The Cubs bounced in and out of first place in early July, splitting a series with the Cincinnati Reds, then dividing a Fourth Of July doubleheader with the Pittsburgh Pirates. The Bruins took the opener of the holiday skirmish by a count of 3–2 in 10 innings. Larry French upped his record to 7–1 with a route-going performance. Stan Hack knocked in the winning run with a single in the tenth, one of his two hits in the game. Frank Demaree, who also had two hits, homered earlier in the game. Mace Brown spoiled the day for Charlie Grimm's troops by stopping them 7–4 in the nightcap. Woody English had a 3-for-3 day in the loss, and losing pitcher Bill Lee was 2-for-2.

The final fan poll for the fourth Major League All-Star Game was announced, and Gabby Hartnett was designated as the National League

catcher for the fourth straight time. He polled 24,643 votes to 16,214 for Gus Mancuso of the New York Giants. Billy Herman, Stan Hack, and Frank Demaree also won positions on the team, while Curt Davis and Lon Warneke were selected for the pitching staff. Mickey Cochrane once again nosed out Bill Dickey for the American League spot by a count of 20,576 to 15,722. The All-Star Game was played at Braves Field on July 7, with Lefty Grove drawing the starting assignment against Dizzy Dean. The game was another fine pitchers duel, with the Cardinal fireballer getting the best of the A's ace, leaving with a 2–0 lead after three innings. The National League pushed over two more scores in the fifth off Schoolboy Rowe and hung on to win 4–3. Gabby Hartnett was credited with the game-winning hit when he tripled in the first run of the game in the second inning. The Cubs catcher caught the entire game, with one hit in four at-bats. Another Cubbie, Augie Galan, homered in the fifth inning, as the Chicago representatives scored all four National League runs, and Lon Warneke got the save. The win was the National League's first in four tries against their American League foes.

When action resumed, Chicago opened with a satisfying 3–1 victory over the New York Giants at the Polo Grounds. Larry French tacked up another win, holding Bill Terry's sluggers to just four hits. Hartnett had 1-for-4 with an assist. According to Gabby's nephew, Fred Hartnett, life in the big leagues could be an adventure. "One of my uncles on my mother's side went to New York. He was looking for a job as a runner on Wall Street. The Cubs were in town to play the Giants, so he spent five days with them in New York. He said they wanted him to go to Philadelphia with them, but he said, 'I would have been dead because they stayed up all night carousing, then they'd play ball. They slept till late morning, played ball in the afternoon, and were off again. It was the same thing day after day.'"[4]

As July drew to a close, the Chicago Cubs were still clinging to the top spot with a record of 58–36, good enough for a one-game lead over St. Louis, with New York another six games behind. The New York Yankees had opened up a 9½-game lead over the Cleveland Indians in the American League race and were widening it day by day. The Chicago Cubs batting leaders included Frank Demaree at .357, Billy Herman at .320, Ethan Allen at .302, and Gabby Hartnett at .301. Demaree had a wide lead in home runs with 13 (versus seven for Augie Galan). Larry French at 10–3, Lon Warneke at 11–6, Tex Carleton at 9–5, and Bill Lee at 11–6 were setting the pace on the mound.

Tex Carleton and Boston Bees right-hander Johnny Lanning crossed

Opposite page: Gabby Harnett was intense on the playing field. Here, he politely lets the umpire know he missed the call. (Roy Hartnett)

swords in a brilliant pitching duel on August 1, with the "Arkansas Hummingbird" eking out a 1–0 victory. Gabby Hartnett singled in the winning run off losing pitcher Bob Smith in the eleventh inning, after Lanning had shut the Cubs down over the first 10 innings. Charlie Grimm's cohorts lost the next two games and fell out of the lead. They never recovered, struggling through a 16–17 month that left them floundering in third place, four games behind the sizzling New York Giants, who won 24 of 27 games during the month, to pass both the Cubs and the Cardinals. Carl Hubbell spearheaded the Giants' surge by winning his last 16 games of the season to finish with a record of 26–6. Only a clutch 1–0 victory by Lon Warneke over the Giants Frank Gabler on the last day of the month kept the Chicagoans within striking range. Ethan Allen's three-bagger and Billy Herman's single in the sixth inning accounted for the only run of the game. Gabby Hartnett had a triple in three at-bats and gunned down two base runners.

September was another sub-.500 month for the Cubbies, as they limped home with a 13–14 record down the stretch, leaving them in a second-place tie with the St. Louis Cardinals. The New York Giants held their own against both teams to win the pennant by five games. Joe McCarthy's Bronx Bombers made a shambles of the American League race, winning 102 games to outdistance the Detroit Tigers by a whopping 19½ games. It was New York's eighth pennant since 1921.

The Yankees were a heavy favorite to defeat the New York Giants in the World Series, and they made the odds stand up as they won the world championship in six games. The Giants made a fight of it for awhile, beating their cross-river adversaries at home in the opening game by a score of 6–1 behind "King Carl" Hubbell. The Bronx Bombers jumped on Hal Schumacher and four relievers from the first pitch in game two, to rout Bill Terry's crew by a score of 18–4. Crosetti and DiMaggio had three hits, and four other players had two hits each, as Lefty Gomez coasted to an easy victory. Bump Hadley outpitched Freddie Fitzsimmons 2–1 in Yankee Stadium in game three, and Monte Pearson beat Hubbell 5–2 the next day, giving the Yanks a three-games-to-one lead. "Prince Hal" Schumacher stopped the rout temporarily with a hard-fought 5–4 win in 10 innings. Returning to their home grounds, the Giants jumped out to a quick 2–0 lead in the first inning off Gomez, but that was all she wrote. The Yankees pounded Fitzsimmons for five runs in 3⅔ innings and went on from there to clinch their fifth world championship with a 13–5 victory. Jake Powell led the Yankee attack with an average of .455. He was followed by Rolfe at .400 and rookie Joe DiMaggio at .346. Dick Bartell hit .341 for the Giants. Lefty Gomez had a perfect 2–0 record for the Yankees.[5]

Paul Waner at .373 and Luke Appling at .388 were the league's batting champions for 1936. Mel Ott and Lou Gehrig with 33 and 49 homers, respectively, were the home run kings, and Carl Hubbell at 26–6 and Tommy Bridges at 23–11 topped the pitchers. Frank Demaree was the leading Chicago Cubs hitter with an average of .350, followed by Billy Herman at .334. Demaree had 16 home runs, while Larry French went 18–9 and Bill Lee went 18–11 on the mound. Billy Herman slugged 57 doubles for the second year in a row, giving him a major league record of 114 doubles in two consecutive seasons. Thirty-five-year-old Gabby Hartnett had another outstanding year, playing in 121 games with a .307 batting average, including seven home runs and 64 RBIs in 424 at-bats. He led the league in fielding with an average of .991, and he allowed only 39 stolen bases against a league average of 50.

Larry French won 90 games for the Cubs between 1935 and 1940.

Bill Dickey allowed 47 stolen bases against a league average of 36. The Yankees backstop did not lead the league in any defensive categories, but he had a sensational year with the bat. He hit a stratospheric .362, with 22 home runs and 107 RBIs, in 423 at-bats. Mickey Cochrane played in just 44 games as his career was winding down. He would play in 27 games in 1937 before suffering an injury that would end his career.

The 1937 season looked to be another dogfight in the National League, with New York, Pittsburgh, and Chicago all vying for the pennant. It would turn out to be an injury-plagued and disappointing season for Charlie Grimm's troops, as Gabby Hartnett, Curt Davis, and Tex Carleton all went down with various afflictions before the season ever got underway. Hartnett tore a muscle in his throwing arm during an infield drill in Phoenix, Arizona, and was out until May 13. Davis tore ligaments in his arm in Yuma, was lost to the team until June 4, and didn't make his first start until early July. And Carleton suffered a chipped elbow in California and didn't make his first start until the third week of May. In one of the few player moves made over the off-season, the Cubs obtained the services of second baseman Lonnie Frey in exchange for Roy Henshaw and Woody English on December 5, 1936.

The season got underway on a down note for the Chicago Cubs. First they lost another spring series to the White Sox, six games to five. The final game, a 7–6, 10-inning White Sox victory, clinched the series. The regular season opener, on April 18, was no better. Cy Blanton, who was 13–15 for the Pirates in 1936, blanked Charlie Grimm's charges 5–0 on five hits. Larry French took the loss. Augie Galan and Stan Hack each had two hits for the losers. It was not a good month for the Cubs, as they dropped six of their first seven games before beating Pittsburgh 7–2 on the last day of the month. Roy Parmelee was the winning pitcher for Chicago, throwing a complete game, while his mates combed Russ Bauers and two relievers for 17 base hits. Demaree, O'Dea, and Hack all ripped three hits, with one of O'Dea's going for two bases. Prior to that game, the injury gremlin had struck the Cubbies twice more. On the 28th in Cincinnati, Larry French went down with a broken hand, putting him on the shelf until May 22. The next day, Gabby Hartnett started a game in Pittsburgh and went 3-for-3 at the plate, but re-injured his arm and went back on the sick list. The press immediately reported that he would be out for the season, but Gabby quickly squelched that rumor and said he was ready to go whenever Charlie Grimm needed him.

The Cubs opened an eastern swing in early May by sweeping three games from the sixth place Philadelphia Phillies. They took their frustrations out on Jimmie Wilson's club by whipping them 14–7 in the opener, then came back with more of the same in game two. Charlie Root was able to enjoy the day, as he was presented with 17 runs by his buddies with the bats, and coasted home a 17–4 winner. Ken O'Dea, who had spent a couple of days on the injury list, returned with a bang. He cracked two singles and a triple and scored two runs. Rookie Joe Marty, an off-season addition from San Francisco of the Pacific Coast League where he hit .359, smashed his second home run in two days and added two singles, good for three RBIs and three runs scored. Demaree hit his second homer in two days, and Rip Collins also went long. Charlie Grimm's cohorts extended their winning streak to six games with a 1–0 victory over the Phillies in a game called because of rain after five innings. Bill Lee became the winner when the Cubs scored the only run of the game in the top of the fifth inning on a single by

Augie Galan and a ringing double to left field by Rip Collins. The streak came to an end the next day when the Brooklyn Dodgers pummeled Clyde Shoun by a 12–1 score. Ken O'Dea had two hits for the Cubbies, and Gabby Hartnett saw action as a pinch hitter in the eighth inning, grounding to shortstop. Brooklyn won the finale of the series 6–5, then headed to New York to do battle against Terry's Giants.

On Monday, May 10, Carl Hubbell won his twentieth straight game, beating the Bruins by a 4–1 count before 36,529 rabid Polo Grounders. Demaree's home run in the ninth was the only score off the screwball artist. Bill Lee, who was the losing pitcher in this battle, was the last man to defeat Hubbell: that victory came on July 13, 1936. Clyde Shoun gave the Cubs a 4–3 victory in game two on home runs by Augie Galan and Rip Collins, but New York captured the get-away game, battering Roy Parmelee 10–1. The Cubs bounced back the next day to take the Boston Bees into camp by a 6–2 score. Charlie Root was the winning pitcher and Rip Collins put one over the wall. The pride of Millville was rushed back into action on the 13th when backup catcher Johnny Bottarini went down with a torn nail in game two. Gabby went 0-for-2, but drew two walks and scored the last run in an 8–6, 12-inning Cubs win. After the game, he reported no ill effects from the action and announced he was ready to play every day. At the age of 36, Gabby Hartnett still played the game with the same enthusiasm he did when he first arrived in Catalina in 1922. When he replaced Bottarini, the Cubs were languishing in fifth place with a 9–10 record, but over the next two months, the man *Baseball Magazine* called the inspirational force behind the Chicago Cubs would bat a sizzling .391, with five home runs and 41 RBIs, in 192 at-bats. On defense, he would gun down would-be base runners at an alarming rate, play nursemaid to a group of scatter-arm pitchers, and give a maximum effort on every play. The team would respond to his leadership by winning 51 of 73 games to take a seven-game lead in the National League race.[6]

The Windy City boys went 12–6 the rest of May, climbing into third place, just 2½ games behind Pittsburgh. On Memorial Day, they dumped the Cardinals twice, 4–2 and 6–3. Bill Lee took the lid-lifter, beating former teammate Lon Warneke. Chicago scored single runs in the second, third, and fifth, and Lee protected the lead the rest of the game. Galan and Jurges had two hits each. In game two, Clay Bryant took the measure of Dizzy Dean, who was ripped for 15 base hits led by Billy Herman's four. Collins had three hits, and Bryant and O'Dea checked in with two each. Galan walked, homered, and scored two runs. The same day, before 61,756 screaming fans at the Polo Grounds, the Brooklyn Dodgers ripped Carl Hubbell for five runs on seven hits in 3⅓ innings, en route to a 10–3 victory in the first game of a doubleheader, ending his amazing winning streak at 24 games. King Carl had run off 16 consecutive wins at the end of 1936 and captured his first eight games in '37 before tasting defeat. New York took the nightcap 5–4.

Billy Herman was the leading Cubs hitter through May with an average of .347, followed by Joe Marty at .333, Lonnie Frey at .328, and Gabby Hartnett at .315. Clay Bryant had a 3–0 record on the mound, and Root and Shoun were both at 4–1.

As the weather warmed up in June, so did the Cubs. They ripped their opponents from stem to stern, winning 16 games against just 8 losses. And the old man, Gabby Hartnett, was the sparkplug, terrorizing enemy pitchers to the tune of .420, with 16 RBIs. On June 4, they tangled with their old friends, the New York Giants, in a Polo Grounds twin bill. They won their eighth straight game in the opener, pounding Carl Hubbell for four runs and 11 base hits in 7⅔ innings, en route to a 6–5, 11-inning victory. A triple by Ken O'Dea and a single by Billy Herman accounted for the winning tally. Hartnett had two hits and an RBI, Herman was 4-for-6 with a triple, and Galan and Hack cracked home runs. Clyde Castleman cooled off the red-hot Cubbies temporarily in the nightcap, beating Bill Lee 4–2 with a three-run rally in the bottom of the eighth. Augie Galan hit a two-run homer in the ninth for the Cubs' only runs. June 8 was a big day in the Windy City. Charlie Grimm's Cubs were closing in on first place, and the White Sox whipped the New York Yankees 5–4 to gain a share of first place in the American League. Southpaw Thornton Lee was the winning pitcher, surviving solo home runs by Joe DiMaggio and Lou Gehrig.

The Bruins moved into first place for a few hours on June 13 after demolishing the Philadelphia Phillies 16–8 in the first half of a twin bill, but dropped back into second place after Jimmie Wilson's battered warriors rose up and defeated their tormentors 4–3 when Cubs castoff Chuck Klein belted a three-run homer over the right field wall in the bottom of the eighth. Clyde Shoun coasted to the win in the opener, backed by a 22-hit attack led by Billy Herman and Rip Collins who had four hits each. Herman, Collins, and O'Dea had home runs. In the nightcap, Joe Marty had two of the Cubs' nine hits. Hartnett had a pinch-hit single in the ninth. Two days later, the Cubs were home to meet the Boston Bees in the first game of a long home stand. Home cooking proved to be just the tonic the team needed as they vaulted over the New York Giants into first place, winning 10 of 15 games over the last two weeks of June, while the New Yorkers were going 10–7. Augie Galan slugged his way into the record books on the 25th. Batting against Freddie Fitzsimmons of the Brooklyn Dodgers in the fourth inning, Galan, batting lefty, put one into the right field seats. Four innings later, batting right-handed against Ralph Birkofer, he homered to left field to

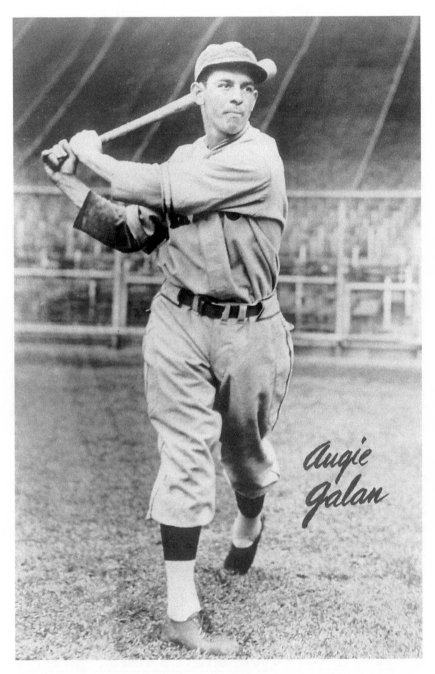

Left-fielder Augie Galan played an important part in the Cubs' 1935 and 1938
National League Championships.

become the first batter to hit home runs from both sides of the plate in the same game. The Cubs won the game 11–2.[7]

When the Cubs were playing at home, Gabby Hartnett, a man of habit, always followed the same routine. Thirty minutes after the game ended, the big catcher was in his car and on his way home. He would be greeted by Martha on his arrival and would sit down to a big dinner with her and the kids. After dinner, he might grab a stack of baseball gloves he kept in the closet, hand them out to the kids in the neighborhood, and play street ball with them until it became too dark to play. Gabby's son Bud was a big hitter like his father, but he was missing one key ingredient in his repertoire. He wasn't blessed with the "Hartnett Arm." Some nights Gabby would give the boys instructions in the proper way to catch a ball, the right way to grip it to throw it, and how to block the plate. And, being a 16-mm. movie nut, he shot reel after reel of Bud and his friends playing ball. Occasionally Gabby would bring one or more of his teammates home to Albion Avenue for a home-cooked meal. Ken O'Dea, Stan Hack, and Charlie Root were frequent visitors. The neighborhood kids thought it was fantastic that Bud had baseball stars at his house, but to Bud they were just family friends.

The Cubs ended the month by dumping the St. Louis Cardinals 9–4, with Charlie Root getting the victory in relief and Gabby Hartnett smashing a double and a home run and gunning down a prospective base stealer. Billy Jurges, who had turned into an offensive machine, went four-for-five. In the American League, the Yankees had reclaimed first place from the White Sox and were beginning to pull away from the rest of the league. From this point to the end of the season, the Bronx Bombers would continually widen their lead, eventually winning the pennant by a whopping 13 games.

July 2 was a sad day in American history as the country's beloved aviatrix, Amelia Earhart, was lost while flying from New Guinea to Howland Island in the Pacific Ocean on the last leg of an around-the-world flight. Ms. Earhart was the first woman to fly the Atlantic Ocean alone, in 1932, and the first woman to fly the Pacific Ocean from Hawaii to California, in 1935. In June, she and her navigator, Fred Noonan, left Miami, Florida, headed east and flew into history. The U.S. Navy would conduct an extensive search of the Pacific Ocean in the vicinity of Howland Island, but after two weeks, the search was called off without finding a trace of the lost fliers.[8]

Charlie Grimm's charges split the first four games in July, then beat the Pirates 10–5 on July 3, with Gabby Hartnett hitting a home run and a single, driving in two runs, scoring two, and racking up another assist. It was the beginning of a surge that would see the Cubbies take 18 of their next 24 games. And Gabby was the catalyst again, like he had been in June. "Old Tomato Face" hit a resounding .403 with two home runs and 16 RBIs. The

big Fourth of July doubleheader turned out to be a no-decision, as the Bruins split with the Pittsburgh Pirates, winning the first game by an 8–5 count
and dropping the nightcap 7–6. Charlie Root was the winning pitcher in
relief in game one, and Collins, Demaree, and Curt Davis supplied the big
lumber by slamming home runs. Hartnett was 1-for-3 in game two and
nabbed two runners on the bases. The next day, the Cubs swept a twin bill
from the St. Louis Cardinals, eking out a dramatic 13–12, 14-inning victory
over the Redbirds in the opener and taking a 9–7 verdict in game two. The
first game was a dogfight from beginning to end, with the Cardinals jumping out to an early 7–1 lead, the Cubs tying it with a six-run outburst against
Ray Harrell in the fourth, St. Louis coming back again to take a convincing 12–7 lead, and the Cubs tying it with four runs in the eighth and one
in the ninth. Forty-two base hits echoed around the Friendly Confines, as
39,240 noisy spectators cheered every Cubs rally over the four-hour-nine-
minute length of the game. The second game, lasted a mere two hours and
14 minutes, witnessed another 23 base hits, as the pitching on both sides
took an afternoon siesta. Frank Demaree had a monster day in the opener,
banging out six hits in seven at-bats with three doubles, and then going 2-
for-4 in the nightcap. Shortstop Billy Jurges had six hits in 10 at-bats with
a double and a triple, and Billy Herman went 4-for-10 with a double. Gabby
Hartnett caught both games and went 3-for-8 with two bases on balls, three
RBIs, and two assists. He was in the middle of both big Cubs rallies in the
opener, rapping two singles in the six-run fourth inning and hitting another
single in the four-run eighth. Charlie Root was the only pitcher to escape
unscathed in the first game, tossing six shutout innings for the victory.

The Chicago race for the pennant was interrupted on July 6 for the
major league All-Star Game. Five Chicago Cubs players were selected for
the game: Demaree, Herman, Jurges, Collins, and Hartnett. The game was
played in Griffith Stadium in Washington before President Franklin D. Roosevelt and 31,390 other baseball fans. "Before the game early arrivals were
surprised to see a young lady appear in the field in the vicinity of the pitchers' warm-up pen. Nobody seemed to know who she was. While she was
attempting to engage Dizzy Dean in conversation, a guy in the upper deck
who obviously had no manners yelled: 'See if she's got a girl friend, Dizzy.'
She finally was persuaded to leave the grounds, but not until she made an
affectionate pass at Gabby Hartnett. The pass was incomplete and Gabby
kicked out of bounds."[9] Dizzy Dean was the starter and loser for the National
League, as the American Leaguers pounded their way to an 8–3 verdict.
With the game scoreless in the bottom of the third, Dean was touched up
for a single by Joe DiMaggio, then gave up a long home run over the right
field fence by Lou Gehrig. After the game, "Dizzy Dean confessed he had

made two big mistakes by not taking advice. Twice in the three disastrous innings he pitched against the heavy hitters of the American League, Dean shook off catcher Gabby Hartnett's signal. Gabby ordered curve balls to Joe DiMaggio and Lou Gehrig, the Yankee sluggers, but Dizzy knew better. He threw them fast ones; they saluted him with a single and a home run. 'Gabby was right. When he asked for a curve against DiMaggio, I shook him off and Joe singled. I was sure I was right on Gehrig. In the first inning, I fanned him with a fast one, but he pickled the fastest one I've got in the third.'"[10] This All-Star Game is best remembered "for Earl Averill's line drive in the third inning, which fractured Dizzy Dean's toe and led to the premature end to his spectacular career. Dean recovered from the broken toe, but tried to resume his pitching too soon. By favoring the toe, he changed his delivery and irreparably injured his pitching arm."[10]

At the break, the Cubs 44–25 record gave them a two-game lead over the New York Giants. The Yankees had widened their lead over Detroit to 5½ games in the American League. Gabby Hartnett was the top Chicago hitter, batting a cool .388 with five home runs and 31 RBIs. Billy Jurges was hot on his tail with a .362 average, followed by Billy Herman at .360 and Frank Demaree at .349.

The Cubs dropped three of their next four games to fall out of the lead and, after losing a 2–1 decision to the Boston Bees, they also lost their manager, Charlie Grimm, who was sidelined with sciatica. In his first managerial experience, Gabby Hartnett was put in charge of the team, who responded to his leadership by running off nine victories in 12 games to regain the top spot in the league standings. The Cubs beat the Bees 5–1 in Gabby's managerial debut, and he contributed two singles in four at-bats and an RBI. Demaree had 3-for-4 with two RBIs, and Herman and Jurges both had two hits. Tex Carleton was the beneficiary of five runs from a team that had scored only six runs in the previous four games. Gabby Hartnett's two hits gave him second place in the National League batting race, 20 points behind Joe Medwick's .411 average.

The Windy City boys moved into the Polo Grounds to take on Bill Terry's determined Giants, who trailed the Cubs by just one game. In the series opener, they had to face King Carl Hubbell, one of the greatest southpaws in baseball history. Hartnett sent Curt Davis to the mound to face the Giants ace, but the 33-year-old veteran didn't survive the first inning, giving up two runs on two hits, a walk, and two hit batters before Charlie Root, in relief, could stem the tide. Root yielded another run in the third to give Terry's troops a 3–1 lead, but he was untouchable after that. Meanwhile, Hartnett's warriors kept chipping away at Hubbell, scoring seven runs on 13 base hits in eight innings, en route to an 11–3 victory. The next day,

Chicago broke a five-all tie with three runs in the seventh inning and went on to a 10–5 win. Hartnett was 2-for-4 with two runs scored. Frey, Herman, Jurges, Marty, and Parmelee also had two hits. One of Frey's was a home run. New York took the get-away game, but Hartnett still handed a two-game lead to Charlie Grimm when the manager returned from his sick bed on the 27th. The Bruins welcomed their boss back with a 5–2 win over the Brooklyn Dodgers, with Tex Carleton picking up the victory. Gabby Hartnett was given the day off by his manager after his two-week double-duty assignment. Demaree had three hits, and Hack and Herman had two each.

Four days later, Carleton three-hit the New York Giants to give the Cubs a five-game bulge over their closest adversaries. At one point, he retired 22 batters in a row, as the Cubs won the game easily 7–1. Gabby Hartnett had a 2-for-3 day, including a bases-loaded double to the wall in right center field off Carl Hubbell, who once again proved to be no puzzle to the Chicago batters. Charlie Grimm's charges kept the pressure on the New Yorkers with a 5–4 11-inning victory to sweep the three-game series. George Stainback, who had seen little service the entire season, came off the bench and lined a bases-loaded single off losing pitcher Rube Melton to send the 30,326 Cub fanatics into a victory dance. The Giants were the mortal enemies of the Cubs as far back as 1903, and every victory over them was sweet. When Chicago beat the Phillies 4–1 on the 3rd, it gave them a big seven-game lead in the league standings. That would be their high-water mark. The season would take a disastrous turn from that point on. On the 9th, Rip Collins broke his ankle when he slid into Pittsburgh Pirate catcher Al Todd and was lost to the team for a month. On the 14th, the Cubbies had their biggest outburst of the season, walloping the last-place Cincinnati Reds by a 22–6 score. Demaree had four hits with a triple, Ken O'Dea had four hits and four RBIs, and Joe Marty had three hits and two RBIs. Root, who relieved Parmelee in the second inning, coasted to the victory. The next day, these same Reds rose up and defeated Grimm's troops; and on the 16th, they beat the Cubs in a twin bill by scores of 13–6 and 9–8. Manager Grimm was puzzled and frustrated by the sudden collapse of his pitching staff. "I can't understand it. What have they got to tighten up about? I've only got five pitchers I can count on in the clutch, but I won't cry about it. I'll go along with what I've got and do the best I can."[12]

Chicago played a doubleheader against the Bees in Boston's Beehive on the 28th, and came away with a split. In the first game, big Lou Fette, all 200 pounds of him, nailed the Cubs with a five-hitter to win 3–1. Tex Carleton pitched a strong game, but was tagged for two runs in the second inning, and that was the ballgame. The nightcap was more interesting.

Chicago took a 4–0 lead after 3½ innings, thanks to the slugging of starting pitcher Charlie Root who singled and scored in the third inning, then sent a Guy Bush fastball into the left field seats for a home run in the fourth. The Bees closed the gap to 6–3 in the fifth, then tied the game off Root and two relievers in the bottom of the ninth. In the tenth, the Cubs loaded the bases, and pitcher Clay Bryant brought them all home with a high fly ball down the left field line that dropped into the seats for a grand slam homer. Three days later, after splitting two games and slipping back into second place, Grimm's plucky warriors recaptured the top spot by nipping the Dodgers 4–2, while the Giants were being pummeled by St. Louis, 8–1. Tex Carleton, one of the five pitchers manager Grimm said he could count on, let the Bums down with two runs, but it took a two-run Chicago rally in the eighth to push over the winning runs. Augie Galan ripped a double and a triple and scored two runs. Herman and Demaree each had two hits, a run scored, and an RBI. Gabby Hartnett had a single in Chicago's game-tying rally in the sixth inning, had three big assists, and guided Carleton, who was touched for eight base hits and four bases on balls in a complete game effort.

Charlie Grimm's weary troops sleepwalked through August with a 15–15 record and saw their seven-game lead whittled down to just one. Hartnett did everything he could to keep the Cubs in contention. He ripped the ball at a .320 pace during the month, with three homers and 10 RBIs, and his defensive play, pitch-calling, and field leadership were flawless; however, the Cubs' second-tier pitchers were ineffective.

Chicago dropped six of their first nine games in September, dropping them three games behind Bill Terry's New York Giants. They cut the lead to two on the 10th when they romped over the Redbirds 11–0 behind Carleton. Gabby Hartnett smashed two home runs good for three RBIs, and he also scored three runs. Phil Cavaretta lashed four hits in four at-bats with a triple and two RBIs. On the 10th, Boston's sixth-place Bees stung the Cubbies with a double dose of poison, routing Tex Carleton 9–4 and whipping Clay Bryant 4–2. An eight-run fifth inning, with seven runs crossing the plate after two outs, was Carleton's downfall. And, as the *Tribune* noted, "For added entertainment of the 13,906 customers, the Bees threw in a triple play at no extra cost." The "Arkansas Hummingbird" bounced back in his next start, humbling the Philadelphia Phillies by a 9–3 count. Rip Collins, back at his station after missing a month with a broken ankle, had a double and a homer in three at-bats, with two RBIs and two runs scored. On September 19th, the Brooklyn Dodgers visited the Friendly Confines, and they were just what Charlie Grimm's cohorts were looking for. The Cubs swept them three straight. In the series opener, Curt Davis scattered seven base hits, Gabby Hartnett put one in the seats with a man on, and the Cubs won 2–1.

George Cisar, just up from the Three-I League where he stole 63 bases, was thrown out trying to steal home, ending the game. Billy Jurges remembered an incident in one of the games, which he described to Gabby's nephew Fred: "The Dodgers had a rookie [Cisar] who thought he was pretty good, and he was going to steal against Gabby. He got on base. He looked down at Gabby and he was going to steal second base, and he did. I'm sure that didn't sit too well. So Gabby went out to the mound. He called Jurges in, and he said to the pitcher, 'The next pitch, pitch out,' and he told Jurges, 'When you see that happen, move over about six feet and in.' So they pitched out and Gabby fired the ball to Jurges, and the kid was going by and they tagged him out at short. Gabby threw the mask and glove down, took the kid by the hand, led him down into the dugout and said, 'Okay, sit there and be a good boy,' and patted him on the head. Then he went back, put his mask on and caught the rest of the game."[12]

The Chicago Cubs went down fighting, racking up 20 victories against 14 losses, but when the Giants smelled a pennant waiting for them at the end of the road, they were blistering. They ran off 24 wins against just seven losses down the stretch and captured the National League flag by three games. The moment of truth came in Wrigley Field between September 21 and 23 when the Cubs tangled with the hated Giants in THE CRUCIAL SERIES of the year. Charlie Grimm's charges needed a sweep of the series. Nothing less would do as they trailed by 3½ games coming in. The Cubbies walloped the New Yorkers in game one, but Rube Melton set them down on six hits the next day to give his team a 6–0 victory, backing the Chicagoans against the wall. Game three was a dogfight all the way. The Giants jumped out to a quick 3–0 lead off Curt Davis; the Cubs came back to tie it in the fourth; Terry's troops recaptured the lead again at 8–3 after 5½ innings, driving Davis to cover under the barrage of base hits; and the Cubs fought back with three runs in the bottom of the same inning to narrow the gap to 8–6. Chicago pushed across one run in the bottom of the ninth, and had two other runners on base with just one out, but Carl Reynolds and Augie Galan were retired to end both the game and the Chicago Cubs' pennant push. The Bruins won eight of their last 10 games, but it was too little, too late.

Gabby Hartnett reached a historic milestone on September 27 when he caught his 100th game. It was the twelfth time in his career that the venerable Chicago backstop had caught 100 or more games in a season, tying him with Ray Schalk for the most 100-game seasons by a catcher in major league history. Schalk's record was established between 1913 and 1925, while Gabby's string began in 1924.

The American League race was once again a New York Yankees runaway, with the Bronx Bombers winning 105 games, good enough for a comfortable 13-game lead over the Detroit Tigers. The Yankees were heavy favorites to polish off the upstart Giants in less than seven games. They did it in five. The Series opened in Yankee Stadium on October 6, with 60,573 noisy Bronxites lending support to their team. Carl Hubbell held a tenuous 1–0 lead after 5½ innings. Then the Yanks fell on him for a big seven-spot in the bottom of the sixth and won going away 8–1. Five singles, four bases on balls, and two errors turned the game into a nightmare for Bill Terry's warriors. The next day, the Yankees bombarded Rube Melton and two relievers for eight runs on 12 hits, and Red Ruffing coasted to another 8–1 victory. The deluge continued when the Series moved to the Polo Grounds. Monte Pearson handcuffed the Giants on five hits, and the Bronx bombers pecked away at Hal Schumacher for five runs in the first five innings and a 5–1 triumph. Hubbell outpitched Bump Hadley 7–3 in game four to give the Giants their first win in the Series. Harry "The Horse" Danning hammered two singles and a double to pace the Giants. But it all ended the next day, as Lefty Gomez tossed a complete game 4–2 win, scattering 10 base hits along the way. Tony Lazzeri was the top hitter for the Yankees, powdering the ball at a .400 clip with two home runs. Red Rolfe and Myril Hoag each batted an even .300. Jo Jo Moore hit .391 for the Giants and Hank Leiber hit .364. Lefty Gomez racked up a 2–0 record, with a 1.50 earned-run-average (ERA).[14]

The individual season batting champions were Joe Medwick at .374 and Charlie Gehringer at .371. The home run kings were Mel Ott with 31 and Joe DiMaggio with 46. And the leading pitchers were Carl Hubbell with a record of 22–8 and Lefty Gomez with a record of 21–11. Gabby Hartnett led the Chicago Cubs batters with an average of .354, 12 home runs, and 82 RBIs. And he led the National League catchers in fielding for the fourth consecutive year with a percentage of .996, while allowing only 47 stolen bases against a league average of 57. His American League counterpart, Bill Dickey, had a sensational season himself, batting .332 with 29 home runs and 133 RBIs. Dickey also led the league in fielding average at .991, being victimized by base stealers just 52 times against a league average of 70.

The Chicago Cubs failure can be traced back to its lack of depth on the pitching staff, as Charlie Grimm had pointed out early in the season. The Cubbies led the National League in runs scored, batting average, slugging average, and fielding average, but their 3.97 team ERA, which was sixth out of eight teams, was 44 points higher than the previous year and 71 points higher than their pennant-winning year of 1935.

11

A Baseball Legend Is Born, 1938

Chicago Cubs owner, Philip K. Wrigley, sat through two disappointing seasons in 1936 and '37 when he expected his team to capture the National League pennant, only to watch in horror as they collapsed down the stretch. He vowed that wouldn't happen again, and manager Charlie Grimm was put on notice that he had to produce a pennant winner in 1938 to keep his job. The Chicago front office made only two player deals during the off-season, and they were minor ones. They signed former New York Yankee second baseman Tony Lazzeri and pitcher Jack Russell who was 2–5 with Detroit in 1937.

When spring training got underway, Gabby Hartnett, the elder statesman of Charlie Grimm's team, "led the rookies and other veterans at a tremendous clip, his round red face glowing like a rising sun. And when he was done with this, he promptly issued a challenge to all and sundry, for a round of golf. Such pep was infectious and the rest of the squad took to the work with vim. The opening drill (except for Hartnett's group) turned out to be little more than a romp, with the photographers getting most of the benefit therefrom. A heavy fog encountered shortly after the S.S. Catalina left the dock at Wilmington delayed the arrival on the island and curtailed the drill somewhat, to say nothing of causing the players no end of annoyance with its accompanying cacophony of whistles and fog horns."[1]

Life was beginning to return to normal in the United States in 1938 after a long, painful depression. People were becoming more financially secure, and leisure time activities like family vacations and spectator sports could be enjoyed once more. And professional baseball players were cavorting on playing fields from California to Florida in preparation for the upcoming season. All was well in America, but not so elsewhere. Dark war clouds were descending on the world scene, as Nazi Germany, Fascist Italy, and the Empire of Japan all undertook military operations against defenseless nations. Japan invaded China in 1931, beginning a territorial expansion that would continue for 14 years. Italian dictator Benito Mussolini's army invaded Ethiopia in 1935, then participated in the Spanish Civil War on the side of General Francisco Franco. And Nazi Germany under Adolph Hitler annexed Austria in1938, relentlessly pursuing one objective, the domination of Europe. Soon the three powers would sign formal nonaggression pacts, plunging the planet into another world war.[2]

One day before the Cubs embarked on their quest for the pennant, the front office completed a major deal, obtaining Dizzy Dean from the St. Louis Cardinals for $185,000 in cash and three players: Curt Davis, Clyde Shoun, and Tuck Stainback. Dean, once the major league's greatest pitcher, was in the twilight of his career at the young age of 27. The right-handed flamethrower went 24–13 for the Redbirds in 1936, but after injuring his toe in the '37 All-Star Game, he slipped to 13–10. The Cubs were hoping he could regain his once overpowering skills and pitch them to a pennant. The addition of Dean made Chicago the favorite to capture the National League Championship, according to the Broadway betting commissioner. Prior to acquiring "Old Diz," the Cubs were picked to finish second behind New York. Now they were 3 to 2 to win it all, with the Giants at 8 to 5, the Cardinals at 4 to 1, and the Pirates at 5 to 1.

Charlie Grimm's charges opened the season in Cincinnati facing the last-place Reds, with Clay Bryant opposing lanky right-hander Gene Schott. It was a good day for the Cubs but a bad day for Bryant, who was sent to an early shower with a four-run barrage in the third inning. Fortunately for the Bruins, they had their hitting shoes on, and they peppered Schott and two relievers for 15 base hits en route to an 8–7 victory. Charlie Root, with three innings of relief, was the winning pitcher. Rip Collins, with two singles, a double, a home run, three runs scored, and two runs-batted-in (RBIs), was the top gunner for Charlie Grimm. Rookie Coaker Triplett, fresh off a .356 season at Memphis, pounded out two doubles and a single. And Billy Jurges had two RBIs. Dizzy Dean started his first game of the season the next day and coasted to an easy 10–4 victory. The Cubbies raked southpaw Lee Grissom for six hits in a little more than one inning, as they crossed the plate nine times in the second inning to give Dean a lot of breathing room. The former Cardinals ace tired after six innings, having pitched just 17 innings during spring training, and was relieved by Jack Russell. He was touched

Dizzy Dean made a significant contribution to the Cubs' 1938 National League pennant.

for eight hits, but held the Reds to just two runs, while fanning three. Tony Lazzeri and Coaker Triplett had four hits each. Gabby Hartnett went 2-for-5 with a double, two RBIs, and a run scored.

When the Chicago Cubs opened their home season on April 23, they entered a much different Wrigley Field than the fans remembered from the previous year. P.K. Wrigley, envisioning a World Series in 1937, undertook a major construction project that summer to increase the beauty of the stadium and provide additional comfort for the patrons. A temporary fence was installed around the outfield to separate the playing field from the construction area, so the team could play their home games while the work was in progress. Construction continued even on game days, but it was halted 30 minutes before the cry of "Play ball!" New bleachers were built in left field; the right field bleachers were replaced" a huge scoreboard, measuring 27 feet high and 75 feet wide, was installed high above the center field fence; and new concession stands and restrooms were strategically located. As a final touch, the red brick walls surrounding the outfield were adorned with a lush ivy covering, making Wrigley Field the most beautiful baseball stadium in the country.

Larry French blessed the new park by blanking the Cardinals 4–0, with Frank Demaree driving in three runs. Dean followed up with a four-hit shutout of his own, beating his old team 5–0. Jurges and Hartnett each had two hits and an RBI. The Chicago express took eight of 12 games during the month to finish in third place, 2½ games behind the New York Giants. Bryant stopped a two-game Cubs slide on the 28th by taking the Reds in tow, 12–5, in a complete game effort. The big right-hander had a shutout until the Reds erupted for five runs in the ninth. Augie Galan ripped a double and a home run, driving in five runs for the Bruins. Billy Herman had a single, a double, and three RBIs, and Ken O'Dea had three singles, an RBI, and two runs scored. Old Diz had to come out of his next start after just 3⅔ innings when his arm tightened up, but the Cubs went on to beat Cincinnati 6–4, with Russell picking up the win. Galan was once again the big gun, smashing a homer and a single with three RBIs. Gabby Hartnett and Tony Lazzeri also hammered homers for Grimm's cohorts. Chicago closed out the month by routing St. Louis by an 11–5 count. Tex Carleton was the beneficiary of the outburst. Stan Hack went 3-for-6, with two RBIs, and Gabby Hartnett contributed a double, a home run, and two RBIs.

Dizzy Dean started against the Philadelphia Phillies in Wrigley Field on May 4 and came away a 5–2 winner, but he had to retire after seven innings with a sore arm. The injury was later diagnosed as a slight tear in the right deltoid muscle, which put the "Great One" on the shelf for an indeterminate period of time. Joe Marty sparked the offense in the game with two singles and a homer, and Gabby Hartnett also put one into orbit for the Cubbies. New York and Pittsburgh followed Philadelphia into the Friendly Confines, but Charlie Grimm's troops couldn't capitalize on their home field advantage and ended the home stand with a five-five split, leaving them a full 5½ games off the Giants' torrid pace. Chicago went 10–5 on the road the last two weeks of the month to cut the New York lead down to 2½ games, with another home stand staring them in the face, but the growing injury list made life uneasy for manager Charlie Grimm. Gabby Hartnett was hit by a pitch thrown by Claude Passeau of the Phillies on June 4 and left the game with a bruised wrist. Gabby had contributed a single, a double, and two RBIs to the Cubs' 5–1 win before being sent to the bench. On the 7th, the Bruins whipped the Phils 7–1 behind Tex Carleton and moved into first place when Cincinnati dumped New York by a 4–1 margin. Gabby Hartnett was spotted in the dugout puffing on a big cigar during the game. If it was a celebratory cigar, the celebration was short lived because Bill Terry's Giants arrived in town to take matters into their own hands. They swept the three-game series from the Cubs by scores of 4–2, 4–1, and 8–5. In the opener of a Wednesday twin bill, Mel Ott's two-run homer in the tenth inning spelled defeat for Larry French. The second game was over in the first inning when the Giants pushed over two runs on a two-out wind-blown triple by Hank Leiber. They added two more runs in the fifth off hard-luck loser Clay Bryant. In the get-away game the next day, Terry's opportunistic crew rallied for three runs in the ninth inning to break a five-all tie and complete the sweep. "Rowdy Dick" Bartell had a double and a home run with two RBIs for the New Yorkers.

The Cubs were in Boston in mid-month during one of their three or four such excursions every year. Gabby Hartnett always looked forward to the Boston trips because it allowed him to get away after the game and visit his family in Millville, often spending a quiet evening with his mother and some of his brothers and sisters at the Great Western Hotel or one of the local taverns. Sometimes he would bring his good friend Dizzy Dean with him, which would cause quite a commotion in the little town, according to Gabby's nephew, Fred Hartnett: "They used to hang out at Oates' Tavern in Mapleville on route 7. They'd be over there and the word would spread that they had some major leaguers in there. Kids would be showing up at 8 or 9 o'clock at night and Dizzy would be sitting on the running board of an automobile signing autographs. Diz only went to third grade, but he would tell them kids 'You guys stay in school and do good,' and all the rest of that stuff."[3]

June was a once-in-a-lifetime month for a young Cincinnati pitcher. Twenty-three-year-old Johnny VanderMeer, in his first full season in the big time, pitched his way into legend by tossing two consecutive no-hitters. He pitched his first no-no against the Bees in Boston, a 3–0 whitewashing sprinkled with four strikeouts and three bases on balls. Future Hall of Fame catcher Ernie Lombardi knocked in two of the runs with a homer. Four days later, the 6'1", 195-pound southpaw turned his blazer loose on the Dodgers in the first night game ever played in Ebbets Field. The final score was 6–0, and Frank McCormick accounted for three of those runs with a homer in the third inning. The game was not as easy as it would seem, however. VanderMeer walked eight men along the way, including three in the ninth after the first man had been retired. Manager Bill McKechnie made a hurried trip to the mound at that point to settle his pitcher down, and it must have worked because the next man up, Ernie Koy, grounded into a force play at the plate, and Leo Durocher ended the suspense by flying out to short center field. The stands exploded when Harry Craft gloved the ball, and hundreds of fans poured onto the playing field trying to reach the new superstar, but his teammates whisked him away to the safety of the clubhouse before any damage could be done. On June 19, Debs Garms of Boston singled off VanderMeer with one out in the fourth inning, ending his consecutive hitless innings streak at 21⅔.

The Cubs plodded through June in a fog, winning just 11 of 25 decisions to end the month in fourth place with a 35–29 record. They now trailed New York, Pittsburgh, and Cincinnati in the standings. Stan Hack led the Chicago Cubs hitters with an average of .312, followed by Gabby Hartnett at .299. Rip Collins had eight home runs and Augie Galan had 43 RBIs. Bill Lee was the leading pitcher with a record of 8–4. After splitting a Fourth of July doubleheader with the St. Louis Cardinals, 4–3 and 3–4, Charlie Grimm's charges had a few days to relax during the All-Star break. The game, played at Crosley Field in Cincinnati on July 6, included three Cubs players: second baseman Billy Herman, third baseman Stan Hack, and pitcher Bill Lee. It was the first time since the inception of the All-Star Game that Gabby Hartnett was not selected as the catcher. The National League won for only the second time in six tries. The score was 4–1 as both VanderMeer and Bill Lee tossed three shutout innings, with VanderMeer picking up the victory. Hack and Herman had one hit each, and Hack scored one of the National's runs.

The Chicago Cubs went 7–6 over the next two weeks when the axe fell. Charlie Grimm was fired and Gabby Hartnett was promoted to manager. P.K. Wrigley decided a change of managers was necessary if his team was going to win the National League pennant. He called Charlie Grimm into his downtown office in the morning of the 21st, and informed him that he was being relieved of his duties. Then he called Gabby Hartnett in and offered him the job, which Gabby quickly accepted. Some sources have claimed the job was first offered to Billy Jurges, but that Jurges turned it down in favor of Gabby. Grimm also recommended Gabby as his replacement. When Gabby and Charlie Grimm posed for photographers after the meeting, Charlie told him, "I know you'll make a good manager. You have everything you need; personality, baseball ability, knowledge of the game." Gabby said, "Charlie, I'm glad you're taking it this way," to which Charlie replied, "What the hell, Gabby. That's baseball." Someone reminded Gabby that one day he would also be fired. Gabby just smiled and said, "When I get fired, I'll enjoy fishing and hunting."[4]

The Wrigley Field clubhouse was flooded with congratulatory telegrams for Gabby as soon as the news hit the wires. He received telegrams from Edgar Bergen, Charlie McCarthy, Lou Costello, Ronald Reagan, George Halas, Ray Meyer, and dozens of other people from the entertainment industry as well as from his relatives and friends back in Millville. The new manager held a short meeting with his players before taking the field for a double-header against the Brooklyn Dodgers. He asked his players for just two things: 100 percent cooperation and 100 percent hustle. He always wanted his players to look sharp and dress nice, and he told them, "Wear good suits, make sure you have a haircut, and smoke good cigars."[5]

A crowd of 25,830 people filled the Friendly Confines to see Gabby's debut, and left three hours later unfulfilled. Clay Bryant gave his new manager a present by taking the measure of Burleigh Grimes' team, 5–2, in game one. Carl Reynolds and Frank Demaree both punched out three base hits, with one of Reynolds' going for two bases. Augie Galan had a single, a triple, and two RBIs. Hartnett went 0-for-3 with a walk and a run scored. The nightcap was not as satisfying. Charlie Root threw a five-hitter at the Dodgers, but his teammates couldn't do anything with the offerings of "Hot Potato" Luke Hamlin, and Chicago went down 1–0 on a second-inning home run by former Cub Dolph Camilli. Two days later, Dizzy Dean, in just his second start after coming off a 10-week stay on the injured list, helped pitch the Cubs to a doubleheader sweep against the hated New York Giants with a complete game five-hitter. The Cubs won 3–1, scoring a run in the first inning and a two-spot in the fourth. Carl Reynolds had a single, a double, and one run scored to lead the attack. Gabby Hartnett was 0-for-3, but knocked in the eventual game winner with a sacrifice fly. Bill Lee captured the opener 7–4 on the strength of a six-run Chicago uprising in the bottom of the second inning. Galan and Reynolds both had two hits, including a double. The Cubs went on to lose three straight to the cellar-dwelling Phillies before ending the month with a 4–3 victory in a seven-inning game called at 6 PM by Pennsylvania law. Manager Gabby Hartnett paced his team with three hits in three at-bats, a run scored, and a stolen base. Charlie Root went the distance for the win. The split left the Bruins in third place with a 51–41 record, 7½ games from the top. Stan Hack was the leading Chicago hitter with an average of .331. The next highest average belonged to Carl Reynolds who was hitting .296. Tony Lazzeri was at .295 and Gabby Hartnett was at .288. Joe Marty had seven home runs and Gabby led the team in RBIs with 41. Dizzy Dean was flaunting a perfect 5–0 record, while Jack Russell was at 4–0, and Bill Lee was at 13–5.

The Cubs opened a big series against Bill Terry's Giants at the Polo Grounds on August 2nd. They took the opener 7–0 behind Clay Bryant, but were routed 8–3 in game two, bringing the wrath of manager Gabby Hartnett down on them. He accused some players of not giving their full effort in the pennant race, and he benched Frank Demaree and Rip Collins who were hitting just .259 and .265, respectively. They were replaced temporarily by Jim Asbell and Phil Cavaretta. The Cubs won six of their next 10 games, and then disaster struck. In a game against the St. Louis Cardinals, Gabby Hartnett caught a foul tip off the bat of Joe Medwick on the tip of his thumb, breaking it, and sending him to the bench for a month. Harry Danning remembered a meeting with Gabby in New York just days earlier: "One night I was having dinner in Toots Shor's Restaurant when Gabby walked in. I was single so I went there often. Gabby was playing in Brooklyn and he came to New York for dinner. We met by accident and had a nice conversation. Gabby was telling me how he was able to play in the major leagues for 17 years without ever breaking his thumb. In those days, you had to cover the ball with your right hand once it was in your glove, and broken thumbs were commonplace for catchers. One-handed catching was not allowed. Gabby said he folded his right thumb into the palm of his hand to protect it when he covered the ball. The next time I saw Gabby, his thumb was all taped up. A foul tip broke it."[6]

Gabby Hartnett's Cubs were still lethargic as August came to an end. They hadn't responded to the managerial change as enthusiastically as the Chicago front office had hoped, and their 16–15 record for the month left them in fourth place, seven games behind the front-running Pittsburgh Pirates as the stretch run got underway. The Cubs' top hitters were Stan Hack at .309 and Augie Galan at .301. Rip Collins had 10 homers. And the leading pitchers were Dizzy Dean at 6–1 and Bill Lee at 16–9. In the American League, the Bronx Bombers of New York owned a commanding 13-game lead over the Boston Red Sox.

The month started slowly for the Cubbies as they dropped two to the Reds by scores of 6–0 and 7–5, with Vance Page and Larry French being treated roughly by the Rhinelanders. They bounced back to nip the Reds the next day by a 2–1 score in 11 innings on a home run by Augie Galan, and followed that up by sweeping Pie Traynor's Pittsburgh Pirates in a twin bill, 3–0 and 4–3. Bill Lee scattered 10 hits in his shutout, while his mates made the most of their five hits, pushing across all three of their runs in the third inning on two singles and two Cincinnati errors. In the nightcap, Clay Bryant outpitched Red Lucas, as the Cubs scored single runs in the eighth and ninth to pull out the win. Doubles by Hack and Herman scored the tying run in the eighth, and a double by Carl Reynolds and a single by Ken O'Dea plated the gamewinner. The Chicago Cubs ran their winning streak to six games by sweeping a three-game series from the St. Louis Cardinals. Demaree starred in the Bruins 7–6, ten-inning win with two home runs and four RBIs. Gabby Hartnett pinch-hit in the game, his first appearance since he broke his thumb more than three weeks before. Clay Bryant stopped the Redbirds 4–2 in the get-away game. The streak brought Hartnett's charges to within 3½ games of Pittsburgh with 22 games to play.

After dropping a 9–1 decision to the Reds, Bill Lee pitched his second straight shutout, beating Cincinnati 2–0. Stan Hack had three hits, including a home run, drove in one run, and scored two. When the Cubs moved into Boston to do battle with the Bees, Gabby Hartnett was back in the pads, directing traffic and running the game from behind the plate for the first time since August 15. His presence on the field was critical to the success of the team, because he was the Cubs' inspirational leader, and his intensity and enthusiasm were contagious. "He sparked the team into a winning streak. The big, red-faced catcher laughed, shouted, cajoled, and sweated. He played each game as though ten devils were after him. Gabby had his Cubs playing the best ball in the league."[7]

His first game back was less than memorable, however, as the Cubs lost to the Bees 5–2, with Bryant absorbing the beating and Gabby drawing the collar in four trips to the plate.

The next day, September 14, was the first day of the Cubs' drive to the top. They began the day four games behind the Bucs. They ended it just 2½ games off the pace. While Pittsburgh was taking a double thrashing from Bill Terry's Giants, 3–0 and 10–3, the red-hot Bruins were taking the measure of the Bees 6–3 on Gabby Hartnett's grand slam homer in the third inning. The big catcher stepped to the plate against hard-throwing Lou Fette, with Hack, Herman, and Reynolds sitting on the sacks, and slammed a 2–2 pitch off the left field foul pole to erase a 2–1 Boston lead. Pittsburgh extended their lead to three games the next day by hitting five home runs to defeat the New York Giants by a score of 7–2, while the Cubs were idle.

Pie Traynor's charges broke even with Boston on the 16th, winning the opener of a twin bill 7–6 and dropping the nightcap 5–4. The Cubs and

Gabby Hartnett was honored by his Millville neighbors in Braves Field in August 1938. (Town of Millville J.G. Fitzgerald Historical Society, Inc.)

Giants were rained out. The next day, the Pirates edged the Bees 2–1, but Gabby Hartnett's streaking Bruins toppled Terry's fading Giants twice by scores of 4–0 and 4–2. Bill Lee, who was in a zone during September, tossed his third consecutive shutout in the opener. A bases-loaded walk to Gabby Hartnett plated the first run of the game. Rip Collins later hit his thirteenth homer of the year, a line drive into the upper right field stands at the Polo Grounds. The Cubs had a scare in the sixth inning when Hartnett took a foul tip off a knuckle of his right hand, but it turned out to be more painful than serious. Stan Hack blasted a two-run homer in the third inning of the nightcap to support Clay Bryant, who recorded his seventeenth victory of the year. Rain, which had postponed the game the day before, caused a delay in this one, and continued to come down throughout the game.[8]

The weather forecast for New York for the 18th called for showers and somewhat warmer temperatures. For Monday the 19th, it called for showers with little change in temperature, with the next day being fair and cooler. The weather forecast was wrong. The Chicago Cubs played a doubleheader against the Brooklyn Dodgers in a drizzle on the 18th, putting a severe strain on the Bruin pitching staff. Root, Dean, and Carleton all pitched in the opener, with Root taking a 4–1 loss after being ko'd in the third inning. The nightcap was called on account of darkness after five innings with the two teams deadlocked at three apiece. The Dodgers loaded the bases with none out in the bottom of the fifth, but couldn't pull the trigger. Jack Russell, in relief of Larry French, fanned Goody Rosen and induced Gilly Campbell to line into an unassisted double play by Billy Herman. The loss, coupled with Pittsburgh's 1–0 win over the Phillies, increased the Bucs' lead to 3½ games over Chicago, with 15 games left on the schedule.

The gods smiled on the Cubs while treating most of the residents of the east coast with disdain, as torrential rains shut down the National League pennant race for three days. The famous hurricane of 1938 pounded the Atlantic coast from New Jersey to Maine, giving the Chicago pitching staff a much-needed rest. The *New York Times* headline for the 22nd screamed, "Hurricane Sweeps Coast." An accompanying story reported that 11 people were dead and 71 were missing on Long Island, and more than 80 people had died in New England. Floods threatened rivers all over the Northeast. Providence, Rhode Island, was buried under a tidal wave, with six feet of water in the streets of the business section. Gabby Hartnett's birthplace of Woonsocket was battered, and 25 national guardsman with drawn bayonets were called out to restore order after youthful looters invaded jewelry and dress stores in search of plunder. One corner of the cemetery was washed out, and several coffins were carried away in the flood waters. The next morning, the *New York Times* reported that the death toll from the storm had risen to 462, with thousands made homeless. Two hundred and fifty people were killed in the Providence area in the storm that was called the worst national disaster in recorded American history. The *Providence Journal* published a four-page newspaper reporting the event, but the paper was actually printed in Woonsocket.[9]

Baseball returned to the east coast on September 22, with the Philadelphia Phillies hosting the Chicago Cubs in a twin bill, and the Dodgers entertaining the Pirates. Both contenders swept their games, with Pittsburgh beating Brooklyn by scores of 6–0 and 11–6 and Chicago dumping the Phillies 4–0 and 2–1. Bill Lee was the Cubs' hero in the opener, tossing his fourth straight shutout, which tied the National League record. It was also his ninth shutout of the season and his twentieth victory. Hack and Herman were the big stickers in the game. Hack had a double in three trips and scored two runs. Herman had a single and a triple, drove in two runs, and scored one. In game two, Clay Bryant took the measure of Claude Passeau, with Billy Jurges rapping a single and a triple, driving in one run and scoring the other. The stalemate left Gabby Hartnett's warriors in a precarious situation. The Cubs still trailed Pie Traynor's Bucs by 3½ games and had only 12 games left in their schedule.

The 23rd was a big day for Chicago. They squeaked out two more wins over the pesky Phillies by scores of 3–2 and 7–6, while Pittsburgh was being toppled by Cincinnati, 5–4 in 12 innings. The City of Brotherly Love was kind to Hartnett's charges, but it wasn't easy. Kirby Higbe and Jack Russell shared pitching duties once again in game one, with Russell tossing five shutout innings to pick up the victory. Augie Galan hit a game-winning homer over the right field wall in the eighth inning. In game two, Carleton was bombed out in the first inning before he could retire a man; but Russell, Root, and French stemmed the tide enough to allow the Bruins' bats to come back and win it. A two-run rally in the eighth and a four-run uprising in the ninth won the day. Rip Collins' bases-loaded double knocked in the winning runs. Collins and Hack each had three hits, while Demaree contributed two. Gabby Hartnett had 1-for-3 with a walk and accounted for two runs. He also picked off one careless base runner.

In another game, in another league, Hank Greenberg of the Detroit Tigers slammed two home runs as his team lost a doubleheader to the Cleveland Indians by scores of 8–1 and 6–5. The homers were Greenberg's fifty-fifth and fifty-sixth of the season, leaving him just four homers shy of Babe Ruth's record with nine games remaining in the season.

With the pennant hanging in the balance, the Cubs returned home to open a critical home stand against the Cardinals and Pirates beginning on the 24th. Charlie Root helped get the Cubbies off on the right foot as he blanked the Redbirds over the last 3⅔ innings, while his mates were exploding for three runs in the sixth and three more in the eighth, en route to a 9–3 triumph. Billy Herman had four hits, Stan Hack chipped in with three, and Gabby Hartnett had a single and a homer to lead the Bruin attack. The big catcher also tossed out one base runner. The win kept Chicago on pace with the Pirates who took the measure of the Reds 4–1. Still trailing Pittsburgh by two games, Hartnett's charges had eight games remaining in the heart-pounding season, two more against the Cardinals, three huge games against the Pirates, and a three-game finale in St. Louis. Both teams won again on Monday, with Clay Bryant stopping the Redbirds 7–2 and Pittsburgh taking the measure of the Redlegs 5–3. By virtue of the victories, both the Giants and the Reds were officially eliminated from the pennant race. The next day, the Cubbies completed the sweep of St. Louis, beating them 6–3 behind Bill Lee. The big right-hander was scored on for the first time in five games, but he didn't care as he rolled to his twenty-first victory of the season. Frank Demaree went 3-for-4 with three RBIs, while Stan Hack had three hits in four at-bats with four runs scored, to pace the Cubs offense. Pittsburgh had an off-day, so many of their players were in Wrigley field to scout the Cubs.

Manager Gabby Hartnett made a gutsy call for the opener of the three-game series against the league-leading Pittsburgh Pirates, selecting the old warhorse Dizzy Dean to take the mound. Dean's last start was on August 20, more than five weeks previous. Pittsburgh manager, Pie Traynor, expressed confidence that his team would maintain their lead: "If we win five of our remaining seven games, it doesn't make any difference how many the Cubs win. And we'll get those five. I'm going to play my three aces — Jim Tobin, Bob Klinger, and Russ Bauers — one right after the other." The biggest series of the year got underway on September 27 with Dizzy Dean facing off against Jim Tobin, and 42,238 crazed Cubs fans filled every nook and cranny of the big park. Old Diz was magnificent. Pitching with nothing but heart, he held the hard-hitting Bucs at bay for 8 2/3 innings, while Reynolds and Jurges knocked in runs off the Pittsburgh right-hander to give the Cubs a tenuous 2–0 lead into the ninth. One time during the game, Gabby went out to the mound and told Diz, "Try to throw the next pitch a little harder." An amused Dean replied, "Gabby, I'm throwing twice as hard as I've ever thrown. I'm throwing harder. I just can't throw as fast." The first man up in the Pittsburgh ninth was Arky Vaughan, and Dizzy hit him with a pitch, but then he settled down and retired Gus Suhr on a pop-up and forced Woody Jensen to hit into a force play. But that was all Dizzy had. His tank was dry, and after Jeep Handley ripped a double to left center field, putting the tying runs on second and third, Gabby Hartnett rushed to the mound and brought in Bill Lee. The Cubs ace immediately wild-pitched a run home and moved the tying run to third, but just when the situation began to look shaky, he fanned Al Todd to wrap up the win. Afterwards, manager Hartnett said of Dean, "All he had was a slow ball, good control, and a lot of heart."

The Cubs had crawled to within a ½ game of first place, the closest they had been to the top since June 8, and the stage was set for one of the greatest games in baseball history. It would be the defining moment in the career of Gabby Hartnett. Clay Bryant, the Cubs' 18-game winner, was on the mound, opposed by 6'3" right-hander Russ Bauers. The game was a tense struggle throughout, with first one team, then the other, mounting rallies. The Cubs jumped out in front 1–0 in the second, but the Bucs came back with a three-spot in the sixth, one on Johnny Rizzo's twenty-first homer of the season. In the bottom of the inning, Gabby Hartnett led off with a double to center and came around to score on Rip Collins' two-bagger to right. Collins eventually scored on an infield out, tying the game at 3-all. The tie lasted into the eighth when Pie Traynor's troops jumped on Page and French for two runs before the fifth Chicago pitcher of the day, Bill Lee, could stem the tide. Once again, the battered Bruins teetered on the brink of defeat, and once again, they came storming back. A single by Rip Collins, a double by the old pro, Tony Lazzeri, and a single by Billy Herman got the

Cubbies even again; but as the ninth inning got underway, darkness was settling over the Friendly Confines, and the umpires, after conferring, decided
to play just one more inning. A tie would necessitate playing a doubleheader
the next day, a prospect that was unappetizing to manager Hartnett whose
pitching staff was decimated, and whose team would be decided underdogs
if they had to play two games in one day, needing victories in both games
to claim first place. Charlie Root, a 39-year-old grizzled veteran, took the
ball in the top of the ninth and shackled the Bucs with an assist from his
37-year-old catcher, Gabby Hartnett. With Paul Waner on first after lacing
a single to left, and two men out, the Pirates right fielder tested the old
man's arm and came out second best, as Gabby gunned him down on an
attempted steal.[10]

Now it was the Cubs' turn to bat, with a tie game looming before them.
Mace Brown, the Pirate's premier reliever, starting his second inning on the
mound, quickly disposed of Phil Cavaretta on a fly ball to center field and
Carl Reynolds on a bouncer to second base. The fate of the Cubs now rested
squarely on the shoulders of their aging manager, Gabby Hartnett. The
ruddy-faced Irishman knocked the clay from his spikes and stepped in to
face the flamethrowing right-hander. Brown threw Gabby a blazer. The man
from Millville swung and missed. Brown threw another one and Gabby
barely got a piece of it, fouling it off. Now, with the count 0–2 and the vis-
ibility almost zero, Brown inexplicably threw Hartnett a high curveball, and
Gabby sent it screaming on a line into left field. Most fans were unable to
follow the flight of the ball in the darkness, but when it settled into the left
field seats for a walk-off home run, Wrigley Field erupted with a deafening
roar that could be heard for blocks. Thousands of half-crazed spectators
came spilling out of the stands screaming and racing toward the diamond.
As Gabby remembered it: "'I swung with everything I had, and then I got
that feeling, the kind of a feeling you get when the blood rushes out of your
head and you get dizzy. A lot of people have told me they didn't know the
ball was in the bleachers. Well, I did. Maybe I was the only one in the park
who did. I knew it the moment I hit it.' On his way to second base, he was
mobbed by his teammates, the fans, the vendors, the ushers, even the cops.
Gabby would've been lost in the throng except for that 'Tomato Face' that
glistened with sweat and a wide grin. 'I don't think I saw third base,' said
Hartnett. 'And I don't think I walked a step to the plate — I was carried in.
But when I got there, I saw umpire George Barr taking a good look — he
was going to make sure I touched that platter.'"[11]

Bud Hartnett added, "I met Pat Pieper on the bus and he told me a
story about Dad's famous home run. Pat was the Public Address Announcer
at Wrigley Field during the day and a waiter at night. In those days the

Gabby Hartnett running out his "Homer in the Gloamin'" on September 28, 1938. Chicago PA announcer Pat Pieper, running alongside, is making sure he touches home plate.

announcer stood on the field with a megaphone and called out the lineups and the batters. When Gabby hit the home run, Pat was standing near third base, and when Gabby rounded third, Pat ran alongside him from third to home. All he could say was 'Step on the plate Gabby. Step on the plate.' He's the man in the cap running alongside Gabby in the famous picture of the 'Homer in the Gloamin.'"[12]

Billy Herman, at second base, wondered why Mace Brown didn't waste a pitch instead of coming right in with it, unless he thought Gabby couldn't see it. "It was so dark, that to this day, I never saw the ball. And I don't think anyone else did either."[13]

Paul Waner watched the drama unfold from his position in right field. "Hartnett swung and the damn ball landed in the left field seats. I could hardly believe my eyes. The game was over and I should have run into the clubhouse, but I just stood out there in right field and watched Hartnett circle the bases, and take the lousy pennant with him. The crowd was in an uproar, absolutely gone wild. They ran onto the field like a bunch of maniacs, and his teammates and the crowd and all were mobbing Hartnett, and piling on top of him, and throwing him up in the air, and everything you could think of. I've never seen anything like it, before or since. So I just stood there in the outfield and stared."[14]

The clubhouse was bedlam as the players filed in. Billy Herman, seemingly in a daze, could only mutter, "Lord God Almighty. Lord God Almighty." Players were hugging and kissing each other, and trying to get to Gabby to hug him.

When the clubhouse celebration finally ended, Gabby Hartnett headed to the Cubs' offices upstairs, only to be greeted by Charlie Grimm who extended his hand and said, "Great, Gabby. It was the greatest ball game I ever saw." Gabby grabbed his hand, whispered 'Thanks Charlie' and continued up the stairs. Later he and Martha headed home to Albion Avenue, but it wasn't a fast trip or a quiet evening. Everyone in Rogers Park knew Gabby's black Lincoln sedan, and they stopped the Cubs' manager at every traffic light to offer their congratulations. When the Hartnetts finally arrived home four hours after the game ended, their evening was just beginning. They were deluged with visits from friends and neighbors wanting to share the moment with them.

The season wasn't over yet. It only seemed that way. And the next day, manager Gabby Hartnett had to gather his troops around him and remind them there was still a long way to go, including an important game against Pittsburgh, which would determine if the Cubs stayed in first place. But the finale of the series turned out to be a cakewalk for the Cubbies. The demoralized Bucs went quietly to their doom before the rapid pitches of Bill Lee. Russ Bauers walked the bases full in the first inning and, after an infield out scored the first run of the game for the Cubs, Gabby Hartnett came through again, drilling a single to center field for two more runs. That was more than enough for Lee who tossed a complete game seven-hitter and won going away, 10–1. The only downside to the afternoon was an accident suffered by Hartnett in the ninth inning. A foul tip off the bat of Johnny Rizzo tore the nail off the third finger of his right hand, an injury that would normally put him on the shelf for a few days. But with the pennant still hanging in the balance, the tough Chicago manager just taped it up and moved on.

On September 30, the high-flying Bruins moved into St. Louis to tackle the always ill-tempered Redbirds. In the opener, the Cubs blew a 6–2 lead in the fifth and had to settle for a 7–7 tie, forcing a doubleheader the next day. Manager Gabby Hartnett, who took a beating behind the plate for 17 years without incurring a serious injury, suffered his fifth injury of the season when he was hit by another foul ball, this one to his right index finger. With two fingers now battered, the old warhorse headed to the bench for the rest of the series. Meanwhile, in Pittsburgh, Pie Traynor's Pirates gained a split with the Cincinnati Reds by taking the nightcap of a doubleheader 4–3 after dropping the first game. The Cubs lost the first game of a twin bill on October 1, but they captured the second game while the Bucs were dropping another decision to the Redlegs. And suddenly the Chicago Cubs were champions of the National League.

The championship celebration was riotous. "When the Cubs got home they nearly had their whiskers pulled out for souvenirs by a wildly hysterical crowd of 5000 at the Illinois Central railroad station. But they hadn't seen anything yet, for it was a 300,000-strong delegation which hailed them as World Series conquerors-to-be from myriad skyscraper windows and on packed sidewalks along their march of triumph." The victory parade made its way through the Loop to City Hall. "Surrounded by politicians, flanked by 'me-too' publicity seekers, Gabby presented his ear-to-ear grin to his public, which numbers a few less than 3,600,000 adoring fans. He rode through the Loop seated on a sailors collar of an open limousine, waved a soft hat that was as green as the grass over which his greatest home run ball recently sizzled. Paradoxically they were 'driven into the snow' as a waste paper blizzard of super-Corriganesque proportions filled the sky and for a time actually carpeted the Chicago River." The ecstatic Cubs manager voiced the feelings of all his players when he said, "Boy, it's really great to be alive. I've had the greatest days of my life the past week."[15]

The National League Championship created excitement all around the Millville-Woonsocket area. Several friends and relatives made plans to attend one or more World Series games in New York or Chicago. Gabby's sister "Charlie," sent him a telegram, wishing him luck in the upcoming World Series: "To Leo Hartnett, Manager Chicago Cubs, Clubhouse, Wrigley Field. 'Wish I were there. Will be listening. Carloads of cake. Anne.'"

Unfortunately for Gabby, the Chicago Cubs had expended all their energies in beating the Pittsburgh Pirates, and they had nothing left for the Yankees, who were well rested after winning their league in a laugher, beating the Detroit Tigers by 13 games. The World Series opened in Chicago on October 5, and Red Ruffing tamed the Bruins 3–1, beating Bill Lee in the process. Lefty Gomez gained a decision over Dizzy Dean in game two by a score of 6–3, Monte Pearson beat Clay Bryant 5–2, and Ruffing closed it out in New York with an easy 8–3 win over Lee. Joe Gordon and Bill Dickey paced the New York attack with .400 averages. The Cubs had some big stickers of their own, with Joe Marty tattoing Yankee pitchers to the tune

Bill Dickey, one of the greatest American League catchers, batted .400 against the Cubs in the 1938 World Series.

of .500, followed by Stan Hack at .471 and Phil Cavaretta at .462. Unfortunately, Billy Jurges at .231 was the only other Chicago batter over .188. Gabby Hartnett, hampered by his injured hand, could manage only one hit in 11 at-bats for a .091 average. He did gun down two out of three would-be base stealers. Dickey shot down both men who tried to steal on him.[16]

The individual season batting leaders were Ernie Lombardi at .342 and Jimmie Foxx at .349. Mel Ott had 36 homers, and Hank Greenberg, who challenged Babe Ruth's single-season record, finished with 58 after failing to homer over the final five games of the season. Bill Lee at 22–9 and Red Ruffing at 21–7 paced the pitchers. Gabby Hartnett, whose career was winding down, hit .274 with 10 homers in 88 games. He and his backup, Ken O'Dea, allowed 40 stolen bases against a league average of 44. Gabby's American League counterpart, Bill Dickey, hit .313 with 27 home runs and 115 RBIs. Defensively, he led the league in putouts and assists and allowed only 52 stolen bases against a league average of 68.

Bill Lee was the Cubs' most valuable player in 1938. "He won 22 and lost 9 and led the league with a 2.66 ERA and nine shutouts. From May 19 through June 3 the General marched through five consecutive victories, pitching three straight shutouts, 32 consecutive scoreless innings, allowing one run in 47, and one extra base hit, a double. Within a space of 17 days in September, Lee tacked up four successive shutouts. He zipped through 37⅓ runless innings against five teams."[17]

Gabby Hartnett became an instant national hero after his historic home run, and Chesterfield cigarettes quickly corralled him to represent their company. Soon, billboards adorned with the slogan "Chesterfield — They satisfy" were sprouting up all over the country, with Gabby's smiling face peering out from behind his catcher's mitt. They even had a billboard on Main Street in the center of Millville, according to John McNamara, "But Gabby didn't smoke cigarettes. He only smoked cigars."

The handsome Hartnett face also graced the Wheaties cereal boxes in grocery stores from California to New York. According to the advertising, Gabby declared, "It's the tops!.... This breakfast of champions."

Gabby spent a few weeks relaxing at home with his family. Then he hit the road to South Dakota with teammates Stan Hack and Charlie Root to hunt deer, elk, pheasant, and rabbit. They spent two weeks in St. Francis, South Dakota, on the Rosebud Sioux Indian Reservation, hunting and socializing, and Hack and Gabby each bagged an elk before returning to Chicago, but Charlie Root came up empty. Gabby had the elk head mounted and, according to his daughter Sheila, "It was in a crate in the garage for a hundred years."

On his return home, Gabby found himself in great demand as an after-

Fred Hartnett points to a picture of his son on a Chesterfield billboard in 1938. Gabby never smoked cigarettes. (Sheila Hartnett Hornof)

dinner speaker at sports banquets and other functions. His recent celebrity, the result of his season-ending heroics, made him a popular guest. And the smiling Irishman, who was always ready to talk, was equipped with a new portfolio of funny stories and baseball experiences. He traveled to a few functions outside Illinois, but did most of his speaking at local events, such as those sponsored by the Elks Club and the Holy Name Society at St. Timothy's Roman Catholic Church in Chicago.

The Chicago Cubs' front office made a major trade on December 6, dealing Billy Jurges, Frank Demaree, and Ken O'Dea to the New York Giants for Dick Bartell, Gus Mancuso, and Hank Leiber.

12

The End of the Trail, 1939–1946

Gabby Hartnett had many exciting moments during his fabulous 17-year major league career, but now his time was running out; his playing days were numbered, and his managerial career would be less than satisfying after 1938. When the players arrived at Avalon in February, several key members of the 1938 National League Championship team were among the missing. Gone were Jurges, Demaree, and O'Dea. In their places were Dick Bartell, Gus Mancuso, and Hank Leiber. Rip Collins was released, as was Tony Lazzeri. Other new additions to the team included first baseman Rip Russell, purchased from Los Angeles of the Pacific Coast League (PCL) after hitting .318 with 21 homers and 114 RBIs for the Angels in '38; outfielder Gee Gee Gleeson, who was coming off a .310 season with Newark of the International League; and Claude Passeau, who would come aboard on May 29 in a trade with Philadelphia, which would send Joe Marty and Kirby Higbe to the Phils. There were also a dozen holdouts, all looking for more money after winning the National League pennant. And Clay Bryant was unhappy because, after winning 19 games, he was offered less money than Dizzy Dean got for winning seven games.

Eventually all the players signed contracts, but not all of them were happy, and many of them were critical of manager Hartnett for his caustic remarks after the World Series. As Warren Bown reported, "On the 'funeral' train from New York to Chicago, following the 1938 World Series, Manager Hartnett in an ill-guarded moment, declared he would be glad to get rid of everyone on his squad before another season started. Hartnett was very mad about it all, and while some made due allowance for his peeve, others were willing to concede that Gabby was as lacking in tact as Rogers Hornsby had been before him."[1]

Gabby's ill-timed remarks may have seriously damaged his ability to manage the ball club over the next two years, and may have indirectly led to his firing. Phil Cavaretta, one of the disgruntled benchwarmers, said, "Some players you can be tough with and let them have it, scream at them, but a lot of them, as the years go by, you can't do that anymore. Going into '39, we didn't absolutely say, 'The heck with this.' We still gave it our best, but deep inside the best wasn't coming out. He was our manager, and we still carried respect for the man because he was our manager, but after the train thing, he lost a lot."[2]

The state of affairs in the real world was even worse. The world order was deteriorating into a quagmire that would lead to a full-blown world war in a matter of a few short months. In September of '38, British Prime Minister Neville Chamberlain signed a treaty with Adolph Hitler that gave the German dictator a large chunk of Czechoslovakia in return for Hitler's guarantee that he would make no more demands for additional territory in Europe. That promise was broken less than six months later when German troops occupied Prague. On September 3, 1939, England and France would declare war on Germany and the carnage would begin.

The outlook for the Chicago Cubs was not bright as the season got underway. They were anchored by a group of graybeards, headed by 38-year-old Gabby Hartnett, 40-year old-Charlie Root, 39-year-old Earl Whitehill, 34-year-old Jack Russell, 33-year-old Gus Mancuso, 32-year-old Vance Page, 30-year-old Larry French, 30-year-old Dick Bartell, and 28-year-old Dizzy Dean, the man with a 50-year-old pitching arm.

The season finally opened in Chicago on April 21 after eight days of rain, and Hartnett's Cubbies took the measure of the Cincinnati Reds by the score of 4-2. Bill Lee pitched a complete game, and Joe Marty and Stan Hack took Curt Davis deep to the delight of the 14,020 Cubs fanatics who braved the wind and cold to root for their heroes. The usual post-game meeting between the manager and the players was a short one, as it always is after a victory.

The year 1939 was Gabby Hartnett's true baptism of fire as a major league manager. In '38, he replaced Charlie Grimm in July, so he wasn't involved in any of the off-season personnel decisions. He was primarily a field manager, an inspirational leader whose job it was to motivate the troops he had and mount a challenge to Pittsburgh's pennant parade. In that, he was eminently successful. His fist pounding the air to celebrate a strikeout, his constant chatter behind the plate, and his clutch base hits sparked his team to victory. In 1939, he was responsible for all aspects of the managerial position: off-season personnel decisions and roster changes, lineup decisions, and game strategy during the season.

One of Hartnett's primary concerns was how to maintain a normal family relationship during the club's home stands without affecting his managerial responsibilities. He tried to follow the same routine he had as a player; leaving the clubhouse at the same time each day after the game, so he would arrive home in time to have dinner with Martha and the children at 6:30. He made it a point never to talk baseball at the dinner table and, although Bud or Sheila would sometimes ask him questions about the game, Martha learned early on that it was better to talk about other things. After dinner, Gabby preferred to spend the evening playing "scat" or some other card game with the family, or work with them on a jigsaw puzzle. The new Chicago manager was in bed by midnight and up by 8 AM. Martha always had a big breakfast and the newspaper waiting for him, because she knew that a long, grueling day awaited him at Wrigley Field. After breakfast, he would play with the children for an hour before leaving for work.

Gabby's day at the park began about 11 AM when he met with the trainer to discuss the physical condition of the players. Next he would meet with his coaches to review the strategy for the game, and then with the players to go over the signals for the day and discuss how to pitch to each of the opposing players. Batting and fielding practice would begin at 1 PM, followed by the game at 3 PM. Then it was home for dinner at 6:30.

On April 30, Lou Gehrig played his last game in a New York Yankee uniform, ending his consecutive game streak at 2,130. The popular first baseman was suffering from amyotrophic lateral sclerosis, a degenerative neuromuscular disease that was incurable, and, after hitting just .143 in eight games, he turned his job over to Babe Dahlgren. Lou Gehrig had only two more years to live.

The Cubs ended the month with a 4-1 win over the St. Louis Cardinals as rookie Gene Lillard, up from Los Angeles after running up a 16-10 record in the PCL, scattered 10 hits for the win. Chicago's 6-3 record in April left them in third place, one game off the top. They slipped back to 14-14 in May, dropping them five games behind Bill McKechnie's front-running Cincinnati Reds. But they finished the month on a high, blanking the Redlegs in both ends of a twin bill. Augie Galan was the leading Chicago hitter through May with a .310 average. Hank Leiber was hitting .290 and Stan Hack was at .281. Leiber also paced the team with five home runs and 21 runs-batted-in (RBIs).

Fred Hartnett recalled one early season visit the Cubs made to Boston: "Dizzy Dean was with the Cubs toward the end of my uncle's career. They were down here in Blackstone at Corbett's Café. It's still there but it's got a different name. They played the Braves on a Saturday afternoon in Boston. He and Diz were here on Saturday night. They left Blackstone about 5 AM on a train. Got the trainer out of bed. Got them in condition to play. Gabby caught both games of a doubleheader. Dizzy pitched the first game and won. Came in the second game in relief in the 9th, and 7 o'clock they were back down at Corbett's. They had a full day."[3]

June got off to a slow start as Gene Moore of the Brooklyn Dodgers tripled off Charlie Root in the bottom of the fourteenth inning, then stole home with the winning run. The play was actually intended to be a squeeze play, but the batter missed the pitch and Cubs catcher Bob Garbark dropped the ball as Moore slid across the plate. The Cubs had scored two runs in the top of the ninth to tie the game at 2–2, and Root had tossed six no-hit innings in relief before yielding Moore's blast. Root ended the month better than he began it. He beat Johnny VanderMeer and the Reds 5–1, helped out by a three-run eighth inning. Gabby Hartnett had a two-for-three day, which was half the Chicago hit total. VanderMeer lasted only 1⅔ innings in this game, leaving after walking five men, four of them in the weird second inning, in which a total of five Cubs walked and three Cubs struck out. According to the *Chicago Tribune*, "The Cubs made two runs in the second inning and left three runners on base without rapping a fair ball of any classification in the entire inning; then in the eighth, they scored their third and fourth runs on a strikeout that should have retired the side. The topsy turvy triumph lopped another game off the lead of the Reds over the Cubs, reducing the margin to five games. At noon on June 18, the margin was ten and a half games and the Cubs were in the throes of a four game losing streak. [Dizzy Dean got the Cubs back on track when he beat Brooklyn 1–0 on a Gabby Hartnett homer.] Since that time the Cubs have won ten out of twelve."[4]

One of the highlights of the month for Gabby was to be able to attend the Baseball Hall of Fame induction ceremonies in Cooperstown, New York, as the manager of the National League champion Chicago Cubs. Many baseball legends were admitted into the Hall in 1939, including George Sisler, Eddie Collins, "Wee Willie" Keeler, and Gabby's former manager Rogers Hornsby.

Hank Leiber at .303 was the only Cubs batter to post a .300 average through June. Gabby Hartnett had eight home runs to lead the team in that category, and Augie Galan had 35 RBIs. Leiber had a big day against the St. Louis Cardinals in the first game of the Fourth of July doubleheader when he smashed three home runs, but the Redbirds hung on to win 6–4.

The All-Star Game gave most of the Chicago Cubs players a few days to rest up for the second half of the season, but Bill Lee, Stan Hack, and Billy Herman, who were selected for the All-Star squad, caught a train to New York City. The game was played in Yankee Stadium on July 11, and the teams were managed by the previous year's World Series skippers, Gabby Hartnett and Joe McCarthy. For the fifth time in seven years, the American League walked off with a victory, winning a close contest by the score of 3–1. Two runs in the fourth inning off the Cubs' Bill Lee spelled the difference in the game. A walk, two singles, and an error by Arky Vaughan did the damage. Twenty-year-old Bob Feller shackled the National Leaguers over the final 3⅔ innings. Manager McCarthy started six players from his New York Yankees squad.

When the second half of the season got underway, the Cubs continued to struggle. Their July record was a sad 14–15, dropping them into fourth place, a distant 13 games behind the first-place Reds. Some of the player problems associated with the Cubs decline surfaced at the end of the month when pitcher Larry French complained directly to owner P.K. Wrigley, saying he hadn't pitched in a month and wanted more playing time. Dizzy started the game against the last-place Phillies on August 1, and his quick exit didn't help his situation any. He lasted only three innings, complaining of a sore arm, and was relieved by French who held the Phils to one run in six innings to pick up the 6–2 victory. Manager Hartnett's efforts to rouse the Cubs from their lethargy were partially successful. They ran up a fine 19–10 slate in August, closing the gap between themselves and the Reds to 7½ games, but it was too little, too late. On August 28, Gabby caught his 1,722nd game, breaking the mark of Chicago White Sox legend, Ray Schalk.

The Bruins played a doubleheader against Leo Durocher's revitalized Dodgers in Ebbets Field in early September, and a promising start ended with a disappointing split. Larry French, recently released from manager Gabby Hartnett's doghouse, knocked off Durocher's boys in the first game by a 6–2 score, with Hank Leiber and Gus Mancuso hammering home runs. But in game two, Lefty Tamulis edged Bill Lee 3–1. The Cubs also visited New York during their east coast swing, and Giants catcher Harry Danning remembered one of the games: "One day the Cubs were hitting in the Polo Grounds against Carl Hubbell. Gabby Hartnett was at bat. Bill Terry came out to the mound and told Hubbell, 'Don't give him anything good to hit, but don't walk him.' Hubbell threw the first pitch outside for ball one. He threw the next pitch two feet outside and Gabby reached over and hit a homer. That's the kind of ballplayer Gabby was."[5]

On the 9th of September, Charlie Root won again, this time 3–2 over the league-leading Cincinnati Reds. A two-run rally in the bottom of the seventh, on a double by manager Hartnett and singles by Rip Russell and Bobby Mattick, gave the Cubbies the victory. The win still left the Bruins eight games behind the Redlegs, and they wouldn't get any closer. When the season ended, Gabby Hartnett's tame Cubbies were comfortably ensconced in fourth place, 13 games behind Cincinnati. St. Louis finished second and Durocher's Dodgers edged the Cubs for third place. Hank Leiber was one of the few Cubs bright spots down the stretch, hitting 10 home runs during the month, including a grand slam off "Sailor" Bill Posedel of the Boston Bees.

The American League race was another runaway for the Yankees, a typical pattern for Joe McCarthy's Bronx Bombers during the late '30s. They finished the season with 106 victories and a 17-game lead over the Boston Red Sox. They were heavily favored in the World Series, and they proved the betting line correct as they swept the Reds in four games, outscoring them 20 to 8. Charlie "King Kong" Keller paced the hitters with a .438 batting average. He was followed by Joe DiMaggio at .313. But this was a Series of pitching, not hitting, as the Yankees mound corps had a brilliant 1.22 earned-run-average (ERA), to 4.33 for Cincinnati.[6]

The individual season batting leaders were Johnny Mize at .349 and Joe DiMaggio at .381. Mize with 28 homers and Jimmie Foxx with 35, showed the way in the long ball contest, and Bucky Walters at 27–11 and Bob Feller at 24–9 paced the leagues pitchers. Hank Leiber at .310, Billy Herman at .307, and Augie Galan at .304 were the top Cubs hitters. Bill Lee with a record of 19–11, Larry French with 15–8, and Claude Passeau with 13–9 were the top pitchers. Manager Gabby Hartnett played in just 97 games, hitting .278 with 12 home runs in 306 at-bats. His .992 fielding average was the highest in the National League, but he didn't play enough games to qualify for the title. Bill Dickey won the American League fielding title with an average of .989.

The Chicago Cubs' disappointment over their failure in the National League pennant race was matched in the important City Series against the White Sox. Hank Leiber launched a three-run homer in the bottom of the ninth inning of game four to bring the Bruins back from the brink of defeat to a thrilling 5–3 victory, giving Hartnett's cohorts a 3-to-1 lead in games. But excitement turned to despair when the Pale Hose rallied from a 5–0 deficit in game five to win it 8–5 in 10 innings. They went on to win the final two games as well by scores of 6–1 and 7–1, to claim the City Series title four games to three. For a Cubs team in highly partisan Chicago, it was as devastating a loss as any World Series loss could have been.[7]

The Hartnett's celebrated the Christmas holiday in their Albion Avenue home, but they kept in touch with all their relatives and friends back in Millville through an imaginative Christmas card that portrayed the four members of the Hartnett family rushing through the snow to "your house" carrying a card that read, "Merry Xmas and a Happy and Prosperous New Year. The Hartnetts." Martha's character added, "This is one message we must deliver personally." To his friend, Margaret [Miles] Gauvin's card, Gabby added a note: "Let's hope you chew Wrigley's gum for the next 50 years. Regards to all the family. I suppose they are all grown up. Leo."

The Chicago Cubs didn't make any significant player moves during the off-season, and the "old" Cubs just got older. Gabby Hartnett's playing career was nearing an end. He would play just 37 games in 1940 and 64 games in 1941 before hanging his mitt up for good. His major league managerial career was winding down also. He was put on notice that he had to win in 1940 to keep his job. "Philip K. Wrigley, who had become an absentee owner — he rarely saw the Cubs play — descended into the trenches. On April 20, 1940, he announced he was taking a six-month leave of absence from his gum company and moving his offices from Michigan Avenue to Wrigley Field for a closer view of the day-by-day operations. 'We have a darned good team,' Wrigley said."[8]

The Chicago Cubs didn't have a "darned good team." In fact, it would be an almost impossible task to win the pennant with the patchwork outfit Gabby had at his disposal. Twenty-three-year-old Bobby Mattick would struggle through one disappointing year at shortstop, batting .218 and fielding .946, then be released at the end of the season. Most of the other players were familiar figures; Hack, Herman, Leiber, Cavaretta, Russell, Galan, French, Lee, and Root. As the *Chicago Tribune* noted, "To win, the Cubs will have to uncover a series of Herculean fielding, hitting, and pitching surprises. Even manager Gabby Hartnett would be surprised by such an unveiling. The pilot knows old age is not only gaining on him, but also on a few of the important men in his command" (9).

The Chicago Cubs opened the 1940 season in Cincinnati on April 16, taking on the defending National League champions. A big crowd of 34,342 fans welcomed their heroes back to Crosley Field, and the Reds responded with a 2–1 victory over the visiting Cubs. Paul Derringer, who went 25–7 in '39, got the best of "Big Bill" Lee, who finished the year at 19–15. The big news on opening day, however, came out of Cleveland where twenty-year-old Bob Feller tossed a no-hitter at the Chicago White Sox, winning 1–0 on an RBI by his batterymate Rollie Hemsley. "Rapid Robert" fanned eight men and walked five in his masterpiece.

Nineteen-forty would be a bad year for the Cubs, but it would be a tragic year around the world. Nazi Germany, after defeating Finland on March 12, would conquer Norway and Denmark in early June, and march down the Champs Elysées in Paris late in the month. In August, the terror-filled blitzkrieg of England would begin, subjecting the civilian populace to months of continuous bombing and rocket attacks, as Hitler tried to bring the island nation to it's knees. Winston Churchill's famous speech about "blood, sweat, and tears" would rally the English people to begin the long fight for freedom. In September, Germany, Italy, and Japan would sign a 10-year military and economic agreement, forming what the allies would refer to as the "Axis." On October 29, the United States, realizing that their entry into the war was inevitable, would begin the first peacetime military draft. The war would not end quickly, nor would it save the more than 20 million people who would die in it, but eventually the "Axis" would be defeated and its leaders eliminated.

On the home front, the Cubbies took the measure of the Boston Bees 8–7 on Al Todd's home run in the tenth inning on April 30. Bill Lee, who came on in the top of the tenth, was the winning pitcher. Hank Leiber, with a single, triple, home run, and four RBIs, and Bill Nicholson, with three singles and two RBIs, paced the Chicago offense. The win brought the Cubs' record for the month to an even 7–7, leaving them in third place, 4½ games behind the undefeated Dodgers. One month later, the struggling Windy City boys were one game under .500 at 18–19. They had settled into fourth place, trailing the first-place Reds by eight games. Leo Durocher's Dodgers had slipped into second place, two games off the pace. The woes of the Cubs were reported in the press: "While the Cubs would dearly love to hoist themselves into the status of a pennant contender, their desires appear to exceed their ability. Their hitting, most of the time, is of the scattergun variety. In hopes of finding a solution, Manager Gabby Hartnett has juggled his lineup repeatedly. One combination has proved no better than another so he'll just have to keep on juggling."[10]

Hank Leiber was the leading Chicago hitter on June 1, with a .338 average, five home runs, and 32 RBIs. Billy Herman was hitting .310 and Bill Nicholson .308. Augie Galan was the biggest disappointment in the early going, hitting just .202, 102 points below his 1939 average. Other disappointments included Bobby Mattick at .222 and Phil Cavaretta, the disgruntled first baseman, at .220. On June 2, the Cubs edged the Dodgers in the Friendly Confines by a score of 4–3 in 12 innings. Catcher Al Todd supplied the punch by hitting a walk-off homer in the bottom of the twelfth. In the top of the inning, Chicago pitcher Jake Mooty beaned "Pee Wee" Reese, sending the Brooklyn shortstop to the hospital with a concussion. The next day, baseball legend Dizzy Dean was optioned to Tulsa of the Texas League, ending three months of turmoil. The Dean saga had begun during spring training when the high-spirited pitcher and his manager had an encounter that led to a $100 fine for insubordination. The man from Lucas, Arkansas, then missed the team train, insisting he was taking a bath and had lost track of the time. Later, on a trip to New York, the pitcher didn't show up for a game, saying he had cut his arm when he fell through a glass cigar counter at the hotel, and the doctor had told him not to use the arm for several days. Manager Hartnett immediately ordered his eccentric pitcher to return to Chicago. He was eventually farmed out after having appeared in 10 games, five of them as a starter, with a 3–3 record and a 5.17 ERA. That was essentially the end of the "Great One's" major league career except for two one-inning guest-shots in '41 and '47.

The Dean melodrama was a microcosm of the entire 1940 season. The team played poorly, and there was constant dissension and turmoil in the clubhouse. Some players, like Cavaretta and Herman, were offended by Hartnett's ill-timed remarks after the 1938 World Series. Some players resented the trade of their All-Star shortstop Billy Jurges to the hated Giants. Others, like Dick Bartell, were known troublemakers. And then there was Dean. The inept performances of the Cubs wore on Gabby Hartnett, making him irritable and short-tempered. It was not a happy time for the smiling Irishman.

The month of June was only moderately better as the team labored to a 16–14 record, good enough for fourth place, 9½ games behind Bill McKechnie's Redlegs. They finished the month by dropping a twin bill to those same Reds in Cincinnati, losing the opener by a 7–4 count and the nightcap 7–6. Jim Gleeson accounted for all the Cubs offense in game one, with a grand slam home run in the sixth inning. Bucky Walters was the winning pitcher, and Vance Page took the loss in relief. In game two, Elmer Riddle beat Larry French with a run in the eighth and the game winner in the ninth. Bill Nicholson hit a three-run homer for the Cubs, who blew a five-run lead over the last five innings. Gabby went back to Cooperstown for the Hall of Fame ceremonies in June, as the Cubs took on the Boston Red Sox in an exhibition game at Doubleday Field. The Cubs won 10–9.

The American League race was becoming a major surprise at the All-Star break, as the highly favored New York Yankees were reposing in fourth place, 8½ games behind the front-running Cleveland Indians. The All-Star Game was played at Sportsman's Park in St. Louis on July 9, and the National League responded to the home field advantage by blanking the American Leaguers 4–0. Paul Derringer beat Red Ruffing, as the Senior Circuit pushed over three runs before a man had been retired in the first inning. Chicago's Billy Herman was in the middle of the rally.

July continued the downward trend of the Cubs. As the month came to an end, Gabby Hartnett's charges dropped a game to the Philadelphia Phillies 7–3, and lost the services of their left fielder at the same time. Augie Galan was carried off the field on a stretcher with a broken kneecap after colliding with the concrete barrier in left field while running down a foul ball in the fifth inning. Manager Hartnett, who started the game behind the plate, went on the injured list himself when he was struck in the head by a bat swung by Mel Mazzera. His pain was even worse after his team dropped their second game in three starts to the cellar-dwelling Phils. Other members of the Chicago hospital brigade included Rip Russell who was recovering from an appendectomy, Phil Cavaretta who was out with a broken ankle, and Clay Bryant who was home in California recovering from some unknown illness. The Cubbie's plight was now hopeless after their 15–16 run in July, because the red-hot Reds went 20–8 over the same period, leaving Chicago in their dust, now a distant 16 games from the top. Second-place Brooklyn was 7½ games out. Detroit had caught Cleveland in the American League chase, making it a two-horse race, although Boston and New York were still within striking distance.

On August 31, the Reds took the measure of the Bruins again, this time by a 5–4 count on Ernie Lombardi's game-winning single in the bottom of the ninth. Vance Page was the victim. Stan Hack went 3-for-5 for the Cubs, and Bobby Mattick went 2-for-4. The loss dropped Chicago even further down the ladder, leaving them in sixth place, 17 games back. Brooklyn was still hanging tough at 7½ back. In the American League, the Indians had opened up a 2½-game lead over Detroit, while New York had sneaked to within five games of the leader.

Gabby Hartnett's wounded and unhappy crew ended the year with identical 13–15 records in August and September, to finish in fifth place, an embarrassing 25½ games behind the pennant-winning Cincinnati Reds. The American League race was a real dogfight down to the wire, with the Tigers finally opening a two-game lead over Cleveland with just three games to play, then clinching the pennant on Floyd Giebell's 2–0 shutout of the Indians on September 27. The never-say-die Yankees kept the pressure on also, and came in third, just two games off the top.

Bill McKechnie's Cincinnati Express defeated the Detroit Tigers in a thrilling seven-game World Series, taking the finale 2–1. Detroit took the opener in Cincinnati by a 7–2 count behind 21-game winner Bobo Newsome. Bucky Walters evened the count at one game apiece with a 5–3 win in game two. The Tigers won games one, three, and five, and the Reds won games two, four, and six. McKechnie's charges rewrote the script in game seven as Paul Derringer outpitched Newsome to capture the world championship. The winning rally in the bottom of the seventh inning consisted of leadoff doubles by Frank McCormick and Jimmy Ripple, a sacrifice bunt, and a sacrifice fly by Bill Myers. Billy Werber led the Reds at bat with a .370 average, and Derringer and Walters won two games apiece. For the Tigers, Bruce Campbell hit .360 and Hank Greenberg was close behind at .357. Bobo Newsome won two games with a 1.38 ERA.[11]

The individual season leaders were Debs Garms (.355) and Joe DiMaggio (.352) in batting, Johnny Mize (43) and Hank Greenberg (41) in home runs, and Bucky Walters (22–10) and Bob Feller (27–11) in pitching. For the Cubs, Stan Hack hit .317, Jim Gleeson hit .313, and Hank Leiber hit .302. Twenty-four-year-old Bill Nicholson blossomed in 1940, hitting .297 with 25 home runs and 98 RBIs. He was nicknamed "Swish" because of his penchant for striking out; but in today's environment, with his 82 strikeouts a year, he would be known as a contact hitter. Hank Leiber was close behind Nicholson with 17 homers and 86 RBIs. Thirty-one-year-old Claude Passeau was the top pitcher with a record of 20–13. Vern Olsen finished at 13–9 and Larry French had 14–14. Gabby Hartnett, limited to 37 games, batted .266 with just one home run in 64 at-bats.

It was a disappointing season for the Cubs, for manager Gabby Hartnett, and for owner P.K. Wrigley. The handwriting was on the wall. It was apparent that Hartnett's reign as skipper of the Cubs was over. Only the date of his dismissal was unknown. And that date, November 12, was badly handled by the Chicago Cubs front office who phoned Gabby minutes after he had learned about his firing from a reporter, who called him at home. "A press conference was called to announce the firing of Gabby Hartnett and the resignation of Charles Webster as Treasurer. At the meeting, Hartnett said to Wrigley, 'Well, thanks anyway Mr. Wrigley; not thanks for firing me, but for coming down here with me to announce it.'"[12]

Gabby took his firing in stride, and was probably relieved to be free of the discord in the Chicago Cubs organization, from the front office to the clubhouse. When he was hired in 1938, he said that if he was fired, he would go fishing and hunting. And that's what he did. He picked up his buddies and took the train to the Sioux Reservation in South Dakota for a little pheasant hunting. When he returned home, he had offers from both Joe Cronin of the Boston Red Sox and Bill Terry of the New York Giants, to join them as a player-coach. Gabby opted for the New York offer so he could stay in the National League where all his friends were.

The change in managers didn't work miracles for the Chicago Cubs as owner P.K. Wrigley hoped. Their 75–79 record in 1940 became 70–84 in 1941 and 68–86 in '42. Gabby's achievements with the players he had at his disposal looked better in retrospect.

The new year got off to a sad start for Gabby Hartnett and the rest of the Hartnett family, when Fred Hartnett died in Woonsocket, Rhode Island, on February 3, just before Gabby was to leave for spring training. Fred had been sick for about six weeks, and many of his sons and daughters visited him in Woonsocket Hospital on a regular basis. Sweetie, who never forgave his father for the breakup of his marriage, refused to attend the funeral.

Gabby however, did come in from Chicago for the funeral, which was celebrated in St. Augustine's Church in Millville, with burial in the family plot in Blackstone Cemetery. Before catching a train to the Giants' camp in Miami, Florida, Gabby noted his father's influence on his baseball career: "My dad was a pretty good semi-pro player, and a catcher at that. He's the fellow who really made a ballplayer out of me. Not many kids are that fortunate."

Reports out of Florida told of a much happier Gabby Hartnett, now that he was out from under the zoo that was Chicago in recent years. "He wasn't exactly laughing-Leo then, for the headaches of handling a ball club that was sagging and harassed by internal strife and front office aloofness caused Gabby to lose his flair for fun and he no longer was the affable guy of the glory days when he was just a brilliant backstopper. He became a grim, dour Hartnett as he sat on that tempestuous kettle of discord."[13]

During the summer for many years, while Gabby was away playing baseball, Martha and the children would take the train east to visit Grandma, Millie, Tina, and Charlie at their home at 329 Murray Street in Woonsocket. This year, Grandma and the girls rented a house in Point Judith on the Rhode Island coast for a month, so six-year-old Sheila and her 11-year-old brother had an even greater summer, sloshing about in the surf and playing on the beach. The ocean was like a new world to them, and they loved it. And when the New York Giants visited Boston, Gabby was able to stop by for a short visit.

The Giants, who had won the National League pennant in 1937, had slipped badly in the last three years, finishing a distant sixth in 1940. And they were not picked to be much better in '41. They too were getting old and were in need of a transfusion of young blood, but it would be more than a decade before they would seriously challenge for the title again. Bill Terry's charges could do no better than a fifth-place finish in 1941, 25½ games behind Leo Durocher's rampaging Dodgers. Thirty-two-year-old Mel Ott was one of the Giants batting leaders, hitting .286 with 27 home runs and 90 RBIs. Babe Young hit .265 with 27 homers and 104 RBIs, and Dick Bartell, back with the Giants, checked in with an average of .303. "Prince Hal" Schumacher was the top pitcher with a record of 12–10. Thirty-eight-year-old Carl Hubbell had 11 wins against nine losses. Gabby Hartnett, in his farewell season, played in 64 games, 34 behind the plate and 30 as a pinch hitter. He batted an even .300 in 150 at-bats, with five homers and 26 RBIs. He was charged with just one error in 34 games for a .994 fielding percent-

Gabby (left) went hunting in South Dakota with teammates Stan Hack, standing on right, and Charlie Root, kneeling on left. (Sheila Hartnett Hornof)

age. Ray Berres of the Boston Braves was the fielding leader with an average of .995.

Gabby Hartnett caught his last major league game in Philadelphia on September 29. It was his 1,990th game. The big catcher went 1-for-4 at the plate, as Tom "Lefty" Sunkel blanked the Phillies 2–0 for his only victory of the year. The tall southpaw had a no-hitter for 8⅔ innings before the spell was broken. Two days before the season ended, the Giants gave Gabby his unconditional release so he could pursue any managerial opportunities that might present themselves. In the meantime, he and his old friend Mickey Cochrane co-wrote an instructional book called *How to Catch*. It was part of *The Instructional Baseball School All-Star* series, intended for a teenage audience.

As baseball took its annual sabbatical, the United States was suddenly and treacherously thrust into World War II. In the early morning hours of December 7, a large Japanese naval task force unleashed a sneak air attack against American warships in Pearl Harbor and aircraft at Hickam Field, scuttling most the country's Pacific fleet, including the battleships Arizona, California, and West Virginia, and destroying 150 aircraft that were on the ground at the airfield. When the carnage ended just minutes later, more than 2,000 American soldiers, sailors, and marines were dead. The next day, President Franklin D. Roosevelt, standing before Congress and referring to December 7 as "a date that will live in infamy," declared war on Japan and her Axis partners, Germany and Italy, beginning four years of sacrifice, both human and economic, on the part of the American people.[14]

Gabby Hartnett began a hectic five-year career as a minor league manager in 1942 when he signed to manage the Indianapolis Indians of the American Association. The Indians finished sixth out of eight teams under their new manager, winning 76 games against 78 losses. It was a 10½-game improvement over their 1941 finish and, with Gabby at the helm, they set a new Indianapolis attendance record. The old warhorse still couldn't stay on the bench, however. He appeared in 72 games behind the plate, but the old skills were no longer in evidence. He hit just .220 and fielded .970.

The world war increased in intensity for the United States in 1942; and on June 7, the tide of the war in the Pacific changed as a small American fleet, led by the aircraft carriers Hornet, Enterprise, and Yorktown, crushed a much larger Japanese force off Midway Island, sinking or damaging 20 warships and destroying 275 Japanese planes. American B-17s and torpedo planes attacked the enemy fleet, sinking three of the four Japanese carriers in a matter of minutes and, without air cover, the other Japanese ships were sitting targets for U.S. planes. From this point on, the United States would be the aggressor, pushing the enemy force back closer and closer to its homeland.

Gabby returned to the New York Giants organization in 1943, to manage their Jersey City franchise. He took over a team that had finished fourth the previous season with a record of 77–75. Gabby found managing a minor league team more enjoyable and satisfying than managing at the major league level because the emphasis was on developing young talent, and he was an outstanding teacher, particularly of pitchers and catchers. But the old warrior was still torn between two worlds because he had been taught, even as a child, that you play the game to win, and when the parent club would raid the farm system, bringing the more promising players to New York to try to breathe new life into the once-great Giants, it frustrated him. Gabby also lost many players to U.S. military service through enlistments and the draft. At one time, he considered enlisting himself, but he was above the draft age and married with children. When President Roosevelt encouraged major league baseball to continue to operate their minor league systems as a valuable morale booster for the people at home, Gabby decided to make his contribution to the war effort on the playing fields of organized baseball.

While the Jersey City manager was evaluating his talent at spring training, the U.S. Marines were engaged in a bloody battle with the Japanese army for control of little Guadalcanal in the Solomon Islands, just northeast of Australia. After six months of hand-to-hand combat in the jungles and mountains of the 2,500-square-mile island, the Japanese evacuated the island, giving Uncle Sam another stepping stone on the road to Tokyo. On March 15, 1943, food and other items were added to a growing list of products that were rationed in the United States due to shortages or military demand. Ration books were distributed to the American people, allowing them to purchase limited amounts of such things as gasoline, automobile tires, sugar, coffee, shoes, silk, and butter.

As Gabby Hartnett's pitiful Jersey City Giants struggled through the spring and summer, the Allies were making large gains on the Atlantic front as well as the Pacific. On May 13, the German Army surrendered its North African territories, with more than 250,000 prisoners taken. Two months later, British and American forces invaded Sicily, and two months after that, the British Eighth Army invaded Southern Italy. Italy officially surrendered to the Allies on September 8, but German forces still occupied the country. An American invasion force landed near Naples within days, driving the Germans north. The Allies reached Naples on October 1, but it wasn't until June 4, 1944, that they were able to take Rome.[15]

Amelia, the Hartnett's maid, left their employ to go to work in a defense plant to help out the war effort during this time. She wasn't replaced. Martha also made a valuable contribution to the war effort. She gave up her car, and she never drove again.

The 1943 Jersey City Giants finished the season in last place, their 60–93 record leaving them 35½ games behind the pennant-winning Toronto club and six games behind seventh-place Buffalo. They had only two bonafide future major league players, pitcher Bill Voiselle and shortstop Buddy Kerr. Kerr hit a barely visible .209 during the season and Voiselle limped home with a 10–21 record. Both players went on to successful major league careers. Kerr enjoyed a nine-year sojourn in New York and Boston, retiring with a batting average of .266. Voiselle also had a nine-year career, finishing with a 74–84 record. In fact, he went 21–16 for the New York Giants in 1944. The Jersey City Giants were shut out 32 times in 1943, causing Gabby Hartnett to call a meeting of his pitchers. According to Voiselle, "He told us we could jump the team if we wanted — and that he'd jump with us. I learned more under him than from any other manager."

Gabby, who had been a renowned beer drinker throughout his major league career, still enjoyed a brew or two in the minors. Joe Stephenson, a Boston Red Sox scout, who played for "Old Tomato Face" in 1943, remembered. "Gabby was my manager at Jersey City. After every game, there were two cases of beer in the clubhouse — one case for Gabby and one case for the players."[16]

Gabby Hartnett was back at the helm of the Jersey City team in 1944, and his 14-year old-son Bud joined him for the summer. They shared an apartment off Journal Square. It was a magical summer for the 14-year-old boy. He had a Giants uniform and worked out with the team every day. He got to play with future New York Giants players like Buddy Kerr, Whitey Lockman, and Danny Gardella. He thought Gardella was a real character, saying, "He always made crazy remarks and spent all his time looking up into the stands trying to find good looking girls. He had one trick he liked to do for the spectators. He would do a handstand, balancing both hands on the barrel of a bat.

"One day, when the Giants were in Baltimore for a game with the Orioles, Hack Wilson met Dad in the hotel and they talked for about ten minutes. Hack didn't look good. I don't know what they talked about. Hack probably wanted to borrow a couple of bucks. When he died my father and a couple of other old timers buried him."[17]

The 1944 edition of the Jersey City Giants were a much better club than the 1943 group. They were still not pennant material, but they managed to finish in fifth place with a 74–79 record, an improvement of 14 games over the previous year. The Baltimore Orioles, who had to play on the road for 10 days in July after fire damaged Oriole Park, captured the pennant by a margin of .007 over the Newark Bears. The next year, Gabby Hartnett was back at the helm of the Giants for his third consecutive year. He had his club in first place on July 4, and was anticipating a run for the pennant, when the parent club burst his bubble. They recalled one of his top pitchers, Sal Maglie, as well as outfielder Whitey Lockman who was hitting .317 in 48 games. The season fell apart after the exodus, and Gabby, who felt the men should have played out the season in Jersey City in view of the fact that New York was not going anywhere in the National League, complained loud and long to upper management, to no avail. A frustrated Hartnett resigned on August 9, as his club finally settled into fifth place with a 71–82 record, 24 games off the pace of the Montreal Royals. Maglie, who often played golf with his manager, said Gabby hit his drives over 300 yards.[18]

Gabby Hartnett traveled to Millville after the season ended to participate in an old-timers' game played on the famous Meadow ball field on October 1 to raise money for a hometown newsletter being mailed to the area's servicemen. Tim McNamara pitched and Gabby played shortstop for Millville against Uxbridge. As can be seen in the photograph, he still swung the bat with bad intentions. Whether he was playing in a pick-up game or in a World Series, Gabby Hartnett always played to win.

Around the world, the war was heating up in both theatres of operation, Europe and the Pacific. The Allies invaded France on June 6, 1944, landing on the beach at Normandy under withering fire from the German defenders, and began their advance toward Germany. American forces in the Pacific moved relentlessly ahead, capturing the Mariana Islands on July 28, and invading the Philippine Islands on October 25. The year 1945 finally brought an end to the greatest war in history. Unfortunately, President Franklin D. Roosevelt didn't live to see it, as he succumbed to a heart attack on April 13. Vice President Harry S. Truman picked up the gauntlet and promised to complete Roosevelt's ambitious programs. In Italy, former Dictator Benito Mussolini was killed by partisans on April 28, and his body was hung upside down from a streetlight. The Allied advance across Europe ended with the unconditional surrender of Germany on May 7, six days after Adolph Hitler had committed suicide in his Berlin bunker. In the Pacific, two horrendous atomic bombs, dropped on Hiroshima and Nagasaki, killed more than 300,000 people, bringing Japan to its knees. The government surrendered on August 11, and the healing began.[19]

The ruddy-faced Irishman didn't stay unemployed for very long after he left Jersey City. He signed to manage the Buffalo Bisons of the International League on November 1, 1945. The Bisons had finished in sixth place in '45, seven games behind Gabby's Jersey City outfit. General Manager Bucky Harris and Gabby worked well together, and the team won 14 more games than the previous season, finishing fifth with a 78–75 record. However, while they finished 25 games out of second place the previous year,

they were just three games from the second spot in '46. Still, it was not enough to save Gabby's job. He was not offered a contract for 1947, so he folded his tent, returned to Chicago, and became a full-time businessman. Bucky Harris also left the Bisons to become the manager of the New York Yankees.

While Gabby was managing Buffalo, peace was being restored around the world, and the boys came marching home. Major league baseball players like Ted Williams, Bob Feller, and Pee Wee Reese restored the quality of baseball at the upper level, while the minor leagues were overflowing with talent. Organized baseball had seen its minor league operations drop from 36 leagues in 1938 to just 12 in 1945. With the war over, the number of leagues increased to 46 in 1946, and to 58 two years later.[20]

Anna "Charlie" Hartnett and her brother Frank "Sweetie" Hartnett at the old-timers' game.

Opposite page: Gabby swung with "bad intentions," even in old-timers' games. (Town of Millville J.G. Fitzgerald Historical Society, Inc.)

13

Into the Sunset, 1947–1972

Charles Leo "Gabby" Hartnett returned to 2638 Albion Avenue in the fall of 1946 to relax with his family, do a little hunting, and play some golf. When he learned he wouldn't be offered a contract to manage Buffalo in 1947, he looked around for other opportunities, and one surfaced almost immediately. His friend Louis Fratini, who owned a bowling alley on Devon Avenue, suggested they build a recreation center with bowling alleys, a lounge, and other facilities. Gabby jumped at the idea, and the two of them went to work immediately on the plans. They bought land in Lincolnwood, just 20 minutes from the center of Chicago, for the recreation center, plus additional land to build houses on, for investment purposes.

The estimated cost of the project was $250,000, but the actual cost more than doubled before the recreation center was open for business. The bank requested a larger down payment to cover the increased cost of the project, so Gabby and Martha gladly sold their house and rented a third-floor apartment on North Washtenaw Street, about two blocks away. Sheila remembered that apartment: "One day my Dad left the house. I was in high school. He rang the bell and said 'Come to the window.' So I opened the window and he said, 'Sheila, throw me my glasses,' and I said, Can you catch them? Was that a mistake! He said 'THROW THE GLASSES,' and turning to his friend Jack Fitzgerald he said, 'Can you believe that? asking me if I can catch.' Another time, he put rubbers on over his shoes. He left them on all winter, and when he took them off in the spring, he discovered he had one brown shoe and one black shoe."[1]

Former Chicago Cubs catcher, Bob O'Farrell, who owned a bowling alley in Waukegan, told Gabby he should open the alleys as soon as possible, even before the entire recreation center was completed, so he could begin generating revenue. Gabby took that advice, and Gabby Hartnett's Recreation Center was up and running within a year, with 20 bowling alleys open for business. A barber shop, a soda fountain, a cocktail lounge, and a sporting goods store soon followed. A sign over the lounge read, "Everyone Shoots Par at Gabby's Bar." There was a shooting range in the basement, as well as a poker table. Gabby sometimes would play gin rummy in the basement all day. Bud said, "He always had a pencil stuck behind his ear. He would go upstairs to the bowling alley occasionally, but if someone stopped him and talked for too long, he would take the pencil from behind his ear and say, 'I've got work to do in the basement,' and he would go back to the card game.

"When the bowling alleys were under construction, I worked there as a security guard. It was a little bit out of the city and we didn't want any kids to get in there and do any damage, so I used to sit in there and kind of watch the property. I would scream and holler at the kids and they would run. I used to sit on a ladder and shoot rats with a .22.

"I was still in high school at St. George's Christian Brothers, where I played football. I didn't play baseball except American Legion ball. I didn't play in high school because I didn't have a good arm. I couldn't hit a wall with a handful of rice. I could hit the ball a long way, but no arm. If they had had a designated hitter, I could have played, but I didn't have much enthusiasm for baseball either."[2]

The recreation center originally had 20 bowling alleys, which were later expanded to 32. And they were state of the art alleys, with one of the first automatic pinsetters in the country. Most alleys at that time relied on pinboys, who sat next to the alley and set up the pins manually after each frame. Gabby's alleys were busy 24 hours a day, with both male and female instructors on duty to teach anyone the fine points of the sport.

The year ended sadly for Gabby, however. He lost his "greatest pal" on November 16, 1947, when his mother Nell died in Woonsocket at the age of 64. Gabby had traveled east to visit his mother several times during the year when her health began to fail. And this time, he and his brother "Sweetie" took the train to Woonsocket to say goodbye. Nell was mourned at a Requiem Mass at St. Charles Church, and burial followed in the family plot in St. Paul's Cemetery in Blackstone. Gabby and Sweetie stayed in Woonsocket a few days after the funeral to visit with their brothers and sisters and look up old friends.

Grandma Nell had been a joy to Gabby's family over the years, and Sheila's memories of her are still vivid: "She was a lot of fun. She was only 17 years older than my Dad. She'd come to visit and she'd stay several months, and she was out with Mom and Dad for dinner or to a bar or anywhere. She didn't want to stay home. She was ready to go at any time. And she had a good time for herself. She was not a little old gray-haired lady with a bun on the back of her head. She liked to get her hair done, and she liked to wear her dress a certain length so her nice ankles and legs could show up. She was cute."[3]

When the recreation center opened, Gabby was there every day to oversee the operation and socialize with the patrons. He particularly enjoyed the kids. He could spend hours with them, talking baseball, hunting, or fishing. His normal daily schedule included a golf game in the morning, lunch, then a trip to the center to check the mail, meet people, and play cards. Martha always waited to see his car pull into the driveway at night, because he always arrived home at 6:30 sharp for dinner. In the evening, he was back at the center, often bowling in one or more of the leagues that kept the alleys humming. He played in one league with his old baseball buddies Ray Schalk, Bob O'Farrell, and Jimmy Archer, catchers all. And he wasn't just a figurehead. He was a good bowler, carrying a 190 average at one time, with at least one "300" game to his credit.

His golfing partners included his friend Jack Fitzgerald, who was a teacher and assistant basketball coach at DePaul University; Bill Chambers, the golf pro at the Sunset Hills Golf Club; former major league catchers Bob O'Farrell and Ray Berres; and his brother Sweetie. Berres was a member of the Pittsburgh Pirates when Gabby hit his famous home run, and he saw it from the bench. Berres, who lived in Twin Lakes, Wisconsin, just a hop, skip, and a jump from Chicago, visited the Windy City often to golf and hunt with Gabby. They hunted pheasants on local farmlands with permission, and they played golf at many semipublic and private courses where

Nell Hartnett was a frequent visitor to Chicago in the 1930s and 1940s. (Sheila Hartnett Hornof)

they were guests. Berres recalled, "I frequently stopped in to see him at his bowling alley. I'd say, 'Come on, you old buzzard, spend some of that World Series money you took away from me. My last visit was a few days before his death. Sick as he was, the humor and big Irish grin were still there."

Sweetie, christened Francis but known as Frank, was a big part of Gabby's life. They often traveled together, played golf together several times a week, and hung out together at the center. Sheila noted, "Frank had a different personality than Dad. Dad would never argue with anyone, but Frank liked the give-and-take of friendly discussions. He liked to pick your brain, stir the pot, argue, and prove a point."[4]

Shortly after the center opened, Bud Hartnett, who had just graduated from St. George's High School, enlisted in the United States Marine Corps and spent the next two years on active duty. His tour of duties included a year in Guam in the Mariana Islands and six months with the Presidential Honor Guard.

The years following Gabby's retirement from baseball were happy and relaxing ones for the Hartnett family. Gabby was a successful businessman, and he was now able to spend the summers, as well as the winters, with Martha and the children. The recreation center kept him busy, but he still had time to enjoy golfing, bowling, and playing cards with his friends. And he still traveled occasionally — to a golf tournament at Hilton Head or Pinehurst, North Carolina, or to speak at a sports banquet somewhere — but he kept the trips to a minimum and didn't travel in the winter. "He played golf at Sunset Hills Golf Club in Highland Park. He never joined a private club because he didn't have to. He always had plenty of invitations to golf at the private clubs in the area, so he was able to golf four or five times a week."[5]

At one of the baseball banquets, Gabby spent some time talking to "Pepper" Martin, the "Wild Horse of the Osage" who had terrorized Mickey Cochrane during the 1931 World Series, stealing everything but his chest protector. Pepper confided to Gabby, "I could steal off anybody except you. Every time I got to second base, the ball was waiting for me."

Gabby socialized with his friends and customers at the recreation center five days a week, but Saturday and Sunday were reserved for the family. He and Martha were able to go out in the evening more, now that he was out of baseball. "They often went downtown to the Loop, to the Chicago Theatre or the Palace to see a movie or a stage show. They also enjoyed going to the Edgewater Beach Hotel for dinner, and dancing on the terrace overlooking Lake Michigan. It was an upscale hotel, very beautiful. My Dad and George Gobel were the last two people in the lounge before they tore the hotel down. Occasionally, Mom and Dad would meet friends in the lounge at the recreation center, and visit."[6]

In 1948 the family took a fishing vacation to Wisconsin. They stayed with Jack Beall, a friend of Gabby's who had a lodge on a lake in Spooner, a tiny town of about 2,000 people in the northwest corner of the state. The 400-mile trip took all day, but the anticipation of a week of complete relaxation made the time pass quickly. Sheila and Gabby spent much of the week fishing out on the boat but Martha preferred to stay on shore in a lawn chair and watch the two fishermen in action. Sheila said her father was not much of a fisherman. She often caught the biggest fish. In fact, she got her name in the local paper for catching two bass on one hook. And they were both "keepers."[7]

When Bud returned home in 1949, he joined his father at the recreation center, running the sporting goods store and helping out wherever he could. He also opened a commercial maintenance business with a loan from his father. When he first mentioned the idea to his father, Gabby said, "OK. Let's do it." So Bud started his own business while still a teenager, cleaning factories and other commercial establishments at night, as well as selling cleaning supplies. He later expanded the business to include home maintenance. The first job brought in a grand total of $14, but sales gradually increased to the $250,000 per year level. He ran the business for 30 years before selling it.

Bud and Gabby were also able to spend more time together outside work. "We used to go hunting all the time. We went out around a little town called Virgil, Illinois. And some people that owned a farm there, the Sauvers, used to let us go hunting there. We hunted pheasant and a few pigeons. Dad used to stand outside the silo next to the barn, and one of the boys would go inside and shoo the pigeons out of the barn. There was a little hole on top of the barn where the pigeons used to come out, one at a time. And Dad would shoot the pigeons with his shotgun as they came out the hole. He was a great outdoorsman. He loved hunting. His brother Frank was just the opposite. He didn't go too much for the shooting. He loved to play golf. Those two guys were very close. Frank was a good guy."[8]

In addition to his other many interests, Gabby followed DePaul basketball, Notre Dame football, the Chicago Bears professional football, and the Chicago Cubs. He became good friends with DePaul basketball coach Ray Meyer and Bears owner George Halas. He also had a favorite tavern he frequented in Morton Grove. The owner of the bar put a plaque on one of the stools that read, "Gabby Hartnett's Private Spot."

Gabby and Martha lived on North Washtenaw Street for six years, then moved to a second-floor apartment at 5448 North Kimball, but that turned out to be a bad decision. There was no parking in front of the building, so Gabby had to park in a parking garage several blocks away and have the

Gabby (left) enjoying a good cigar and the company of his brother and best friend, "Sweetie," during the 1960s. (Sheila Hartnett Hornof)

attendant drive him home. Eventually the Hartnetts moved again, this time to a sixth-floor apartment in Des Plaines. The building had an elevator and adequate parking, so they lived there until Gabby died in 1972. Martha was still there in 1981 when the apartments went condo. She wasn't interested in buying the condo so she moved again, this time to a small one-bedroom apartment in Glenview. She was only there one month when she had a stroke and went to live with Sheila in Creve Coeur near St. Louis.

On November 23, 1948, Gabby's old friend Hack Wilson passed away in Baltimore. Life had not been kind to the former ballplayer after his retirement from the game in 1934. His drinking got worse, and he bounced from job to job, working at one time or another as "a bartender, a bouncer in a honky-tonk, a freight handler, and a stevedore. He wound up as a laborer in the Baltimore park district, and died penniless at the age of 48."[9] Former Chicago Cubs manager Joe McCarthy attended the interment in Martinsburg, West Virginia. "He unveiled the monument and soberly said the final words about his favorite slugger. 'I know you will say a fervent prayer for the great Hack. And may God rest his soul.' He turned to Grimm and Cuyler and added, 'He was a wonderful little fellah.'"[10]

Bud was married to Jane Maasmann in Skokie in 1950, and they rented an apartment in Chicago and started to raise a family. His only son, Steven, was born in 1952, and his first daughter, Hope, was born in 1954. Bud's maintenance and chemical supply company was renamed Hope Chemical after his daughter. This marriage and two subsequent marriages produced six more daughters: Joanne, Donna, Kathleen, Peggy, Anna, and Martha.

Gabby's daughter Sheila attended Marquette University in Milwaukee, Wisconsin, in the early 50s, then transferred to Mundelein College in Chicago. She married Bob Hornof on November 24, 1956, and the newlyweds moved into a small apartment at 824 West Gunnison, not far from the lake. It was a shared first-floor apartment. They had the first three rooms, and another couple had the other three rooms, with privacy at a minimum. Their first son, Tim, was born on October 24, 1957. Later additions to the family included Susie, Nancy, and Tom. When their finances permitted, the Hornofs bought a house in Morton Grove. They moved to St. Louis in 1971 when Bob, who was western regional manager of the American Felt & Filter Company, was transferred.

The grandchildren made Gabby's life complete. Since he had missed so much of his own children's growing years, being away from home every summer for 20 years, he showered attention on the grandchildren. Bud said his children called Gabby "Boo," because he was always jumping out of a hiding place and scaring them by yelling, "boo."

Sheila said, "Dad was very quiet except when the grandchildren were around. He was a wonderful grandfather, and he visited us often. He didn't play baseball much with Bud and I when we were young because he was gone a lot. But when he visited us, he would go out on the street and play ball with all the kids on the block. He would throw the ball around with them, and show them how to throw the ball and catch it with two hands. And when he was real ill and dying in a hospital bed in Mom and Dad's apartment, all of those kids came to see him. They all got together as a group and someone drove them out to Des Plaines so they could say goodbye.

"Dad loved to do magic tricks and card tricks. He did them with Bud and I when we were little, and he did them with my kids. And he was good. He would drop Mom off at my house every morning, then he'd go bowl or play cards or whatever, and pick her up at five o'clock. Sometimes he'd stay for dinner, but not often. He'd walk in, and me, my husband, and my mother would be sitting there, and he'd say, 'Where is everybody?' If there wasn't a kid in the room, it was like no one was there. We all said, 'Who are we?'"[11]

The year 1955 was the high point in Gabby Hartnett's life. On January 26, his friends at the Sunset Hills Golf Club heard on the radio that he had been elected to the National Baseball Hall of Fame in Cooperstown, New York. They immediately notified him at the recreation center, just minutes before radio, television, and newspaper hordes descended on the place. A dazed but happy Gabby spent the evening accepting congratulations from friends and relatives and giving interviews, while his proud wife and daughter looked on.

On February 16, Gabby and Sweetie traveled by train to Woonsocket to participate in the annual Mardi Gras celebration and visit their family. They stayed with their sister Dorothy Rynn at her home at 21 Kermit Street, and were thrilled to visit with all their other sisters and brothers, some of whom they hadn't seen since their mother's funeral seven years before. It was a noisy and fun-filled day at the Rynn home, and it carried over into the evening at one of the local taverns. Gabby attended many of the events of the weeklong celebration, including a reception at the home of Vincent Carney and the Trinity Club Valentine Mardi Gras Ball at Dreyfus Hall, where he was honored. He was also interviewed on radio stations WWON and WJAR in Pawtucket, Rhode Island. And he found time to visit some of his old baseball buddies in Blackstone and Millville, such as his old batterymate Tim McNamara and pitcher Chet Nichols, who threw in the National League between 1926 and 1932. Chet Nichols Jr. also pitched in the major leagues, between 1951 and 1964.

Five months later, the Hartnett clan, including Gabby, Martha, his daughter Sheila, Sheila's fiancé, Bob Hornof, and Sweetie, drove to Cooperstown, New York to participate in the annual National Baseball Hall of

Fame Induction Ceremony. Bud had to stay in Chicago to take care of his business. The inductees, in addition to Gabby, were Joe DiMaggio, Ted Lyons, Dazzy Vance, Frank "Home Run" Baker, and Ray Schalk. Other Hartnett relatives and friends made the journey from the Woonsocket-Millville area. The 11 AM ceremony took place on a portico set up in front of the Hall of Fame on Main Street. Ford Frick, the Commissioner of Baseball, during his speech, referred to Gabby as "Mr. Personality with the tomato face." Gabby was the last of the inductees to give his acceptance speech, and it was the shortest one: "This is one day I'll never forget. I have always said that catching was one of the toughest jobs in the business, and it's nice that the baseball writers have honored me and my profession. I wish every catcher could receive this recognition. They certainly deserve it. It's a great feeling to become a baseball immortal and enter Baseball's Hall of Fame."[12]

After a photo session and a luncheon reception, a baseball game was played on Doubleday Field between the Milwaukee Braves and the Boston Red Sox. John McNamara, who traveled to Cooperstown from Millville by car with his uncle Tim and Chink Duffy, recalled the trip: "In one of the induction ceremony photos with Gabby at the podium, right behind him is Chink Duffy. He got up on the stage. He had a lot of moxie, believe me. He said he was Gabby's brother so they let him right up.

"We drove out. The Braves were playing the Red Sox. Gabby had a place for all the people from Millville in the left field stands. They're open stands, you know. Wooden bleachers is what they are. So we're all up there sitting there and all of a sudden Joe DiMaggio came up and stood before us and said, 'You people are all going to have to move.' And I said, 'Like hell.' I was just out of the Marine Corps. Why should we move for Joe DiMaggio because he wanted to move some of his buddies in? Gabby happened to come along and he said, 'What's going on here?' I said, 'This guy wants us to move,' and he said, 'Hey Joe, go find some other place for your buddies. Leave these people alone.'"[13]

Fred Hartnett, Gabby's nephew who was 13 at the time, has his own memories of Joe DiMaggio and the festivities: "DiMaggio came in with his agent. Landed on Lake Otsego in a seaplane. A guy went out and picked him up and brought him in. He had a couple of dolls with him. It was right after the Marilyn Monroe stuff. I remember seeing him elsewhere in the course of the events and the girls always stayed away from him when he walked. Only his agent walked next to him. The girls and others walked behind him.

"I drove out to Cooperstown with my mother and two aunts. We stayed right on the lake. Dazzy Vance and his family were there. Gabby's sisters Tina, Charlie, Mary, and Dottie attended. In the afternoon, I was down on

Gabby and his family enjoying a meal at the Hall of Fame celebration in 1955. Left to right: Sheila, Gabby, Bob Hornof, and Martha. (Printed with permission of the *Call*, Woonsocket, RI)

the field before the baseball game. Because of Gabby, I was allowed to walk around. Hank Aaron was there. So were Del Crandall, Lew Burdette, and Joe Adcock. Players were coming through the crowd. A guy slapped Ted Williams on the back. Williams turned and said, 'Hey, screw. Do I look like a piece of meat to you?' I went 'Oh, God.' I was scared to death. Pretty soon I heard someone say, 'Hey kid.' I looked down and it's Ted Williams. 'Yeah, you. Come here.' So I go down in the dugout. He asks my name and stuff, and he makes the connection right off the bat. There were some adults leaning over the dugout trying to get his autograph, and he says to me, 'Look at these dizzy bastards,' and he reaches back and picks up a bat and he's whacking the top of the dugout, you know, so I'm sitting there with him and he's talking to me about baseball, about hitting, about using the wrists, and he says, 'Stay right here. I'll be right back. If anyone tells you to leave, tell them I said to stay.' So he went up and took batting practice. There were

Gabby making his acceptance speech in Cooperstown on July 25, 1955. (Printed with permission of the *Call*, Woonsocket, RI)

people sitting on their porches [beyond the right field wall] and he was hitting balls off their houses. Then he came back and he brought Cy Young down into the dugout, and he said, 'Did you ever meet Cy Young?' And I said, 'No.' 'C'mon down.' So down we went, moving reporters. 'Cy, I want you to meet Gabby Hartnett's nephew.' I shook his hand. He was 88 years old. So I tell people, 'I was introduced to baseball's greatest pitcher by baseball's greatest hitter.'"[14]

Sheila was another family member who had a magical trip east. "We had a wonderful time. The Hall of Fame was just beautiful. We drove out there. Bob and I weren't married. Uncle Frank and Sylvia, and Frank's daughter and son, Pat and Mike, followed us. Frank had four children. Two boys died. It was just very much fun for me to meet DiMaggio. He got in with my Dad you know, by the baseball writers. Then there were four others that got in through the old timers. I remember standing out on a veranda overlooking Lake Otsego, and my Dad said, 'I want you to meet someone,' and I hurried over and it was DiMaggio, and I was thrilled. And then he said, 'Come on over here. And I went over and met this old man. It was Cy Young. Got a picture of my Dad and Cy Young. And then over here. 'C'mon Sheila.' It was Ty Cobb. And I was just having a ball.

"Then at the ball game we met Ted Williams and Jimmy Piersall. We just had a wonderful time. I was just in seventh heaven. And my mother, I told you, didn't like publicity, and I remember 'Home Run' Baker got in and she called him, not to his face, 'No-Hit' Baker. And I said, 'Mom, it's 'Home Run' Baker,' and she said, 'OK, that's right.' She could have cared less."[15]

Ted Williams started in left field for the Red Sox, hit a home run in the first inning, then left Cooperstown with a police escort to keep another appointment. Gabby estimated that he signed over 500 autographs for fans during the afternoon.

Gabby and the other inductees were invited to be the guests of the New York Yankees for the rest of the week, participate in Hall of Fame ceremonies at Yankee Stadium on Saturday, and play in the old-timers game, if possible. There were 20 Hall of Famers at the stadium on Saturday, including Young, Cobb, Vance, DiMaggio, Mickey Cochrane, Charlie Gehringer, Lefty Grove, and Bill Terry. The Hall of Famers, with Gabby catching, lost the two-inning game to the Yankee old-timers before a packed house by the score of 7–3.

"We had a wonderful trip to New York. Bob and I took a cab and went to Harlem. We walked into this place and Bob gave the guy two bucks for a table and we were sitting right behind Count Basie's table. When they got off the stage, they sat at a front table, and Bob and I were right next to them.

Mom and Dad didn't do much 'night-lifeing.' Mom and I had a room, and Bob and Dad had a room. That's how it was in those days.

"We were walking in downtown Manhattan and a young cop came up — I mean he was a young man — and he said, 'Gabby Hartnett,' and he stopped the traffic and let us walk across the street. We went to Toots Shor's Restaurant. We met Toots Shor. There were a lot of movie stars there. Don Ameche came up to our table, and I'm thinking, 'Oh my gosh. This is really something.' And he's been doing this all his life, you know. All my life I thought he was just Dad who came home at 6:30 for dinner — and boy we had to have dinner at 6:30 by the way. He was so prompt.

"They used to come to our house for dinner, Mom and Dad, at say 6:00. And they'd pull up in front of our house. They wouldn't come in at five [minutes to] or a minute after. They'd walk in at 6 o'clock. Very, very prompt. And I don't know if that was my Mom or my Dad. They were never late for anything in their life. People would ask, 'What's it like to have Gabby Hartnett for a Dad?' Well, I mean, he's my Dad. My Dad never, ever talked sports or baseball at the dinner table. When he came home, he wasn't Gabby Hartnett anymore. He was quiet. He was just a normal dad. I didn't know how to answer that question. To me, he was my father."[16]

Life began to slow down for Gabby after 1955. He was a full 10 years removed from his career in professional baseball. He had scaled the summit of baseball greatness. Gone was the excitement of designing, building, and operating his own recreation center. He still traveled to sports banquets and golf tournaments, but the trips were becoming fewer and fewer each year. He still managed to squeeze in a couple of hunting trips during the year, and he still played golf and bowled, but he found he had more time on his hands. The ruddy-faced Irishman watched television in the morning and in the evening. His favorite shows were the *Ed Sullivan Show* and the game shows. And he enjoyed spending time with his grandchildren.

Gabby lived through several family tragedies in the late 50s. His brother Chickie, who had worked out with the Cubs at Catalina in 1934, succumbed to lung cancer in 1958 at the age of 45, leaving behind a wife and two children. His brother Buster died the following year, leaving a wife and a son.

But life went on, and Gabby kept busy at the center. In 1960, he traveled to Pinehurst, North Carolina, to participate in the Pro Baseball Players Golf Tournament, and he had another thrilling experience. He scored a hole-in-one and couldn't wait to get on the phone and tell the folks back home. He finally got his son-in-law, Bob Hornof, on the line, and gave him the good news: "I got my hole-in-one. I'm in the Hall of Fame, and I bowled 300. All I have to do now is beat Patterson [heavyweight boxing champion, Floyd Patterson] and my life will be complete."[17]

In 1963, Gabby's partner Louis Fratini died and Gabby thought it was time for him to get out of the business and take life a little easier. He was 62. He finally sold his interest in the recreation center to the Fratini family in September 1964, but the center retained his name. Gabby now had more time to spend with his family and play cards with his friends. But that all changed in January 1965 when the Quarterback Club roasted him at a gala event in Chicago. Dozens of friends, relatives, and celebrities attended the all-male festivities, including his son Bud, his brother Sweetie, Sweetie's son Michael, Charles O. Finley, the owner of the Kansas City Athletics, and numerous media people. During the dinner, Finley, never one to miss a publicity opportunity, recruited Gabby to coach for the A's.

"Old Tomato Face," with Martha's blessing, headed south in February to join Kansas City at their spring training site in Bradenton, Florida. He was in charge of the catchers, and he worked with them, teaching them how to shift their body with the pitch, how to guard the plate, and how to get their throws off as quickly as possible. Doc Edwards, one of the A's catchers, thought he was the greatest coach he ever had. "Everyone on the team knew all the great things Gabby had accomplished during his major league career, yet he was very low key, humble, and unassuming. He never said, 'I did this, and I did that.' He never ordered catchers to do something a certain way. He always said, 'I think this is the best way to do it,' and because of his reputation, he commanded respect, and you just did what he suggested.

"He was a hard worker, and he worked his catchers hard. If the program was set up to run extra laps, he would say, 'Run 'em and run 'em all. If you can't run 'em, don't come to me.' After we finished running the laps, he would come over and say, 'You're my kind of guy. Let's go have some fun now.' And he would hit us pop-ups or fungoes. During the game, he was on the bench along with the manager, offering his input. Off the field, he was just one of the guys, a great human being. He was one of the two guys I always liked being around. The other one was Birdie Tebbetts."[18]

Jimmie Dykes and Luke Appling, who played for the Chicago White Sox during the thirties and coached for Kansas City for several years, played against Gabby in the Chicago City Series. They were both well aware of Gabby's intensity and hard-nosed play on the field, and they both voiced the opinion that "Gabby's a great guy, but you wouldn't want to run into him on a ball field."[19]

Rene Lachemann, another of the Kansas City catchers said, "Gabby was always happy and had a great sense of humor. I was only 19 at the time, and he took a liking to me and took me under his wing and worked with me. I got into 92 games that year, which was unusual for a 19-year-old kid. Unfortunately, I hurt my arm, which ended my career.

"He was a legendary beer drinker. People used to say he could drink 30 or 40 beers at one time. One day in Washington, DC, about five of us, including Gabby, went to a bar. I think Catfish Hunter was with us. We had a contest to see who could drink the most beer. They had schooners that held about three beers, and most of us had to stop after three schooners, but Gabby downed 10 of them. And he never showed any effects of it.

"Gabby was the life of the party. He was just a great person. I have met a lot of people in baseball, and he was one of the best. He will always have a special place in my heart. You couldn't find a better man."[20]

Rick Monday, who went on to star with the Oakland A's, Chicago Cubs, and Los Angeles Dodgers, met Gabby at spring training and was duly impressed by the baseball legend, saying, "Gabby Hartnett was the most gentle human being I have ever been around."

The A's were not a very good team in 1965. They went through two managers to no avail and finished in the basement in the 10-team American League with a record of 59–103, a distant 43 games behind the Minnesota Twins. The following year, Alvin Dark was signed to manage the club, and he brought them home in seventh place, with a 74–86 record. For some reason, he didn't want Gabby for a coach, and the 65-year-old baseball legend spent the year scouting and doing public relations work. He retired at the end of the season, bringing to an end a lifetime of baseball experiences.

In 1967, Gabby was following the athletic careers of his grandchildren, and Sheila remembered one particular occasion: "My son's team was playing at Loyola Academy's football field, and it was a big deal for the kids. And my Dad went to the game, and it was October, and it was raining, and Dad had on a black raincoat all buttoned up to the neck and a dark hat and slacks. And he went up to buy a ticket and the kid selling them said, 'Oh, no charge for you Father.' And my Dad said, 'Well son, I'm not a priest, but I am out of work, so I'll take the pass.'"[21]

Gabby's health was beginning to fail as the 60s drew to a close. "My Dad probably had arthritis, but he never went to a doctor so I don't know for sure. But he wore a copper bracelet and carried an acorn, if you can believe it. He always attributed everything to an old baseball injury."[22]

In May 1969, the beginning of the end visited the great Chicago Cubs catcher. He was stricken on the golf course and began spitting blood. He was rushed to the hospital where he underwent surgery for a bleeding ulcer. Two months later, still recuperating from his operation, he was persuaded to go to Washington, DC to attend the 100th anniversary celebration of the beginning of professional baseball, where baseball's greatest team and baseball's greatest "living team," selected by a special committee, were to be announced. Gabby was led to believe he would be among those honored.

He wasn't. And although he was greatly disappointed at the apparent deception on the part of the event's organizers, he did get to meet President Nixon at the White House, attend the All-Star Game at R.F.K. Memorial Stadium on July 23, and saw the National League pound the American League 9–3 behind two home runs by Willie McCovey and one by Johnny Bench.

Gabby's health continued to deteriorate in the months that followed. His spleen was removed in 1970, and his sisters Tina and Millie came to Des Plaines to help care for him. But he never fully regained his strength. The end came in 1972. His health took a turn for the worse late in the year, and Martha had a hospital bed brought to the house. His friends and relatives visited him frequently, and the kids from Sheila's neighborhood came to see him one last time. "His brother Frank drove 45 minutes every day to give Dad a shave. He wouldn't let anyone else shave him, just Frank. He was very devoted to my Dad."[23]

Gabby was rushed to Lutheran General Hospital in Park Ridge on December 7 suffering from a liver ailment. The doctors wanted to operate again, but Gabby said no. He was ready for whatever God had in store for him. Two of the last people to see him were his son Bud and his good friend Jack Fitzgerald. Gabby died at 5:20 AM, on Wednesday, December 20, 1972, exactly 72 years to the minute after he was born. The doctors had told the family he was going to die the previous week. They said he couldn't last another day, but Martha said, "The doctors are wrong. He'll die on his birthday." When Bud telephoned Uncle Frank with the news, Frank didn't say anything. He just hung up the phone. He wouldn't go into the funeral parlor to visit Gabby because he didn't want to see him like that.

Sheila met a lot of people at her father's wake, and she was overwhelmed by the amount of love and respect people had for him, saying, "George Halas came to my Dad's wake just after he had hip replacement. The conditions were cold and icy but he came anyway. I thanked him for making the trip, and he said, 'I could never repay him for what he did for me.' I always wondered what he meant by that, but I didn't ask him.

"Dad was a very generous person. When he died, several people contacted us, little farm people from Illinois, and tried to pay back money Dad had lent them. Dad would never let them pay it back.

"He had a great sense of humor — liked to tell jokes. Never told the same joke twice. Liked the quick one-liners. And he loved to play cards. Rummy was his favorite, and he would bet on himself, but he never bet on any sport. He would never bet on a baseball game or a football game or anything like that."

The wags, who knew how much Gabby loved a good joke, threw him a couple of one-liners at his wake. One of them said, "Well, he went out in par." To which George Halas added, "But now he's six under."[24]

Gabby's life was celebrated with a Requiem Mass in Our Lady of Perpetual Help Church in Glenview on December 23. Interment followed in All Saints Cemetery in Des Plaines.

Martha moved in with her daughter Sheila in Creve Coeur, near St. Louis, after suffering a stroke in 1981, but she lived only one more year. She had a second stroke in 1982 and died on March 6 of that year. She is buried next to Gabby.

Sweetie moved to Oregon to be near his son after Gabby's death. He died in Portland several years later.

Bud left Chicago in 1990, moving to Westfield, Wisconsin, a little town of about 2,000 people. He still lives there and although officially retired, he works three or four hours a day at "Green Thumb" a government-sponsored enterprise.

Looking back over the life of Gabby Hartnett, it is apparent he was born with exceptional athletic ability. And his father brought that ability to the surface through diligence and hard work. Fred, whose early marriage and growing family doomed any thoughts he might have had of a major league baseball career, may have experienced that career vicariously through his son with whom he shared many personal and physical characteristics. Both men were tall, rugged, and good looking. They both had friendly, outgoing personalities and enjoyed socializing. Neither man smoked cigarettes, but they loved big cigars. They both maintained close religious affiliations, and they liked nice clothes, a good card game, and a friendly wager. And both were avid outdoorsmen and hunters. On the baseball field, they were outstanding defensive catchers with powerful throwing arms.

On the other hand, there were significant differences between the two men. Gabby had a father who pushed him to achieve excellence, and who managed his career until he became a professional. Fred didn't have that advantage. Gabby was blessed with good luck that put him in the right place at the right time. Injuries to his competitors propelled him into the starting catcher position in both Worcester and Chicago. And his historic home run in 1938 catapulted the Cubs to the National League pennant and made him a legend. Fred's decisions were often ill-timed, beginning with his marriage at the age of 18. And while Gabby's 43-year marriage was still strong at the time of his death, Fred's marriage ended in separation after 25 years. And there was one last difference. Fred was a teetotaler while Gabby loved a good beer.

Under different circumstances, Fred Hartnett might have enjoyed a long, productive major league baseball career himself. But fate ruled otherwise. It was left to his son to carry the torch.

14

Gabby Hartnett's Legacy

The accolades and honors continue to pour in for Gabby Hartnett decades after his death.

On May 18, 1972, seven months before his death, Gabby was inducted into the Rhode Island Heritage Hall of Fame. He was too ill to attend the ceremony, but his sister Mildred accepted the trophy for him. Three years later, the East Woonsocket Little League named one of their fields "the Gabby Hartnett Field."

On November 12, 1982, a section of route 122, running from Millville to Blackstone, was dedicated as the "Charles L. 'Gabby' Hartnett Memorial Highway." Author James Murphy spoke at the dedication: "Leo Hartnett, the people of Millville have not forgotten you. We still love you and are very proud of you." Representative Richard T. Moore, the master of ceremonies, read a proclamation from Governor Edward J. King, designating November 11 as "Gabby Hartnett Day." Gabby's brother Frank and nephew Fred W. Hartnett helped unveil the newly placed sign, and Frank added, "If my heart could speak out loud, you would receive the warmest reception you ever had in your life." Longfellow Elementary School pupils sang "Take Me Out to the Ballgame" accompanied by the high school band.[1]

Twelve years later, Gabby Hartnett (he preferred to be called Leo) was inducted into the Greater Woonsocket Hall Of Fame, which also included the great Nap Lajoie, considered by many to be the greatest second baseman in baseball history.

And, not surprisingly, he was selected as the catcher on the all-time Chicago Cubs baseball team, going back to 1876.

Gabby Hartnett was the acknowledged leader of the Chicago Cubs for 17 years. His trademarks were his red face, a big cigar, and a hearty laugh

Left to right: "Sweetie," Massachusetts Representative Richard T. Moore, and Gabby's nephew Fred Hartnett at the dedication of the Charles L. "Gabby" Hartnett Memorial Highway in 1982. (Town of Millville J.G. Fitzgerald Historical Society, Inc.)

and, on the field, his boundless energy, typified by his constant chattering behind the plate, his loud, throaty yell, and his clenched fist pumping the air to urge his team on. On a hot day, his face would be so red it would resemble a ripe tomato ready to explode — which gave him his nickname, "Old Tomato Face." He was always visible and vocal on the field, encouraging, cajoling, prodding, and even chastising his pitchers and teammates to give their best at all times. If he saw someone dogging it, or not giving a maximum effort, he let them know about it in no uncertain terms.

His accomplishments on the field were legendary. He was the first of the all-around catchers, combining strong offense with flawless defense. He broke the mold of the good-field, no-hit catcher of the early twentieth century. In today's game, the pendulum has swung the other way. Modern-day catchers are selected primarily for their offense, and for many of them, defense is a lost art. As Harry Danning said, "There are receivers and there are catchers. Receivers just catch the ball. Today they are just receivers, always looking into the dugout for a sign. A catcher looks out for everything. He gives the signals. He guides and directs the pitcher. He's always ready to throw. Gabby ... he could do it all."[2]

Gabby Hartnett dropped only three foul pop-ups in 20 years. He was the first catcher to hit more than 20 home runs in a single season, hit 200 home runs in a career, and drive in 1,000 runs. During his long career, he averaged 20 home runs and 101 runs-batted-in (RBIs) for every 550 at-bats, to go along with a .297 batting average. He led the league in fielding average seven times, assists six times, and double plays six times, more than any other modern-day catcher. He also routinely allowed fewer stolen bases than his American League counterparts Bill Dickey and Mickey Cochrane. His estimated 53 percent caught-stealing rate is an all-time #2 behind Roy Campanella. He reportedly had the strongest throwing arm in major league history. He held numerous major league and National League records during his career, including most seasons catching in 100 or more games (12), most games caught in a career (1,793), most consecutive chances without an error (452), most home runs by a catcher in a season (37), and most home runs by a catcher in a career (236). He still holds the major league record for participating in 163 double plays in a career. And, according to the baseball historian Walt Wilson, he caught 114 shutouts, which may be another major league record.

The testimonials from his contemporaries, in addition to the impressive offensive and defensive statistics noted above, establish Gabby Hartnett as one of the great catchers in baseball history. Sheriff Blake, a great admirer of Hartnett, said, "Gabby was the greatest catcher I ever saw.... He was so good with his pitchers. Now if you got a man on first base who was a good base runner, you didn't have to keep your mind too much on him; you could concentrate on the hitter. Because if the runner got too far off first, Hartnett would pick him off. When he threw to second base, the pitcher had to fall to the ground in a hurry or get hit, the ball came so fast and so straight. He'd throw to second as easy and as accurate as throwing a strike over the plate. Besides that, Gabby was a great guy, always laughing and joking. I never saw him mad once. Everybody liked him."[3]

Paul Richards was another Hartnett admirer. "The best throwing arm I ever saw on a catcher probably belonged to Gabby Hartnett. Better than Bench? Yes. The fans used to come out early to watch infield practice just to watch Hartnett throw the ball around. He made a theatrical performance out of it."[4]

Casey Stengel called Gabby Hartnett the greatest catcher that ever played the game. And Casey saw every catcher from Roger Bresnahan to Johnny Bench.

Joe McCarthy said, "Gabby Hartnett was the perfect catcher. He was the greatest catcher I ever saw. He was super-smart. Nobody ever had more hustle, and nobody could throw with him. There have been few great clutch hitters, and he was the best." McCarthy was particularly impressed with Hartnett's ability to take control of a game, as he lived up to his nickname by constantly yelling at his infielders and pitchers. "Sometimes if he felt the pitcher wasn't bearing down enough, he'd fire the ball back to the mound like a rifle shot. That caught the fellow's attention, believe me."

Another of baseball's legends, Bill Klem, known as "The Dean of Umpires," who umpired in the National League for 36 years, and who had seen all the great catchers between 1905 and 1939, selected Gabby Hartnett as the catcher on his all-time All-Star team.

Harry Danning was a catcher with the New York Giants from 1933 to 1942. He was a .285 hitter who played in two World Series and two All-Star Games. He played against Gabby Hartnett for eight years; saw Mickey Cochrane play for five years; saw Bill Dickey play for 10 years and played against him in the World Series twice; and saw Berra, Campanella, and Bench many times. "Gabby Hartnett and Bill Dickey were the two greatest catchers I ever saw. They could do it all."[5]

Ray Berres, a catcher who played against Gabby in the National League from 1934 to 1941, noted, "Gabby was a great catcher who possessed one of the best throwing arms in baseball. He also swung a good bat. He was a leader. He was a good competitor and a good guy. I will never forget his 'homer in the gloamin.' I was present as I was a member of the Pittsburgh club at the time. He had a terrific sense of humor, often reflected in his Irish face. He enjoyed teasing and being teased."[6]

Teammates Billy Jurges and Lonnie Frey called Gabby Hartnett the best catcher they ever saw.

"Hartnett was a master in using the 'pitchout,' stopping base stealers before they started. Charlie Grimm, Chicago's manager in the 1930s, depended on Hartnett to tell him when to bring in relievers."[7]

Dizzy Dean thought Gabby knew every batter's weakness and every pitcher's strengths, and he called the pitches like he would make moves in a chess game, to exploit the opponents weakness. Dean once said, "If Gabby would have caught me, I never would have lost a game."

Carl Hubbell was quoted as saying, "Hartnett was the toughest hitter I ever faced. He always scared me." P.K. Wrigley noted Gabby's intensity and enthusiasm: "He was one of those ballplayers we used to have in those days who played baseball for the sheer joy of it."

And Bill Voiselle, former New York Giants pitcher, who pitched for Gabby in Jersey City, considered him an outstanding manager. "I learned more under Gabby than from any other manager."

A scientific study and statistical analysis of the top 25 catchers in baseball history, conducted by the author, confirmed the above statistics and testimonials. The forthcoming book on the subject verified Gabby Hartnett's status as the greatest all-around catcher in baseball history. Gabby trailed Mickey Cochrane by a small margin as an offensive threat, but led him by a wide margin as a defensive catcher. He led Bill Dickey, Yogi Berra, and Johnny Bench in both categories. Only Roy Campanella came close.[8]

But his legacy is much more than his baseball expertise. Charles Leo Hartnett was even more outstanding off the field. Harry Danning said that Gabby was one of the nicest men in the league, well liked and well respected.

As noted previously, Rick Monday called him "the most gentle human being I ever met." And Rene Lachemann said, "He was just a great person. He will always have a special place in my heart."

Chicago sports writer Bill Gleason paid him one of the highest compliments: "Gabby was, in the language of Chicago, 'an old neighborhood guy,' which means that he never forgot where he came from, that the friends from the neighborhood were given top billing above the celebrities who were so proud to say they knew him."[9]

Jimmy Powers, columnist for the *New York Daily News*, watched Gabby Hartnett in action for 20 years. "Hartnett was a genuinely happy man. When he laughed, he laughed all over and his big frame shook. He had the capacity of getting along with everyone."[10]

DePaul University basketball coach Ray Meyer was another admirer of the great Cubs catcher. "Gabby was a genuine down-to-earth person loved by all. At our games, he always had time for the young people — signing autographs, talking to children. He loved people, and people loved him. Gabby was a big man because he had time for the little ones."[11]

His daughter Sheila said her father "enjoyed a good joke whether he initiated it or whether it was on him. He was always happy, and always had a smile on his face."

Ken Smith, former Director of the Baseball Hall of Fame, noted, "The first point anyone would think of is his hearty, high-spirited personality, distributed by his Irish smile, loud and active voice, and friendly demeanor, all emitting from his 6'1", 218-pound frame. On the field, he was a swashbuckler who knocked over anybody who got in the way. But off the field, there wasn't a more friendly character you'd run into around the circuit."[12]

Gabby Hartnett achieved greatness in two separate and distinct arenas. He is the greatest catcher in major league baseball history and he was a great human being, who proved that nice guys do finish first.

Rudyard Kipling's famous poem "If" captured the essence of the man. A few excerpts from that poem are presented here:

> "If you can meet with Triumph and Disaster
> And treat those two imposters just the same,
> If you can talk with crowds and keep your virtue,
> Or walk with kings — nor lose the common touch,
> If you can fill the unforgiving minute
> With sixty seconds worth of distance run,
> Yours is the earth and everything that's in it,
> And — which is more — you'll be a Man, my son!"

Charles Leo "Gabby" Hartnett was a man.

Chapter Notes

1. In the Beginning, 1900–1919

1. *Woonsocket Call*, Tuesday July 26, 1955, p. 13.
2. Sheila Hartnett Hornof, interview with the author, May 3, 2003.
3. John McNamara, interview with the author, December 11, 2002.
4. Ibid.
5. James M. Murphy, unpublished manuscript, pp. 21, 30.
6. Ibid., p. 41.
7. *Providence Sunday Journal*, May 21, 1972, p. D2.
8. *New York Times*, December 21, 1972.
9. James M. Murphy, unpublished manuscript, pp. 21–22.
10. Ibid., pp. 22–23.
11. Ibid., p. 27.
12. John McNamara, interview with the author, December 11, 2002.
13. James M. Murphy, unpublished manuscript, p. 23.
14. James M. Murphy, unpublished manuscript, pp. 28–29.
15. Ibid., pp. 35–36.
16. Ibid., p. 36.
17. *The Sporting News*, 1936.
18. James M. Murphy, unpublished manuscript, undated. p. 26.
19. Ibid., pp. 32–33.
20. Ibid., p. 39.
21. "The Open Road for Boys," p. 6.
22. The Dean Megaphone, 1919, p. 33.
23. Ibid., p. 35.
24. Ibid.
25. James M. Murphy, unpublished manuscript, undated, p. 44.
26. Fred W. Hartnett, interview with the author, December 11, 2002.
27. Paul Sann, *The Lawless Decade*, p. 56.
28. *Woonsocket Call*, August–October, 1919.
29. "Big League Stars In Action Program," October 11, 1954.
30. William F. McNeil, "Ruth, Maris, McGwire and Sosa," p. 31.

2. On the Road to the Major Leagues, 1920–1921

1. James M. Murphy, unpublished manuscript, undated, pp. 67, 70.
2. *Woonsocket Call*, July–August 1920.
3. Fred W. Hartnett, interview with the author, Dec. 11, 2002.
4. Ibid.
5. Sann, *The Lawless Decade*, pp 38–39.
6. *Sporting News*, 1936.
7. Fred W. Hartnett, interview with the author, Dec. 11, 2002.

8. *Berkshire Eagle*, May 2–3, 1921.

9. Ibid., May 17, 1921.

10. Jocelyn Wilk, Columbia University Archives, correspondence with the author, Jan. 7, 2003.

11. John McNamara, interview with the author, Dec. 11, 2002.

12. James M. Murphy, unpublished manuscript, undated, pp. 90–91.

13. *Berkshire Eagle*, July 3, 1921. .

14. James M. Murphy, unpublished manuscript, undated, p. 95.

15. *Berkshire Eagle*, September 3, 1921.

16. "The Open Road for Boys," p. 50.

17. *Berkshire Eagle*, Sept. 13–14, 1921.

18. Ibid., Sept. 15–16, 1921.

19. Ibid., Sept. 26, 1921.

20. "The Open Road for Boys," p. 7.

21. Sann, *The Lawless Decade*, p. 65.

22. Ibid.

3. Breaking in with the Chicago Cubs, 1922–1923

1. James M. Murphy, unpublished manuscript, p. 100.

2. Jack Zanger, *Great Catchers of the Major Leagues*, p. 88.

3. Eddie Gold & Art Ahrens, *The Golden Era Cubs 1876–1940*, pp. 133–134.

4. Warren Brown, *The Chicago Cubs*, p. 84.

5. Gold and Ahrens, *The Golden Era Cubs, 1876–1940*, p. 103.

6. Ibid., p. 94.

7. James M. Murphy, unpublished manuscript, undated, p. 107.

8. Al Hirshberg, *Baseball's Greatest Catchers*, p. 73.

9. Zanger, *Great Catchers of the Major Leagues*, p. 89.

10. *Chicago Times*, March 1922.

11. *Chicago Tribune*, March 1922.

12. *New York Times*, April 13, 1922, p. 15.

13. James M. Murphy, unpublished manuscript, pp. 117–118.

14. Gold and Ahrens, *The Golden Era Cubs, 1876–1940*, p. 98.

15. Ibid., p. 87.

16. Ibid., pp. 83, 101–102.

17. Ibid., p. 100.

18. Craig Carter, editor, *Daguerreotypes*, 8th Ed., p. 222.

19. *New York Times*, April 26, 1922, p. 7.

20. Richard M. Cohen and David S. Neft, *The World Series*, pp. 92–96.

21. Sann, *The Lawless Decade*, p. 39.

22. *The Baseball Research Journal*, 1979, p. 20.

23. Sheila Hartnett Hornof, interview with the author, April 28, 2003.

24. *The Baseball Research Journal*, #14, 1985, p. 31.

25. *New York Times*, April 19, 1923, p. 16.

26. Ibid., April 21, 1923, p. 7.

27. Ibid., April 25, 1923, p. 7.

28. Ibid., April 28, 1923, p. 10.

29. Gold and Ahrens, *Golden Era Cubs 1876–1940*, p. 96.

30. Sann, *The Lawless Decade*, pp. 81–82.

31. Ibid, p. 89.

32. *The New York Times*, Sept. 17, 1923.

33. Gene Brown, Arleen Keylin, David Lundy, editors, *Sports of the Times*, p. 27.

34. Cohen and Neft, *The World Series*, pp. 97–101.

35. *Woonsocket Call*, January 30, 1965.

4. A Major League Star at Last, 1924–1925

1. Joseph L. Reichler, editor, *The Baseball Encyclopedia*, 4th ed., pp. 349–350.

2. *Chicago Tribune*, April 16–17, 1924.

3. *New York Times*, June 6–8, 1924.

4. Sheila Hartnett Hornof, interview with the author, April 28, 2003.

5. John McNamara, interview with the author, December 11, 2002.

6. *New York Times*, June 12, 1924.

7. James M. Murphy, unpublished manuscript, undated, pp. 149–150.

8. Ibid., pp. 150–151.
9. *New York Times*, June 26, 1924.
10. Ibid., June 28, 1924.
11. Ibid., August 2, 1924.
12. Gold and Ahrens, *The Golden Era Cubs, 1876–1940*, p. 113.
13. Cohen and Neft, *The World Series*, pp. 102–106.
14. *SABR Baseball Research Journal* 1979, p. 20.
15. Brown, Keylin, Lundy, editors, *Sports of the Times*, p. 28.
16. John McNamara, interview with the author, December 11, 2002.
17. Gold and Ahrens, *The Golden Era Cubs, 1876–1940*, p. 136.
18. *Woonsocket Call*, January 9, 1925.
19. Jimmy Powers, *Baseball Personalities*, pp. 226–227.
20. *New York Times*, April 15, 1925.
21. Ibid., May 9, 1925.
22. Ibid., May 22, 1925.
23. *New York Times*, Sept. 6 and 27, 1925.
24. Arts & Entertainment television special, "The St. Valentines Day Massacre," 2003.

5. Refining His Skills, 1926–1927

1. James M. Murphy, unpublished manuscript, undated, p. 158.
2. Bob Chieger, *The Cubbies*, pp. 23, 213.
3. *New York Times*, April 22–26, 1926.
4. *Chicago Tribune*, May 1–3, 1926.
5. *New York Times*, May 7–10, 1926.
6. Ibid., May 10, 1926.
7. Ibid., June 1, 1926.
8. Chieger, *The Cubbies*, pp. 218–219.
9. *New York Times*, June 27–July 1, 1926.
10. Sann, *The Lawless Decade*, p. 155.
11. *New York Times*, Sept. 3, 1926, p. 10.
12. Ibid., Sept. 24, 1926, p. 1.
13. Cohen and Neft, *The World Series*, pp. 114–119.
14. Gold and Ahrens, *The Golden Era Cubs, 1876–1940*, p. 117.
15. *New York Times*, May 9, 1927.
16. Eugene Converse Murdock, *Baseball Players and Their Times*, p. 200.
17. Sann, *The Lawless Decade*, p. 102.
18. *Chicago Tribune*, June 6, 1927.
19. *New York Times*, July 1, 1927 p. 17.
20. Gold and Ahrens, *The Golden Era Cubs, 1876–1940*, pp. 115–116.
21. *Chicago Tribune*, July 5–8, 1927.
22. *New York Times*, July 19–20, 1927.
23. Ibid., August 7, 1927.
24. *Chicago Tribune*, August 10, 1927.
25. Gold and Ahrens, *The Golden Era Cubs, 1876–1940*, p. 99.
26. Ibid., p. 107.
27. Marshall Smelser, *The Life That Ruth Built*, p. 355.
28. Cohen and Neft, *The World Series*, pp. 120–123.
29. Grantland Rice, *The Tumult and the Shouting*, pp. 151–154.
30. Sann, *The Lawless Decade*, p. 136.

6. The Best of Times, the Worst of Times, 1928–1929

1. Gold and Ahrens, *The Golden Era Cubs, 1876–1940*, pg.125.
2. Edward Burns, *The Sporting News*, 1936.
3. *Woonsocket Call*, May 17, 1928.
4. Ibid., January 30, 1965.
5. Ibid., May 17, 1928.
6. John Warner Davenport, *Baseball's Pennant Races*, pp. 57–58.
7. Frank Graham, *McGraw of the Giants*, p. 234.
8. Cohen and Neft, *The World Series*, pp. 124–127.
9. Reichler, *The Baseball Encyclopedia*, 4th ed. pp. 369–370.
10. Brown, Keylin, Lundy, editors, *Sports of the Times*, p. 48.
11. *Chicago Tribune*, January 29, 1929.
12. Sheila Hartnett Hornof, interview with the author, July 8, 2003.

13. Arts and Entertainment Network, "The St. Valentines Day Massacre," 2003.

14. Powers, *Baseball Players and Their Times*, p. 196.

15. *Woonsocket Call*, April 16, 1929.

16. Shatzkin, editor, *The Ballplayers*, p. 308.

17. Cohen and Neft, *The World Series*, pp. 128–131.

18. Chieger, *The Cubbies*, p. 270.

19. Robert M. Hoffman, editor, *News of the Nation, 1925–1929*, pp. 1, 3.

7. The "Year of the Hitter" and Beyond, 1930–1931

1. *Chicago Tribune*, February 25, 1930.

2. Daniel Okrent and Steve Wulf, *Baseball Anecdotes*, p. 93.

3. *Chicago Tribune*, May 1, 1930.

4. Chieger, *The Cubbies*, p. 226.

5. *Chicago Tribune*, May 3 and 4, 1930.

6. Ibid., May 31, 1930.

7. Gold and Ahrens, *The Golden Era Cubs, 1876–1940*, p. 128.

8. *Chicago Tribune*, July 14, 1930.

9. *SABR Baseball Research Journal*, #29, pp. 27–29.

10. William F. McNeil, *The Dodgers Encyclopedia*, pp. 243–244.

11. Chieger, *The Cubbies*, p. 97.

12. *SABR Baseball Research Journal*, #30, 2001, p. 84.

13. Cohen and Neft, *The World Series*, pp. 132–136.

14. Gold and Ahrens, *The Golden Era Cubs, 1876–1940*, p. 120.

15. Fred W. Hartnett, interview with the author, December 11, 2002.

16. Brown, Keylin, Lundy, editors, *Sports of the Times*, p. 53.

17. Hoffman, editor, *News of the Nation*, No. 36. p. 3.

18. Jerome Holtzman and George Vass, *The Chicago Cubs Encyclopedia*, p. 50.

19. *Chicago Tribune*, April 15, 1931.

20. Gold and Ahrens, *The Golden Era Cubs, 1876–1940*, p. 130.

21. *Chicago Tribune*, June 7, 1931.

22. Ibid., August 1, 1931.

23. Bruce Nash and Allan Zullo, *Baseball Hall of Shame*, p. 11.

24. Donald Honig, *A Donald Honig Reader*, p. 108.

25. Cohen and Neft, *The World Series*, pp. 137–141.

26. *SABR Baseball Research Journal*, History of the Chicago City Series, p. 22.

27. Sheila Hartnett Hornof, interviews with the author, May 27 and July 8, 2003.

28. Bud Hartnett, interview with the author, June 17, 2003.

29. Sann, *The Lawless Decade*, p. 215.

8. A World Series — and Gabby Plays, 1932–1933

1. Honig, *A Donald Honig Reader*, p. 110.

2. Holtzman and Vass, *The Chicago Cubs Encyclopedia*, p. 51.

3. Graham, *McGraw of the Giants*, p. 251.

4. Chieger, *The Cubbies*, p. 263.

5. Editors of Time-Life Books, *Crimes and Punishments*, pp. 71–71.

6. *Chicago Tribune*, April 19, 1932.

7. Chieger, *The Cubbies*, p. 270.

8. *New York Times*, May 17–19, 1932.

9. McNeil, *The Dodgers Encyclopedia*, p. 345.

10. Gold and Ahrens, *The Golden Era Cubs, 1876–1940*, pp. 145–146.

11. Honig, *A Donald Honig Reader*, pp. 118–119.

12. Ibid., p. 469.

13. Holtzman and Vass, *The Chicago Cubs Encyclopedia*, p. 51.

14. *Chicago Tribune*, August 7, 1932.

15. Gold and Ahrens, *The Golden Era Cubs, 1876–1940*, p. 128.

16. *Chicago Tribune*, September 1 and 4, 1932.

17. *Chicago Tribune*, September 21, 1932.

18. Honig, *A Donald Honig Reader*, p. 111.

19. Gold and Ahrens, *The Golden Era Cubs, 1876–1940*, pp. 116, 135.

20. Holtzman and Vass, *The Chicago Cubs Encyclopedia*, p. 51.

21. Gold and Ahrens, *The Golden Era Cubs 1876–1940*, p. 141.

22. Hoffman, editor, *News of the Nation*, Nos. 36 and 37.

23. Tot Holmes, *Brooklyn's Babe*, p. 179.

24. *Chicago Tribune*, April 4, 1933.

25. *Chicago Tribune*, July 1, 1933.

26. Holmes, *Brooklyn's Babe*, p. 182.

27. Ibid., p. 184.

28. *Chicago Tribune*, September 15, 1933.

29. Cohen and Neft, *The World Series*, pp. 147–150.

9. The National League's MVP, 1934–1935

1. Chieger, *The Cubbies*, p. 61.

2. *Chicago Tribune*, April 18–19, 1934.

3. Holmes, *Brooklyn's Babe*, pp. 186–187.

4. *Chicago Tribune*, June 14, 1934.

5. Edward Burns, The Sporting News, 1936.

6. Maury Allen, *You Could Look It Up*, p. 113.

7. J. Roy Stockton, *The Gashouse Gang*, pp. 53–54.

8. McNeil, *The Dodgers Encyclopedia*, p. 346.

9. Cohen and Neft, *The World Series*, pp. 151–156.

10. *Chicago Tribune*, April 17, 1935.

11. Ibid., May 12, 1935.

12. Gold and Ahrens, *The Golden Era Cubs, 1876–1940*, p. 114.

13. *Chicago Tribune*, June 11 and 13, 1935.

14. "Open Road for Boys," p. 7.

15. *Chicago Tribune*, August 1, 1935.

16. Fred Hartnett, interview with the author, December 11, 2002.

17. Gold and Ahrens, *The Golden Era Cubs, 1876–1940*, p. 144.

18. *Chicago Tribune*, September 5, 1935.

19. Powers, *Baseball Personalities*, p. 228.

20. Chieger, *The Cubbies*, p. 211.

21. *Chicago Tribune*, September 25, 1935.

22. Honig, *A Donald Honig Reader*, pp. 114–116.

23. Chieger, *The Cubbies*, p. 30.

24. Cohen and Neft, *The World Series*, pp. 157–161.

25. Hoffman, editor, *News of the Nation*, No. 37, p. 3.

10. Reaching for the Top, 1936–1937

1. Edward Burns, *The Sporting News*, 1936.

2. Gold and Ahrens, *The Golden Era Cubs, 1876–1940*, p. 157.

3. *Chicago Tribune*, June 13, 1936.

4. Fred W. Hartnett, interview with the author, December 11, 2002.

5. Cohen and Neft, *The World Series*, pp. 162–166.

6. Ralph Cannon, *Baseball Magazine*, 1937.

7. Gold and Ahrens, *The Golden Era Cubs, 1876–1940*, p. 155.

8. *Universal Standard Encyclopedia*, vol. 7, p. 2579.

9. *Chicago Tribune*, July 8, 1937.

10. Ibid.

11. John Thorn, Pete Palmer, Michael Gershman, and David Pietrusza, editors, *Total Baseball*, 5th Ed., p. 244.

12. Ralph Cannon, *Baseball Magazine*, 1937.

13. Fred W. Hartnett, interview with the author, December 11, 2002.

14. Cohen and Neft, *The World Series*, pp. 167–170.

11. A Baseball Legend Is Born, 1938

1. *Chicago Tribune*, February 25, 1938.

2. *Universal Standard Encyclopedia*, vols. 10 and 13.

3. Fred W. Hartnett, interview with the author, December 11, 2002.

4. *Chicago Tribune*, July 21, 1938.

5. John McNamara, interview with the author, December 11, 2002.

6. Harry Danning, interview with the author, June 17, 2003.

7. Powers, *Baseball Personalities*, p. 229.

8. *Chicago Tribune*, September 18, 1938.

9. *New York Times*, September 18–23, 1938.

10. *Chicago Tribune*, September 27–30, 1938.

11. Gold and Ahrens, *The Golden Era Cubs, 1876–1940*, p. 133.

12. Bud Hartnett, interview with the author, June 17, 2003.

13. Gold and Ahrens, *The Golden Era Cubs, 1876–1940*, p. 149.

14. Lawrence S. Ritter, *The Glory of Their Times*, p. 343.

15. *Chicago Daily News*, October 3, 1938.

16. Cohen and Neft, *The World Series*, pp. 171–174.

17. Gold and Ahrens, *The Golden Era Cubs, 1876–1940*, p. 153.

12. The End of the Trail, 1939–1946

1. Brown, *The Chicago Cubs*, p. 179.

2. Peter Golenbock, *Wrigleyville*, p. 275.

3. Fred W. Hartnett, interview with the author, December 11, 2002.

4. *Chicago Tribune*, July 1, 1939.

5. Harry Danning, interview with the author, June 13, 2003.

6. Cohen and Neft, *The World Series*, pp. 175–178.

7. *SABR Baseball Research Journal*, 1979, p. 23.

8. Holtzman and Vass, *The Chicago Cubs Encyclopedia*, p. 61.

9. *Chicago Tribune*, April 16, 1940.

10. Ibid., June 1, 1940.

11. Cohen and Neft, *The World Series*, pp. 179–183.

12. Golenbock, *Wrigleyville*, p. 277.

13. Unknown newspaper, article.

14. Hoffman, editor, *News of the Nation*, No. 38, p. 1.

15. Ibid., No. 39, pp. 1–3.

16. Chieger, *The Cubbies*, p. 232.

17. Bud Hartnett, interview with the author, May 10, 2003.

18. Lloyd Johnson Miles Wolff, editor, *The Encyclopedia of Minor League Baseball*, p. 215.

19. Hoffman, editor, *News of the Nation*, No. 40, pp. 1–4.

20. Wolff, *The Encyclopedia of Minor League Baseball*, pp. 193–237.

13. Into the Sunset, 1947–1972

1. Sheila Hartnett Hornof, interview with the author, April 28, 2003.

2. Bud Hartnett, interview with the author, May 10, 2003.

3. Sheila Hartnett Hornof, interview with the author, June 3, 2003.

4. Ibid., June 10, 2003.

5. Ibid., May 3, 2003.

6. Ibid., May 27, 2003.

7. Ibid., July 8, 2003.

8. Bud Hartnett, interviews with the author, May 10 and June 16, 2003.

9. Gold and Ahrens, *The Golden Era Cubs, 1876–1940*, p. 119.

10. Ibid., p. 112.

11. Sheila Hartnett Hornof, interview with the author, April 28, 2003.

12. *Woonsocket Call*, July 26, 1955.

13. John McNamara, interview with the author, December 11, 2002.

14. Fred W. Hartnett, interview with the author, December 11, 2002.

15. Sheila Hartnett Hornof, interview with the author, June 3, 2003.

16. Ibid., June 3, 2003.

17. Ibid., June 3, 2003.

18. Doc Edwards, interview with the author, July 8, 2003.

19. Ibid., July 8, 2003.

20. Rene Lachemann, interview with the author, July 25, 2003.

21. Sheila Hartnett Hornof, interview with the author, April 28, 2003.

22. Ibid., April 23, 2003.

23. Ibid., May 27, 2003.

24. Ibid., April 28, 2003.

14. Gabby Hartnett's Legacy

1. *The Woonsocket Call*, November 12, 1982.

2. Harry Danning, interview with the author, June 18, 2003.

3. Murdock, *Baseball Players and their Times*, pp. 196–197.

4. Honig, *A Donald Honig Reader*, p. 599.

5. Harry Danning, interview with the author, June 18, 2003.

6. Ray Berres, correspondence with the author, June 16, 2003.

7. Zanger, *Great Catchers of the Major Leagues,* p. 23.

8. William F. McNeil, *Bench, Berra, Campanella, and Hartnett—The Search for Baseball's Greatest Catcher.*

9. Chieger, *The Cubbies,* p. 69.

10. Powers, *Baseball Personalities,* p. 228.

11. *Woonsocket Call,* 1983.

12. *The Tocsin,* August 18, 1972, p. 1.

Bibliography

Ahrens, Art, and Eddie Gold, *The Golden Era Cubs, 1876–1940*, Chicago: Bonus Books, 1985.

Allen, Maury. *You Could Look It Up*, New York: Times Books, 1979.

Arts and Entertainment Network. "The St. Valentines Day Massacre," 2003.

Benson, Michael. *Ballparks of North America*, Jefferson, NC, McFarland & Company, Inc., 1989.

Berkshire Eagle, 1900–1972.

Berres, Ray. Correspondence with the author, June 16 and 26, 2003.

Bevis, Charlie. *Mickey Cochrane, The Life of a Baseball Hall of Fame Catcher*, Jefferson, NC: McFarland & Company, 1998.

"Big League Stars In Action," Program. North Attleboro, MA, October 11, 1954.

Boston Globe, Boston, MA., 1921–1972.

Brown, Warren. *The Chicago Cubs*, New York: G.P. Putnam's Sons, 1946.

Burns, Edward. *The Sporting News*, February 27, 1936.

Cannon, Ralph. "The Cubs' Rocky Road," *Baseball Magazine*, 1937.

Carroll, Margaret. Interview with the Author, December 11, 2002.

Caruso, Gary. *The Braves Encyclopedia*. Philadelphia, PA: Temple University Press, 1995.

Chicago Cubs Information Guide. Chicago, IL., 1998.

Chicago Times, 1922–1972.

Chicago Tribune, 1921–1972.

Chieger, Bob. *The Cubbies*. New York: Atheneum, 1987.

Coberly, Rich, *The No-Hit Hall of Fame*. Newport Beach, CA: Triple Play Publications, 1985.

Cohen, Eliot, editor. *My Greatest Day in Baseball*, New York: Simon and Schuster, 1991.

Cohen, Richard and David S. Neft. *The World Series*. New York: Macmillan Publishing Co., 1986.

Crimes and Punishments. Alexandria, Virginia: Time-Life Books, 1991.

Daguerreotypes, 8th ed., Carter, Craig, ed., St. Louis: The Sporting News Publishing Co., 1990.

Danning, Harry. "The Horse," Interviews with the author, June 13 and 17, 2003.

Davenport, John Warner. *Baseball's Pennant Races: A Graphic View*, Madison, WI, 1981.

Dean, John. Interview with the author, December 11, 2002.

The Dean Megaphone, Franklin, MA., Dean Academy, 1919.

Edwards, Howard "Doc," Interview with the author, July 8, 2003.

Frommer, Harvey. *Baseball's Greatest Managers*. New York: Franklin Watts, 1985.

Gallagher, Mark and Walter LeConte, *The Yankee Encyclopedia*. Champaign, IL: Sports Publishing, Inc., 2000.

Golenbock, Peter. *Wrigleyville*. New York: St. Martin's Press, 1996.

Graham, Frank. *McGraw of the Giants*. New York: Putnam Books, 1946.

Hartnett, Bud. Interviews with the author, May 2, May 10, June 17, July 8, and July 31, 2003.

Hartnett, Fred W. Interview with the author, Millville, MA, December 11, 2002.

Hirshberg, Al. *Baseball's Greatest Catchers*. New York, G.P. Putnam's Sons, 1966.

Hoffman, Robert M., editor. *New of the Nation*. Englewood Cliffs, NJ: 1975.

Holmes, Tot, *Brooklyn's Babe*. Gothenburg, NE: Holmes Publishing, 1990.

Holtzman, Jerome, and George Vass, *The Chicago Cubs Encyclopedia*. Philadelphia: Temple University Press, 1997.

Honig, Donald. *A Donald Honig Reader*. New York: Simon & Schuster, 1988.

Hornof, Sheila Hartnett. Interviews with the author, April 28, May 3, May 27, June 3, June 10, July 8 and July 21, 2003.

Hornof, Sue. Interview with the author, April 28, 2003.

Kachline, Cliff. "37 Innings to Finish One Game," *The Baseball Research Journal*, (2001).

Kaplan, Jim. *Lefty Grove: American Original*, Cleveland, OH: Society for American Baseball Research, 2000.

Lachemann, Rene. Interview with the Author, July 25, 2003.

Light, Jonathan Fraser, *The Cultural Encyclopedia of Baseball*, Jefferson, NC: McFarland & Company, 1997.

McCoy, Alfred M. "Gabby Hartnett Up," *Open Road for Boys*, May 1938.

McNamara, John. Interviews with the author, Millville, MA, December 11, 2002 and May 29, 2003.

McNeil, William F. *Bench, Berra, Campanella, Hartnett—The Search for Baseball's Greatest Catcher* (work in progress).

_____, *The Dodgers Encyclopedia*. Champaign, IL: Sports Publishing, Inc., 2000.

_____, *Ruth, Maris, McGwire and Sosa*, Jefferson, NC: McFarland & Company, 1999.

Monday, Rick. Interview with the author, January 27, 2003.

Murdock, Eugene Converse, *Baseball Players and Their Times*, Westport, CT: Meckler Publishing, 1991.

Murphy, James M. *Gabby Hartnett: The Way It Was—And Will Never Be Again*, (unpublished manuscript, undated).

Murphy, Jim. "Shattered Dreams, Pleasant Memories," *Baseball Research Journal* (1985): pp 30–32.

Nash, Bruce, and Zullo, Allan. *The Baseball Hall of Shame*, New York: Pocket Books, 1985.

Nemec, David. *Great Baseball Feats, Facts, and Firsts*. New York: New American Library, 1987.

Okrent, Daniel, and Steve Wulf, *Baseball Anecdotes*. New York: Harper & Row Publishers, 1989.

Owens, Thomas S. *Great Catchers*. New York: Metro Books, 1997.

New York Times, 1921–1972.

Powers, Jimmy. *Baseball Personalities*. New York: Rudolph Field, 1949.

Providence Sunday Journal, May 21, 1972.

Reidenbaugh, Lowell. *Baseball's Hall of Fame, Cooperstown, Where the Legends Live Forever*. New York: Arlington House, Inc., 1988.

Rice, Grantland. *The Tumult and the Shouting*. New York: A.S. Barnes & Company, 1954.

Ritter, Lawrence S. *The Glory of Their Times*. New York: William Morrow, 1984.

Rothe, Emil H. "History of the Chicago City Series," *Baseball Research Journal* (1983).

Sann, Paul. *The Lawless Decade*. New York: Crown Publishers, 1960.

Shatzkin, Mike, editor. *The Ballplayers*. New York: Arbor House, 1990.

Singletary, Wes. *Al Lopez — The Life of Baseball's El Senor*. Jefferson, NC: McFarland & Company, 1999.

Smelser, Marshall. *The Life That Ruth Built*. Lincoln, NE: University of Nebraska Press, 1975

Brown, Gene, Arleen Keylin and Daniel Lundy, editors. *Sports of the Times*. New York: Arno Press, 1982.

Stockton, Roy J. *The Gashouse Gang*. New York: Barnes, 1945.

Thorn, John; Pete Palmer; Michael Gershman and Pietrusza, editors. *Total Baseball*, 5th ed. New York: Viking, 1997.

"The Tocsin," Cooperstown, N.Y. August 18, 1972.

Universal Standard Encyclopedia. New York: Unicorn Publishers, Inc., 1955.

Van Riper, Guernsey, Jr. *Behind the Plate: Three Great Catchers*. Champaign, IL: Garrard Publishing Company, 1973.

Wilk, Jocelyn, Assistant Director, Columbia University Archives. Correspondence with the author, January 3, 2003.

Wilson, Walt. "Hack Wilson in 1930," *The Baseball Research Journal* (2000).

Woonsocket Call, 1910–1972.

Zanger, Jack. *Greatest Catchers of the Major Leagues*. New York: Random House, 1970.

Index

326 Index